Problems in Value Theory

Online resources to accompany this book are available at: www.bloomsbury.com/problems-in-value-theory. Please type the URL into your web browser and follow the instructions to access the Companion Website. If you experience any problems, please contact Bloomsbury at: companionwebsites@bloomsbury.com

ALSO AVAILABLE FROM BLOOMSBURY

An Ethical Guidebook to the Zombie Apocalypse, by Bryan Hall
Debating Christian Religious Epistemology, edited by John M. DePoe and Tyler Dalton McNabb
Epistemology: The Key Thinkers, edited by Stephen Hetherington
Explaining Evil, edited by W. Paul Franks
Problems in Epistemology and Metaphysics, edited by Steven B. Cowan
Philosophy of Language: The Key Thinkers, edited by Barry Lee

Problems in Value Theory

An Introduction to Contemporary Debates

**EDITED BY
STEVEN B. COWAN**

BLOOMSBURY ACADEMIC
LONDON • NEW YORK • OXFORD • NEW DELHI • SYDNEY

BLOOMSBURY ACADEMIC
Bloomsbury Publishing Plc
50 Bedford Square, London, WC1B 3DP, UK
1385 Broadway, New York, NY 10018, USA

BLOOMSBURY, BLOOMSBURY ACADEMIC and the Diana logo are trademarks of
Bloomsbury Publishing Plc

First published in Great Britain 2020

Copyright © Steven B. Cowan and Contributors, 2020

Steven B. Cowan has asserted his right under the Copyright, Designs and Patents Act,
1988, to be identified as Editor of this work.

For legal purposes the Acknowledgements on p. xii constitute an extension
of this copyright page.

Cover design: Louise Dugdale
Cover image: © Busà Photography / Getty Images

All rights reserved. No part of this publication may be reproduced or transmitted
in any form or by any means, electronic or mechanical, including photocopying,
recording, or any information storage or retrieval system, without prior
permission in writing from the publishers.

Bloomsbury Publishing Plc does not have any control over, or responsibility for, any
third-party websites referred to or in this book. All internet addresses given in this
book were correct at the time of going to press. The author and publisher regret any
inconvenience caused if addresses have changed or sites have ceased to exist,
but can accept no responsibility for any such changes.

A catalogue record for this book is available from the British Library.

A catalog record for this book is available from the Library of Congress.

ISBN: HB: 978-1-3501-4738-6
PB: 978-1-3501-4739-3
ePDF: 978-1-3501-4740-9
eBook: 978-1-3501-4741-6

Typeset by Deanta Global Publishing Services, Chennai, India
Printed and bound in Great Britain

To find out more about our authors and books visit www.bloomsbury.com and
sign up for our newsletters.

Contents

List of Contributors viii
Acknowledgments xii

Introduction *Steven B. Cowan* 1

PART ONE Problems in Ethics and Aesthetics

Introduction to Part One *Steven B. Cowan* 17

1 Is Morality Relative? 28

Morality Is Relative *Michael Ruse* 28
Morality Is Objective *Francis J. Beckwith* 37

Responses 50
Beckwith's Response to Ruse 50
Ruse's Response to Beckwith 55

2 What Makes Actions Right or Wrong? 60

Consequences Make Actions Right *Alastair Norcross* 60
Respect for Persons Makes Actions Right *Mark Linville* 71

Responses 84
Linville's Response to Norcross 84
Norcross's Response to Linville 88

3 Does Morality Depend on God? 93

Morality Depends upon God *Matthew Flannagan* 93
Morality Does Not Depend on God *Graham Oppy* 105

Responses 117
Oppy's Response to Flannagan 117
Flannagan's Response to Oppy 121

4 Is Beauty in the Eye of the Beholder? 127

Beauty Is Relative *James Mock* 127
Beauty Is Objective *Carol S. Gould* 138

Responses 151
Gould's Response to Mock 151
Mock's Response to Gould 155

5 What Is the Meaning of Life? 160

The Meaning of Life Is Found in God *Douglas Groothuis* 160
The Meaning of Life Can Be Found without God *Christine Vitrano* 171

Responses 182
Vitrano's Response to Groothuis 182
Groothuis's Response to Vitrano 185

Essay Suggestions 191
For Further Reading 193

PART TWO Problems in Political Philosophy

Introduction to Part Two *Steven B. Cowan* 197

6 Do We Need Government? 205

We Do Not Need Government *Roderick T. Long* 205
We Need Some Government *Alex Tuckness* 218

Responses 230
Tuckness's Response to Long 230
Long's Response to Tuckness 234

7 Should Wealth Be Redistributed? 240

Wealth Should Be Redistributed *Jon Mandle* 240
Wealth Should Not Be Redistributed *Jan Narveson* 253

Responses 265
Narveson's Response to Mandle 265
Mandle's Response to Narveson 269

8 When May the Government Wage War? 274

    The Government Should Never Wage War *Andrew Alexandra* 274
    The Government May Sometimes Wage War *Nathan L. Cartagena* 284

    Responses 297
    Cartagena's Response to Alexandra 297
    Alexandra's Response to Cartagena 301

Essay Suggestions 305
For Further Reading 307

Index 309

Contributors

Andrew Alexandra (B.Phil., Oxford University) has worked in the Australian Research Council Special Research Centre for Applied Philosophy and Public Ethics (CAPPE) at the University of Melbourne since 2000. Among his many publications in the areas of political philosophy and professional and applied ethics are his coauthored books, *Reasons, Values and Institutions* (Tertiary Press, 2002), *Police Ethics* (Allen and Unwin, 2nd ed., 2006), *Ethics in Practice* (UNSW Press, 2009), *Integrity Systems for Occupations* (Ashgate, 2010), and *Media, Morals and Markets* (Wiley-Blackwell, 2011), and his co-edited collection *Private Military Companies: Ethics, Theory and Practice* (Routledge, 2008). He is currently working on a book on pacifism.

Francis J. Beckwith (Ph.D., Fordham University) is Professor of Philosophy and Church-State Studies at Baylor University where he also serves as Associate Director of the Graduate Program in Philosophy. His many books include *Defending Life: A Moral and Legal Case Against Abortion Choice* (Cambridge University Press, 2007); *Politics for Christians: Statecraft as Soulcraft* (InterVarsity Press, 2010); and *Taking Rites Seriously: Law, Politics, and the Reasonableness of Faith* (Cambridge University Press, 2015), winner of the prestigious American Academy of Religion's 2016 Book Award for Excellence in the Study of Religion in the category of Constructive-Reflective Studies.

Nathan L. Cartagena (Ph.D., Baylor University) is an assistant professor of Philosophy at Wheaton College, and Liaison to Wheaton's ROTC Program. His teaching and scholarship focus on moral and political philosophy, retrieving and extending medieval teachings to address contemporary issues and questions about race, emotions, virtues, and warfare.

Steven B. Cowan (Ph.D., University of Arkansas) is Professor of Philosophy and Religion at Lincoln Memorial University. He specializes in the philosophy of religion and the metaphysics of free will, topics on which he has published numerous articles in academic journals and popular magazines. He has authored or edited several books including (with James Spiegel) *Idealism and Christian Philosophy* (Bloomsbury, 2016) and *The Love of Wisdom: A Christian Introduction to Philosophy* (B&H, 2009).

CONTRIBUTORS

Matthew Flannagan (Ph.D., University of Otago) is a New Zealand-based theologian and ethicist. He currently teaches philosophy, theology, ethics, and religious studies at St. Peters College in Auckland. Matthew regularly participates in local and international conferences, panel discussions, and public lectures, and is the author of numerous articles on ethics and philosophy and contributor to several books. His most recent work has been on divine command metaethics and the ethics of killing. He recently coauthored (with Paul Copan) *Did God Really Command Genocide? Coming to Terms with the Justice of God* (Baker, 2014).

Carol Steinberg Gould (Ph.D., SUNY Buffalo) is Professor of Philosophy at Florida Atlantic University. She publishes widely in aesthetics, ancient Greek philosophy, philosophy of psychiatry, and, more recently, Japanese philosophy. From 2011 to 2013, she was a scholar for a program at the New York-based Aquila Theatre Company called "Ancient Greeks / Modern Lives: Poetry-Drama-Dialogue," a major initiative funded by the National Endowment for the Humanities. She co-edited *Ethics, Art, and Representations of the Holocaust* (Lexington Books, 2013). She is finishing a book tentatively titled, *Glamour, Beauty, Persons, and Aesthetics* (Bloomsbury, forthcoming).

Douglas Groothuis (Ph.D., University of Oregon) is Professor of Philosophy at Denver Seminary. He specializes in philosophy of religion and the thought of Blaise Pascal. He has published thirty academic articles in journals such as *Inquiry, Religious Studies,* and *Philosophia Christi* as well as dozens of articles in magazines and newspapers. His thirteen books include, *Walking through Twilight: A Wife's Illness—A Philosopher's Lament* (InterVarsity, 2017), *Philosophy in Seven Sentences* (InterVarsity, 2016), *Christian Apologetics* (InterVarsity, 2011), *On Pascal* (Wadsworth, 2002), *Truth Decay* (InterVarsity, 2000), and (co-edited with James Sennett) *In Defense of Natural Theology* (InterVarsity, 2005).

Mark D. Linville (Ph.D., University of Wisconsin-Madison) is Senior Research Fellow and Philosophy Tutor for the PhD program in Great Books at Faulkner University. He co-edited (with David Werther) *Philosophy and the Christian Worldview* (Bloomsbury, 2012) and has published articles in various journals as well as book chapters on ethics and philosophy of religion, including "The Moral Argument" in the *Blackwell Companion to Natural Theology* (Blackwell, 2009).

Roderick T. Long (Ph.D., Cornell University) is Professor of Philosophy at Auburn University. He also serves as president of the Molinari Institute, editor of the *Molinari Review*, and coeditor of *The Journal of Ayn Rand Studies*. His publications include *Reason and Value: Aristotle versus Rand* (Objectivist Center, 2000); (co-edited with Tibor R. Machan) *Anarchism/Minarchism:*

Is a Government Part of a Free Country? (Ashgate, 2008); (co-edited with David M. Hart, Gary Chartier, and Ross Miller Kenyon) *Social Class and State Power: Exploring an Alternative Radical Tradition* (Palgrave Macmillan, 2018); and *Wittgenstein, Austrian Economics, and the Logic of Action: Praxeological Investigations* (Routledge, forthcoming). A senior fellow at the Center for a Stateless Society, Long blogs at *Austro-Athenian Empire*, *Bleeding Heart Libertarians*, and *Policy of Truth*.

Jon Mandle (Ph.D., University of Pittsburg) is a Professor in the Philosophy Department at the University at Albany (SUNY). He is the coeditor (with David Reidy) of *The Cambridge Companion to Rawls* (Cambridge, 2015) and *A Companion to Rawls* (Blackwell, 2014). He is the author of three books, as well as articles on justice, metaethics, and the history of ethics.

James Mock (Ph.D., Syracuse University) has been on the faculty at the University of Central Oklahoma for 26 years. He is a Professor of Philosophy specializing in aesthetics, philosophy of music, and American philosophical thought. He also teaches cultural overview courses, specializing in both American history and the Enlightenment. He has been recognized for teaching and service with, among others, the provost's Modeling the Way Award, the president's Vanderford Initiative Award and the College of Liberal Arts Outstanding Service Award, Faculty Member of the Year Award, and Lifetime Achievement Award. He is Director of the Applied Liberal Arts Program. He has presented many academic papers at national and international conferences as well as published articles and book chapters, many focused on the implications of the work of David Hume and others on the continuing relevance of the work of John Dewey.

Jan Narveson (Ph.D., Harvard University) is Distinguished Professor Emeritus of the University of Waterloo in Canada. He has published seven books, notably *The Libertarian Idea* (1988 and 2001), *Moral Matters* (1993/1999), *You and The State* (2008), and *This is Ethical Theory* (2010), and several hundred articles and reviews in philosophical journals and collections, among them "Pacifism, a Philosophical Analysis" (1965); "A Puzzle About Economic Justice in Rawls' Theory" (1976); "Deserving Profits" (1995); "The Invisible Hand" (2003); and "Cohen's Rescue" (2010). In 2003 he was made an Officer of the Order of Canada. He has for decades led the Kitchener-Waterloo Chamber Music Society.

Alastair Norcross (Ph.D., Syracuse University) has taught Philosophy at the University of Colorado-Boulder since 2007. He previously taught at Southern Methodist University and Rice University. He has published extensively on theoretical and applied ethics. His work in applied ethics focuses mainly on issues concerning the treatment of nonhuman animals. In theoretical ethics, he articulates and defends a version of act utilitarianism—scalar utilitarianism—which holds that actions, people, institutions, and anything else of ethical interest should be evaluated comparatively (as better or worse) with relevant alternatives, as opposed to absolutely (as right or wrong).

Graham Oppy (Ph.D., Princeton University) is Professor of Philosophy at Monash University. He is the author of *Ontological Arguments and Belief in God* (Cambridge University Press, 1996), *Philosophical Perspectives on Infinity* (Cambridge University Press, 2006), *Arguing about Gods* (Cambridge University Press, 2006), *Reading Philosophy of Religion* (Wiley-Blackwell, 2010, with Michael Scott), *The Best Argument against God* (Palgrave, 2013), *Reinventing Philosophy of Religion* (Palgrave, 2014), and *Describing Gods: An Investigation of Divine Attributes* (Cambridge University Press, 2014). He is also editor of *The History of Western Philosophy of Religion* (Acumen, 2009, with Nick Trakakis), and the *Handbook of Contemporary Philosophy of Religion* (Routledge, 2015).

Michael Ruse (Ph.D., Bristol University) is Lucyle T. Werkmeister Professor of Philosophy and Director of the Program in the History and Philosophy of Science at Florida State University. The founding editor of *Biology and Philosophy*, he is the author or editor of over sixty books, including *Can a Darwinian be a Christian?* (Cambridge, 2001), *Darwinism as Religion: What Literature Tells Us about Evolution* (Oxford, 2017), and most recently, *On Purpose* (Princeton, 2017).

Alex Tuckness (Ph.D., Princeton University) is Professor at Iowa State University in the departments of Political Science and Philosophy. He is the author of *Locke and the Legislative Point of View* (Princeton University Press, 2002) and *The Decline of Mercy in Public Life* (with John Michael Parrish, Cambridge University Press 2014). His other publications include articles in the *Journal of Political Philosophy, American Political Science Review, Journal of the History of Philosophy*, and the *American Journal of Political Science*.

Christine Vitrano (Ph.D., City University of New York Graduate Center) is Associate Professor of Philosophy at Brooklyn College, City University of New York. She has published articles in academic journals on happiness, well-being, and the meaning of life. She is the author of *The Nature and Value of Happiness* (Westview Press, 2014), coauthor of *Happiness and Goodness: Philosophical Reflections on Living Well* (Columbia University Press, 2015), and coeditor of *Happiness: Classic and Contemporary Readings in Philosophy* (Oxford University Press, 2008).

Acknowledgments

I wish to express my appreciation to the staff at Bloomsbury Publishing for allowing me to undertake the project of editing this series, and especially Colleen Coalter, Helen Saunders, and Becky Holland for all of their advice and support through the many months it has taken to bring it to completion. Many thanks also to the contributors to this work; without them it would not exist. And, as always, I am grateful to my lovely wife, Ronda, and my precocious son, Oliver, for their love and patience while I wrapped up work on the manuscript. I am truly blessed to have a family such as them.

Introduction

Steven B. Cowan

The unexamined life is not worth living.
—SOCRATES

All men by nature desire knowledge.
—ARISTOTLE

At the beginning of every Introduction to Philosophy course, I tell my students two things. First, I tell them that the study of philosophy is the most practical course of study they will take in college. Second, I tell them that *not* engaging in some philosophical study at some point in their lives can be dangerous. These statements are likely to strike you the same way they strike my students at first. Maybe you are thinking: "Isn't philosophy about a lot of impractical, abstract ideas far removed from daily life? How can it be practical? And how can not doing philosophy be dangerous? I'm doing fine so far!"

My response to this reaction is this: Studying philosophy is practical because the kinds of questions and issues that philosophers address can have a big impact on how you choose to live. And not studying philosophy is dangerous because, whether you realize it or not, you are bombarded with philosophical ideas every day, some of which, if you accept them, may lead you astray. Let me explain.

What Philosophy Is All about

Philosophers study the most fundamental questions that people can ask. Sometimes these are called the "Big Questions." Here are a few examples:

- What is ultimately real?—Matter? Spirit? Both?
- Why is there something rather than nothing?

- Does God exist?
- Is there life after death?—If so, how? What's it like?
- What are human beings?—Collections of atoms? Do we have a soul?
- Do we have free will or is everything we do determined?
- How do we know things?—What are the sources of human knowledge?
- *Can* we know anything?
- Is morality just a matter of cultural preferences?
- How do we discover what is morally right and wrong?
- Where does civil government get its authority?

These are just some of the questions that philosophers ask and seek to answer. Many of these questions are abstract; they are not the stuff of daily life. Nonetheless, the answers one gives to such questions have important practical implications. *Ideas have consequences.* For example, if you believe that matter (i.e., atoms, molecules, physical energy) is ultimately what is real, then you won't believe that God exists, and you probably won't believe in life after death. That's bound to affect some of your lifestyle choices. Also, if you believe that people do not have free will, that will influence what you believe about things like criminal punishment, raising your children, and the assessment of your own behavior. The point here is that *what you believe matters*. It matters for how you live. And some of what you believe is *philosophical*. Look back at the above list of philosophical questions. Don't you already have beliefs about some or all of these things? Of course, you do. Do you think it might be good to be right about such beliefs if you can? If you agree, then you already see the importance of studying philosophy.

This leads me to the danger of not studying philosophy. You already have some philosophical beliefs, as we have seen. But where did you get them? Most likely, you did not get them from the formal study of philosophy. Many of them you no doubt inherited from your parents. Perhaps you acquired them from your church or from peers at school. But where did *they* get them, and are they the right ones? As we have noted, philosophers deal with questions and ideas that can be very abstract and removed from everyday life. This is why many people think that philosophy is just an "ivory tower" activity. And in many ways it is. The trouble is that philosophical ideas that begin in the ivory tower never stay there. Philosophers usually enter the ivory tower trying to answer a question or solve a problem. And when they think they have the answer, they tell other people about it. And so philosophical ideas always make their way down from the ivory tower to the "person on the street."

I mentioned some of the potential sources for how you got your philosophical beliefs. Let me mention another. Possibly the most significant way that philosophical ideas are communicated to the wider culture is through *the arts*. This includes the fine arts—paintings, sculpture, classical music—but especially the popular arts: pop music, novels, films, and so on. Whenever you read a novel or watch a movie, you are being taught some philosophical idea, whether you realize it or not. If you don't realize it, you can be led to believe that idea without any critical reflection. This can be dangerous since it may turn out that the idea being taught is false (and keeping in mind, of course, that what you believe matters).

By way of example, let's briefly discuss three movies starring the acclaimed actor, Tom Hanks. All three movies are about the meaning of life, and they all teach different messages about it. The first is the comedy *Joe vs. the Volcano* in which Hanks plays a man named Joe who works at a meaningless job under dreary conditions and with very unlikable people. He wonders whether his life has any significance. While on a sea voyage, however, Joe has a profound religious experience that convinces him that, despite its difficulties, life is meaningful because it is a gift from God who helps to make sense of it all. The second is the movie *Castaway*. In this film, Hanks portrays a man who is stranded on a deserted island for four years. What keeps him clinging to life is the hope of being reunited with his fiancé. When he is finally rescued, though, he finds that his fiancé presumed he had died and had married another man. Through these tragic events, Hanks's character learns that the meaning of life is an arbitrary subjective choice that each person makes for himself. The third movie is *Forrest Gump* in which Hanks plays a man with a mental disability who, through a series of fortuitous events, manages unexpectedly to go to college, survive the Vietnam War, become a millionaire, and eventually win the heart of his childhood sweetheart. Near the end of the movie, Forrest remarks, "I don't know if we each have a destiny, or if we're all just floatin' around accidental like on a breeze. But I think maybe it's both." The message seems to be that life is a paradoxical mixture of chance and fate (though perhaps with an emphasis on chance as symbolized by the feather floating in the wind at both the beginning and the end of the film). These three perspectives on the meaning of life cannot all be true, and the point here is that studying philosophy can, first, help you discern what a movie (or novel or song) is trying to convince you to believe, and, second, enable you to evaluate the merits of that perspective.

All of this is why the ancient Greek philosopher, Socrates (c. 470–399 BC), said that "the unexamined life is not worth living." Whatever else may be required for a worthwhile life, surely it involves knowing *what you believe and why*—and thus knowing why you have chosen to live the way you live for the things you choose to live for. This, by the way, is the ultimate goal of philosophy. The word "philosophy" comes from two Greek words: *philo* (love) and *sophia* (wisdom). So, etymologically and ideally, philosophy is "the love of wisdom." The lover of wisdom—the philosopher—seeks to follow the admonition of Socrates to examine his life with the ultimate goal of *wise living*.

The Approach of This Series

I noted that philosophers seek to answer the "Big Questions" such as "What is real?" or "How do we know?" It is the nature of these questions to be *difficult*. This is evident in the fact that philosophers have been discussing many of the same questions for centuries. And the fact that philosophers often *disagree* on the right answers underscores their difficulty as well. You might say that these tough questions present us with puzzles or mysteries to solve not unlike the questions that scientists pursue in their work. So, another way to characterize philosophy is that it seeks to *solve problems*—problems related to answering the Big Questions. Call these *philosophical problems*. There are many such problems, as many and more as there are Big Questions. Sometimes these problems are so well known and so specific that they have special names, for example, the Gettier Problem, the Mind-Body Problem, the Problem of the One over the Many, and so on.

It's because philosophy involves solving philosophical problems that the two volumes in this series are entitled *Problems in Epistemology and Metaphysics* and *Problems in Value Theory*. They are designed to introduce students to some of the most important and interesting philosophical problems and the ways in which philosophers have attempted to solve them. The problems addressed in the two volumes come from three major areas of philosophy: (1) *epistemology*, which deals with questions related to knowledge, (2) *metaphysics*, which deals with problems having to do with the nature of reality, and (3) *value theory*, a broad area that covers problems related to ethics, aesthetics, and political philosophy. The current volume is devoted to addressing problems in value theory, while the other addresses problems in epistemology and metaphysics.

Each chapter in each volume contains a "point-counterpoint" debate, two major essays by contemporary philosophers arguing for different answers to the philosophical question posed in the chapter. After each set of point-counterpoint essays, the authors also offer critical responses to their philosophical opponent's essay.

The advantages of this approach are twofold. First, it allows students *to explore different perspectives on philosophical problems with those who hold the actual views in question.* Rather than having all sides of a debate presented and evaluated by a single author (who no doubt has his or her own biases), the point-counterpoint format allows the student to read the arguments for skepticism presented by an actual skeptic, the arguments for God's existence defended by a theist, the arguments for consequentialism defended by a consequentialist, and so on. Learning about a particular viewpoint on any topic from the "horse's mouth," so to speak, is almost always preferable to the alternative. Second, the approach of this series lets the student *see how philosophy is actually done today.* Students can observe firsthand how professional philosophers in the field today make a case for a solution to a philosophical problem and interact with one another to advance philosophical discussion.

A word of warning, though. The point-counterpoint format of this book necessitates that only two sides of each philosophical topic are represented. The reader should not get the impression from this that there are or have been only two possible solutions to a philosophical problem. In many cases, there are *several* options that philosophers have explored and debated. Covering all the options in a book in which philosophers debate and respond to one another would, however, be too long and too complicated for an introductory text. So I have chosen the two perspectives on each topic that seem to me to allow the beginning philosophy student the best exposure to the major aspects of the problem under discussion.

To aid both students and instructors, I have also included in the book some pedagogical features. First, at the beginning of each essay, I have provided a list of "Study Questions." These questions are designed primarily to facilitate reading comprehension, to help the reader follow the author's train of thought and understand the major points and arguments presented. They can also be used by instructors to enable students' classroom preparation. Second, at the end of every chapter are "Questions for Reflection." These questions require students to critically evaluate what they have read in the chapter and to explore additional related issues. These questions can be utilized to facilitate classroom discussions or provide small group exercises. They could also be used for writing assignments.

At the end of each part of the book, I have included a third pedagogical aid in the form of "Essay Suggestions." These are potential topics for philosophy papers. I have included at least one suggestion related directly or indirectly to each philosophical problem discussed in the book. Also at the end of each part of the book, I have provided a list "For Further Reading." Each list is comprised of books that will allow the student to expand his or her knowledge of the areas of philosophy and the specific problems addressed in the book.

Online Resources

Bloomsbury Publishers provides some additional online resources for students and instructors to accompany the two volumes of *Problems in Epistemology and Metaphysics* and *Problems in Value Theory*. First, there is a set of *historical essays*. The plan and format of this series focuses on contemporary debates in philosophy. Though most of the contributors do provide some historical background to the problems they discuss, no doubt many instructors would like their students to have the opportunity to explore this background in more depth. The online historical essays are organized into sections that parallel the eighteen chapters in the two volumes of this series.

Second, we have provided online an appendix on *How to Write a Philosophy Paper*. Instructors who assign students to write essays or term papers on philosophical topics should direct their students to read this appendix for helpful guidance for completing their assignment.

The Philosopher's Toolkit

Every profession has its tools. Carpenters have hammers, saws, and blueprints. Scientists have microscopes, test tubes, and double-blind experiments. Philosophers are no different. There are three major "tools" they use to solve philosophical problems.

Arguments

A great deal of philosophical work involves the construction, defense, and evaluation of arguments utilizing the principles of logic.[1] An *argument* is a group of statements some of which provide reasons or grounds for accepting one of the others. The statements given as reasons are called the *premises*, and the statement they provide reasons for is called the *conclusion*.

Arguments come in two major types: deductive and inductive. A *deductive* argument is one which purports that the premises provide conclusive grounds for accepting the conclusion. In a good deductive argument, it is impossible for the premises to be true and the conclusion false. Consider the following arguments:

> All men are mortal.
> Socrates is a man.
> Therefore, Socrates is mortal.

If an NFL football team makes a touchdown, they get six points.
My favorite NFL football team made a touchdown.
Therefore, my favorite NFL team got six points.

You can see that if the first two statements in each of these arguments (the premises) are true, then the last statements (the conclusions) also have to be true. Deductive arguments like these are said to be *valid*. This means that an argument has the right kind of form or structure so that the premises, if true, guarantee the truth of the conclusion. Here are the forms of these arguments:

All M are P
All S are M
Therefore, all S are P

If P, then Q
P
Therefore, Q

Any argument that matches these forms is valid because such arguments transfer truth from the premises to the conclusion. This doesn't mean that the conclusion or the premises of a valid deductive argument *are*, in fact, true. An argument can be valid even if every statement in the argument is false as in this example:

All dogs are collies.
All collies are police dogs.
Therefore, all dogs are police dogs.

Every statement here is obviously false. Yet, *if* the premises were true (just pretend), then the conclusion would be true, too. So validity has to do with the form of an argument, not with the truth or falsity of any of its statements. However, when an argument is valid *and* it has true premises, then the argument is said to be *sound*. A good deductive argument is both valid and sound.

Care must be taken in evaluating deductive arguments, however, because they can also be *invalid*. An invalid argument fails to have the appropriate form to transfer truth from the premises to the conclusion. With an invalid argument, the conclusion does not follow logically from its premises. Consider these argument forms:

All P are M
All S are M
Therefore, all S are P

If P, then Q
Q
Therefore, P

Any argument that follows these patterns is invalid. To see why, consider the following arguments that match these forms:

> All cats are animals.
> All dogs are animals.
> Therefore, all dogs are cats.

> If George Washington was assassinated, then he is dead.
> George Washington is dead.
> Therefore, George Washington was assassinated.

In both of these arguments, the premises are true, but the conclusions are false. Clearly, the conclusions do not follow from their premises. Since valid arguments preserve truth from the premises to the conclusion, any arguments that have these patterns must be invalid. There are many more valid and invalid forms of argument, but these will suffice to show you what it means to have a good (or bad) deductive argument.

An *inductive* argument is an argument in which the premises, if true, provide *some* support for accepting the conclusion. In a very good inductive argument, the truth of the premises can make the conclusion highly probable. But, unlike deductive arguments, even good inductive arguments do not guarantee the truth of the conclusion. Here is a simple example:

> Most Republicans are pro-life.
> Jim is a Republican.
> So, it's likely that Jim is pro-life.

Supposing that the premises of this argument are true, they certainly provide some grounds for believing the conclusion, perhaps strong grounds. Nevertheless, the conclusion could be false since Jim might be among the small percentage of Republicans who are pro-choice. There are many different kinds of inductive arguments: statistical syllogisms like the one above, arguments from analogy, generalizations, causal inferences, arguments to the best explanation, and more. Regardless of type, when the premises of an inductive argument are true, and the probabilistic connection between premises and conclusion is strong, the argument is said to be *cogent*.

The reader of this book will encounter many arguments of several types within its pages, both deductive and inductive. It will be your job to evaluate these arguments to decide whether they are valid, strong, sound, and cogent.

Definitions

Another tool in the philosopher's toolkit is *definitions*. Sometimes a philosophical problem can be illuminated or even resolved by getting clear on the meaning of a key term (or terms) in the debate. Famously, the eighteenth-century philosopher David Hume (1711–1776) believed that the age-old debate over whether or not free will is compatible with determinism could be resolved simply be giving clear definitions of "free will" and "determinism." (Most subsequent philosophers have disagreed with Hume on this.) On other occasions, a philosophical problem itself *just is* the matter of finding a correct definition, as is the debate over the meaning of "knowledge" (see Chapters 1 and 3 of Volume 1). Further, a premise in an argument may take the form of a definition, so that an adequate evaluation of the argument requires considering the adequacy of the definition.

There are many different kinds of definitions but not all are relevant to doing philosophy. For example, a *lexical definition* is the kind you find in a dictionary. Lexical definitions merely list the ways that a term is commonly used in a given language. What philosophers are primarily concerned with, however, are *descriptive* or *analytic definitions*. An analytic definition sets out the necessary and/or sufficient conditions that something has to meet in order to be that kind of thing. A simple example involving geometrical shapes will help you see what I mean. Consider this definition of a square:

A geometrical figure is a *square* if and only if:

(i) it has four straight sides,

(ii) its sides are of equal length, and

(iii) it has four right angles.

Using the expression "if and only if" (sometimes abbreviated "iff") indicates that this definition is an attempt to set forth both the necessary and sufficient conditions for a figure's counting as a square. This means that anything that meets the three conditions is a square, and anything that doesn't meet all three conditions is not a square. That is, meeting all these conditions is *sufficient* for being a square; and meeting each condition is *necessary* for being a square.

The "square" example is fairly straightforward. When you are trying to define more complex concepts, however, coming up with the correct set of necessary and sufficient conditions can be difficult (as you will see in several chapters of this book). So, philosophers have devised ways to evaluate the adequacy of definitions. The most important way is to design, if possible, a *counterexample* to the definition. This involves doing one (or both) of two things: (1) identifying something that *doesn't* meet one or more of the conditions but clearly is an example of the kind of thing being defined (thus showing that one or more of the conditions are not necessary); or

(2) identifying something that meets all the conditions but clearly *is not* an example of the kind of thing being defined (thus showing that the conditions are not sufficient). Suppose, for example, that you were presented with this definition:

A geometrical figure is a *square* if and only if:

(i) it has four straight sides, and

(ii) it has four right angles.

This definition fails to provide a sufficient condition for a figure being a square. A (non-square) rectangle would meet these conditions and is a counterexample of the second kind. Now consider this definition:

A geometrical figure is a *rectangle* if and only if:

(i) it has four straight sides,

(ii) its sides are of equal length, and

(iii) it has four right angles.

While a square (a kind of rectangle) meets all these conditions, there are many rectangles that fail to satisfy condition (ii), thus providing a counterexample of the first kind.

Even though philosophers often seek to provide analytic definitions that state both necessary and sufficient conditions, often they will attempt to give incomplete definitions that state only necessary conditions or sufficient conditions but not both. Here are two examples:

A geometrical figure is a *rectangle* if it is a square.

A geometrical figure is a *square* only if it has four sides.

The first of these examples provides a sufficient condition for being a rectangle. Being a square is *enough* to count as a rectangle (though other shapes can be rectangles too). The second example provides a necessary condition for being a square. Whatever else something has to have, nothing counts as a square *unless* it has four sides. In order to know whether an analytic definition states a necessary condition, a sufficient condition, or both, pay careful attention to the connectives that are used: "if," "only if," or "if and only if." The following table will help you keep it straight:

An analytic definition states...	...if it uses the connective...
a sufficient condition	if
a necessary condition	only if
necessary and sufficient conditions	if and only if

The reader will come across several discussions of definitions throughout this book. Be prepared to use the "counterexample method" to determine the adequacy of these definitions.

Thought Experiments

When constructing or evaluating an argument, one of the things that must be considered is whether or not the premises of the argument are true. Truth, of course, is a necessary condition for even a valid argument to be *sound* (see the above section on arguments). But what determines if a premise is true? Often philosophers will offer additional arguments in support of the premises of an argument. And in some cases, the premises of these additional arguments will be defended with still more arguments. Eventually, however, one comes to a point where there are no additional arguments to give. At this point, a philosopher will typically appeal to what is called *rational intuition*. He or she will claim, that is, that a particular premise or statement is intuitively true, or known by intuition. Sometimes the same thing is meant by saying that a statement is "self-evident." Before you balk at this notion, you should realize that you, the reader, have used rational intuition as a source of knowledge more than once while reading this introduction. How did you know, for example, that the first deductive argument I presented earlier (the one with "Socrates is mortal" as its conclusion) is valid? You could just "see" it, right? How do you know simple mathematical truths like "$3 - 4 = -1$"? Answer: rational intuition. So philosophers sometimes justify the premises of arguments by appealing to intuition.

But what if philosophers don't share the same intuitions? Or what if a philosopher presents a claim that he or she can't defend by argument and that he or she thinks may prove controversial? This is where the third item in the philosopher's toolkit comes in. Philosophers seek to justify (or sometimes criticize) appeals to intuition by using *thought experiments*. A thought experiment is a hypothetical scenario or case study in which intuitions are tested. They very frequently take a narrative form. The basic idea is to imagine the implications or consequences of the story and determine what, if any, intuitions are supported by the story. Consider the following thought experiment offered by Judith Jarvis Thomson to justify abortion:

> But now let me ask you to imagine this. You wake up in the morning and find yourself back to back in bed with an unconscious violinist. A famous unconscious violinist. He has been found to have a fatal kidney ailment, and the Society of Music Lovers has canvassed all the available medical records and found that you alone have the right blood type to help. They have therefore kidnapped you, and last night the violinist's circulatory system was plugged into yours, so that your kidneys can be used to extract poisons from his blood as well as your own. The director of the hospital now tells you, "Look, we're sorry the Society of Music Lovers did this to you—we would never have permitted it if we had known. But still, they did it, and the violinist is now plugged into you. To unplug you would be to kill him. But never mind, it's only for nine months. By then he will have recovered from his ailment, and can safely be unplugged from you."[2]

Thomson grants, for the sake of argument, that an unborn human fetus has a right to life. No matter, Thomson argues. In this thought experiment, it is clear that you are not obligated to remain plugged up to the violinist. You are perfectly within your rights to unplug and walk away even though the violinist will die. Applied to the case of abortion, the thought experiment seems to support the conclusion that it is morally permissible for a woman with an unwanted pregnancy to "unplug" from her fetus by having an abortion.

Of course, like arguments and definitions, thought experiments can be criticized. A couple of ways to undermine a thought experiment are (1) to show that the thought experiment doesn't really support the intuition or conclusion its author claims it does, but rather *some other* conclusion; and (2) to show that the thought experiment is based on faulty assumptions. Thomson's violinist scenario may be criticized on both fronts. First, it has been argued that the thought experiment, at best, supports abortion only in cases of pregnancies resulting from rape. After all, the person in the thought experiment was kidnapped and hooked up to the violinist against her will. Second, we may question whether the thought experiment is really analogous to typical cases of pregnancy. In the normal pregnancy, a woman does not have to be bedridden for nine months. Moreover, abortion does not involve merely "walking away" from the fetus as in the violinist case, but it involves actively killing the fetus.

Many of the essays in this book make use of thought experiments. Some of them can be quite clever and imaginative, and they all are designed to drive your intuitions in a certain direction. You will have to think hard and use your own imagination to decide if you are being driven in the right direction.

Notes

1 *Logic* is a branch of philosophy to which many books and college courses are devoted. One commonly used textbook of logic is Patrick J. Hurley, *A Concise Introduction to Logic*, 12th ed. (Stamford, CT: Cengage Learning, 2015).
2 Judith Jarvis Thomson, "A Defense of Abortion," *Philosophy & Public Affairs*, 1:1 (Fall 1971): 47–66.

PART ONE

Problems in Ethics and Aesthetics

Introduction to Part One

Steven B. Cowan

Axiology (or Value Theory) is the branch of philosophy that studies value. Broadly speaking, it asks questions like "What has worth or value?" and "What kinds of things are valuable?" and "What are the different sorts of value?" As for the last of these, philosophers usually make a distinction between *intrinsic value* and *instrumental value*. Something has intrinsic value if it is valuable for its own sake; it is valuable in and of itself, apart from anything else. Something has instrumental value if it is only valuable for gaining something else. A good example of something that has merely instrumental value is paper money. People value paper money not for its own sake but for what they can do with it, namely, buy other things that they value more.

But what has *intrinsic* value? This is the subject of intense debate among philosophers. Some argue that nothing really has intrinsic value. People might treat some things *as if* they had intrinsic value—that is, they may attribute intrinsic value to something, say fame or fortune or human life, but this attribution is simply a matter of *preference*, a preference that not everyone will share. Those who take this perspective on intrinsic value hold what is called *value subjectivism*. Other philosophers hold to *value objectivism*, contending that there are things that are intrinsically valuable in themselves independently of our preferences. Of course, value objectivists differ on what they think is objectively valuable. Some—those called *value monists*—think that there is only one thing that is intrinsically valuable, but they differ on what that one thing is. For example, *hedonism* is the view that the one intrinsically valuable thing is pleasure, while *perfectionism* is the view that developing those traits (whatever they are) that are distinctive of human beings is the only intrinsically valuable thing. Most philosophers, however, adhere to *value pluralism,* which holds that there are multiple things that are intrinsically valuable such as happiness, knowledge, human life, etc.

Besides addressing fundamental questions about the nature of value, the field of axiology has three major subdivisions. They are ethics, aesthetics, and political philosophy. Since political philosophy is a very large and complex discipline in its own right, I have devoted Part Two of the book to addressing problems in that area. Here in Part One, we will focus on matters related to ethics, aesthetics, and the difficult-to-classify but deeply existential problem concerning the meaning of human life.

Ethics

The philosophical discipline of *ethics* is typically divided into three subfields. *Metaethics* deals with fundamental questions concerning the meanings of ethical concepts such as "good," "bad," "right," and "wrong," as well as the metaphysical status of moral values (e.g., Are they subjective or objective?). *Normative ethics* seeks to develop and justify an ethical theory about what makes actions right or wrong and therefore delineate what our actual moral obligations are. Finally, *applied ethics* applies normative ethical theories to resolve real moral issues such as abortion, capital punishment, affirmative action, and so on. Part One will not include any discussion of issues in applied ethics (though the political issues discussed in Chapters 7 and 8 of Part Two could count as ethical issues). However, we will address two metaethical problems: the question of the status of moral values (specifically, the question of whether or not they are relative or objective) and the problem of the relationship between God and ethics. In between those issues, we will deal with a key debate in normative ethics over what makes actions right or wrong.

Moral Relativism versus Moral Objectivism

Surely you have noticed that people seem to have disagreements about what is right and wrong. Some people believe that abortion on demand is morally permissible, but others strongly oppose abortion. Many people believe that capital punishment is the penalty that murderers deserve while many others think the death penalty is atrocious. Homosexuality is believed by some to be morally offensive, yet others claim it is a perfectly acceptable alternative lifestyle. In some African societies, the practice of female genital mutilation is believed to be morally obligatory, but people in most other cultures find this practice to be barbaric. People in most Western and Eastern societies believe that the elderly should be protected and cared for until they die of natural causes. But in earlier Eskimo culture, the elderly were expected to leave home and family and wander into the wilderness to freeze to death when they could no longer contribute to the survival of the clan.

All these differences of opinion on moral issues have led many people to embrace *moral relativism*, the view that what counts as right and wrong is a matter of individual or cultural preference. For the moral relativist, there are no universally binding moral principles or values. Nothing is objectively or intrinsically right or wrong. As the definition suggests, however, there are two versions of moral relativism. *Moral subjectivism* sees morality as based on individual preferences. Whether or not a particular course of action is right or wrong is up to each individual person to decide for himself. *Conventionalism* (or cultural relativism) places the focus on groups of people, organized societies or cultures. For the conventionalist, whether or not an action is right is determined by the preferences of the culture as a whole.

The most common justification given for either subjectivism or conventionalism is the phenomenon noted earlier: there are lots of disagreements over morality. So, for example, a conventionalist might offer the following argument for his view:

Premise: Different cultures have different systems of morality.

Conclusion: Morality is a matter of cultural preferences.

There is an obvious problem with this argument, however. It is logically *invalid*. That is, even granting that the premise is true,[1] it simply does not follow that morality is relative to cultures. It's possible that some cultures get morality right and others just get it wrong. An analogy may help to get the point. It's a fact that people disagree over the shape of the earth. The so-called Flat Earth Society (yes, it really exists) believes that the earth is flat, while the rest of us (I'm assuming that includes you) believe that the earth is round. But none of us believes that the fact that this disagreement exists implies that whether the earth is flat or round is a matter of cultural preference! No, one group has simply gotten the geological facts wrong. Likewise, the mere fact of disagreement about moral issues does not by itself prove that there is no objective truth in morality. So, despite all the apparent moral disagreement that exists, *moral objectivism*—the view that there *are* objective, universally binding moral principles—could be true.

Still, we have not proven that moral relativism is false. Morality could still be relative even if disagreements don't prove it so. Nonetheless, the majority of philosophers (and probably most nonphilosophers, too) embrace moral objectivism. Why? Well, one reason is that moral relativism, as we have defined it, comes at a very great cost. Let us assume for the sake of argument that conventionalism is true. And let us ask, on this assumption, what *else* would be true? In other words, let's ask what *implications* follow from conventionalism. It turns out that the implications are very difficult to accept. (Most of what follows applies, with some minor adjustments, to subjectivism.)

First, if conventionalism is true, then *we cannot say, for example, that Hitler and the Nazis did anything morally wrong* when they invaded and enslaved other countries and murdered six million Jews (and many millions of others, too). Why not? Because the Nazis were acting in accordance with the moral principles accepted by their culture. And as long as their culture believed that their violent actions were moral, then—if conventionalism is true—they *were* moral! But, surely, that cannot be right, can it?

Second, if conventionalism is true, then *moral progress is logically impossible*. Moral relativism will not allow us to say that one moral perspective or lifestyle or action is morally better or worse than another. So, for example, when the United States abolished slavery, we did not, indeed *could not*, have improved morally as a society. But, we *did* improve morally, didn't we? If so, then conventionalism must be false.

Third, conventionalism implies that *there are no moral disagreements*. This is because moral relativism of either variety reduces moral statements to mere statements of preference. To say, for example, "Capital punishment is wrong," simply means, for the relativist, "I (or we) don't like capital punishment," and to say, "Capital punishment is right," is to say, "I (or we) like capital punishment." But this is just like when one person says, "I like chocolate ice cream," and another says, "I like vanilla." They are not disagreeing with each other. They are simply stating their preferences. This implication is somewhat ironic given that the major reason given in favor of conventionalism is the fact that people of different cultures seem to disagree about morality! In any case, most of us think that people do have genuine moral disagreements (which explains why people can get very emotional about the moral issues that divide us). If real moral disagreements exist, then that spells trouble for conventionalism (and subjectivism).

There are other adverse implications and criticisms of moral relativism but these will do to show that it is problematic at best. And this is why few philosophers defend it. Nevertheless, there are many related questions that are still worth exploring. Even if we grant that moral objectivism is true, for example, it might be helpful to know *why* that is so. And perhaps there are other forms of moral relativism and/or other challenges to objectivism that are not subject to the criticisms outlined above.

With this in mind, in Chapter 1, Michael Ruse (Florida State University) rejects the problematic kind of moral relativism discussed above for some of the same reasons. At the level of "substantive ethics" it is not the case that "anything goes." He argues, however, that evolutionary biology presents us with a more nuanced but real form of moral relativism. On the Darwinian theory of evolution, morality is an adaptation that aids survival just like every other human feature that has evolved. Morality, on this view, is not objective in the sense that the principles and values that comprise it have to be what they are. Morality takes the form it does because of the kinds of beings that we have evolved into. If evolution had made us different—say, more like insects—then our moral beliefs would be different and they would be "right."

Moral objectivism is defended by Francis Beckwith (Baylor University). He begins by delineating several moral propositions—such as "It is wrong to kill human persons without justification," and "One should not take another's property without good cause"—that everyone (or almost everyone) intuitively knows are true. He then argues that any disagreements associated with these propositions actually presuppose an objective morality and are concerned not with the truth of the propositions per se, but with their proper application.

Normative Ethics: Consequences versus Principles

Suppose you have a friend who has just lost his job and he desperately needs some money to pay his rent this month. Out of compassion and friendship, you give him the money he needs. Your friend is greatly happy and relieved and he and his family are able to avoid being evicted from their home. Everyone would agree that in this situation you did the *right* thing. Or suppose that one of your coworkers gets the promotion that you expected to get. Angry and jealous, you key her new car when you leave work that afternoon, costing her hundreds of dollars for a new paint job. Surely, your action in this case was *wrong*. But why? What is it about your actions in these two cases that made them, respectively, right and wrong?

Among other things, a normative ethical theory is supposed to tell us *what makes our actions right or wrong*. In the history of ethics, two approaches to this question have dominated. *Consequentialism* is the view that *consequences* are what make an action right or wrong. If the results of your action are good, then your action was morally right; but if things end up badly because of your action, then it was wrong. In the first example above, according to consequentialism, your action was right because it resulted in relieving your friend's financial burden and/or making him happy. In the second case, your action was wrong because it cost your coworker a lot of money and (presumably) made her unhappy.

Consequentialism comes in several variations, depending upon what counts as a good (or bad) consequence. One version of consequentialism, *ethical egoism*, says that the consequence our actions should aim for is *self-interest*. An action that promotes my interests is a good action; one that doesn't is a bad action. However, the most prominent variety of consequentialism is *utilitarianism*. For the utilitarian, what counts as a good consequence is the *maximization of happiness for the greatest number of people*. More specifically, if an action results in an overall balance of happiness over unhappiness for the group of people affected by the action, then the action was good; otherwise it's bad. So, in the first case above, the action was right because it generated a great deal of happiness for all involved—your friend and his family, and probably you, too. The action in the second case was wrong, we might say, because your coworker's unhappiness outweighed whatever brief satisfaction you got from keying her car.

The second dominant approach to normative ethics is *deontology*, the view that acting on the correct rules or principles, regardless of consequences, is what makes an action right. Failing to follow such principles makes an action morally wrong. So, for example, in the first case above, the deontologist might say that we have a duty to follow a *principle of benevolence* that requires us to help others in need when doing so is within our means. And in the second case, the principle *do no harm* indicates why keying your coworker's car was wrong.

Just as with consequentialism, there are different variants of deontology, but the most influential one is *Kantianism*, developed initially by the eighteenth-century philosopher, Immanuel Kant (1724–1804). He believed that there was one supreme rule of morality, what he called the Categorical Imperative which basically states (by way of a simple paraphrase): *Do only those actions that can be universalized*. In other words, we should only do an action that, if everyone did it, would not entail a contradiction or some other kind of absurdity.

The defense of consequentialism is made in Chapter 2 by Alastair Norcross (University of Colorado-Boulder). After clarifying the essential features of what he calls "Core Consequentialism," Norcross then addresses some of the most common objections to a consequentialist approach to ethics. He contends that these objections only apply to some versions of consequentialism but not to consequentialism per se, or they ignore crucial distinctions such as that between judgments of character and judgments of actions, or they are based on intuitions about the nature of rights that the consequentialist believes are unjustified.

Following an aspect of Kant's deontological theory, Mark Linville (Faulkner University) defends the "Respect-for-Persons" principle as the central feature of what makes actions right. Actions are right, that is, if they treat people with due respect, and wrong if they fail to do so. In defending this principle, Linville starts with what he calls our "pre-theoretical" or bedrock moral beliefs—basic moral beliefs like "Babies should not be strangled," which we simply know intuitively. Then he asks what normative ethical theory best accounts for and supports these bedrock moral beliefs. Linville argues that the only ethical theory that adequately upholds our most basic moral intuitions is one that places the inherent dignity of persons at the center.

God and Morality

The famous Russian novelist, Fyodor Dostoyevsky (1821–1881), wrote, "If God does not exist, everything is permitted." He believed that without God to serve as a foundation for morality, there could be no objective moral values or obligations. Atheism, in other words, implies moral relativism. Dostoyevsky's belief about this is not uncommon. Even many atheists have agreed. Friedrich Nietzsche (1844–1900), for example, built his philosophy of the "will to power" (the idea that *might makes right*) on the assumption of atheism. J.L Mackie (1917–1981), a prominent twentieth-century atheist philosopher wrote, "Moral properties constitute so odd a cluster of qualities and relations that they are most unlikely to have arisen in the ordinary course of events without an all-powerful god to create them."[2] And Michael Ruse, who defends a version of moral relativism in this volume (see Chapter 1), writes, "Morality is just an aid to survival and reproduction . . . and any deeper meaning is illusory."[3]

So, is it really the case that objective morality depends upon the existence of God? In Chapter 3, Matthew Flannagan (St. Peter's College, Auckland) argues in favor of the dependence of morality on God. Specifically, he defends a version of the *Divine Command Theory* (DCT), according to which moral wrongness is identical with the property of being contrary to God's commands. Flannagan rebuts the standard objections to the DCT, such as the charge that it makes morality arbitrary. And he argues that secular accounts of morality (i.e., accounts of morality that don't depend on God) fail to deliver because they cannot adequately explain key features of objective morality such as the prescriptivity and authority of moral requirements.

The view that morality is independent of God is supported by Graham Oppy (Monash University). He begins by affirming a worldview called *naturalism*—in his words, the view that "there are none but natural entities involving none but natural properties." This view, of course, entails that God does not exist. He also affirms *moral realism*, the view that moral judgments at least sometimes represent real moral facts that obtain independently of our preferences (roughly equivalent to what I've called moral objectivism), and he defends it against fellow atheists who deny that there are such moral facts. Given naturalism and moral realism, it follows that morality does not depend on God. But Oppy further defends the independence of morality by arguing that moral facts are necessarily true just like mathematical and logical facts. But, he argues, necessary truths do not depend upon anything else for their existence. So, moral truths do not depend upon anything else for their existence.

Aesthetics

Aesthetics is a branch of value theory concerned with beauty, taste, and the appreciation of art. Several important questions are dealt with by aestheticians, such as the following: What is art? What is the purpose or function of art? What is the connection, if any, between morality and art? Is beauty in nature the same quality as beauty in art? These and many other aesthetic problems deserve our attention. Unfortunately, space will allow us to address only one: namely, *Are our aesthetic judgments objectively true?*

We have all heard the expression, "Beauty is in the eye of the beholder." The idea here is that whether or not something is beautiful is a matter of individual taste, and no one's taste is any more authoritative than anyone else's. I may look at a painting such as Van Gogh's (1853–1890) *Starry Night*, and say, "That's beautiful." But, you might look at it and say, "No, I think it's kinda ugly." Someone who thinks that beauty is in the eye of the beholder would say that we are *both* right; it's just a matter of personal preference. This view is called *aesthetic relativism*, and a great many people today accept this view.

The opposite of aesthetic relativism is *aesthetic objectivism*. According to this view, some things are truly beautiful and some things just aren't—beauty is *not* merely in the eye of the beholder.[4] Or, put another way, some aesthetic judgments (e.g., "*Starry Night* is beautiful") are objectively true, and some are false. This implies, of course, that some artworks (and other things) can be better or worse aesthetically than others.

One consideration in favor of objectivism is that there are works of art that are valued by people of diverse cultures and across many centuries. People everywhere for many centuries, for example, have admired the sculptures of Michelangelo, the paintings of Da Vinci, and the architecture of the Aztecs. What explains this fact that some art survives the "test of time" and some does not? The objectivist explains it by claiming that the art that survives is aesthetically better than the art that doesn't. The relativist must explain—*how?*—why there are no objectively better or worse works of art despite this phenomenon.

James Mock (University of Central Oklahoma) leads off in Chapter 4 arguing for a form of aesthetic relativism he calls "rational relativism." Borrowing primarily from the aesthetic theories of David Hume, John Dewey (1859–1952), and George Santayana (1863–1952), Mock argues that in art appreciation, "there can be better responses at a point in time, but not one single response for all time." The idea seems to be that art objects (paintings, sculptures, etc.) have objective features that elicit aesthetic responses, and that such responses can be better or worse, accurate or inaccurate, to the degree that a person is educated and practiced in recognizing and appreciating those features. But aesthetic responses are also informed and molded by a person's cultural background and personal experiences, so that they will differ from place to place and from time to time. In this way, Mock claims to avoid the naïve relativism that reduces aesthetic judgments to mere personal preferences, while also denying that there is only one legitimate aesthetic response to a given art object.

Carol Gould (Florida Atlantic University) provides a defense of aesthetic objectivism, arguing that aesthetic judgments can be true or false. She begins by responding to standard objections to objectivism such as the claim that beauty is relative simply because beauty is experienced subjectively, or because there are cultural differences in standards of beauty. Despite the presence of subjectivity and cultural diversity, there are typical features shared by things that are judged as beautiful such as symmetry and the golden ratio. Gould goes on to argue that there are shared criteria that can be utilized to settle aesthetic disagreements once one is willing and able to approach art with the appropriate level of disinterestedness, sympathy, and attentiveness.

The Meaning of Life

Perhaps the one philosophical question that almost every human being contemplates at some time or another is the question of life's meaning. We ask questions like "Why are we here?" or "Why am *I* here?" or "What is the purpose and significance of human life?" or "What makes life worthwhile?" Such questions are not new, either. They have been asked by people as far back as historical memory goes. "Meaningless! Meaningless! All is meaningless!" says the Preacher in the biblical book of Ecclesiastes, who goes on to ask, "What advantage does a man have in all his work which he does under the sun?" (Eccl. 1:3, NASB)—and the implied answer is that it's very difficult to say. Socrates, the ancient Greek philosopher, raises the question when he declares: "The unexamined life is not worth living." And Hamlet, in Shakespeare's famous play, states, "To be or not to be. That is the question."

There have been three basic answers to the problem of discerning life's meaning.[5] First, there is the *theistic solution*. On this approach, meaning in life is found in relationship to a personal God. For those who hold this view, without God, life can have no real meaning. But, since God actually exists (they believe), life can and does have meaning. Second, there is the *pessimistic naturalist solution* (nihilism). Those who take this approach agree with theism that without God there would be no meaning to life. The problem, though, as they see it, is that there is no God—or at least there is no good reason to believe in God. Therefore, for the pessimistic naturalist, life has no meaning. It is literally meaningless or absurd. The third solution is that of the *optimistic naturalist*. Like those who take the previous approach, those in this camp deny the existence of God; however, they do not think that life is therefore meaningless. They believe, instead, that God's existence is irrelevant to the question of whether or not life has meaning. They hold that life can have meaning even if there is no God. Optimistic naturalism, however, divides into two subcategories: (1) *Objective optimism* holds that human life has an objective meaning that does not depend on people's desires and preferences; rather, meaning is found when people live in accordance with certain inherently valuable conditions. (2) *Subjective optimism* claims that what constitutes a meaningful life varies from person to person depending upon their subjective desires or goals; it has nothing to do with matching one's life up to some objective reality, whether it's God or some natural conditions.

Douglas Groothuis (Denver Seminary) opens Chapter 5 with a defense of the theistic solution to the problem of life's meaning. He claims that there are at least three things that are necessary for human life to have real meaning: (1) that our existence or being not be an accident, but, rather, is intentional; (2) that our lives have an objective purpose or direction; and (3) that our lives and the purpose they serve have intrinsic value. Theism, Groothuis argues, meets these conditions. Our lives are not accidents because God intentionally chose to create us. We have a God-given purpose, namely, "to glorify God and enjoy him forever." And because we are created in God's image, we have intrinsic value and dignity. Atheism, however, cannot satisfy these conditions according to Groothuis. On the atheistic worldview, human beings are accidents of the big bang and evolution, existing for no reason or purpose. Thus, there is no basis for human value and no basis for meaning.

Christine Vitrano (Brooklyn College) defends the subjective optimistic version of optimistic naturalism. On her view, a meaningful life is a life characterized by happiness, where happiness is understood as "life satisfaction." And the key to achieving such happiness is the pursuit of projects that one finds "deeply engaging and that make you happy." A person who is happy (i.e., satisfied) with her life has a meaningful life. In response to the objection that a person might be happy leading a life filled with doing horrible things to other people, Vitrano qualifies her view with the requirement that the happiness that constitutes meaning cannot be acquired by violating commonsense moral norms. Against objectivist theories of meaning (which includes theism and objective optimism), she argues that they depend upon the concept of objective values, a concept that she finds seriously problematic.

Notes

1 Though we will not pursue the topic here, there is reason to doubt that this premise is exactly true. While there are obvious disagreements on many moral issues, all cultures around the world appear to share the same core moral values. For more on this, see Edward O. Wilson, *On Human Nature* (New York: Bantam Books, 1979).

2 J. L. Mackie, *The Miracle of Theism* (Oxford: Clarendon Press, 1982), 115.

3 Michael Ruse, "Evolutionary Theory and Christian Ethics," in *The Darwinian Paradigm* (London: Routledge, 1989), 269.

4 I should point out here that beauty is not the only aesthetic property that art and other things can have. We focus on beauty here, however, for the sake of simplicity.

5 Here I follow the taxonomy of Joshua Seachris in *Exploring the Meaning of Life: An Anthology and Guide*, ed. Joshua W. Seachris (Malden, MA: Wiley-Blackwell, 2012), 10–13.

1

Is Morality Relative?

Morality Is Relative

Michael Ruse

Study Questions

1. What are the two levels of "morality" that Ruse distinguishes?
2. What is meant by "relativism"? In what sense, according to Ruse, is substantive morality *not* relative? In what sense *is* it relative?
3. What problems does Ruse find with grounding metaethics in God?
4. What problem does Ruse find with saying that morality is like mathematics?
5. What is Kant's view of morality? How does it avoid relativism?
6. What is Darwin's threefold argument for evolution?
7. What does the Darwinian say about morality? In what sense would Darwinian morality be relativistic?
8. What objection to Darwinian morality could be raised in terms of game theory? How does Ruse respond?
9. What two implications follow from the idea that morality is an evolutionary adaptation?
10. How does Ruse respond to the person who thinks he can live immorally now that he knows morality is ultimately subjective?

Meanings: Substantive Morality

Normal human beings find philosophers intensely irritating. You ask them a question and, instead of answering it, inevitably they say, "Well it depends what you mean by . . . ." They cannot get on with the job but lose everything in a snowstorm of words and definitions and ambiguities and metaphors and all of the rest. By the time they have finished you are totally confused, and probably have lost interest in the answer. Which may have been their intent all along. Actually, however, in defense of philosophers—in defense of Ludwig Wittgenstein (1889–1951), who famously commented, "Philosophical problems arise when language goes on holiday,"[1]—they are not necessarily always wrong in what they do. How often has one got into an argument with someone, say, about the existence of God, and finds long into the discussion that each is talking about a completely different notion of the deity? You may be denying the identity of an old white-haired gentleman who liked to walk in the garden and who takes an intimate interest in what we do every minute of the day, while your opponent may be arguing about an entity much like a mathematical concept, outside time and space and about as far from being a person as it is possible for anything to be.[2]

Taking this as a caution, let us turn to the matter of morality and relativism. Ask first what you mean by "morality."[3] Philosophers have been here before you. First, there is the level known as "substantive" or "normative" morality. This has to do with conduct. What should I do? What should you do? Claims like: Do not kill. Do not steal. Do not rape. And the multitude of rules of conduct we have for daily life: Let others go first. Don't leave the dirty dishes for your mother to clean up. And—a favorite among philosophers—don't mark up library books with a yellow pen and make sure you get them back on time. Then there is the level known as "metaethics." This has to do with justification. Why should I do what I should do? Many people would say: You should do what you should do because that is what God wants. Others, even those who believe in His existence, want to keep God out of things. You should do what you should do because there are eternal, moral truths just as there are eternal truths of mathematics. 2+2=4 is true because that is the way things are. *Rape is wrong* is true because that is the way things are. Anyone who cannot see this is "morally blind."

Well, what about "relativism"? I take it that relativism in some sense means "subjective," not part of nature but part of our desires or wishes or hopes or hates. I like Verdi. I cannot stand Wagner. You would rather go to Grand Ole Opry. That is as relativistic, as subjective as you like. But usually "subjective" means more than that. It means that it is all your choice and—this is important—no one can fault you for making that choice. They may stop you from acting on that choice. It is you who says that you don't like broccoli. It is your mother who says that you are not getting down from the table until your plate is clean. And no slipping it to the dog underneath, who probably doesn't like broccoli anyway!

Now I suspect that there are few if any who are going to say that at the level of substantive ethics, morality is or could be relative. The whole point about morality is that, in some sense, it is not a matter of choice. It is binding on you. Rape is always wrong, even though at the end of the Second World War Russian soldiers raped German women without end. It doesn't mean that you never do wrong. I suspect that there are few of us who can say genuinely that we have always stood right up and told mother that we will do the dishes. There are even some of us who have been known to return library books late—only nonphilosophers like sociologists would ever mark up a book with a yellow pen—but the point is that we would still be wrong.

So morality—meaning substantive morality—is not relative in this sense. There is another sense, though, when it can be, and often is, relative. Moral claims do not occur out of context. We are always in a specific situation when they arise, and, depending on the situation, that means what is the right moral claim can change. Morally, if someone doesn't like their job, the employer might keep them until the end of their contract, but then they must be free to go. I find that I don't much like teaching at Florida State University—the emphasis on football seems to me quite wrong—so morally I must be free to give up the job. My employer might insist that I stay until the end of term, but that must be it. In wartime, though, the solider cannot just call it a day and move back into civilian life. You are stuck for the duration. Morally, you have no right to quit the job and perhaps a strong moral dictate to stay on the job. Here there appear to be different, opposing, moral claims. But the underlying morality is the same. It is just that the circumstances are different.

Meanings: Metaethics

What about the metaethical side to things? That is, what about questions of justification? How about the reasons behind one's substantive moral judgments? In a way, it is a bit funny to ask if metaethics is relative. It is not the sort of thing that could be relative. A bit like asking if Tuesday is tired. Of course, you can ask if people tend to be more tired on Tuesdays than on other days of the week. So, in that sense, there might be a genuine and interesting question lurking behind asking if metaethics can be relative. And there is. Does metaethics point to subjectivity? Are the foundations of substantive morality objective or subjective? Well, once again, it all depends on what you mean!

If you believe in God—at least if you believe in the Judaeo-Christian God—presumably, in any basic sense, morality is objective. Note that it has to be this kind of God. The God of Aristotle, the Unmoved Mover, probably doesn't even know of our existence, so even if morality is objective, and even if the Unmoved Mover has a role in this objectivity, it isn't because the Unmoved Mover cared at all or had any decision in things.[4] For the Jew or Christian (or Muslim), the God of Abraham really does care and we are to do what He—I will call him a He, although this is tradition rather than essential theology—wants. We should not kill because God doesn't want us to kill.

Actually, though, you are still not entirely away from relativism. The *Euthyphro* problem—named after Plato's (427–347 BC) dialogue of that name—rears its ugly head. Is that which is good, good because God wants it, or does God enforce a separate objectively good morality? If the latter, then God seems irrelevant to morality; and if the former, we are back with relativism in spades. If God wanted killing to be okay, then it is okay. To be honest, something along these lines seems to be the position in the book of Job. I made the rules. Obey them. "Where wast thou when I laid the foundations of the earth? Declare, if thou hast understanding. Who hath laid the measures thereof, if thou knowest? Or who hath stretched the line upon it?"[5] Morality, on this view, seems to be completely relative, although it is not for us humans to do the deciding.

Obviously—with or without God—if you think that morality is like mathematics and that the latter is objective, then morality is objective. It is "out there" in some kind of sense, binding on us no less than $2+2=4$.[6] But even if you believe this sort of thing, you are still not trouble-free. What exactly is the nature of this world outside the world of nature, in which we live? And how are we able to connect to it? Are mathematics and morality things we can access through a kind of supernatural Skype? I know what it is to see a stone or a dog. I am not quite sure what it means to say that I know "$2+2=4$" or "Do not kill." How does our brain, a natural phenomenon, connect with mathematics or nonnatural ethics? You might say that it is not the brain that does the connecting but the mind, but in a way this is even more mystifying because the brain is obviously involved somehow and so now you don't just have the mind-ethics/mathematics connection to worry about, but a mysterious mind-brain connection is also involved somewhere.

Suppose then you decide not to go with the notion of objective meaning out there, although what "out there" means exactly if it is all a matter of mind is pretty obscure. Suppose you decide that it is all in the mind, as it were. You are not then plunged into some kind of extreme relativism, or, indeed, relativism at all for that matter. The great German philosopher, Immanuel Kant, argued that although things like mathematics and morality are in the mind (they are *a priori* as opposed to a posteriori, meaning natural or physical), they are not simple analytic truisms (like "All bachelors are unmarried").[7] They are, in some sense, part of the way things are—synthetic. However, what Kant argued was that the "synthetic *a priori*" was nonrelativistic and necessary in some sense. They are the required conditions of thinking rationally at all. In the case of morality, Kant argued that the supreme condition of morality, what he called the Categorical Imperative, demanded that you treat people as ends and not as means. Thus, for instance, rape is wrong because you are just satisfying your own lust and using the other person's body as a means to do this. You don't care about them as a person but only as a means to your own sexual gratification.

But why should you take the Categorical Imperative as binding—as necessary and not just a matter of choice? Because to do otherwise would get you into a contradiction—not a logical contradiction but a natural contradiction. If everyone thought as you do, against the Categorical Imperative, society would break down—it would be impossible, in a state of contradiction. In his rather convoluted way, Kant wrote:

> Because the universality of the law in accordance with which effects happen constitutes that which is really called nature in the most general sense (in accordance with its form), i.e., the existence of things insofar as it is determined in accordance with universal laws, thus the universal imperative of duty can also be stated as follows: So act as if the maxim of your action were to become through your will a universal law of nature.

Basically what Kant has in mind is a situation where, let us say, no one had any regard for the truth. Then, pretty soon that society would break down because you couldn't trust anyone, anywhere. To use a philosopher's example, suppose no one bothered to return library books. You simply couldn't run a library if you had to keep buying a new copy every time anyone borrowed a book. So with Kant, at the metalevel, you do have a kind of subjectivity, but it is one with no place at all for relativism, and hence if you mean by "objective" not so much "out there" as something you must obey without choice, you might think that calling such a system objective is really not out of place.

What about a case where you really do think that the foundations of morality are subjective? Let us agree that if you are going to have genuine substantive ethics you cannot just have: "If it feels okay, then it is okay." That is not morality. Perhaps you could have something that is relative within societies but not without. Of course, thanks to culture we already have something like this down here on earth. Take the Mormons in the nineteenth century. Most Americans thought you should have one wife and only one wife. The Mormons not only thought it was permissible to have more than one wife, but it was, for some people at least, obligatory. Two different substantive moral systems. Is that an end to matters? Do we simply judge the two systems as of equal value and argue that the Mormons only lost out in the end because they were the smaller group and the larger group simply had more bigots? I suspect most of us would say that although this is all a matter of culture, it is still possible to take a broader view and to judge that one side was simply wrong. You should not have two wives any more than during the Third Reich was it morally permissible to persecute Jews. Demeaning other human beings is cross-cultural—even if in the end you want to say that it is all relative or subjective with respect to human beings here on earth.

Darwinism

How then might we have different, relative systems that go beyond mere cultural differences? Biology comes at once to mind. Could biology make for different systems with different moral codes? Charles Darwin's (1809–1882) theory of evolution, published in his *On the Origin of Species* in 1859, has a threefold argument. First, picking up on the ideas of the political economist Thomas Robert Malthus (1766–1834), he argued that population pressures lead to an ongoing "struggle for existence," and, more importantly, to a struggle for reproduction. Second, he argued that new variations—what we today would call "mutations"—are always appearing spontaneously in natural populations. Third, he argued that this leads to a natural winnowing or selection.

> Let it be borne in mind in what an endless number of strange peculiarities our domestic productions, and, in a lesser degree, those under nature, vary; and how strong the hereditary tendency is. Under domestication, it may be truly said that the whole organisation becomes in some degree plastic. Let it be borne in mind how infinitely complex and close-fitting are the mutual relations of all organic beings to each other and to their physical conditions of life. Can it, then, be thought improbable, seeing that variations useful to man have undoubtedly occurred, that other variations useful in some way to each being in the great and complex battle of life, should sometimes occur in the course of thousands of generations? If such do occur, can we doubt (remembering that many more individuals are born than can possibly survive) that individuals having any advantage, however slight, over others, would have the best chance of surviving and of procreating their kind? On the other hand, we may feel sure that any variation in the least degree injurious would be rigidly destroyed. This preservation of favourable variations and the rejection of injurious variations, I call Natural Selection.[8]

Given enough time this leads to evolution, but note it is not just any-old-kind of evolution, but change in the direction of organisms having features that help in the struggle—features that are known as "adaptations," and are design-like such as the hand and the eye.

Now the whole point about morality—substantive morality—for the Darwinian is that it is an adaptation, no less than the hand and the eye.[9] Humans are social beings and hence morality is seen as an aid to sociality—no less than, say, the fact that humans don't come into heat and thus don't have the social disruptions that that would cause. (Imagine trying to teach intro philosophy if half the class were males and a couple of the females were in heat.) But since morality is an adaptation, there is nothing sacred about it. Nothing that says it must take the form that it does. Mammals can get from A to B by walking (humans), running (dogs), flying (bats), jumping (kangaroos), and so on. So with morality. Darwin, in his *Descent of Man* (1871), spotted this himself: "If, for instance, to take an extreme case, men were reared under precisely the same conditions as hive-bees, there can hardly be a doubt that our unmarried females would, like the worker-bees, think it a sacred duty to kill their brothers, and mothers would strive to kill their fertile daughters; and no one would think of interfering." And continuing: "The one course ought to have been followed, and the other ought not; the one would have been right and the other wrong."[10] In this scenario, Darwin is assuming that people like us are reared like ants. And he seems to suggest that it is culture that counts. We seem to have an extreme version of the Mormon example. But suppose it were all biology, and we had exoskeletons and six limbs. In other words, suppose in some sense we really were insects. Of course, we wouldn't be very humanlike if we were insects, but Darwin's point is that we could still be moral—though our morality would be different.

Of course, you might say that whatever the substantive morality, certain rules of game theory might have to apply. For example, morality would break down if one's highest moral code—one's Categorical Imperative—were to lie and cheat. You must have some kind of reciprocation, or it could never have evolved. If you don't get something out of morality—not necessarily consciously and not necessarily every time, but certainly on average—morality is not going to evolve. But while all of this is true, the fact that we are obeying certain formal rules of game theory does not itself make for morality. We could just do things on a basis of reason and self-interest. No morality. I want something from you. You want something from me. Let's trade. No morality. I have no obligation to do something for you or conversely. Kant spotted this: "What concern of mine is it? Let each one be as happy as heaven wills, or as he can make himself; I won't take anything from him or even envy him; but I have no desire to contribute to his welfare or help him in time of need."[11]

Kant argues that in real life this wouldn't go too far because it takes out the human need of sympathy and feeling. I suspect that a stronger reason why we have evolved beyond this is that time is money in real life, and working out the cost-benefits would be ruinously expensive—it would take way too long. Morality is a quick and dirty way of getting along. Sometimes it breaks down—someone cheats on us, for example—but usually it works. But I can certainly imagine real humans—not ant-humans—with a different moral system. Suppose that, rather like John Foster Dulles (1888–1959) (President Eisenhower's secretary of state) in the 1950s dealing with the Russians, instead of thinking that you should love your enemies, you thought you should hate your enemies, that this was a moral obligation. However, you knew your enemies felt the same about you and so you cooperated with them—as did Dulles and the Russians. So now you have two functioning moral codes. It just so happens you have developed one rather than the other. But you could have developed the other. Which is the true one? Who can say? And before you say that at least there was one true code, notice that its truth seems inessential to your belief system (you can function and survive whether it's true or not), and that is surely antithetical to what we understand by objective moral standards.

Implications

Let me make a couple of points about morality—substantive morality that is—on the assumption that it is all a matter of biology. If you think that morality is an adaptation, like hands and eyes, that evolution has put in place to make us successful animals (where "successful" put in evolutionary terms means good at surviving and reproducing, or if not good then at least better than competitors), then what follows?

First, morality like this is going to be relative in an almost literal sense. Many people, the philosopher Peter Singer is one, think that morality is something that applies indifferently to all people.[12] I have the same obligation to (let us say) a child in Syria as I have to my own children. I suspect that in this era of President Donald Trump, many of us feel uncomfortable at denying this. But I suspect that biology does suggest a greater obligation to relatives and friends than to others. This is nothing new to biology, of course. St Paul said, "I seek not yours but you: for the children ought not to lay up for the parents, but the parents for the children" (2 Cor. 12: 14). Nor would Hume disagree: "A man naturally loves his children better than his nephews, his nephews better than his cousins, his cousins better than strangers, where everything else is equal. Hence arise our common measures of duty, in preferring the one to the other. Our sense of duty always follows the common and natural course of our passions."[13] Charles Dickens (1812–1870) makes this point brutally in his great novel *Bleak House*.[14] He has withering scorn for the philanthropist Mrs. Jellyby who ignores her own family to campaign on behalf of a "hundred and fifty to two hundred healthy families cultivating coffee and educating the natives of Borrioboola-Gha, on the left bank of the Niger." She ignores her children Caddy and Peepy, to say nothing of the poor and needy in her own society—Jo the crossing sweeper, for instance. As Dickens (like Paul and Hume) would say, this is not to say we have no obligations to strangers, but simply that charity does begin at home.

Second, we have to be deceived by our biology into thinking that morality is objective—even if it isn't! "Reason is as cunning as it is powerful. Cunning may be said to lie in the intermediative action which, while it permits the objects to follow their own bent and act upon one another till they waste away, and does not itself directly interfere in the process, is nevertheless only working out its own aims."[15] The proposition *Rape is wrong* may be without objective foundation, but it means rape is wrong—it is morally prohibited—even if the whole world thinks it is okay. It was wrong to be prejudiced against Jews even though eighty percent of Germans under the Third Reich thought it acceptable. What is essential to morality is the sense of absoluteness. The meaning of moral statements includes objectivity.[16] "Rape is wrong" means it is objectively wrong to rape. And it doesn't take much to see why evolution added this element to the pie. If we thought it was all feeling, then the temptation to cheat would be overwhelming and substantive ethics would break down almost immediately. Because we think morality is binding on us, we do not cheat—at least, if we do cheat, we know that it is wrong.

These are my answers to the question about whether morality is relative. In the system, it cannot be, otherwise we don't have morality. With respect to foundations, it could be—my own strong suspicion, based on the fact that we are creatures of evolution rather than made in the image of a creator god—that morality is subjective. But if we thought that morality was subjective at the metaethical level, morality at the substantive level would break down. Our biology has to trick us into thinking that morality is objective. And if you respond that, now you know the truth, you can go out and be immoral, let me assure you that you are mistaken. The truth does not set you free. More strongly, you simply won't be able to go against your deepest biological instincts. We all know that self-abuse makes you go blind. There are very good reasons for you to stop, especially given that you already have to wear glasses. It makes no difference. The day you stop abusing yourself, forever, will be the day that I believe you can now be immoral, forever.

Notes

1 L. Wittgenstein, *Philosophical Investigations* (Oxford: Blackwell, 1953).

2 M. Ruse, *Atheism: What Everyone Needs to Know* (Oxford: Oxford University Press, 2015).

3 M. Ruse, *Taking Darwin Seriously: A Naturalistic Approach to Philosophy* (Oxford: Blackwell, 1986).

4   D. Sedley, *Creationism and Its Critics in Antiquity* (Berkeley: University of California Press, 2008).

5   Job 38: 4–5.

6   This seems to have been the position of G. E. Moore, the British philosopher active at the beginning of the last century. He spoke of "nonnatural properties" and openly identified himself as a Platonist—Plato was one who explicitly thought there is a supersensible world of eternal truths (see G. E. Moore, *Principia Ethica* [Cambridge: Cambridge University Press, 1903]; and see also for background detail S. Cunningham, *Philosophy and the Darwinian Legacy* [Rochester: University of Rochester Press, 1996]).

7   I. Kant, *Foundations of the Metaphysics of Morals* (Indianapolis: Bobbs-Merrill, 1959).

8   C. Darwin, *On the Origin of Species by Means of Natural Selection, or the Preservation of Favoured Races in the Struggle for Life* (London: John Murray, 1859), 80–81.

9   M. Ruse, *The Philosophy of Human Evolution* (Cambridge: Cambridge University Press, 2012).

10 C. Darwin, *The Descent of Man, and Selection in Relation to Sex* (London: John Murray, 1871), 1, 73.

11 Kant, *Foundations*, 41.

12 P. Singer, "Famine, Affluence and Morality," *Philosophy and Public Affairs*, 1 (1972): 229–43.

13 D. Hume, *A Treatise of Human Nature* (Oxford: Oxford University Press, 1978), III, 2, i.

14 C. Dickens, *Bleak House* (Oxford: Oxford University Press, [1853] 1948).

15 G. F. W. Hegel, *Logic,* trans. W. Wallace (Pacifica, CA: Marxist's Internet Archive, [1830] 2008), 447.

16 J. L. Mackie, *Ethics* (Harmondsworth, Middlesex: Penguin, 1977).

Morality Is Objective*

Francis J. Beckwith

Study Questions

1. What does it mean to say that morality is objective?

2. Why is it no objection to objective morality to point out that moral claims exist in the mind?

3. What does Beckwith mean by "morality"? How do moral "oughts" differ from other types of "oughts"?

*© Francis J. Beckwith, 2020.

4. According to Beckwith, why should we not be surprised to find disagreement among those who believe in objective morality?
5. What uncontroversial moral propositions does Beckwith list? Why does he think they are uncontroversial?
6. What does the disagreement between President Bush and Bill Maher imply about courage and cowardice?
7. What do exemptions to the universal prohibition against homicide require? What do disagreements about these exemptions show and not show?
8. Are people always entitled to their property, according to Beckwith? Why? Does this undermine the objectivity of property rights? Why?
9. What evidence does Beckwith offer for the moral obligation of truth telling? What might justify exceptions to this rule?
10. Why is the principle of tolerance important? What limits may it have? Why?

Everywhere you turn you are confronted with moral questions. Is abortion the unjust taking of a human life? Is this particular war justified? Is it ever permissible to lie? Should a business for the sake of diversity take race into consideration when hiring? How much of my paycheck should I contribute to charity? Unsurprisingly, intelligent and informed people give differing and sometimes contrary answers to these and other moral questions. For this reason, the claim that morality is objective—that there could be true answers to some moral questions—seems to be a mistake. And yet, many people, including some of the most respected thinkers in history, believe that morality is objective. For example, the great American civil rights leader, Martin Luther King, Jr. (1929–1968), in his famous Letter from a Birmingham Jail, writes that "an unjust law is a code that is out of harmony with the moral law,"[1] implying that there is an objective morality by which we can judge the civil and criminal laws of our nation.

In this essay we will see why people like King believe in objective morality and show why you should accept their view. But first, we have to do some philosophical housekeeping, which simply means that we have to define and clarify some of the terms we will be using.

Philosophical Housekeeping

To say that morality is *objective* is to say that it is a belief whose truth does not depend on how someone may feel about it. We think this way about other subjects. So, for example, we say that it is objectively true that George Washington (1732–1799) was the first president of the United States, that 2+2=4, or that the Yankees play in New York City—and we say these things even if someone were to say that they felt that John Adams (1735–1826) was the first president, that 2+2 really equals 5, or that the Yankees play in Torre Del Greco, Naples. In the same way, for the moral objectivist, claims like "it is wrong to torture children for fun," "courage is a virtue," or "one ought to make fair judgments" are true even if someone were to say that they felt that it is okay to torture children for fun, that cowardice is a virtue, and that it is permissible to make unfair judgments.

But could not someone say that there is something fundamentally different about moral claims in comparison to claims about presidents and baseball teams? After all, presidents and baseball teams are outside one's mind, while moral claims are inside one's mind. That's certainly true. But whether a claim is objective—in the sense we are using it here—does not depend on where it is located. Certain objective truths—about Adams, Washington, and the Yankees—are about particular things, while other objective truths—about mathematics, conceptual claims, and morality (at least for the moral objectivist)—are about universal things, which by their very nature are not particular things and not necessarily outside our minds.[2] Perhaps an analogy will help. Consider a principle of criminal law: "The basis of our system of criminal justice is that a person, although charged with an offence, is considered innocent until proved guilty of the offence."[3] This principle is not a claim about a particular person to which one may point, for example, "John Wilkes Booth, accused of murder by the prosecution, is innocent until proven guilty." Rather, it is a universal claim that applies to all persons as such, and yet, it is not outside anyone's mind, as is a president or a baseball team. (It is, of course, written down, but the text, a mere inscription of the rule, has its source in a mind.) Yet, it is objective in exactly the same way that the moral objectivist believes "it is wrong to torture children for fun" is objective.

Now that we have clarified what we mean by "objective," it is time to clarify what we mean by "morality." This is a bit more difficult, since the claims of morality often overlap other claims that we do not ordinarily think of as moral ones. For example, suppose we say that morality is about what one ought to do. So, we reason, one ought not to steal, murder, or torture children for fun. There are, however, other kinds of "oughts" that do not obviously seem to be about morality, for example, you ought to reason well, pay your taxes, and brush and floss your teeth every day. But is that entirely correct? After all, one could think of these "oughts" as moral by saying that there seems to be something immoral about someone who intentionally reasons badly, violates the tax code, and shows no concern for their own dental well-being. (There is a sense in which intellectual recklessness, lawbreaking, and carelessness about one's health reveal bad character, which is a moral judgment.) Nevertheless, certain conditional "oughts" do not seem to have anything to do with morality, for example, if you want to go to the basketball game, you ought to buy tickets; if you want to get that job, you ought to invite the boss' husband to the party; and so forth.

Morality is also often said to be about what is good as opposed to what is bad or wicked. So, for example, most of us believe that kindness, fairness, and courage are good, whereas meanness, unfairness, and cowardice are bad. Those beliefs seem to be about morality. On the other hand, most of us believe, among other things, that an increase in one's wealth, a well-played football game, a beautiful sunset, a way with words, and a highly skilled plumber are good. Although these latter beliefs do not seem to be about moral goods, they may play a role in a moral action: increased wealth may allow one to donate more money to charity; cooperation in successful sporting endeavors often requires the good of friendship; the beauty of nature may inspire one to perform acts of virtue to protect the environment; attractive and compelling prose written for a good end may arouse others from moral apathy; a home absent disrepair makes it easier for the homeowner and her family to engage in tasks ordered toward the common good. Nevertheless, there do seem to be many goods, in and of themselves, that have virtually nothing to do with morality, for example, a good hammer, a good bottle of Scotch, or a good pair of glasses.

So, what then is morality? Although, as we have seen, it is difficult to precisely define, it seems fair to say that morality concerns the evaluation of human conduct, motives, and ends, usually in the form of judgments about goodness, badness, virtue, and vice. Thus, we say that the people who house and shelter widows and orphans are good, and that the people who intentionally create widows and orphans are bad and that they ought not to do it. Morality often concerns what is just or unjust. This is why we say that someone who does not give others their due or takes advantage of the weak and vulnerable commits an injustice. Although these moral beliefs are often reflected in a society's laws and religious traditions (e.g., criminal statutes, the Ten Commandments, the Golden Rule, The UN Declaration on Human Rights), the bulk of these moral beliefs are unwritten, though the expectation is that no competent adult can plausibly feign ignorance of their authoritative nature.[4] So, for example, even if there were no civil or criminal laws that prohibited child abandonment, our unwritten customs, informed by certain moral beliefs, tell us that it is deeply wicked for parents to intentionally abandon their children when rearing them is no longer convenient.

Now that we know what it means to say that morality is objective, we can move on to see why many people, including many philosophers, believe that it is true that morality is objective.

Why Morality Is Objective

Aristotle (384–322 BCE) once wrote that when we study morality we should not expect from it the sort of exactitude we find in other disciplines: "For it is the mark of an educated man to look for precision in each class of things just so far as the nature of the subject admits; it is evidently equally foolish to accept probable reasoning from a mathematician and to demand from a rhetorician scientific proofs."[5] This is because, as Aristotle notes, our moral judgments and opinions are influenced by everything from self-interest and unruly passions to lack of self-restraint. This is why the tax-evader driven by greed, and thus engaged in a wrong, tries to justify his action by appealing to some good that he is claiming to vindicate, such as, "my family needs the money," "I can spend it in better ways than the government can," "the tax rates are too high," and so forth. So, when we discuss morality and whether it is objective we should not be surprised that we discover there is disagreement among those who seemingly believe in objective morality. For this reason, to quote Aristotle yet again, "We must be content, then, in speaking of such subjects and with such premises to indicate the truth roughly and in outline."[6] In other words, in arguing that morality is objective the best we can do is to show that belief in its truth explains a lot more than the belief that it is false.

Now let us consider several apparently uncontroversial moral propositions. (We could, undoubtedly, add other propositions to this list, but these five will do.)

(1) Courage is a virtue, and cowardice is a vice.

(2) It is wrong to kill human persons without justification.

(3) One should not take another's property without good cause.

(4) One should not intentionally tell a falsehood to someone who is entitled to the truth.

(5) Society (or at least the legal system) ought to exhibit a generous amount of tolerance toward its citizens, though there are limits.

I say these propositions are morally uncontroversial, since I am fairly certain that any person who reads them, no matter their cultural background, religious convictions, or political beliefs, will immediately agree that they are true.[7]

They seem to be beliefs that, in the words of J. Budziszewski, "we can't not know."[8] And if that's the case, there exists an objective morality. The devil, of course, is in the details. For if we go through each one of these beliefs we will begin to think about disagreements that may arise about how, to what, and to whom these propositions should be applied. Nevertheless, the nature of these disagreements, as I will argue, presupposes an objective morality. So, let's go through each of these beliefs.

Courage and Cowardice

Only hours after the terrorist attacks of September 11, 2011, President George W. Bush delivered these words to the American people: "Freedom itself was attacked this morning by a faceless coward. . . . Make no mistake: the U.S. will hunt down and punish those responsible for these cowardly acts."[9] On his ABC television show, *Politically Incorrect*, comedian Bill Maher responded to the president's account with a different take: "We have been the cowards, lobbing cruise missiles from 2,000 miles away. That's cowardly. Staying in the airplane when it hits the building, say what you want about it, it's not cowardly."[10]

Although it is clear that in this dispute there is no disagreement with the claim that cowardice is a vice and courage a virtue, there is a disagreement over whether in this particular case the acts of the terrorists (or the United States) could appropriately be labeled one or the other. Nevertheless, this does show that we not only have an intuitive sense of what courage and cowardice are, but also can, in fact, reason about them without abandoning the idea that the goodness of courage and the badness of cowardice are objectively true.

For instance, we often think of courage as a kind of inner strength exhibited in the face of adversity, which may include risk of death or bodily harm. That, however, does not seem entirely correct, since some of the world's most pernicious criminals, such as Bonnie and Clyde, were "courageous" in this sense, but it seems wrong to say that they displayed *virtue* while committing their crimes. As Aristotle put it, "Men, then, as well as beasts, suffer pain when they are angry, and are pleased when they exact their revenge; those who fight for these reasons, however, are pugnacious but not brave; for they do not act for honour's sake nor as the rule directs, but from strength of feeling; they have, however, something akin to courage."[11] In other words, to call pernicious risk-taking criminals "courageous" would be like saying that an instance of rape is a case of "making love" simply because both involve sex.

We also have an intuitive sense of what cowardice is. We often think of it as a kind of inner *weakness* exhibited in the face of adversity, which may include risk of death or bodily harm. So, we think of the soldier who abandons his platoon and betrays his country as exhibiting cowardice. Yet, if we begin to think deeply about it, we will likely conclude that not all cases of withdrawal or restraint in the face of adversity is cowardly (even though we may wind up disagreeing about specific cases). When, for example, Germany and Japan surrendered to the Allied Powers at the end of the Second World War, their leaders were not acting as "cowards." Rather, they assessed their predicaments wisely and came to the conclusion that continued fighting would not only be futile, it would mean further destruction of what remained of their respective societies and cultures.

Life

The good of life is so fundamental to our moral intuitions that we demand an explanation or justification for the cause of an intentional death but not if somebody just happens to be alive. So, for example, upon hearing that Mr. Jones committed suicide, one is apt to immediately ask, "Why did he do that?" but it would be thought odd if upon my telling you that I saw Mr. Jones today as alive as he was last week, you were to inquire, "Why did he do that?"

So, it is unsurprising that every society in the history of humanity has had both customary and legal prohibitions against homicide. Even though these prohibitions have not been absolute, the exemptions that do exist always come with justification. Thus, in cases of self-defense, war, capital punishment, euthanasia, or abortion, the one defending the act offers reasons as to why this is an exemption from the ordinary ban on killing. In self-defense, it is the appeal to necessity: to save an innocent life against unjust aggression, one had to act in a way that resulted in the death of the assailant.[12] With a particular war, the defender of it argues that the nation was justified in waging war since it was the only means by which it could repel another nation's unjust invasion or attack.[13] Supporters of the death penalty argue that taking the life of a capital offender is just retribution for the offender's robbing an innocent person of his life.[14] Euthanasia proponents defend it on the grounds that terminal patients who are suffering have a right to rid themselves of their burden, even if it results in their deaths.[15] On the matter of abortion, some argue that the fetus is not a person and thus not a moral subject,[16] while others argue that even if it is a moral subject it has no right to use another's body against her will.[17]

Of course, each of these exemptions has its critics who disagree with the supposed justifications.[18] But this does not mean there is no objective morality; it simply means that people disagree as to the proper application of the principle that they all believe is true: it is wrong to kill human persons without justification. (Supreme Court justices have over time disagreed as to the precise meaning and application of the free speech clause of the US Constitution's First Amendment; but that does not mean that there is no right to free speech!) So, once again, on the issue of abortion, both pro-choice and pro-life advocates agree that unjustified homicide is wrong. Where most of them disagree is on the question of who counts as a moral subject. That is not so much a moral disagreement as it is a disagreement over a metaphysical question: Who and what is a human person?

Property

To almost everyone, it seems obvious that theft is a moral wrong, though that does not mean that people are always entitled to their property. Consider this case. I borrow my neighbor's gun so that I can go hunting with my friends. After returning, he calls me and asks me to give him back his gun. He tells me that he needs it right away so that he can shoot his wife this evening. I think I am justified in not agreeing to his request, and in believing that what I am doing is not an act of theft.

Even in societies where private property is not as sacrosanct as many wish it ought to be, people defend the communal use or ownership of property or fungible goods by offering justifications. So, for example, socialized medicine, eminent domain law, the taking of a loaf of bread by a starving person, or high inheritance tax rates may be justified by appealing to necessity or the common good. Even the communist believes that someone who takes more than his "fair share" is stealing, and the thief is probably more careful than most in protecting his property. So, it seems that everyone, including the thief and the communist, believes that theft is wrong, even if we differ on what precisely constitutes a justified taking. Thus, the principle—one should not take another's property without good cause—seems practically undeniable, regardless of one's cultural beliefs or political predilections.

Truth

Years ago, when I was on the faculty of the University of Nevada, Las Vegas, I was teaching an ethics course in which we were discussing the issue of moral relativism (which is the denial that morality is objective). One of my brightest and most active students raised her hand and asked the question, "Why is the truth important?" I paused for a moment and answered, "Do you want the true answer or the false one?" She correctly assumed that she was entitled to the truth, that had I intentionally given her a false answer I would have wronged her. But this reaction is not unique to just that student. It seems obvious to almost everyone that one should not intentionally tell a falsehood to someone who is entitled to the truth. Even con-men must rely on the veracity of this principle, since one cannot be a successful grifter unless human beings, including the grifter's victims, consider truth telling a prima facie moral obligation. It is so embedded in the very fabric of every human society that its most important institutions and transactions—for example, marriages, courts, contracts—presuppose the normativity of promise keeping.

However, most people believe—and most societies affirm—that there are justified exemptions to this general rule. Consider what constitutes "someone who is entitled to the truth." For virtually everybody, for example, enemy combatants in a just war and criminals seeking out innocent victims are not entitled to the truth. In fact, soldiers wear camouflage, which is really communicating to the enemy, "There's no soldier here. I'm just a clump of foliage." In ordinary life, we try to come up with ways to answer awkward question by being purposely vague or ambiguous about the total truth. So, when my wife asks me, "Does this dress make me look fat?" it is wise for me to respond by saying, "Honey, I think you look better in that other outfit. This one does not do justice to your beauty."

There are, of course, differing views as to what counts as a justified exemption, but such a dispute would have never arisen unless all the parties in it had already accepted the principle that one should not intentionally tell a falsehood to someone who is entitled to the truth.

Tolerance

If Aristotle is correct, human beings are rational animals,[19] meaning that we have certain rational powers that distinguish us from animals that are not rational. Some, including Aristotle, say that this is manifested in our ability to know universal truths, such as one's knowledge of a perfect circle or the essence of human nature, even if it has no empirical referent in the material world to which we can point. (In other words, because no physical circle can ever be perfect and no individual human being is the same as his essence, the rational power by which we abstract these and other concepts makes available to us universal truths that other creatures cannot know.)

These rational powers, as some contemporary philosophers have argued,[20] also allow us to philosophize, which often leads us to differing conclusions about a variety of important issues, such as the nature of the good life, whether or not God exists, with whom one should seek friendship, what profession one should pursue, in what community one should take up residence, what art and music is the most beautiful, whether one should marry and have children, and so forth. But given that our rational powers, even when properly exercised, will lead us to a diversity of opinions on these matters, most people believe that society (or at least the legal system) ought to exhibit a generous amount of tolerance toward its citizens. But there are limits, often guided by other moral beliefs about what constitutes the common good. So, for example, a tolerant society allows freedom of worship, but it is not so tolerant that it should allow worship that requires human sacrifice. Ironically, in those few ancient societies where human sacrifice was required, it was only performed because it was widely believed that the gods (or God) required it, meaning that the presumption was against it unless a divine sovereign that has the power and authority to issue such orders says otherwise.

But there are, of course, cases that are not that clear to even the most tolerant among us in today's day and age. Take, for example, the debates in the United States and Europe over whether certain wedding vendors ought to be forced to participate in same-sex ceremonies contrary to their religious beliefs, whether parents should be permitted to exempt their school-age children from compulsory government education, whether it should be lawful for observant Muslim women to wear their traditional religious scarf (the hijab) in public, or whether the state should allow certain forms of so-called "hate speech." These contested questions arise precisely because free societies embrace the principle of tolerance as well as other principles that many believe are essential to a well-ordered society and may (or may not) force us to place limits on tolerance (e.g., antidiscrimination laws, the good of uniform educational standards, the fraternal benefit of cultural assimilation, the wrong of dignitary harms).

We would like to think that tolerance is a principle unique to modern Western societies, and thus lacks the universality that seems to be the case with the principles arising from the goods of courage, life, truth, and property. But that is not entirely accurate. For even long before the term "tolerance" began to dominate our political and moral discourse, there were always debates about the limits of dissent and disagreement with prevailing societal or religious norms (not unlike the contested questions already mentioned). Take, for example, the comments from the thirteenth-century Catholic philosopher St. Thomas Aquinas (1225–1274) on whether human law should prohibit all vices:

> Now human law is framed for a number of human beings, the majority of whom are not perfect in virtue. Wherefore human laws do not forbid all vices, from which the virtuous abstain, but only the more grievous vices, from which it is possible for the majority to abstain; and chiefly those that are to the hurt of others, without the prohibition of which human society could not be maintained: thus human law prohibits murder, theft and such like.[21]

Aquinas, to be sure, was no paleo-liberal, but even he understood that a society's common good *may be* inhibited if a certain degree of tolerance is not extended to citizens he (and the majority of other citizens) believed were deeply mistaken in their beliefs and practices.[22] So, it turns out that the "tolerance" of Aquinas and his medieval Catholic compatriots is not so different from the "tolerance" advanced by some of our contemporaries who believe that certain state actions—such as the forbidding of "hate speech," the coercion of wedding vendors who dissent from same-sex marriage, and the prohibition of Muslim women from wearing their religious garb in public—*may or may not* be proper applications of the principles of a tolerant secular society.

Conclusion

Although it is undoubtedly true that individuals and cultures disagree on a variety of moral questions, it is also true that beneath these disagreements is a common objective morality. To be sure, given its generality, this is a modest conclusion, but it is not an insignificant one. In an age in which so many of our compatriots have bought into moral relativism hook, line and sinker, it is important to know that one can marshal a strong case against it.

Notes

1. Martin Luther King, Jr., "Letter from a Birmingham Jail" (April 16, 1963), available at https://www.africa.upenn.edu/Articles_Gen/Letter_Birmingham.html.
2. I say "not necessarily," because some philosophers, such as Plato, believe that certain ideas that they call "universals" do have real existence in some heavenly realm called the world of forms. But that's another subject for another chapter.
3. Legal Services Commission of South Australian, "General Principles of Criminal Law," http://www.lawhandbook.sa.gov.au/ch12s02.php.
4. Some defenders of objective morality admit that some competent adults may get some aspects of morality wrong, but not in its entirety. St. Thomas Aquinas, for example, writes: Consequently we must say that the natural law [objective morality], as to general principles, is the same for all, both as to rectitude and as to knowledge. But as to certain matters of detail, which are conclusions, as it were, of those general principles, it is the same for all in the majority of cases, both as to rectitude and as to knowledge; and yet in some few cases it may fail, both as to rectitude,

by reason of certain obstacles (just as natures subject to generation and corruption fail in some few cases on account of some obstacle), and as to knowledge, since in some the reason is perverted by passion, or evil habit, or an evil disposition of nature; thus formerly, theft, although it is expressly contrary to the natural law [objective morality], was not considered wrong among the Germans, as Julius Caesar relates. (St. Thomas Aquinas, *Summa Theologica*, I-II.Q94.art6, 2nd and rev., literally translated by Fathers of the English Dominican Province [1920], online edition, http://www.newadvent.org/summa/2094.htm#article6)

5 Aristotle, *Nicomachean Ethics* (350 BCE.), trans. W. D. Ross, BkI.3, available at http://classics.mit.edu/Aristotle/nicomachaen.1.i.html.

6 Ibid.

7 There will, of course, be the very rare exception, such as the sociopath, who simply cannot "see" these moral truths. But that no more counts against objective morality than would the existence of a color blind person count against the existence of colors. In fact, when we hear of the sociopath and his strange beliefs, we immediately think that there is something wrong with him, which in itself means we believe that the human person has certain proper functions that, when neither missing nor deformed, constitute a kind of fulfillment or perfection of his nature.

8 J. Budziszewski, *What We Can't Not Know*, rev. ed.(San Francisco: Ignatius Press, 2011).

9 John Gerstein, "Terror Attacks Spark Cowardly Debate," *ABC News* website (September 26, 2001), available at http://abcnews.go.com/Politics/story?id=121312&page=1.

10 Ibid.

11 Aristotle, *Nicomachean Ethics*, BkIII.8, available at http://classics.mit.edu/Aristotle/nicomachaen.3.iii.html.

12 See Judith Jarvis Thomson, "Self Defense," *Philosophy and Public Affairs*, 20:4 (April 1991): 283–310.

13 See David D. Corey and J. Daryl Charles, *The Just War Tradition: An Introduction* (Wilmington, DE: ISI Books, 2012).

14 See Louis Pojman, "In Defense of the Death Penalty," *International Journal of Applied Philosophy*, 11:2 (Winter/Spring 1997): 11–16.

15 See Stephen W. Smith, *End-of-Life Decisions in Medical Care: Principles and Policies for Regulating the Dying Process* (Cambridge, UK: Cambridge University Press, 2012).

16 See Mary Anne Warren, "On the Moral and Legal Status of Abortion Rights," *The Monist*, 57:4 (1973): 43–61.

17 See Judith Jarvis Thomson, "A Defense of Abortion," *Philosophy and Public Affairs*, 1:1 (1971): 47–66.

18 For example, on the matter of abortion, I take the position that abortion, in virtually all cases, constitutes unjustified homicide. See Francis J. Beckwith, *Defending Life: A Moral and Legal Case Against Abortion Choice* (New York: Cambridge University Press, 2007).

19 Aristotle, *Nicomachean Ethics,* Bkl.13, available at http://classics.mit.edu/Aristotle/nicomachaen.1.i.html.

20 See, for example, John Rawls, *Political Liberalism*, expanded edition (New York: Columbia University Press, 2005).

21 St. Thomas Aquinas, *Summa Theologica*, I-II.Q96.art2, available at http://www.newadvent.org/summa/2096.htm#article2.

22 Even on the matter of religious toleration—where one would expect the starkest disagreement between our beliefs and those of the medieval philosopher—one finds in Aquinas a modest case for it:

> [T]hough unbelievers sin in their rites, they may be tolerated, either on account of some good that ensues therefrom, or because of some evil avoided. Thus from the fact that the Jews observe their rites, which, of old, foreshadowed the truth of the faith which we hold, there follows this good—that our very enemies bear witness to our faith, and that our faith is represented in a figure, so to speak. For this reason they are tolerated in the observance of their rites.

> On the other hand, the rites of other unbelievers, which are neither truthful nor profitable, are by no means to be tolerated, except perchance in order to avoid an evil, for example, the scandal or disturbance that might ensue, or some hindrance to the salvation of those who if they were unmolested might gradually be converted to the faith. For this reason the church, at times, has tolerated the rites even of heretics and pagans, when unbelievers were very numerous (St. Thomas Aquinas, *Summa Theologica*, II-II.Q11.art3, available at http://www.newadvent.org/summa/3011.htm#article3).

RESPONSES

Response to Ruse[*]

Francis J. Beckwith

> ### Study Questions
> 1. On what three things does Beckwith agree with Ruse?
> 2. How does Beckwith respond to Ruse's concern about "immaterial realities"?
> 3. Why does Beckwith think that Ruse's "Darwinian morality" isn't really a form of relativism?
> 4. What problem does Beckwith have with Ruse's notion that morality is a trick played on us by our genes?
> 5. Why does Beckwith think that the price of accepting Ruse's view is the "undermining of everything we believe"?

There is much in Professor Ruse's well-crafted chapter with which I agree. First, like me (and most philosophers), he believes that relativism is very difficult to defend at the level of "substantive" or "normative" morality. That is, it seems to virtually everybody that there exists an objective moral law that tells us that certain kinds of action are categorically wrong (e.g., rape, torturing children for fun, theft, and murder, even if some of our compatriots do not live up to these prescriptions).

Second, Ruse correctly observes that there is a sense in which the moral law is relative: "Moral claims do not occur out of context. We are always in a specific situation when they arrive, and, depending on the situation, that means what is the right moral claim can change" (p. 30). So, for example, one may say that Bob has the right to life. But suppose Bob violently attacks Fred, and Fred kills Bob in self-defense. How do we morally evaluate Fred's action vis-a-vis Bob's right to life? It depends on whether lethal force was necessary to ward off Bob's attack. If it wasn't, then Fred violated Bob's right to life. But if it was, then Fred's right to secure his own right to life justifies Fred's use of lethal force. Thus, Ruse is correct that a moral claim may change depending on the situation, even though the principle on which the moral claim is based—in this case, the right to life—is unchanging.

---

[*] © Francis J. Beckwith, 2020.

Third, on the matter of "metaethics"—how we may justify or ground the moral law—Ruse is surely right that there are a variety of different approaches, including appeals to God and Kant's Categorical Imperative, and that there is no consensus among philosophers as to which approach wins the day. But, even if we set the question of justification aside, Ruse points out that there seems to be something inscrutably mysterious about morality if we insist that it is part of the furniture of the universe, "out there" or objective, "binding on us no less than 2+2=4" (p. 31). To believe there are immaterial normative realties—both mathematical and moral—to which we must measure up when doing our sums and exercising our wills is too high a price for Ruse to pay, since it seems to require that human beings, material creatures, have an immaterial aspect to their nature by which they access these apparent immaterial realities. This, according to Ruse, just doubles the mystery, since it means that the physical brain—that undoubtedly is involved with our acquisition of knowledge—must interact with an immaterial mind in order to access immaterial realities, which are already inscrutably mysterious.

Materialism and Darwinian Morality

Here I want to register my first disagreement with Professor Ruse. Why can't one say that our knowledge of mathematics and morality implies that there may be something wrong with materialism, and thus this alleged inscrutable mystery is no less mysterious for the materialist as it is for his critic? After all, for most people, denying what seems obvious about mathematics and morality—that they are normative immaterial realities—is just too a high a price for them to pay. They may reason: better to live with the inscrutable mystery and reject materialism than to abandon what seems obviously true.[1]

Professor Ruse, a materialist, believes that the way around this is to argue that our sense of morality, or what I have called "the moral law," can be fully accounted for by biological evolution. Thus, it is superfluous to claim that our moral sense refers to anything immaterial and unchanging. (He does not specifically address what to do with mathematics, but one suspects that he would tell a similar story.)

According to Charles Darwin, all our parts and powers are the consequence of adaptations. Organisms that survive, do so by adapting to their environment. Over long eons of time, these adaptations result in a variety of different types of organisms (or species) that develop certain parts and powers that allow them to more efficiently survive and pass on their genes. So, for example, having hands with opposable thumbs (for human beings), wings (for bats), or long necks (for giraffes) are adaptations that aid in their survival. Morality, argues Ruse, is no different. For this reason, if human beings had developed bee-like or insect-like attributes instead of the ones we currently possess, our "morality" would have been different. On this point, Ruse quotes from Darwin's *Descent of Man*: "If, for instance, to take an extreme case, men were reared under precisely the same conditions as hive-bees, there can hardly be a doubt that our unmarried females would, like the worker-bees, think it a sacred duty to kill their brothers, and mothers would strive to kill their fertile daughters; and no one would think of interfering."[2]

It is in this sense that Ruse claims to be a relativist. He is arguing that what we think is the moral law is not absolute, but relative to the sort of creatures we have become as a consequence of biological evolution. For, given the nature of biological evolution, we could have just as well become intelligent, social, and culture-creating insects rather than intelligent, social, and culture-creating hominids.

Explaining Morality Away

Here I register my second disagreement with Professor Ruse. I don't think this is relativism at all, but simply a Darwinian version of what many traditional moralists, who are hardly relativists, have noted about morality and its dependence on human nature. St. Thomas Aquinas, for example, argued that there is no such thing as good in the abstract, that what counts as good depends on the essence or nature of the thing we are talking about.[3] Thus, when I say "Phydeaux is a good dog" I mean something different than when I say "Michael is a good human being." The first may refer to Phydeaux's obedience to his master when being walked on a leash, while the second may refer to Michael's kindness, generosity, and honesty. Thus, what seems perfectly good for the canine Phydeaux seems like a violation of the dignity of the homo sapiens Michael.

Professor Ruse goes on to argue that there is another sense in which biological evolution supports moral relativism: "We have to be deceived by our biology into thinking that morality is objective—even if it isn't" (p. 36). What he means by this is that our common belief that there is a moral law is the result of a trick played on us by our genes, since believing that there is a moral law, even though there really is not one, best contributes to the reproductive success of the human race. As Ruse notes in a famous article he coauthored with E. O. Wilson:

> Morality, or more strictly, our belief in morality, is merely an adaptation put in place to further our reproductive ends. Hence the basis of ethics does not lie in God's will—or in the metaphysical roots of evolution or any other framework of the Universe. In an important sense, ethics as we understand

it is an illusion fobbed off on us by our genes to get us to cooperate. It is without external grounding. Ethics is produced by evolution, but not justified by it, because, like Macbeth's dagger, it serves a powerful purpose without existing in substance.[4]

For Ruse, there is a kind of paradox here: in order for our "selfish gene" to get where it needs to go, it must reside in an organism that developed dispositions that incline it to do and not do certain things—for example, acting altruistically or not succumbing to the allure of exciting safari trips—that oftentimes seem completely unselfish. That is, our social mores are derived from a shared moral sense, nimble in its ability to negotiate between communitarian and individual interests, that nevertheless arises from ruthlessly efficient and purely material biological mechanisms that are at root "selfish."

What should we make of this? If one begins, as Ruse does, with the belief that materialism is the correct view of things, his position is compelling. But this is also true of other philosophical projects that rely on One Big Idea. Marx can explain everything through the prism of class struggle. For Heraclitus (c. 500 BC), there are no stable substances, and for Parmenides (c. 515 BC), nothing ever changes. In our own day, certain social movements see all dissent from their views as hate. But in each case, the same One Big Idea that so powerfully explains so much does so at the price of *explaining away*, rather than engaging, what would otherwise undermine the plausibility of the One Big Idea. (For example, if citizens dissenting from secular progressivism are not motivated by hate but by reasonable assumptions about human nature, then there is a possible defeater to the truth of secular progressivism; and thus when one stubbornly sticks with secular progressivism by simply repeating that all dissent is hate, one not only begs the question of, but also insulates oneself from, possibly discovering the truth.)

The Real Price of Ruse's Relativism

Here I conclude by registering my third disagreement with Professor Ruse. The price of accepting his theory is nothing short of *undermining everything that we believe*. Think about it: if our belief in the moral law can be attributed entirely to our genes tricking us into believing that there really is a moral law, why not extend that same analysis to all other beliefs that arise from the same organism's mind? After all, the same mind that entertains belief in the moral law also entertains beliefs about art, literature, science, philosophy, mathematics, and the existence of other people. Perhaps these beliefs also refer to nothing re. If "ethics as we understand it is an illusion fobbed off on us by our genes to get us to cooperate," maybe art, literature, science, philosophy, mathematics, and the existence of other people are illusions fobbed on us by our genes to get us to cooperate.

To get a better sense of why this is a fatal problem for Ruse's view, consider these comments made at the end of his chapter: "Our biology has to trick us into thinking that morality is objective. And if you respond that, now you know the truth, you can go out and be immoral, let me assure you that you are mistaken." So, according to Ruse, our biology tricks us into believing that there is a natural moral law, but it *doesn't* trick us into believing that biology tricks us into believing that there is a natural law. Because this seems implausible, why can't the unrepentant amoralist just do what he wants, since all our beliefs may be just one big collection of tricks played on us by our biology?

It seems then that abandoning the belief that there is an objective and real moral law is just not worth it, especially if you are a Darwinian.

Notes

1 For arguments that the mind is immaterial and that there may be other immaterial realities such as numbers and moral properties, see the essays by Paul Gould and Charles Taliaferro in this volume.

2 Charles Darwin, *The Descent of Man, and Selection in Relation to Sex* (London: John Murray, 1871), I, 73, as quoted by Ruse, p. –.

3 Aquinas writes:
> Since, however, good has the nature of an end, and evil, the nature of a contrary, hence it is that all those things to which man has a natural inclination, are naturally apprehended by reason as being good, and consequently as objects of pursuit, and their contraries as evil, and objects of avoidance. Wherefore according to the order of natural inclinations, is the order of the precepts of the natural law. Because in man there is first of all an inclination to good in accordance with the nature which he has in common with all substances: inasmuch as every substance seeks the preservation of its own being, according to its nature: and by reason of this inclination, whatever is a means of preserving human life, and of warding off its obstacles, belongs to the natural law. Secondly, there is in man an inclination to things that pertain to him more specially, according to that nature which he has in common with other animals: and in virtue of this inclination, those things are said to belong to the natural law, "which nature has taught to all animals" [Pandect. Just. I, tit. i], such as sexual intercourse, education of offspring and so forth. Thirdly, there is in man an inclination to good, according to the nature of his reason, which nature is proper to him: thus man has a natural inclination to know the truth about God, and to live in society: and in this respect, whatever pertains to this inclination belongs to the natural law; for instance, to shun ignorance, to

avoid offending those among whom one has to live, and other such things regarding the above inclination (St. Thomas Aquinas, *Summa Theologica*, I-II.Q94.art2, 2nd and rev., literally translated by Fathers of the English Dominican Province[1920], online edition, http://www.newadvent.org/summa/2094.htm#article2).

4 Michael Ruse and E. O. Wilson, "The Evolution of Ethics: Is Our Belief in Morality Merely an Adaptation Put in Place to Further Our Reproductive Ends?" *The New Scientist*, 108 (October 1985): 51–52.

Response to Beckwith

Michael Ruse

Study Questions

1. What failure or deficiency does Ruse think Beckwith's discussion of objective morality have?

2. What options does Ruse suggest Beckwith might embrace for defining objective morality? What problems might these options have?

3. In what way, according to Ruse, does Beckwith confuse "subjective" with "relative"? Why does Ruse think this is a problem?

4. In what sense, then, is Ruse a moral relativist?

It is not easy commenting critically on someone like Francis J. Beckwith in his article "Morality is Objective," when his basic decency shines through on every page and when—even worse—you find yourself agreeing with just about everything he says! His reply would be, of course, "You do agree and the reason why you agree is because you are a fellow human being and you share an appreciation of—we are both subject to—the same objective moral law." So what then do I say?

What Is Meant by "Objective" Morality?

Well, for a start, I don't think it unfair to ask for a bit more information about the nature of this objective morality. To use the kinds of examples he uses, I am quite happy saying that the computer on which I am typing this response is objectively a Lenovo and not a Mac. And if someone challenges this, we know how we might set about putting them right: Show them the receipts.

I paid a lot less for a Lenovo than I would have for a Mac! Now what about mathematics? I suppose most or all of us would want to say that it is objective in not being up for grabs. I am with Beckwith here. You cannot make 2+2 equal 5 just because you feel like it. Some people, I think Bertrand Russell (1872–1970) was one at one point, would say that "2+2=4" exists just as independently as my Lenovo, even though it might not be exactly part of the furniture of the world, if you know what I mean. It exists in some kind of Platonic heaven. Others probably want to say that it is all a matter of relations—"2+2=4" isn't about a thing, any more than "Nobody beat me" is about nobody, a person. But it is objective in the sense that these relations are not arbitrary, nor are they a matter of personal choice. They are binding.

Move now to morality. "Rape is unpleasant" is perhaps an objective fact of reality, like computers. Women don't like being raped, no matter what the locker room talk may be. "Rape is wrong" is something else. Are we to suppose that it exists in the Platonic heaven of "2+2=4"? If so, tell us a bit more about this heaven and why we should believe in it and how it interacts with our physical world. Is it just a matter of relations? But how is this? If I take two books and two more books, I expect to have four not five books. The person who says five books is wrong. How do I speak to the person who says that all women really like it and rape is not really wrong? I should speak to such a person (that is not the debate), but how do I speak to the rape-is-wrong denier?[1]

You might want to bring in God, in which case you run up against the Euthyphro problem. Does God think rape is wrong because it is objectively wrong, in which case why bring in God? Or does God think rape is wrong simply because that is what He decided, in which case it doesn't seem that a *moral* case is being made here. Rather, it's one of fear of crossing God. To be honest, though, I am not sure that the Euthyphro problem is quite the defeater that so convinces first-year undergraduates.[2] Certainly, the God of Job has more flexibility in this area. I created everything. I make the rules. Shut up and obey. Why shouldn't that be morality? It is certainly objective.

On top of this, one can go the route of Catholic moral theology and put the burden on natural law. To use an example given by Charles Darwin in his *Descent of Man*, if God had made us like the bees, then it would be acceptable for females to shut men out when the cold weather comes, even though it leads to the deaths of the males. But God didn't make us bee-like. He made us humanlike, where society needs males as much as females and where therefore it would be crazy—against nature—to let males starve when winter comes. God determines morality, but it isn't arbitrary, for it depends on how God has shaped the physical state of affairs. God couldn't make 2+2=5 and he couldn't make us humanlike and yet subject to bee morality.

Well, this is all well and good, but what happens if you don't believe in God? Does this mean you have no objective morality or at least no reason to call morality objective? Some would say that this is precisely the case. I suspect that Alvin Plantinga might argue this way,[3] although I am not sure that Francis Beckwith would. Either way, I think we are owed a little more in an essay promoting the objectivity of morality about the source or nature of this objectivity. Lay your cards on the table, Professor Beckwith, so we can see that you don't have an illicit ace up your sleeve!

Confusing Subjective with Relative

So much for a start. For a second, let me suggest that while Beckwith may not have an ace up his sleeve, there is a little bit of the "three-card trick" going on here. Beckwith talks in lofty terms about objectivity and it does seem to be something in opposition to subjectivity. I take it that if there are no humans around, rape is still wrong to the objectivist, whereas the subjectivist is inclined to say that the whole talk about morality in this case is otiose. It is not that rape is now okay, but that the very talk of rape and rightness and wrongness in the absence of humans simply does not make sense.

I am happy with this discussion thus far, but then suddenly Beckwith slips in the word "relative." He writes: "I was teaching an ethics course in which we were discussing the issue of moral relativism (which is the denial that morality is objective)" (p. 44). I say, hang on for a moment Professor Beckwith. Let us stop and look at this relativism. Take an intentionally vile example, say, eating excrement. I take it that our feeling of disgust is about as subjective as you can get. It is truly all a matter of human feelings. You might invoke natural law—a diet of turds seems hardly healthy—but even here matters are a little dicey. It is thought that inhaling the smoke of dried elephant dung clears up sinus problems. (I confess I know this only from rumor although I am fully prepared to admit that one's sinuses may never be the same again.) Either way, a plate full of excrement and French fries seems less than appetizing.

But hardly relative. I don't want such a plate but neither do you nor does the person down the road or the chap in the Brazilian forest who wears only a thong and carries a blowpipe. Of course, I suspect that if you scour the world far and wide you will find those who like the practice. In fact, there is even a word for it: coprophagia. Usually it refers to such animals as dung-beetles who find eating the waste of other animals a valuable food source, but sometimes it applies to humans. Generally, though, these are humans with identifiable mental illnesses. In any case, the fact that there are exceptions no more makes excrement-eating relative in any meaningful sense than the fact that there are—as Beckwith would surely acknowledge—folk who are morally blind about rape makes the immorality of rape relative. It isn't, and those who think otherwise are missing part of what it is to be a mature human being.

I have made my case for saying that morality is subjective, so I won't argue it more here. I will simply reiterate: First, if morality is objective, then where's the beef? Spell out a bit more what you mean by this so we can look at your foundations, as it were. Second, don't confuse subjective with relative, concluding that if one is a subjectivist then one is a relativist. Students often emerge from sociology classes convinced that morality is all relative. They don't get that message from my philosophy classes.

Relative or Not?

And so to my final paragraph. Given that I am the author of the companion piece "Morality is relative," how on earth could I have argued in this response that morality is subjective but not relative? Have I completely changed my mind? Not at all! Look at what I said. First, morality is always a question of moral norms plus physical circumstances. If I have the training of a surgeon, it is moral for me to take out your appendix. Not otherwise. If you are my child, I have special obligations to you that I do not have to the children of others. Saint Paul is a pretty good guide here: "I seek not yours but you: for the children ought not to lay up for the parents, but the parents for the children" (2 Cor. 12:14). Second, morality is not relative here on earth between us humans. Saint Michael Ruse is a pretty good guide here: "In the system, it cannot be, otherwise we don't have morality." On Andromeda, perhaps there are rational beings with three sexes. Polyamory or some such thing is obligatory. Not down here, I am afraid, says he with just a twinge of regret.

Notes

1 For arguments for and against a "Platonic heaven" in which things like numbers and "objective morality" exist as real entities, see the essays by Paul Gould and Joseph Melia in this volume.

2 For a discussion of the question of whether or not morality depends upon God, see the essays in this volume by Graham Oppy and Matthew Flannagan.

3 See A. Plantinga, *Where the Conflict Really Lies: Science, Religion, and Naturalism* (New York: Oxford University Press, 2011).

Questions for Reflection

1. Do you agree with Ruse and Beckwith that radical moral subjectivism—the view that what counts as right and wrong is just a matter of personal or societal preference—is unacceptable? Why?
2. If morality is an evolutionary adaptation, as Ruse argues, then would a person have a reason to be moral if it wasn't in his interest? Why?
3. What significance, if any, does a person's view of the nature of reality (materialism vs supernaturalism, say) have for his or her view of morality?
4. Do you think Beckwith is right that Ruse's view would undermine everything we believe? What, if anything, could Ruse say in response?
5. Beckwith has argued that there are objective moral principles. Does he have to explain why and how these principles exist as Ruse demands? Why?

2

What Makes Actions Right or Wrong?

Consequences Make Actions Right

Alastair Norcross

Study Questions

1. What reason does Norcross provide for thinking that some things, perhaps including happiness and unhappiness, are intrinsically good or bad?
2. What is "Core Consequentialism"? What are its two crucial features?
3. What is the "motivating idea" behind consequentialism?
4. What is "maximizing act utilitarianism"? Why is it sometimes said to be too demanding? How does Norcross respond to this charge?
5. What is the Problem of Motives? What examples are used to explain it? Why does Norcross think it is not a serious problem of consequentialism?
6. According to Norcross, how does consequentialism explain why some character traits are bad?
7. What is the consequentialist intuition regarding the causal route from action to consequences? How does Norcross employ this intuition to criticize the distinction between killing and letting die along with other nonconsequentialist constraints?
8. What does Norcross see as the problem with relying on moral intuitions?

In one of the first great works in ethics in the Western tradition, *The Nicomachean Ethics*, Aristotle begins Book I Chapter 1 as follows: "Every art and every inquiry, and similarly every action and pursuit, is thought to aim at some good; and for this reason the good has rightly been declared to be that at which all things aim." He continues, in Chapter 2:

> If, then, there is some end of the things we do, which we desire for its own sake (everything else being desired for the sake of this), and if we do not choose everything for the sake of something else (for at that rate the process would go on to infinity, so that our desire would be empty and vain), clearly this must be the good and the chief good. Will not the knowledge of it, then, have a great influence on life?[1]

Likewise, early in the first chapter of his treatise *Utilitarianism*, John Stuart Mill (1806–1873) declares:

> From the dawn of philosophy, the question concerning the *summum bonum*, or, what is the same thing, concerning the foundation of morality, has been accounted the main problem in speculative thought. . . . All action is for the sake of some end, and rules of action, it seems natural to suppose, must take their whole character and colour from the end to which they are subservient.[2]

Both Aristotle and Mill are talking about what is *intrinsically good*, that is, what is good for its own sake, simply in and of itself. Another way to put this, as Mill does, is to talk about what is *intrinsically desirable*, or worth desiring or pursuing for its own sake. Most, though not all, philosophers believe that some things are intrinsically good. The most common such thing, and the foundation of the best-known consequentialist theory, *Utilitarianism*, is happiness or well-being, often taken to include the well-being of nonhuman animals, too. Likewise, most philosophers also believe that some things are intrinsically bad, such as unhappiness, or suffering. This doesn't entail that happiness can't be *instrumentally bad*, or that unhappiness can't be *instrumentally good*. That is, a particular person's happiness may lead to unhappiness for others. Suppose that a mugger gets a lot of happiness out of stealing from others. The fact that he gets such happiness could lead him to steal more and more, causing unhappiness to others. Likewise, a talented blues singer and composer may be very unhappy, leading her to compose and sing wonderful songs, which cause others to be happy.

    The claim that some things, at least including happiness, are intrinsically good, and others, at least including unhappiness or suffering, are intrinsically bad, is appealing, and almost certainly true. To appreciate the appeal of the view, suppose that a friend tells you that they heard yesterday of a momentous event occurring in a distant country. Although they distinctly remember hearing of such an event, they can't quite remember what it was, because they were a little distracted and inebriated at the time. You press them to remember, and they tell you that they are pretty sure that it was one of two things: either (i) there was a terrible natural disaster in the relevant country, painfully killing and maiming hundreds of thousands of people and animals, or (ii) a discovery was made, enabling the country to eradicate a terrible disease, which had been painfully killing and maiming hundreds of thousands of people and animals. You, obviously, have no control over which of the two events actually took place. It would be strange, however, if you didn't hope that it was (ii) rather than (i). And, surely the reason you would hope it was (ii) rather than (i) is that you believe it would be better if hundreds of thousands of people and animals were *spared* from painful death and maiming rather than having it inflicted on them. And the reason for this is that the suffering caused by painful death and maiming is intrinsically bad, and the happiness caused by eradicating such things is intrinsically good. This much is relatively uncontroversial. Most philosophers, and certainly most who work in ethics, believe that some things, such as happiness and unhappiness, are intrinsically good and bad, and so they believe that, other things being equal, things go better (that is, the world is better) when there's more of the former and less of the latter.

Core Consequentialism

So far, so good, but we don't yet have the materials for a complete ethical theory. Ethics is not only concerned with discovering or evaluating situations or, as philosophers like to say, "states of affairs" as good or bad, but is also, some would say especially, concerned with evaluating *conduct*. Knowing that some things are intrinsically good and others are intrinsically bad, and that the world would be better if there's a larger net quantity of good, doesn't, by itself, tell me what choice to make in any particular situation. Among other things, an ethical theory is supposed to help guide actions, by giving criteria for evaluating choices. Fortunately, there is an easy and obvious way to connect a theory of the goodness (or badness) of states of affairs (including the maximal state of affairs that philosophers usually refer to as "the world") with a theory of the moral evaluation of different options in a situation of choice. It's simply this:

> An action is morally better or worse than available alternatives to the extent that the world containing it is overall better or worse than the worlds containing the alternatives.

Call this theory "Core Consequentialism" (CC for short). Most accounts of consequentialist approaches to ethics talk of "the consequences" of actions, and propose evaluating actions by comparing their consequences with the consequences of alternatives. This is potentially misleading, because it suggests that there is a sharp distinction between an action itself and its consequences. Whether it's possible to make such a distinction or not, it is no part of the consequentialist approach that actions themselves are not part of the states of affairs to be evaluated as better or worse than alternatives. An action itself may, for example, be pleasurable or painful. Clearly the pleasure or pain of the action is just as relevant to assessing it as is any pleasure or pain that follows the action. Likewise, talk of "the world" that contains the action makes clear that *any* difference an action makes to overall states of affairs is at least potentially relevant to its evaluation compared with available alternatives. Although I may sometimes talk about "the consequences" of an action, or compare the consequences of one action with the consequences of another, this will only be for convenience. The strict interpretation will always be in terms of worlds containing the different actions.

I would like to point out two crucial features of CC. First, the fundamental evaluation of actions, for a consequentialist, is always comparative. This is because the role of an ethical theory, when it comes to *actions*, is to guide *choices*, and it does this by providing reasons to act one way rather than another. Second, there is no mention in CC of an action being "right" or "wrong," or of morality "demanding" or "requiring" or "commanding" that certain things be done or avoided. This is not because consequentialists don't talk about such things. Most (though not all) of them do. But what makes consequentialism a distinctive kind of ethical theory is its approach to the general moral evaluation of actions, not to specific categories of evaluation, such as right and wrong, permissible, impermissible, demanded, required, etc. For a consequentialist, the only consideration of direct relevance to the moral evaluation of an action (as opposed to the character, blameworthiness, etc. of the agent) is the comparative value of its consequences. In evaluating the consequentialist approach, as opposed to particular consequentialist theories (such as maximizing utilitarianism), it is important to see that no particular account of right and wrong, permissible, impermissible, and the like (including an account that ignores those notions) is essential to the approach itself.

Here then, roughly, is the motivating idea behind consequentialist approaches to morality. We care, or at least we should care, about how good or bad the world is. It matters to us. Through our behavior, we can make a difference, often small, but sometimes significant, to how good or bad the world is. To the extent that we can make a difference, it is better, morally better that is, for us to make the world a better place rather than a worse place, and the bigger the positive difference we can make, the better. It is hard to deny the force of this motivating idea. Most philosophers feel its attraction, and accept that the difference our behavior makes to the overall goodness of the world provides moral reasons for choosing to behave in some ways rather than others. Where some disagree with consequentialism is with the claim that such reasons are the *only* reasons that are directly relevant to the moral evaluation of behavior. Perhaps, they claim, there are other considerations that, at least sometimes, compete with consequentialist reasons, undercutting or overriding them. In the remainder of this article, I will consider some of the most common reasons given for rejecting consequentialism, and explain why I don't find them persuasive.

The Demandingness Objection

As I said above, most consequentialist theories do include accounts of what makes actions right or wrong, permissible, impermissible, and related notions. It is worth briefly examining one of the most common, and influential, consequentialist theories, *maximizing act utilitarianism*, because it turns out that one of the most common objections to consequentialism is really an objection to the particular structure of this theory, and not to consequentialist approaches in general.

Utilitarianism, most famously articulated and defended by Jeremy Bentham and John Stuart Mill, is a consequentialist theory with a welfarist account of the good. That is, according to pretty much all versions of utilitarianism, the only thing that is intrinsically good is the well-being, or happiness, of creatures capable of conscious awareness (or "sentient" creatures, for short). Unsurprisingly, the only thing that is intrinsically bad is unhappiness, or suffering. The early utilitarians defined happiness in terms of pleasure, and unhappiness in terms of pain, though they didn't restrict the notions of pleasure and pain to physical or bodily sensations. Some modern utilitarians follow in this tradition (broadly defined as "hedonism"), while others give differing accounts of well-being or welfare. As far as the deep disagreements between consequentialists and nonconsequentialists are concerned, nothing turns on the differences between rival accounts of well-being. Most modern utilitarians adopt a maximizing account of rightness, which can be roughly expressed as follows:

> **MU**: An action is right, if and only if there are no available alternatives that result in a larger net amount of well-being, otherwise it is wrong.

MU (Maximizing Utilitarianism) tells us that only the best action in any given choice is right (unless there is a tie for first place, in which case all tied optimal actions are right). The notion of a right action is often left unexplained, but is usually understood to mean an action that the moral theory demands be done, or an action that must be done, in order for the demands of morality to be met. Thus, if you don't perform the action with the best consequences, you haven't met the demands of morality, and thus have behaved wrongly.

It seems that MU is quite demanding—in fact, many would say too demanding. Consider taking a trip to the movies, at which you spend a total of $12 on a ticket. Given the amount of unrelieved suffering in the world, and the existence of well-organized and efficient charities, how likely is it that you couldn't do more good by donating the $12 to charity than by spending it on a movie ticket (or three or four cups of coffee)? But, if you can do more good by donating the money to charity, it would be wrong to spend it on a movie ticket, and MU thus *demands* that you don't do it. Perhaps you'll say that's fine. It *would* be wrong to spend the money on a movie when you could, perhaps, supply a much-needed vaccination to an at-risk child instead. But the same reasoning will apply to the next time you consider seeing a movie, or buying a cup of coffee, or eating out, or a whole host of other seemingly unremarkable things. In fact, given how much unrelieved suffering there is in the world, and how little most affluent people are doing about it, MU seems to tell all of us that we should be working almost full-time for the benefit of others, and only devote as much time to our own well-being as is strictly necessary to maintain our physical and emotional health in order to keep working for the benefit of others. To the extent that this seems to count against MU, it is known as the "demandingness objection," and is one of the most commonly cited reasons for rejecting the theory. Notice that the objection only applies, if it applies at all, to a consequentialist theory that demands maximization. A consequentialist theory that gives a different, perhaps *non*maximizing, theory of rightness, or one that denies that consequentialism *demands* anything at all, wouldn't be subject to this criticism.

It is interesting to note that neither Bentham nor Mill employed a maximizing account of rightness. Here is Bentham: "An action . . . may be said to be conformable to the principle of utility . . . when the tendency it has to augment the happiness of the community is greater than any it has to diminish it."[3] And here is Mill: "The creed which accepts as the foundation of morals, Utility, or the Greatest Happiness Principle, holds that actions are right in proportion as they tend to promote happiness, wrong as they tend to produce the reverse of happiness."[4] Neither Bentham nor Mill demands that an agent maximize, and Bentham's formulation doesn't suggest any demands at all. Mill's talk of actions being "right in proportion" to their consequences suggests that he thinks that actions can be more or less right or wrong, without any suggestion that morality "demands" maximal rightness.

It is possible to combine CC with an account of rightness that demands maximization, or with an account that sets the standard for rightness as, at least sometimes, somewhat short of maximization (perhaps as "good enough"), or with some other nonmaximizing account of rightness, or with no account of rightness at all, and no claim about demands. Indeed, there are good reasons to opt for the last option, as I have argued elsewhere,[5] but here is not the place to wade into that somewhat complex debate. The main point to emphasize here is that the so-called demandingness objection is not actually an objection to consequentialism itself, but to certain, admittedly currently popular, versions of consequentialism.

The Problem of Motives

So much for demandingness. What other reasons might there be for rejecting a consequentialist approach to ethics? There are two, sometimes overlapping, lines of criticism that have been highly influential. The first is that consequentialism doesn't allow for constraints on actions that don't themselves necessarily affect the value of consequences. These constraints may be embodied in the language of rights (for example, the right to life), or they may be expressed independently of such a notion, as, for example, the claim that it is seriously wrong to kill the innocent. The second line of criticism is that consequentialism doesn't allow the mental states of agents, for example, the motives or intentions with which they act, to be directly relevant to the moral evaluation of actions. I say that the lines of criticism are sometimes overlapping, because some critics refer to motives or intentions in formulating nonconsequentialist constraints on action. Something like this idea might underlie the common sentiment that it is important to do the right thing "for the right reason." Let's consider this approach in a bit more detail.

Rosalind Hursthouse describes a (presumably hypothetical) situation in which one of her colleagues speaks a somewhat uncomfortable truth at a meeting.[6] She is, at first, inclined to praise him for his honesty, but then discovers that he is usually quite deceptive and manipulative, and only spoke the truth on this occasion because he knew it would upset another colleague, and wanted to upset the colleague. On learning this, she says, she would judge that "he would have done better to hold his tongue." This suggests that the colleague's act of telling the truth would have been right, or honest, if done from certain motives, but wrong, or at least less than morally optimal, if done from others. Likewise, consider a surgeon, Dr. Fabulous, who dedicates his life to his craft, becoming the preeminent surgeon in his region, performing many life-saving and life-enhancing surgeries. Given the undoubtedly good consequences of the surgeon's behavior, a consequentialist would probably judge it favorably. But now suppose that you discover that Dr. Fabulous used to enjoy cutting up live animals as a child, and only became a surgeon because he really enjoys the experience of cutting human flesh. He would prefer that his patients not be anesthetized, but he is resigned to the fact that he won't be able to get away with cutting up unanesthetized patients, so he contents himself with imagining their screams of agony while he is cutting them. He also knows that the better he is at his job, the more opportunities he will have to cut; so that is why he has worked so hard at becoming a superb surgeon. If we discover this, we will probably be horrified, and completely change our attitude toward Dr. Fabulous. Whereas earlier we judged him to be admirable, now we judge him to be despicable. Doesn't this show that, at least sometimes, motives or intentions are relevant to our assessment of actions?

The key to understanding why the sorts of considerations raised in the previous paragraph don't tell against the consequentialist approach to ethics is a crucial distinction that is often overlooked or ignored by critics. In describing Dr. Fabulous's *behavior*, I said that the consequentialist would judge *it* favorably. I then said that, upon learning the details of his motivations, we would judge *him* to be despicable. What this demonstrates is that we can separate our judgment of actions from our judgment of character. Often, maybe usually, the two kinds of judgments go hand in hand, but sometimes they can come apart. When we judge that someone has done well, made a good choice for example, we usually thereby think highly of the person. But sometimes we can discover aspects of someone's motivations that reflect badly on their character. From the consequentialist perspective, we judge character traits according to *the probable effects of those traits*. The kind of sadism displayed by Dr. Fabulous usually results in actions that promote suffering, rather than well-being. In this case, due to the institutional safeguards of the medical establishment, Dr. Fabulous's sadism is actually channeled beneficially, but that doesn't prevent us from judging his character negatively, because we judge character by the effects that it *typically* has rather than the particular effect in the circumstance. In fact, the very expression "doing the right thing for the wrong reasons" suggests that we understand the distinction between evaluating an action and evaluating the motives behind it. If the action of Hursthouse's colleague would have been right in that situation from different motives, it would also be right from his actual motives. We may *say* that his action is no longer admirable, when we discover that his true motive was spite, but what we really mean is that we no longer think of *him* as being admirable for his honesty. Once we understand that our judgments of character and of actions can come apart, these kinds of examples don't trouble the consequentialist approach.

Suppose that our judgments of character did infect our judgments of actions, so that Dr. Fabulous's actions themselves (his successful surgeries) received a negative evaluation because they were performed from disgraceful motives. Now suppose that your child requires some serious, complicated, and risky surgery. The only two surgeons available are Dr. Fabulous and Dr. Mediocre, who is an average-level, reasonably competent surgeon, who has had his fair share of failures and qualified successes. Dr. Fabulous, on the other hand, has never had anything less than an unqualified success. If all you know about the two surgeons is their respective track records, the choice is easy. Obviously, you prefer that Dr. Fabulous perform the surgery on your child (assuming you care for your child). Now suppose that you discover the details of Dr. Fabulous's motivations. Do you change your preference about who should perform the surgery? Remember, although Dr. Fabulous would like to inflict pain on his patients, there is actually no chance that he will, because the protocols in place will ensure that your child is properly anesthetized, and Dr. Fabulous knows that he must continue to perform flawless surgeries in order to keep performing more of them. You certainly don't have to like Dr. Fabulous's *attitude* toward your child, but in this case you know that his attitude will have no negative effects on her well-being. Speaking as a parent, I cannot imagine changing my preference about who should perform the surgery. I may no longer have warm fuzzy feelings toward Dr. Fabulous himself, but I certainly don't change my evaluation of his actions.

Not only does the distinction between action and character demonstrate that such examples are no threat to the consequentialist approach, but consequentialism itself provides the most plausible explanation for why some character traits themselves are bad. Consider the sadism of Dr. Fabulous, or the less extreme malice of Hursthouse's colleague. Clearly, such character traits are morally problematic. But is it just a brute fact that sadism, malice, self-centeredness, etc. are bad character traits, and kindness, compassion, and generosity are good? And if it is just a brute fact, how do we know it? This raises important questions of moral epistemology, which I don't have space to explore here, but it is worth pointing out that consequentialism can provide a simple, appealing, and unified answer to the question of what makes character traits good or bad, to which I have already referred. Sadism, malice, etc. are bad character traits, because their possession *usually* leads to bad consequences, whereas kindness, compassion, and generosity *usually* lead to good ones. The sadistic or malicious person usually promotes suffering rather than well-being. Likewise, dishonest behavior usually has bad effects. This approach, then, allows us to judge behavior and character with respect to the very same basic good that underlies whichever version of consequentialism we espouse.

Other Nonconsequentialist Constraints

So much for motives. What of other sources of nonconsequentialist constraints? Perhaps we think that, although we prefer the world to be better rather than worse, there are certain ways of making the world better that are themselves forbidden, or at least bad enough in themselves to outweigh a gain in overall goodness. Perhaps, for example, it is better to let one person die, than to let five people die, but worse to kill one person than to let five people die, because, even though the world in which one person is killed and five live is better than the world in which five die and one lives, killing is itself a morally bad way to produce the better consequences. Many objections to consequentialism are of this form. Sometimes, the objection directly claims that a feature, such as the distinction between killing and letting die, makes a moral difference to the status of actions. Sometimes the feature is indirectly supported, as when it is embodied in a claim about rights or "dignity" or "respect." Sometimes, the objection consists simply in presenting a hypothetical case, in which it is claimed that the consequentialist gives the wrong answer. Though usually the latter kind of objection is then explained as an illustration of the relevance of some nonconsequentialist constraint.

A core consequentialist intuition is that the details of the causal route from action to consequences don't matter morally, except inasmuch as the different routes themselves differ in goodness. It is better to get a friend to agree with a plan by rational persuasion than by torture, but that is because rational persuasion is (at least usually) far less unpleasant than torture. It doesn't matter whether you save five innocent lives by letting a sixth person die or by killing them, unless one death involves more suffering than the other. Suppose, however, we think that the details of the causal routes themselves do matter morally. Now imagine visiting a friend, who insists that you wipe your feet on the mat, before entering the house. This is fine, you think, because the consequences of wiping your feet are that the carpets are protected from dirt. But now suppose that your friend insists that you wipe your feet in the order right-left, rather than left-right, not because this makes any difference to the resulting dirt on the floor—it doesn't—but because the right-left wiping order is said to be much better, in itself, than the left-right wiping order. In fact, your friend thinks that it would be terrible to wipe in the left-right order, much worse than not wiping at all. You ask why, and they say that it's just obvious that one order is good, and the other is terrible. You would rightly be bemused by this claim, and probably worried about your friend's sanity.

Now suppose you learn that your friend is part of a religious sect, whose historical tradition included the claim that god commanded the right-left order. Furthermore, the sect are all descended from people who used to live in a secluded region, whose strange atmospheric conditions resulted in bad effects from the left-right order, but not from the right-left order. Your friend doesn't believe in the god who supposedly commanded the right-left order, and his descendants moved away from the secluded region many generations ago (and the atmospheric conditions have since changed), but the prohibition on left-right wiping is so deeply ingrained in him and his relatives that it just seems *obvious* to him that there is something objectionable about it, even though he freely admits that it has no effect on the consequences of the wiping. He can't be a consequentialist, he says, because consequentialism can't explain the prohibition on left-right wiping.

As soon as we understand the origins of the prohibition on left-right wiping, we can see that it poses no threat to consequentialism. The fact that some people still strongly object to left-right wiping is no reason at all to accept such a prohibition as morally justified. Although it is easy for us to dismiss the left-right prohibition, it may be much harder to dismiss other prohibitions that are deeply ingrained in our own psyches, because of a long historical and/or religious tradition. For example, the common view that killing is morally worse than letting die is a vestige of a time when saving lives was not nearly so easy and pressing as it is now, and when the most likely connection between your behavior and the death of another was through you killing them, rather than letting them die. One of the most influential religious codes, the Ten Commandments, prohibits killing, but not letting die. Furthermore, because the view has always been in the interests of the powerful in society, it has been nurtured by inegalitarian and hierarchical structures. If it were generally accepted that letting people die is as bad as killing them, this would place a much larger moral burden on the rich and powerful, who have the resources to save countless numbers, than on the comparatively powerless. The persistence of the view, then, serves mostly to rationalize large-scale neglect of the vulnerable by the powerful.

For many ethicists, it is possible to understand the sorts of considerations discussed in the previous paragraph, and still feel very strongly that killing is worse than letting die, or at least to have the intuition that particular examples involving killing are worse than examples involving letting die, even when there are no other relevant differences between the examples. Moral intuitions are largely driven by emotions, which are themselves somewhat impervious to rational debunking. A large key to understanding, and accepting, a consequentialist approach is the realization that our intuitive responses to cases, and perhaps to some statements of principles, are often, perhaps usually, unreliable guides to what morality actually says. Once we see that, we can see that nonconsequentialist constraints on action may serve as rough and ready guides to promoting the good in some circumstances (and hindrances to promoting the good in other circumstances), but they are not morally justified in themselves.

Conclusion

Consequentialism is rooted in the appealing and widely shared view that making a difference to how good or bad the world is matters morally. Other features of our choices, such as the motives from which they are performed, or whether they violate a nonconsequentialist constraint, don't directly affect the morality of our actions, though they may be indirectly relevant because of what they tell us about the likely effects of our behavior, either in this case or in general.

Notes

1 Aristotle, *Nichomachean Ethics*.
2 John Stuart Mill, *Utilitarianism* (Indianapolis: Hackett Publishing, 2002).
3 Jeremy Bentham, *Introduction to the Principles of Morals and Legislation*, Ch. 1, para. 6.
4 Mill, *Utilitarianism*, Chapter 2.
5 See, for example, Alastair Norcross, "Reasons without Demands: Rethinking Rightness," in *Contemporary Debates in Moral Theory*, ed. James Dreier (Malden, MA: Blackwell, 2006).
6 Rosalind Hursthouse, "Are Virtues the Proper Starting Point for Morality?" in *Contemporary Debates in Moral Theory*.

Respect for Persons Makes Actions Right

Mark Linville

Study Questions

1. What is the Philosophical Question about Morality (PQAM)? How does the Respect-for-Persons principle (RFP) answer this Question?
2. What does Linville mean by "pre-theoretical" or "bedrock" moral beliefs? What role do they play in moral theorizing?
3. What is meant by an ethical theory having "iniquitous consequences"? According to Linville, what should be our stance toward such theories?
4. What is the distinction that Linville makes between direct and indirect duties? How does he employ this distinction to argue against ethical egoism?

5. How does the Divine Command Theory answer PQAM? What is the problem faced by its unmodified form? What about the "modified" versions?
6. What is the central concern of Virtue Ethics? How does it address PQAM?
7. What problem does Linville find with Virtue Ethics? How, according to Linville, is a Kantian account of virtue superior to standard Virtue Ethics?
8. On RFP, what does it mean to say that a person is wronged? What does this imply?
9. What does it mean to say that the rights implied by RFP are natural and inherent?
10. What reason might there be to think that persons actually have the dignity entailed by RFP?

The Philosophical Question about Morality

If you believe as I do that morality is objective—so that some acts *really are* right and others wrong—then we face the central question of this essay: "What *makes* right acts right and wrong acts wrong?" Call that question the *Philosophical Question About Morality* (PQAM).[1]

In the study of normative ethics, we are confronted with an array of different and competing ethical theories, and one of the most important differences among them is the way in which each answers PQAM. In this essay, I aim to defend what I shall call the principle of *Respect-for-Persons* (RFP) and, of course, the ethical theory that features it. I'll argue that what *makes* an act morally right is that it treats persons with due respect, and what *makes* a wrong act wrong is that it does not.[2] To take what I hope is an obvious—if disturbing—example, rape is an instance of a morally wrong act, and what *makes* it wrong is that it fails to treat a person—the victim—with the respect due her as a person. To borrow from philosopher Immanuel Kant, such an act treats a person "merely as a means to an end"—as one might use a tool to achieve one's *own* purposes—and fails to treat that person as an "end-in-itself." To borrow from Terry Pratchett's (1948–2015) character Granny Weatherwax: "And sin, young man, is when you treat people as things. . . . That's what sin is. . . . People as things, that's where it starts."[3] Rape, she would say, is an act that "treats people as things."

PQAM and Theory Assessment

My proposed answer to PQAM is only one of many such proposals in the history of Western moral philosophy. Confronted as we are with competing answers to our question, how ought we to proceed in assessing the relative merits of competing ethical theories? I appeal to certain of our "pre-theoretical" moral beliefs as touchstones for evaluating the plausibility of any proposed ethical theory. They are "pre-theoretical" in the sense that one need not be in the grip of some theory or ideology in order to have them. They are moral beliefs that I daresay you, my reader, likely share with me, and they are among the "beliefs of common life," right along with our shared beliefs that there is a world external to the imaginings of our own minds and that back of those perceived bodily behaviors of our companions are conscious minds like our own. You or I could readily draw up a list of the sorts of moral beliefs I have in mind. Consider our beliefs regarding the wrongness of rape, sadistic torture, or genocide, or our agreement with G. K. Chesterton's (1874–1936) darkly humorous example in his exchange with atheist Robert Blatchford (1851–1943): "Babies should not be strangled."[4] And you likely agree with me that it is right to work for justice and equality, to seek peace with our fellows as far as possible, and for parents to care for and nurture their children.

We do not argue *to* such beliefs as conclusions. Rather, we argue *from* them as premises to conclusions about the plausibility of ethical theories. They are among the data that a good ethical theory should explain, similar to the way that empirical observations are explained by a good scientific theory. It is one thing, then, to say that such "bedrock" moral beliefs neither require nor are open to *demonstration*. It is another question as to whether they are open to further *explanation*. I may *know*—or think I know—that genocide and slavery are wrong but still not know what it is about the acts that *makes* them wrong. We do not, then, *begin* with some ethical theory and its supreme moral principle and, once that is in hand, attempt to demonstrate that such acts are wrong. We *begin* with such moral beliefs as *epistemically basic* first principles and then ask what sort of moral principle seems to make sense of their being true. We believe that rape is morally wrong. What theory of morality provides the best explanation for this seemingly obvious moral fact?

In light of such considerations, I maintain that, *all else being equal, preference is given to the theory that best explains certain of our pre-theoretical moral beliefs*. The "all else equal" clause leaves open the possibility that some line of evidence or argument *could*, in principle, force us to revise such beliefs. But the default position is that they are "innocent until proven guilty" so that in the absence of a compelling argument otherwise, we are justified in holding them. My approach, then, involves an inference to the best explanation of what would make such beliefs true.

PQAM and "Iniquitous Consequences"

British philosopher Mary Midgley (1919–2018) once wrote: "An ethical theory which, when consistently followed through, has iniquitous consequences is a bad theory and must be changed."[5] Her point is that if a theory, when followed consistently, implies the moral rightness of the obviously wrong, then, all else equal, we have good reason to hold out for a better theory. Such an approach is standard fare in moral philosophy, as when critics of utilitarianism charge that there is more than one way to maximize human happiness—as that theory requires—and some of those ways involve some morally repugnant act R (rape, baby-strangling) as means to that end. Few utilitarians will reply that, yes, the theory *does* imply the rightness of R, and so we must accept that R is right. Rather, we find them implicitly agreeing with our criterion and replying that the theory, when properly interpreted, is in alignment with our pre-theoretical moral beliefs.

There is more than one way for an ethical theory to have Midgley's "iniquitous consequences." Perhaps we think first of the above sorts of examples in which some critic charges that the theory implies the rightness of the obviously wrong, or even the wrongness of the obviously right. But it is also possible for a theory to have all of the intuitively *right* implications—which acts are right and which are wrong—for all of the intuitively *wrong* reasons. I shall argue that certain ethical theories essentially involve such implausible answers to PQAM and that this is a reason for rejecting them. And I'll defend the principle of Respect-for-Persons on the grounds that it—or a principle very much like it—offers a much more plausible answer to PQAM. Indeed, RFP essentially provides what is noticeably lacking in other theories. I believe RFP is embedded within the judgments of commonsense morality, and so, to whatever degree we are justified in those commonsense beliefs, RFP finds its justification as their ground.

Three Theories and PQAM

Before defending RFP, however, let's first briefly examine three competing theories to see how they ultimately run afoul in their respective answers to PQAM.

Ethical Egoism

The ethical egoist, insofar as he is consistent in his egoism, must say that what *makes* an act right or wrong is determined by whether it benefits the *agent*. One might think that egoism has "iniquitous consequences" in that it seems to prescribe, "Do whatever you can happily get away with." That is not a theory of ethics; it is license for licentiousness.

Not so, our more circumspect egoist friend may tell us. Marcus Aurelius once insisted: "That which is not good for the bee-hive cannot be good for the bees." Or, as Jerome K. Jerome (1859–1927) once suggested: "We are so bound together that no man can labor for himself alone. Each blow he strikes in his own behalf helps to mold the universe."[6] And so we are told that how one treats one's fellows must inevitably have consequences for oneself. With this bit of wisdom in mind, the *ideal* egoist will realize that his *own* interests are best served by considering and respecting the interests of *others*. The ideal egoist, we are told, will agree that rape and torture are morally wrong and that benevolence is better than malice.

Now, my own view is that we *can* labor for ourselves without molding the universe. It seems entirely possible for one to cheat, swindle, and embezzle one's way through life without facing negative consequences. At least, one may do so if one is sufficiently clever—or has got hold of Gyges's Ring.[7] But even if we were to make a gift of this point and suppose that a world populated by egoists would be all buttercups and rainbows and unicorns, deeper flaws of the theory would remain.

The egoist's explanation for the wrongness of torture has the same structure as a plausible explanation for the wrongness of vandalism. Though the vandal has *damaged* the car, there is no good sense in which he has *wronged* it. That is, he has not violated any sort of *direct* duty *to* the car itself! Rather, he has violated a *direct* duty to the car's *owner*, and this direct duty carries with it an *indirect* duty *regarding* the car.

Let's say that something has *moral standing* just in case it is the appropriate object of *direct* moral duties. Thus, the car's owner—not the car itself—has moral standing. Similarly, on egoism, one has direct duties only to oneself. Thus, on egoism—and from the perspective of each agent—only the agent has moral standing. If the ideal egoist is civil and charitable, it must be because he believes his self-interested direct duties have in tow various *indirect* duties *regarding* others. And if rape is wrong it can only be because it, in one way or another, harms or wrongs *the rapist*! But surely, if rape is morally wrong at all, any plausible explanation of *why* it is wrong must begin with a *direct* concern for the *victim*. Egoism lacks the conceptual room for assigning actual moral standing to anyone other than the agent, and so the egoist cannot, so long as he remains true to his theory, say the obvious: *Rape is wrong because it wrongs the victim*. On egoism, other people may, of course, be *harmed*, but they cannot, from the perspective of each agent, be *wronged*—no more than the vandalized vehicle is wronged. And this, I say, counts heavily against even the most enlightened version of egoism. The "deep structure" of the theory is flawed regardless of whatever moral prescriptions it makes near the surface.

Divine Command Theory (DCT)

The Divine Command Theorist answers PQAM not by appeal to principle or consequences, but to the commands of God: Right acts are right because God commands them; wrong acts are wrong because God prohibits them. In its unmodified form, DCT faces daunting objections. It seems to imply that God's commands are morally arbitrary, because if the *commands themselves* are the ultimate source of the distinction between right and wrong, good and bad, then God cannot have any prior moral reason for commanding as he does—else, that distinction is grounded in something other than, and prior to, God's commands. But then it would appear that God *could* command rape or genocide, in which case such acts would be morally right. This strikes most of us as an "iniquitous consequence" of the theory.

"Modified" versions of DCT, drawing from a mainstream theological tradition, hold that God's *commands* are always consistent with God's *necessarily good* nature—as essentially loving and just—thus precluding the very possibility of his issuing such morally repugnant commands. Insofar as such modified theories remain divine *command* theories, they claim that, whereas God's nature grounds moral *values* (what is *good*), God's commands are required in order to ground moral *obligation* (what is *right*). The common reasoning here is that we are not morally *obligated* to do everything that it is morally *good* for us to do, such as baking a pie for the new neighbors, and so divine commands mark off those morally *good* things that are also morally *obligatory*. While such modifications seem to be an improvement over the unmodified form of the theory, I am inclined to think that even the modified form offers an unsatisfactory answer to PQAM. Echoing the question of Plato's *Euthyphro*, we might ask, "Is rape wrong because God prohibits it, or does God prohibit it because it is wrong?" If, consistent with the theory, we say that all right acts are right *because* God commands them and all wrong acts are wrong *because* God prohibits them, then we are committed to saying that what *makes* rape an instance of a morally wrong act is the fact that God prohibits it.

But, first, it is hard to see why anything like a divine command is needed in order to ground the obligation to *refrain* from such an act. In the absence of a divine command, would it be merely "good"—but not obligatory—for us to refrain from such acts in the way that baking the pie for the neighbor is merely good but not obligatory? Second, it appears that the wrongness of rape is thus explained not on the ground that it wrongs the *victim* but because it wrongs *God* by disobeying his commands. The point, of course, is not that whether God is wronged is somehow irrelevant. Rather, it is that DCT seems to exclude our having direct duties to one another. Were DCT to acknowledge that such an act is wrong because it violates a direct duty to the victim then it would abandon the central claim that all moral obligations are grounded in divine commands. If persons have moral standing, then that standing is, of itself, sufficient for grounding at least some of our moral obligations. In fact, at least when it comes to an obviously wrong act such as rape, divine commands seem neither necessary nor sufficient for establishing that wrongness. Insofar as DCT must deny such moral standing in order to maintain its theoretical integrity it offers an implausible answer to PQAM.

Virtue Ethics

True to its name, Virtue Ethics (VE) is concerned with the cultivation of the virtues or, what is the same thing, the formation of moral character. The first thing to note, then, is that *our* central question is not also the central question of VE. This is because VE is concerned, first and foremost, with the *goodness of agents* and then, only secondarily, with the *rightness of acts*. In her account of the virtue ethics of antiquity Julia Annas writes: "The framework for ancient ethics is given by claims about the form my final end should take and the place that virtue should have, rather than by claims about actions that are required or permitted or about ways to bring about certain consequences."[8] "The form my final end should take" refers to what it is to live well—to *flourish*—as a human being. Aristotle identified such flourishing with *happiness*—for which the Greek word is *eudaimonia*—and so VE is sometimes referred to as *eudaimonism*. On that account, then, a *virtue* is a character trait that is either conducive to or is a constituent part of such flourishing or happiness. This concern for being virtuous and behaving virtuously is what provides guidance in determining how we ought to live and what sorts of acts are appropriate or inappropriate for us. The central question is not "What is my moral duty?" but, rather, "What is the virtuous thing to do?"

Rosalind Hursthouse explains that on VE the moral consideration for helping someone is grounded in neither principle nor consequences but by "the fact that helping the person would be charitable or benevolent."[9] I ought, first and foremost, to desire to cultivate such virtues, and the reason I ought to do so is that these are part and parcel of a well-lived life as a human being. Robert N. Johnson observes that such theories make "an ideal of the person, rather than duty or value" the "foundation of ethics" so that "what makes an action a moral duty and what makes something of value is its relationship to some ideal of the person."[10] To paraphrase Johnson's highly formalized statement of VE's account of moral rightness, an act is right just in case doing it "is or would be characteristic of a flourishing human life."[11] Thus, the virtue ethicist routes her answer to PQAM through the consideration of whether a given act is the sort of thing that a person who is truly flourishing (i.e., the "ideal person") would do. As Monika Betzler has it: "The standard of right action is to do whatever an entirely virtuous person would do."[12] The flip side of this, of course, is that an act is morally *wrong* if it is what the good or ideal or entirely virtuous person would *not* characteristically do. Rape is wrong because it is an act such that *refraining* from it "is or would be characteristic of a flourishing human life."

Now, we shall certainly agree that rapists and baby-stranglers are neither ideal persons nor entirely virtuous nor good, but this seems to grossly understate the case and hardly gets at the real matter of what it is *about* the act that *makes* it wrong. Does VE afford us the conceptual room for saying simply that what *makes* rape wrong is that it *wrongs the victim*, that is, violates a direct duty owed her? It seems not. Hursthouse notes that virtue ethicists largely "have eschewed any attempt to ground virtue ethics in an external foundation."[13] For VE, the buck stops with considerations of what a good or ideal or excellent or flourishing person would do. This is because, as Johnson observes, on such standard accounts of VE "admirable character traits [are] more basic than the notions of right and wrong conduct." And so the latter are explained by appeal to the former and not the other way around. This precludes any appeal to the moral standing of persons and the direct duties owed them.

Happily, the insights of VE can and ought to be incorporated into a theory that *does* ground moral duties on an external foundation such as RFP. Johnson argues that virtues play an important role in Kant's ethics, though Kant's theory is structurally different from standard accounts of VE.

> Kant's account of virtue presupposes an account of moral duty already in place. Thus, rather than treating admirable character traits as more basic than the notions of right and wrong conduct, Kant takes virtues to be explicable only in terms of a prior account of moral or dutiful behavior. He does not try to make out what shape a good character has and then draw conclusions about how we ought to act on that basis. He sets out the principles of moral conduct based on his philosophical account of rational agency, and then on that basis defines virtue as the trait of acting according to these principles.[14]

Consider the difference between Johnson's account of Kantian virtue and standard VE theory. Ask the virtue ethicist, "What makes compassion a virtue?" and the answer—as determined by the "deep structure" of the theory itself—will be that compassion characterizes the person who lives well or flourishes, and we should all aim for this as our "final end." Though the compassion itself is genuinely altruistic, the value of cultivating that altruistic virtue is self-referential from the perspective of the agent. The deep structure of the theory entails that my ultimate reason for being compassionate is found in the role it plays in my own flourishing, perhaps on the ground that a psychologically healthy and happy person will develop the capacity for a full range of human emotions, including altruistic feelings and sympathies. Here, the direct *concern* we should have for the other is not grounded in any direct *duty* that we *owe* them. Ask the same question of the Kantian, who appeals to the "external foundation" of RFP, and the answer will be that compassion is a virtue because it is a morally appropriate attitude to have toward persons given their dignity. Thus, for VE, *good character* is basic and *right action* is derivative. For the Kantian, precisely the reverse is true: first, we ground our answer to PQAM in a moral principle such as RFP, and *then* we understand good character in terms of a settled disposition to act in accordance with that principle.

Let's sharpen the point. We see that VE is committed to saying that a morally wrong act is one that a perfectly virtuous person will refrain from doing. We raised a *Euthyphro*-inspired question of DCT regarding the wrongness of rape. We may ask a similar question of VE: Is rape wrong *because* it is an act from which a morally good person would refrain, or would a morally good person refrain from the act *because* it is wrong? From all of this it follows that VE is committed to the first option: rape is wrong because it is the sort of act that a good person would never do. VE *cannot* say that rape is wrong because it violates a duty owed another person or that it is inconsistent with her dignity as a person. As Nicholas Wolterstorff observes, "to add the idea [of the worth of persons] is to give up eudaimonism." He adds:

> What [the eudaimonist] says about life-goods is that they are all activities and that each of us must choose among them with the goal in mind of enhancing one's own happiness. There is no room in this scheme for the worth of persons and human beings, and hence none for one's right against others to their treating one a certain way on account of one's worth.[15]

But then the VE answer to the question "What *makes* rape wrong?" cannot be simply that it wrongs the victim. That sort of answer must appeal to something on the order of RFP. A doctrine of virtue ultimately grounded in RFP provides, I think, a rich and compelling account of the moral life. Lacking such grounding, standard VE offers an impoverished and implausible answer to PQAM.

PQAM and Respect-for-Persons

Thus far our case for RFP has been largely negative, as we have set out to show where certain other theories fall short of a plausible answer to PQAM. But to see the shortcomings of these competing theories is, at the same time, to draw attention to what it is that they lack, namely, the conceptual resources for affording *moral standing* to persons. RFP is the sort of theory required in order to be able to say, simply, "Rape is wrong because it *wrongs the victim"*—explaining the moral wrongness of the act by appeal to the effect that the act has upon the *victim herself* directly and primarily—apart from its effect upon anyone or anything else.

To say that the victim is *wronged* is to say that she is done an *injustice*. And the concern for justice on RFP implies the concept of *rights*. The wrongness of rape is explained in part by the fact that it violates a certain right that the victim has—call it the right of *personal autonomy*—in virtue of her humanity or personhood and, negatively, this is a right *not* to be treated in certain ways. It is a right not to be treated "simply as a means"—as though she is a mere thing to be used according to one's own purpose and pleasure—but to be treated as an "end." As a *person* she has ends or purposes of her own and, perhaps most notably, is a rational and moral agent capable of directing her own behavior in a principled and autonomous manner. To treat her simply as a means, then, is to discount her autonomy and, with that, her personhood.

The rights implied by RFP are *natural* and *inherent*. To say that they are inherent is to say that they stem simply from the nature and worth of persons *as* persons. That worth, according to RFP is not merely instrumental—as if the value of a person depended upon, say, her performance in achieving some purpose or in her contribution to society or to individuals—but intrinsic to their nature *as* persons. It is a worth that Kant called *dignity*, and he contrasted dignity with a "market price." The value of mere things, such as my guitar, may be expressed in terms of fair price in cash or barter. Not so with people. To regard a person's worth in terms of market price is just to treat "people as things" or simply as means. The institution of slavery, which treats people literally as property—even to be bought and sold at "market price"—is as direct a violation of this principle as can be imagined, and I maintain that the obvious wrongness of that institution is best explained on just such a principle.

To say that such rights are natural is to say that, unlike *civil* or *legal* rights, they are not legal or social *constructs* and are neither conferred by, say, some legislative body nor do they originate in any sort of social contract such as the US Constitution. Natural rights are thus grounded in the very nature of things—human nature, in particular—and are thus anterior to and transcendent of any and all social arrangements. As James Wilson (1742–1798), one of the

American Founding Fathers, wrote: "Those rights result from the natural state of man; from that situation in which he would find himself, if no civil government was instituted." Wilson maintained that government exists for the purpose of "securing and enlarging" the exercise of such natural rights, and "every government, which has not this in view, as its principal object, is not a government of the legitimate kind."[16] Martin Luther King, Jr. made this same appeal in his "Letter from a Birmingham Jail," when he insisted that "an unjust law is no law at all." King continued, "An unjust law is a human law that is not rooted in eternal and natural law. Any law that uplifts human personality is just. Any law that degrades human personality is unjust."[17] His reference to that which "degrades human personality" is closely akin to our Kantian notion of treating persons merely as means. Thus, the American Civil Rights Movement may be seen as the natural extension of the original vision of the Founders. They too looked to those same "inalienable rights" and that same natural "equality" to which the Founders appealed, and they insisted that natural justice is served and equality achieved only when it applies consistently to *all* persons in virtue of the dignity of their shared humanity without the insertion of arbitrary restrictions based upon race or other human differences. The concern for social justice and for equal rights, then, is best understood against the backdrop of a doctrine of human dignity and a concern for the respect that is morally required of persons.

The central question of this essay has been "What *makes* right acts right and wrong acts wrong?" I contend that the most plausible answer to that question—particularly when we consider those acts that just seem self-evidently wrong—appeals to the dignity of persons, respect for that dignity, and the natural and inherent rights that it entails. Any theory that excludes this appeal fails to capture fully the height and breadth and depth of the wrongness of such heinous acts as rape or of such institutions as slavery. Thus, if we are to make sense of our most deep-seated moral beliefs, we require an ethic of respect for persons.

What remains to be argued—and must be left unargued in this brief essay—is that persons *do*, in fact, have the sort of inherent worth that our moral judgments seem to presuppose and that RFP entails. The project of arguing for the dignity of persons essentially involves an appeal to some feature that is unique to persons and upon which that special worth or dignity supervenes. I can only hint at the direction that such an argument might take.

Stephen Hawking (1942–2018) once said that the human race is "just a chemical scum" on a "moderate planet" orbiting an "average star"—a less than flattering view of our place in the grand scheme of things. Immanuel Kant might have countered that, whereas everything in the universe—including chemical scum—behaves in accordance with law, "only a rational being has the power to act *in accordance with his idea* of laws."[18] If we are scum, we are a scum that has "the moral law within," which Kant regarded as both a source of wonder and the ground of our dignity.

> Two things fill the mind with ever new and increasing admiration and awe, the more often and more steadily we reflect on them; the starry heavens above me and moral law within me . . . . The former view of a countless multitude of worlds annihilates, as it were, my importance as an animal creature, which must give back to the planet (a mere speck in the universe) the matter from which it came, the matter which is for a little time provided with vital force, we know not how. The latter on the contrary, *infinitely raises my worth as that of an intelligence by my personality, in which the moral law reveals a life independent of all animality and even of the whole world of sense.*[19]

It was with such observations in mind that G. K. Chesterton observed: "Man is not merely an evolution but a revolution" in the way he stands out from the rest of the natural order. Attempting to view humanity only through the lens of its commonality with the rest of the animal kingdom is to see that one of the animals has gone "entirely off its head." He suggests, "It would be more like seeing one cow out of a hundred cows suddenly jump over the moon" or one of the birds to abandon its nest building to take up Gothic architecture.[20] The Western intellectual tradition has not failed to note our uniqueness in the order of things, and a long tradition has argued from human uniqueness to human dignity. Whether any of those arguments succeed is a topic for another essay.[21]

Notes

1 The term was coined by Marcus G. Singer in his ethics lectures.
2 *Minimally*, persons are deserving of respect. Should we develop a principle that also affords moral standing to animals, that, too, will involve *direct* duties to *individual* animals, which is incompatible with the theories assessed here, and for the same reasons.
3 Terry Pratchett, *Carpe Jugulum* (New York: Harper Collins, 1998).
4 G. K. Chesterton, "Mr. Blatchford, Persecution, and Other Things," *Clarion* (November 20, 1903), 3.
5 Mary Midgley, "Duties Concerning Islands," in *People, Penguins and Plastic Trees*, ed. C. Pierce and D. VanDeVeer (Belmont, CA: Wadsworth Publishing, 1986), 156–64.
6 Jerome K. Jerome, *Idle Thoughts of an Idle Fellow* (Rockville, MD: Serenity Publishers, 2009), 27.

7 Discussed in Plato's *Republic*, the Ring of Gyges renders its wearer invisible—just like the "one ring to rule them all."
8 Julia Annas, *The Morality of Happiness* (Oxford: Oxford University Press, 1993), 136.
9 Rosalind Hursthouse, "Virtue Ethics," *Stanford Encyclopedia of Philosophy*, http://plato.stanford. edu/entries/ethics-virtue/ (accessed February 28, 2017).
10 Robert N. Johnson, "Was Kant a Virtue Ethicist?" in *Kant's Ethics of Virtue*, ed. M. Betzler (Berlin: De Gruyter Verlag, 2008), 58.
11 Ibid., 60.
12 Monica Betzler, "Kant's Ethics of Virtue: An Introduction," in *Kant's Ethics of Virtue*, 8.
13 Hursthouse, "Virtue Ethics."
14 Robert N. Johnson, "Kant's Moral Philosophy," *Stanford Encyclopedia of Philosophy*, https://plato.stanford.edu/entries/kant-moral/ (accessed February 28, 2017).
15 Nicholas Wolterstorff, *Justice: Rights and Wrongs* (Princeton: Princeton University Press, 2010), 179.
16 James Wilson, in *The Works of the Honorable James Wilson*, ed. Bird Wilson (Philadelphia: Lorenzo Press, 1804), 466.
17 James M. Washington, ed., *A Testament of Hope: The Essential Writings of Martin Luther King, Jr.* (New York: HarperCollins, 1991; reprint HarperCollins, 2003), 293.
18 Immanuel Kant, *Groundwork of the Metaphysics of Morals*, trans. H. J. Paton (New York: Harper Torchbooks, 1964), 80.
19 Immanuel Kant, *Critique of Practical Reason*, trans. Lewis White Beck (Indianapolis: Bobbs-Merrill, 1956), 166 (italics added).
20 G. K. Chesterton, *Everlasting Man* in *G.K. Chesterton: Collected Works*, vol. 2 (San Francisco: Ignatius Press, 1986), 169.
21 I attempt this in "A Defense of Human Dignity," *Faith and Philosophy*, 17:3 (July 2000): 320–32.

RESPONSES

Response to Norcross

Mark Linville

> **Study Questions**
>
> 1. Does Linville accept that human happiness is an important value? Why?
> 2. What is the Problem of Justice that Linville raises for consequentialism?
> 3. What inconsistency does Linville find in Norcross's discussion of moral intuitions? How does Linville respond to the "Let your intuitions be hanged!" objection?
> 4. What is the "more common" response of consequentialists to the Justice Problem? How does Mill's Rule Utilitarianism provide an example of this response?
> 5. What deeper structural problem does consequentialism/utilitarianism have, according to Linville?
> 6. What "absurd" or "bizarre" implications does Linville think utilitarianism has?

Professor Norcross thinks that we should seek to make the world a better place. And a world is better or worse depending upon the net balance of intrinsically good and bad—better if there is a greater balance of good, and worse if there is more bad than good. He goes on to observe that almost everyone thinks that happiness is intrinsically good and unhappiness and suffering are intrinsically bad. Who can argue with that?

Now, the central claim of my main essay is that what *makes* an act right or wrong is whether it is respectful of the dignity of persons. If persons have dignity, then we ought, all else being equal, to promote human happiness and prevent human misery. And so, generally, worlds populated by happy people are better than worlds filled with miserable sufferers. Consequentialists do not have a monopoly on consequences.

The trouble brews when some consequentialist principle is taken for "the foundation of morality" or "the ultimate source of moral obligations," as John Stuart Mill describes his Principle of Utility.[1]

The Problem of Justice

Professor Norcross effectively turns away some common objections to his sort of theory. But in my experience, a more common—and perhaps more serious—objection comes from the consideration of what might be called the *Problem of Justice*: *There is no necessary connection between an act's being the one that produces the best overall consequences and its being fair or just.* It seems easy to imagine scenarios in which the most effective way of achieving "a larger net quantity of good" involves doing some very bad things to some people. The charge is that, given various sets of circumstances, a *consistent* consequentialist would be found justifying acts that are just obviously wrong, so that we may find ourselves even in what Thomas Nagel called "the abyss of utilitarian apologetics for large-scale murder."[2]

Consider Josef Mengele (1911–1979), who performed gruesome experiments upon captive children and adults at Auschwitz. Mengele was a sadistic monster, and it is doubtful that his experiments led to any significant medical breakthroughs. But they might have. Suppose that Mengele's otherwise nefarious work led to a cure for Dread Disease (some horrible pandemic) that would never otherwise have been discovered. Though we might still condemn Mengele for the monster that he was[3] we might, as utilitarians, praise the act itself as morally right. But this seems an absurd and morally repugnant implication of the theory.

Consequentialist Responses to the Justice Problem

Now there are basically two ways in which the consequentialist might defend his theory against this charge. On the one hand, when told that his theory has counterintuitive implications, the consequentialist may reply, "Let your intuitions be hanged!" I am not entirely sure how to read Norcross on this point. In some places he seems to invoke something very much like moral intuitions, observing that this or that account of value or the goodness of consequences is "appealing" or that "most philosophers" believe it or "feel its attraction," and he even speaks of a "core consequentialist intuition." In his reply to the demandingness objection, he notes that "many would say" that certain versions of consequentialism are "too demanding" (p. 65), and he argues that his own version does not suffer that defect—implicitly acknowledging the force of what the many would say. But then he seems to dismiss appeals to intuition as "largely driven by emotions" (p. 70) and suggests that once we realize that our intuitions are largely unreliable, the way is clear to the acceptance of consequentialism. It is not clear to me whether Norcross would say that Midgley's "iniquitous consequences"—such as a consequentialist justification for some moral atrocity—are not so iniquitous after all. It is tempting to read him in this way, as his debunking explanation for certain common intuitions seems tied to his aim to throw off any nonconsequentialist constraints on action. At any rate, I am not sure that I have seen good reason for thinking that we should be persuaded by what "the many" find appealing when this supports a consequentialist theory while throwing a wet blanket over such appeals when they challenge the view. Nor, of course, am I convinced that Mengele's experiments would have been morally right—or a good thing—if only the consequences had been happier. It was an obvious atrocity regardless of the outcome.

More common, I think, is for consequentialists to reply to the Problem of Justice by arguing that their theory does not have such counterintuitive implications.[4] Mill's Rule Utilitarianism might be seen in this light, as he holds that there are times when one ought morally to "abstain" from an act even though the consequences are "beneficial," and this is because "the action is of a class which, if practised generally, would be generally injurious."[5] Indeed, Mill develops an account of justice and of individual rights that he thinks is not merely consistent with the Principle of Utility but, in fact, *derived* from it. Briefly, that principle generates moral rules that imply the general rightness or wrongness of acts based upon the tendency of each *type* ("class") of act, "if practised generally," to promote either general happiness or unhappiness. Now, it is possible for two or more rules to apply so that it is impossible to obey both. But some rules are more important than others in that they are closer to the core concern for human welfare and happiness, and in such dilemmas the aim is to discern which of the competing rules has the greater moral weight (i.e., utility). We might say that the weightier rule (e.g., against killing) "trumps" the lesser rule (e.g., against lying), and so we are morally justified in violating the lesser for the sake of the weightier. And some utilitarian rules protect human and other goods that are so essential to overall human welfare that it is difficult if not impossible to imagine weightier rules that would trump them. These are the rules of justice, and their (near) inviolability is grounded in their utility—their importance as a means to achieving overall good consequences.[6]

Mill also speaks of individual rights, and these amount to the right to be treated in accordance with the rules of justice. He says that to have a right is to have "something which society ought to defend me in the possession of." When asked *why* society ought so to defend it, he replies, "I can give . . . no other reason than general utility."[7] Given all of this, Mill may have the resources in place to reply that his theory simply never implies the rightness of the obviously wrong.[8] For Mill and other consequentialists who reply in such a manner, I am inclined to make a gift of the point and assume, for the sake of argument, that the reply succeeds in turning away the charge that their theory runs aground on the Problem of Justice. The trouble lies deeper.

Structural Problems

Mill's "rights" are not natural or inherent but provisional, based upon the best policy for achieving good consequences—general utility. Now, it will come as no surprise to hear that Mill is not, after all, a natural rights theorist. His predecessor, Jeremy Bentham, famously called talk of natural rights "nonsense on stilts." But my concern here is with the *structure* of the utilitarian explanation of the rightness or wrongness of acts: If society ought to defend me in my possession of life and liberty, then it ought to do so *for the sake of society*—general utility—and not for my own sake. Smith's torturing Jones may be wrong, and Mill might even insist that it violates Jones's "rights," but if asked why Jones should be thought to have such rights, Mill can "give no other reason than general utility." Dr. Mengele's experiments were wrong because they hindered rather than promoted general utility, *not* because they wronged the victims. The suffering of the victims mattered because it decreased general utility. Even Mill's "rights" do not allow for *direct* duties *to* individuals. Utilitarianism fails on the criterion for plausibility that I defend in my main essay.

My ethics professor, Marcus Singer, used to say in his lectures that the Prime Directive for the utilitarian is a sort of weird abstraction, that is, to maintain a "Number" in the universe. That Number represents something like Professor Norcross's "net quantity of goodness," and the higher that Number the better. Think of the Number as assigned to worlds taken in their totality, each number representing the total happiness factor in that world and thus ranking them in a sort of hierarchy. Our aim, then, is to do what we can to increase our world's number and thus to promote it in the ranks. One absurd implication is that the wrongness of rape is found in the fact that it reduces the Number. The victim's suffering is relevant for the same reason and not simply for her own sake. Another oddity is the relative value of persons and their happiness. Should we be concerned to create as much happiness as possible because we have a prior conviction that *people* have intrinsic worth and that, therefore, we should care to make them happy? That is my own view. Happier worlds are better because *people* get on better, and people matter. But that is not a consequentialist view.[9] Rather, the idea is that *happiness itself* is intrinsically good or desirable, and so the more of that intrinsically valuable mental state the better. The bizarre implication is that the very value of people

Notes

1 John Stuart Mill, *Utilitarianism* (Indianapolis: Hackett Publishing, 2002), 1, 26.
2 Thomas Nagel, "War and Massacre," *Philosophy and Public Affairs*, 1:2 (Winter 1972):126.
3 But perhaps not if Mengele aimed to make the world a better place.
4 "These objections seem to me to be just unsympathetic," writes R. B. Brandt in *Morality, Utilitarianism, and Rights* (Cambridge: Cambridge University Press, 1992), 200.
5 Mill, *Utilitarianism*, 19.
6 "Justice is a name for certain classes of moral rules, which concern the essentials of human well-being more nearly, and are therefore of more absolute obligation, than any other rules for the guidance of life" (Ibid., p. 59).
7 Ibid., 54.
8 A reply that implicitly acknowledges the force of the intuition—similar to what we see in Professor Norcross's reply.
9 Should the consequentialist say otherwise then he is perhaps not far from the Kingdom. He is importing elements of a nonconsequentialist, respect-for-persons theory.

Response to Linville

Alastair Norcross

Study Questions

1. Why does Norcross have a problem with Linville's appeal to "common-sense" moral judgments?

2. What basic principle is included in most consequentialist theories? How is this principle relevant to respect for persons?

3. What are the two "fatal flaws" with Linville's appeal to rationality to ground respect for persons?

4. What does Norcross find ironic about Linville's criticism of egoism?

I would like to thank Mark Linville for his thoughtful and carefully argued essay. There is much in this that I agree with. I share his rejection of egoism, divine command theory, and traditional versions of virtue ethics, and his view that the central problem with all three approaches is that they misidentify what is centrally morally problematical with behavior such as murder, rape, and theft. My main complaint about Linville's treatment of these theories is that he takes the time to argue against them at all, at least with respect to the first two. Egoism and divine command theory are simply low-hanging fruit. Almost no contemporary philosophers take either theory seriously as an account of morality. Virtue ethics is clearly taken more seriously, and rightly so (though I share Linville's worries about it). I also agree with the claim that respect for persons is extremely important. Where we disagree is with his claim that respect for persons is, itself, something like the foundational principle of morality. My view is that a more fundamental principle both explains the importance of respect for persons and provides the most plausible account of how that principle should be employed and understood.

The Limitations of Moral Intuitions

First, I have a methodological point to make. Linville puts great weight on intuitive "commonsense" judgments (what he calls the "beliefs of common life"). While it is clear that an appeal to some moral intuitions is unavoidable, I am deeply suspicious of putting much, if any, weight on any but the most general and enduring intuitions. Until relatively recently, moral "commonsense" viewed women as having an inferior moral status in comparison to men, and some races as having an inferior status compared to others. These judgments were not restricted to the philosophically unsophisticated. Such illustrious philosophers as Aristotle and Hume accepted positions of this nature. Aristotle, notoriously, defended the moral permissibility of slavery. The moral wrongness of rape, one of Linville's examples of a moral touchstone, is a relatively recent commitment among even the philosophically sophisticated. Rape was primarily thought to be wrong, not because of what it did to the victim, but because it violated the property rights of the male relations (husband, father, etc.) of the victim (and, regrettably, this attitude toward rape still exists). The view that rape within a marriage is impossible, because wives don't have the right to refuse their husbands, was prevalent until quite recently, and hasn't entirely disappeared. It is certainly encouraging that the vast majority of Linville's acquaintances, and my own, take as a matter of moral commonsense that rape, murder, genocide, and torture are wrong. But to assume that our judgments should carry the kind of weight that

Linville assumes is to ignore the evidence of history. It would be the height of complacency to believe that we just happen to have the good fortune to be alive at a time when the "beliefs of common life" are finally in alignment with the truth about morality.

The Inadequacy of the Respect for Persons Principle

So, what of respect for persons? As I said earlier, I agree that it is an extremely important moral principle. One feature of consequentialist theories that I didn't have space to explore in my original piece is their radical egalitarianism. The good-making features of the world, such as the well-being of sentient creatures (including human persons), are equally good, no matter where they are instantiated. The same goes for the bad-making features, such as suffering. All creatures who can experience well-being and suffering have an equal *interest* in experiencing well-being and avoiding suffering. A basic principle of almost all consequentialist theories is that the like interests of all should be considered equally. The suffering of a man is of no more or less moral significance than the like suffering of a woman. The suffering of a member of one race or social class is likewise of no more or less significance than the like suffering of a member of another race or social class. Racist actions and policies fail to respect some persons precisely because they embody the view that the interests of some people are less significant (perhaps even of no significance) than the interests of others. The attitude toward rape that views it as perpetrating a wrong against a male family member, and not directly against the victim, fails to respect persons for the same reason. The demand for equal consideration of interests embodied in consequentialist theories, such as utilitarianism, is precisely what it *means* to respect individuals. It is only when I weigh your interests equally with the interests of all others whom I can affect that I adequately respect you (and them). Deontological constraints, like Linville's, function to disallow the consideration of certain interests in certain circumstances. Thus they, at least sometimes, *prevent* us from respecting certain individuals.

The principle of respect, embodied in Linville's respect for persons, is both properly grounded in, and delineated by, the principle of equal consideration of interests that lies at the heart of most consequentialist theories. However, Linville's version of the principle, grounded in something like the rational autonomy of human persons, is clearly too narrowly, and arbitrarily, circumscribed to serve as the basic principle of morality. This is because it applies primarily (perhaps exclusively—Linville doesn't expand on this) to those individuals who possess personhood. As Linville says: "The project of arguing for the dignity of persons essentially involves an appeal to some feature that is unique to persons and upon which that special worth or dignity supervenes" (p. 81). In hinting at what such a feature might be, Linville quotes Kant: "Only a rational being has the power to act in accordance with his idea of laws."

Linville's and Kant's appeal to a certain form of rationality, to justify attributing a superior moral status to humans over other sentient creatures, is part of a long philosophical tradition, dating back at least to Aristotle. However, any such appeal suffers from at least two fatal defects. First, whatever kind and level of rationality is selected as justifying the attribution of superior moral status to humans will either be lacking in some humans or present in some animals. To take one of the most commonly suggested features, many humans are incapable of engaging in moral reflection. For some, this incapacity is temporary, as is the case with infants, or the temporarily cognitively disabled. Others who once had the capacity may have permanently lost it, as is the case with the severely senile or the irreversibly comatose. Still others never had and never will have the capacity, as is the case with the severely mentally disabled. If we base our claims for the moral superiority of humans over animals on the attribution of such capacities, won't we have to exclude many humans? Won't we then be forced to the claim that there is at least as much moral reason to use cognitively deficient humans in experiments and for food as to use animals? Perhaps we could exclude the only temporarily disabled, on the grounds of potentiality, though that move has its own problems. Nonetheless, the other two categories would be vulnerable to this objection. Although this problem is well known, no philosopher has yet produced a satisfactory answer to it.[1]

The second, and deeper, problem with the appeal to rationality is that it confuses the categories of moral agent and moral patient. What is the moral relevance of rationality? Why should we think that the possession of a certain level or kind of rationality renders the possessor's interests of greater moral significance than those of a merely sentient being? In the words of the famous utilitarian philosopher Jeremy Bentham: "The question is not, Can they reason? nor Can they talk? But, Can they suffer?"[2] Moral rationality is relevant to certain moral judgments. If a being is incapable of moral reasoning, then it cannot be a moral agent. It cannot be subject to moral obligations. That animals (and some humans) can't be moral *agents* isn't relevant to their status as moral *patients*. Most humans are both moral agents and patients. Most, perhaps all, animals are only moral patients. It is somewhat ironic that Linville's well-taken criticism of egoism—that it can't explain what makes acts like rape wrong—applies equally to a Kantian account of the wrongness of cruelty to animals (and nonrational humans). Notoriously, Kant claimed that cruelty to animals is wrong, because of what such behavior does to the perpetrators themselves, not directly to the animals. But the wrongness of torturing an animal, or a human, stems from what it does to the *victim*. Animals, like humans (rational or otherwise), have an interest in avoiding suffering. Only the consequentialist approach can adequately explain this wrongness.[3]

Notes

1 For a detailed analysis of the problem, attempts to answer it, and explanation of why they all fail, see Norcross, "Puppies, Pigs, and People: Eating Meat and Marginal Cases," *Philosophical Perspectives,* 18 (2004): 229–45.
2 Jeremy Bentham, *Introduction to the Principles of Morals and Legislation*, chap. 17.
3 For more on this, see Norcross, "Puppies, Pigs, and People."

Questions for Reflection

1. How trustworthy are our moral intuitions? What should (or can) we do when people's intuitions differ?
2. Who does a better job at explaining the role of respect for persons in ethical theory, Linville or Norcross? Why?
3. Do humans have greater moral significance than other sentient beings (e.g., animals)? Why?

3

Does Morality Depend on God?

Morality Depends upon God

Matthew Flannagan

Study Questions

1. What is the "autonomy thesis"? In response to it, what two contentions does Flannagan make?
2. What is the divine command theory (DCT)? What is the DCT *not*, according to Flannagan?
3. What is the "anything goes" objection to DCT? How does Flannagan respond to it?
4. Why does Flannagan think that DCT does not make morality arbitrary? What error does he think Shafer-Landau's version of the objection commits?
5. What is the "vacuity objection" to DCT? Why does Flannagan think it misses the point?
6. What does it mean to say that moral requirements are prescriptive? Why does Flannagan think such prescriptions are inexplicable on secular accounts of ethics?
7. Why, according to Flannagan, does secular ethics have difficulty accounting for moral authority?

"If God does not exist everything is permitted."[1] This phrase from Dostoyevsky's novel, *The Brothers Karamazov*, sums up a common intuition held by many people: that in the absence of God, there cannot be things like moral requirements or obligations. Thinkers as diverse as Kant,[2] Locke, Berkeley,[3] Sartre, and J. L. Mackie[4] have held or defended this intuition as did much of the utilitarian tradition before Bentham. In fact, until recently, this was a majority view. William Bristow writes that most thinkers associated with the Enlightenment held that "morality requires religion, in the sense that morality requires belief in a transcendent law-giver and in an after-life."[5]

Of course, the fact that large numbers of people have believed something doesn't mean it's true, and today most philosophers would dismiss this intuition out of hand. Instead, they hold to what is called the *autonomy thesis*: the thesis that there can be moral requirements to engage in an action regardless of whether or not God commands, desires, or wills that people engage in that action.

In this article, I will argue that, despite its popularity, the autonomy thesis is not well supported by the evidence. In doing so, I will defend two contentions:

(1) That attempts to refute a divine command theory of ethics—the theory that moral rightness and wrongness consist in agreement and disagreement, respectively, with God's commands[6]—have failed.

(2) That secular accounts of morality are subject to important skeptical challenges.

What Is a Divine Command Theory?

Before doing so, it's important to distinguish what a divine command theory (DCT) is from common misunderstandings. According to DCT, the property of ethical wrongness is (identical with) the property of being contrary to God's command.[7] God is understood here, in a fairly orthodox fashion, as a necessarily existent, all-powerful, all-knowing, essentially loving and just, immaterial person who created, and providentially orders, the universe.

Note three things. First, this is an account of the nature of moral *wrongness*, not an account of "goodness" in general. The concept of the morally obligatory is not identical to the concept of what it is good to do. It might be good, even saintly, for me to give a kidney to benefit a stranger, but it is not an act I am obliged to do.[8] Obligatory actions are actions we are required to do and another person can legitimately demand we do them. Omitting to do them without an adequate excuse renders one guilty and blameworthy, and others can justifiably censure you, rebuke you, and even punish.

Second, DCT is not the claim that the word "wrong" means "contrary to God's command"; nor is it the claim that persons cannot recognize or know what is wrong unless they believe in God. Instead, the postulated relationship between moral requirements and God's commands is one of identity; moral wrongness is identical with the property of being contrary to God's commands. The example of light illustrates this distinction. People knew how to use the word "light" long before they discovered its physical nature. And they knew the difference between light and darkness long before they understood the physics of light.[9] In the same way, divine command theorists contend we can know the meaning of moral terms such as right and wrong, and know the difference between right and wrong, without knowing that wrongness is identical with the property of being contrary to God's commands.

Third, to claim that moral requirements are identical with God's commands is not to claim that our moral requirements are identical with the commandments laid down in a particular sacred text such as the Koran or the Bible. While many divine command theorists do accept that God has revealed his commands in an infallible sacred text, some do not. Moreover, that God's commands are contained in some particular sacred text is not part of, or entailed by, DCT itself, but by other theological commitments one has. One could consistently be a divine command theorist without holding this.

Consequently, one cannot refute DCT by noting that atheists can be good people, or that the word "good" doesn't mean "commanded by God," or by citing various biblical texts and maintaining that what they teach is immoral. Instead, one must address the claim in question, which is that the best account of the nature of moral obligations, the most adequate answer to the question of what moral obligations are, is that they are divine commands.

Has a Divine Command Theory Been Refuted?

This brings me to my first contention: *that all attempts to refute a divine command theory have failed.* This contention will no doubt surprise many. It's widely claimed that DCTs were refuted 2000 years ago by a line of argument pressed by Socrates in Plato's dialogue, *The Euthyphro*. In reality, however, the original argument is somewhat obscure, and it's hard to find in Plato's text a compelling argument.[10] Most people who attack DCT today ignore the original dialogue and, instead, appeal to three arguments that are loosely associated with Plato's dialogue. They are (1) the anything goes objection, (2) the arbitrariness objection, and (3) the vacuity objection. In the following paragraphs I will argue that they all fail.

The Anything Goes Objection

Perhaps the most common objection to DCT is that such theories have the counterintuitive implication that anything at all could be right or wrong. David Brink's version is typical:

> If God's attitudes had been very different and he had approved of very different things, then different things would be good or bad . . ., for example, had God not condemned genocide and rape, these things would not have been wrong, or, if God were to come to approve these things, they would become morally acceptable. But these are awkward commitments, inasmuch as this sort of conduct seems necessarily wrong.[11]

This objection can be summarized as follows:

(P1) If the DCT is true, then if God commanded us to rape we would be required to rape.

(P2) It is absurd that we could be required to rape.

(P3) God could command us to rape.

(C1) Therefore, DCT is absurd.

The key premise is (P3), the assumption that it is possible that God could command atrocious things like rape. But (P3) seems dubious. As noted, divine command theorists work with a conception of God whereby God is understood to be an immaterial person who is all powerful, all knowing, loving, and just. So, as terms are defined, the claim that it is possible for God to command people to rape others would hold only if it's possible for an all knowing, loving, and just person to command rape. This is unlikely. The very reason critics use the example of rape, is that they view it as a paradigm action that no virtuous person could ever knowingly entertain.

Suppose, however, for the sake of argument, that it is possible for a just and loving, omniscient person to command rape. Rape, then, would only be commanded in situations where a just and loving person, aware of all the relevant facts, could endorse it—and under these circumstances, it's hard to see how (P2) could be maintained.

These considerations suggest that the objection is unsound. (P2) and (P3) cannot both be true.

The Arbitrariness Objection

A variant of this objection is the contention that a divine command theory makes morality arbitrary. It is contended that if a divine command theory is true, then God's commands must be arbitrary. Seeing that nothing is right or wrong prior to God's commanding, God can have no reasons for issuing the commands he does rather than some other commands.

This objection, however, involves a non sequitur—the conclusion drawn does not follow from the premises in question. If nothing is right or wrong prior to God's commands, then it does follow that God cannot command or prohibit actions *because they are right or wrong*. However, this leaves open the possibility that God has *other reasons* for issuing the commands he does. God could, for example, command certain actions because they are cruel or harmful or unjust or detrimental to human happiness. And a loving and just God would oppose actions like this.

Russ Shafer-Landau offers a different version of the arbitrariness objection. He presents the following dilemma: "Either there are, or there are not, excellent reasons that support God's prohibitions. If there are no such reasons, then God's choice is arbitrary, i.e. insufficiently well supported by reason and argument."[12] Alternatively:

> If God is, in fact, issuing commands based on excellent reasons, then it is those excellent reasons and not the fact of God's having commanded various actions, that make those actions right. The excellent reasons that support the requirements of charity and kindness are what make it right to be charitable and kind.[13]

This argument is based on a subtle equivocation. Shafer-Landau states that if God has excellent reasons for his commands, then those reasons, and not the command, *make* the commanded action right. But this claim is ambiguous. Stephen Sullivan has noted the word "make" can, in this context, be used in two very different senses.[14] The first sense refers to what Sullivan calls a *constitutive* explanation: On a hot February day, I pour a glass of water with the aim of drinking it and quenching my thirst. There is a legitimate sense in which I can say that what makes me pour a glass of water is the fact that I am pouring a glass of H20. When I speak like this, I use the word "makes" to refer to a relationship of identity. I am explaining one thing (the pouring of the water) but citing the existence of another thing that I take to be identical with it.

The second sense involves what Sullivan calls a *motivational* explanation, such as when I state that what makes me pour a glass of water is the fact that I am thirsty. Motivational explanations don't explain an action by referring to something taken to be identical with it; rather, they attempt to tell us why an agent acted the way he or she did by giving us the reasons and/or motivations the agent acted upon.

Now let's turn to Shafer-Landau's claim: *If God's commands are based on reasons, then it is those reasons and not God's commands that make the commanded actions right*. If Shafer-Landau is using the word "makes" to refer to a motivational explanation, then this premise is correct. If God has reasons for commanding as he does, then those reasons do motivate God's decision to command what he does. The problem is that in this sense of the word "makes," the conclusion Shafer-Landau draws is compatible with DCT. For Shafer-Landau's argument to have a bite, the word "makes" must be used to refer to a constitutional explanation. When a divine command theorist claims that God's commands "make" an action wrong, he or she is not claiming that God's commands provide a motivational explanation for why actions are wrong. God's reasons for commanding something obviously is not that he has commanded it. As we noted earlier, divine command theorists typically contend that ethical wrongness is identical with the property of being contrary to God's commands. They offer a constitutive explanation of the nature of moral obligations.

Shafer-Landau's premise must, therefore, be rendered thus: *If God's commands are based on reasons, then it is those reasons and not God's commands that are identical with moral rightness*. However, this premise is clearly false. Some analogies will show this. Suppose that a university had good reasons for conferring a degree on a doctoral candidate. Shafer-Landau's premise would entail that those reasons are identical with the conferral of a degree. Or suppose John has good reasons for being a bachelor, Shafer-Landau's premise would entail that those reasons would be identical with being a bachelor. None of these inferences, however, follows.[15]

The Vacuity Objection

At this point, critics usually fall back on what's known as the *vacuity objection*. If a divine command theory is true, then God can't be morally good in any nonvacuous sense. A person is morally good only if that person has both moral duties and acts in accord with them. Yet, according to a divine command theory, the wrongness of an action consists in its being forbidden by God; given that God does not issue commands to himself, it follows that God has no duties and so God can't be morally good. To say, "God is good," then, is to say no more than the vacuous "God does what he commands."

This objection, however, misses the point. Even if it's true that God doesn't have moral duties, it doesn't follow that God can't have certain character traits such as being truthful, benevolent, loving, gracious, merciful, etc. Nor does it mean he is not opposed to certain actions such as murder, rape, torturing people for fun, and so on. If God has no duties, then he isn't under any obligation to love others, or to tell the truth, or what have you, but that does not mean he cannot love others or tell the truth. God does not have to have a duty to do something in order to do it.

The "anything goes," "arbitrariness," and "vacuity" objections, therefore, all fail. This is significant because these are the three reasons commonly given for rejecting DCT. Almost everyone who dismisses the claim that morality is dependent upon God cites these three objections as decisive. Seeing that these objections all fail, one cannot in the absence of further argument proclaim with any confidence that a divine command theory is an inadequate account of the nature of moral obligation.

Skeptical Challenges to Secular Meta ethical Theories

Of course, even if one grants that DCT is an adequate or defensible account of the nature of moral requirements, one could argue that better secular accounts are available. This brings me to my second contention: *that secular accounts of morality are themselves subject to important skeptical challenges*. There are several reasons for thinking this. Here I will focus on just two.

The Problem of Moral Ontology

The first skeptical challenge comes from philosopher John Mackie. Mackie argues that, in the absence of God, we lack what philosophers call an adequate moral ontology. That is, we can't point to anything in reality that plausibly accounts for or explains the existence and nature of moral requirements.[16]

Why does Mackie think this? He takes for granted that moral requirements are *prescriptive*—they direct our behavior; they demand, forbid, prohibit, or require certain kinds of conduct. Mackie argues that *moral* requirements are prescriptions of a certain type. First, moral requirements are *objective*: they transcend demands made by human beings or human institutions. If an action (like the sadistic and brutal rape of a 10-year-old) is wrong, then we are required to refrain from that action "irrespective of whether any person," or "group or society of persons, requires or demands or prescribes or admires it."[17] If our companions or society fails to prohibit the brutal rape of a 10-year-old or demand that we engage in such rapes, the action remains wrong and it is our companions and society that are in error. Objectivity is necessary to account for the fact that "we worry that we can be mistaken in our moral judgments,"[18] that neither we nor society can "eliminate all moral requirements just by not making any demands."[19] These facts all presuppose that what we or our society demands and what morality demands are distinct things.

Skeptics often assume moral objectivity when they criticize religious ethics or institutional religion by citing biblical or Koranic passages that they maintain are immoral, or refer to atrocities done by believers in the name of God. In doing this, they acknowledge that what an individual believer (or that believer's community) endorses and teaches is right can, in fact, be morally wrong.

Second, moral requirements are *categorical* prescriptions. Exactly what is meant by "categorical" is subject to some ambiguity. In various places, Mackie and some of his followers, such as Richard Joyce,[20] understand categoricity in terms of inescapability: the idea that moral requirements apply to us irrespective of whether following them contributes to any ends or aims we currently desire. To see that moral requirements are inescapable, consider a criminal who stands in the dock convicted of a crime. The criminal openly admits the crime, is unrepentant, and informs us that he or she wanted to kill and torture and doing so did not frustrate any of his or her desires. Do we withdraw our moral condemnation of the criminal when we discover that he or she really does desire to kill and maim? Obviously not! Moral requirements can't be escaped or begged off by noting that they don't fulfill one's goals or ends.[21]

Interestingly, that moral requirements are both objective and inescapable is implicit in many of the objections skeptics raise against DCT. In the previous section, I discussed the "anything goes objection" to DCT. It was contended that if moral requirements are identified with divine commands, anything at all could be deemed "right" as long as God commanded it, even rape or genocide. We saw that this objection against DCT failed because God has certain character traits essentially. What's less appreciated is that an analogous line of argument can be made against any metaethical theories that contend that moral requirements are not objective. Suppose moral requirements aren't objective: They don't hold "irrespective of whether any person," or "group or society of persons, requires or demands or prescribes or admires" the action in question. Then it follows that, if I or my society demands that I commit rape or genocide, rape and genocide are not wrong. Unlike God, humans aren't essentially loving and just, and so there is nothing incoherent or impossible about the prospect of my or my society's doing this.

A similar line of argument applies to the rejection of inescapability. Suppose moral requirements aren't inescapable but apply to human beings only if compliance with them contributes to ends or aims we currently desire. It follows that any action, including rape and genocide, can become permissible for a person provided raping and killing contribute to certain goals and ends a human being desires. The testimony of history tells us it's possible, and sometimes actual, for humans to have such goals.

More recently, some writers have suggested that "categorical" should be understood in a further sense. For example, Stephen Darwall argues that there is a conceptual link between something being morally obligatory and something being blameworthy; moral requirements conceptually are like demands people make on each other for which they can hold each other accountable through practices of blaming, reproaching, and guilt.[22] Robert Adams similarly notes this link. He imagines a situation in which there are compelling reasons to support your not walking on the lawn. However, suppose that these reasons give you no grounds for feeling guilty if you do, and they provide no reasons for other people to make you feel like you must stay off the lawn or to blame and reproach you for doing so. Adams concludes, plausibly, that while there would be a sense in which you ought not to walk on the lawn, you have no obligation not to do so.[23] Moral requirements are not *just* prescriptive; they are a certain type of prescription—a prescription that involves a demand which you must comply with, for which others can hold you accountable by blaming and reproaching, and so forth. If I have done wrong, I need to engage in certain practices of expiation such as admitting my guilt, and seeking reparation and forgiveness.

This combination of objectivity and categorical demandingness is readily explicable if God exists. A command is a paradigmatic example of a prescription that involves a demand for which we hold people accountable through standard practices such as blaming. Similarly, divine commands are inescapable. If God commands people to do something, then this fact obtains regardless of whether we believe he did, or whether his command is conducive to our current goals. It's also an objective fact whether or not God commands something; the fact that people might disagree with the demand or might choose to issue different demands themselves makes no difference to whether it, in fact, exists.

However, from a secular perspective, this combination of objectivity and categorical demandingness is, at least prima facie, "odd" or "queer" in Mackie's words. Something transcending human institutions is calling for us to behave in certain ways, demanding of us to act in those ways, condemning us and rendering us blameworthy if we don't. But no objective natural property we know of seems to be able to do this sort of thing. Such things as the rules of etiquette or human laws and institutions can make categorical demands on people's conduct in this way, but these demands aren't objective. Certain natural properties such as the property of causing harm or suffering are objective, but such properties are not the sort of thing that can categorically prohibit, demand, or condemn people's behavior.

Richard Garner sums up Mackie's point: "Queerness of a different magnitude would belong to any property or fact that by itself called for humans to act one way rather than another. Even the most vile of poisons does not say 'Don't drink me.'"[24] Similarly, Gerald Harrison:

> The chair I am sat in cannot bid me sit in it. It does not have a mind. And the same holds true for the natural features of any act or state of affairs. The fact an act hurt someone cannot itself be the disfavouring of me performing it.

> It may give rise to a disfavouring of the act being performed, but it cannot itself be the disfavouring. The non-agential natural world cannot bid us do things.[25]

So, secular accounts of morality face important ontological challenges. A good chunk of contemporary metaethics is motivated by this problem. Descriptivists tend to argue that moral requirements are objective, but have trouble accounting for the prescriptive nature of moral requirements. Expressivists tend to capture something of the prescriptive feature of moral requirements and want to jettison objectivity. As Mackie stated: "Yet each gains much of its plausibility from the felt inadequacy of the other."[26]

The Problem of Moral Authority

Suppose, however, that one could come up with a plausible moral ontology. There is a second skeptical challenge to secular ethics. This concerns the *authority* of moral requirements. In an influential article, Philippa Foot (1920–2010) noted a third way that moral requirements are understood to be categorical. A moral requirement "necessarily gives reasons for acting."[27] Robert Adams refers to the intuition that "moral judgments have an action- and preference-guiding force that they could not have unless everyone had reason to follow them in his actions and preferences."[28] Not only do they give everyone subject to them reasons for acting but these reasons are supposed to be decisive. If an action is morally wrong, then we *have* to refrain from it. The fact that there might be other reasons in favor of doing it, such as that it enhances our perceived self-interest, or it meets our goals, or that it makes us popular, doesn't override our moral duty.

This moral authority is explicable if God exists; if a person who was fully informed, (omniscient), flawlessly rational, and loves us and our loved ones commanded us to do something, then we have reasons to do it. Similarly, if the world has been created and providentially ordered by a loving and just God, then there is no ultimate conflict between what morality requires and one's long-term happiness. God's justice would entail that the world is providentially ordered so that a commitment to always doing the right thing is not inconsistent with one's long-term happiness. If God does not exist, however, then absent some religious doctrine such as Karma, this doesn't seem to be the case. Consider the following example:

> Ms. Poore has lived many years in grinding poverty. She is not starving but has only the bare necessities. She has tried very hard to get ahead by hard work, but nothing has come of her efforts. An opportunity to steal a

large sum of money arises. If Ms. Poore steals the money and invests it wisely, she can obtain many desirable things her poverty has denied her: cure for a painful (but nonfatal) medical condition, a well-balanced diet, decent housing, adequate heat in the winter, health insurance, new career opportunities through education, etc. Moreover, if she steals the money, her chances of being caught are very low, and she knows this. She is also aware that the person who owns the money is very wealthy and will not be greatly harmed by the theft . . . . Ms. Poore faces the choice of stealing the money or living in grinding poverty the rest of her life. In such a case, I think it would be morally wrong for Ms. Poore to steal the money; and yet, assuming there is no God and no life after death, failing to steal the money will likely deny her a large measure of personal fulfilment, that is, a large measure of what is in her long-term best interests.[29]

When such cases occur, moral reasons will point in one direction and our self-interest, goals, and desires in another. This possibility generates the skeptical question: "Why be Moral?" What reason do I have, in such cases, to follow the dictates of morality and not my self-interest? Certainly one can't answer this question by pointing out that it would be immoral not to do what's right. The question, after all, is *why* be moral? Nor can it be answered by appealing to desires or goals that would be fulfilled because the case is one where morality and such things are in conflict. This question has proved to be another central problem in contemporary secular metaethics. It is difficult to find any answer to this question.

In light of the earlier discussion of the arbitrariness objection, the inability to answer this question takes on new significance. If there is no reason to follow morality as opposed to following one's self-interest and goals, then the decision to follow morality is ultimately arbitrary. The fact that DCT was supposed to have this implication, of course, was one of the major reasons people gave for dismissing divine command theories out of hand. But we see now that secular metaethics is the view that really suffers from this problem.

Conclusion

I think a fair assessment of the literature supports two contentions. First, DCT is a defensible account of the nature of moral obligations—an account that hasn't been refuted by the considerations brought against it.

Second, secular accounts of morality face important skeptical challenges. They face ontological challenges, trying to locate the existence of objective, categorical demands in a godless world. And they face challenges explaining the authority of morality—why a person should do what is morally required when it conflicts with his or her goals or interests.

In light of this, it's not enough for people to simply dismiss the claim that morality can't exist without God. Defenders of the autonomy thesis need to show what's wrong with theories that make morality dependent on God, and they need to show that better secular theories exist that aren't plagued by even more serious problems.

Notes

1 Fyodor Dostoevsky, *The Brothers Karamazov*, trans. Richard Pevear and Larissa Volokhonsky (San Francisco, CA: North Point Press, 1990), 589.
2 Immanuel Kant, *Critique of Practical Reason*, trans. Lewis White Beck (Indianapolis, Indiana: Bobbs-Merrill, 1788).
3 Stephen Darwall, "Berkeley's Moral and Political Philosophy," in *The Cambridge Companion to Berkeley*, ed. Kenneth Winkler (Cambridge: Cambridge University Press, 2005), 311.
4 Mackie, *Ethics: Inventing Right and Wrong* (Harmondsworth: Penguin Publishing, 1977), see pp. 48, 231–32.
5 William Bristow, "Enlightenment," in *Stanford Encyclopaedia of Philosophy*, available at https://plato.stanford.edu/entries/enlightenment/ (accessed April 19, 2017).
6 Robert M. Adams, "Moral Arguments for Theism," in *The Virtue of Faith*, ed. Robert Adams (New York: Oxford University Press, 1987), 145.
7 Robert M. Adams, "Divine Command Meta-Ethics Modified Again," *Journal of Religious Ethics*, 7:1 (1979): 76.
8 Example from C. Stephen Evans, *Kierkegaard's Ethic of Love: Divine Commands and Moral Obligations* (Oxford: Oxford University Press, 2004), 16.
9 This example comes from William Lane Craig, "Opening Statement," in *Is the Foundation of Morality Natural or Supernatural? A Debate between Sam Harris and William Lane Craig*, transcript available at http://www.mandm.org.nz/2011/05/transcript-sam-harris-v-william-lane-craig-debate-%E2%80%9Cis-good-from-god%E2%80%9D.html (accessed July 29, 2013).
10 See, for example, Richard Joyce, "Theistic Ethics and the Euthyphro Dilemma," *Journal of Religious Ethics*, 30 (2002): 49–75; and Thomas Carson, "Divine Will/Divine Command Moral Theories and the Problem of Arbitrariness," *Religious Studies*, 48:4 (2012):445–68.
11 David O. Brink, "The Autonomy of Ethics," in *The Cambridge Companion to Atheism*, ed. Michael Martin (Cambridge: Cambridge University Press, 2007), 152.
12 Russ Shafer-Landau, "Introduction to Part IV," in *Ethical Theory: An Anthology*, ed. Russ Shafer-Landau (Malden MA: Blackwell Publishing, 2007), 237.
13 Ibid., 238.

14 Stephen Sullivan, "Arbitrariness, Divine Commands, and Morality," *International Journal of Philosophy of Religion,* 33:1 (1993): 33–45.
15 These points are made cogently by Stephen Sullivan, "Arbitrariness, Divine Commands, and Morality," 37–39. See also Matthew Flannagan's, "Is Ethical Naturalism More Plausible than Supernaturalism: A Reply to Walter Sinnott-Armstrong," *Philo,* 15:1 (2012): 19–37.
16 John L. Mackie, *Ethics: Inventing Right and Wrong.*
17 John L. Mackie, *The Miracle of Theism: Arguments for and against the Existence of God* (Oxford: Clarendon Press, 1982), 238.
18 Adams, *Divine Command Meta-Ethics Modified Again.* 74.
19 Robert M. Adams, *Finite and Infinite Goods: A Framework for Ethics* (New York: Oxford University Press, 1999), 247.
20 Richard Joyce, *The Myth of Morality* (Cambridge: Cambridge University Press, 2001).
21 Richard Joyce, "Mackie's Arguments for an Error Theory," *Stanford Encyclopaedia of Philosophy,* available at https://plato.stanford.edu/entries/moral-anti-realism/moral-error-theory.html (accessed April 20, 2017).
22 Stephen Darwall, *The Second-Person Standpoint: Morality, Respect, and Accountability* (Cambridge, MA: Harvard University Press, 2006).
23 Adams, *Finite and Infinite Goods,* 238.
24 Richard Garner, "On the Genuine Queerness of Moral Properties and Facts," *Australasian Journal of Philosophy,* 68:2 (1990): 137.
25 Gerald K. Harrison, "The Euthyphro, Divine Command Theory, and Moral Realism," *Philosophy,* 90:1 (2015): 121.
26 Mackie, *Inventing Right and Wrong,* 32.
27 Philippa Foot, "Morality as a System of Hypothetical Imperatives," *The Philosophical Review* 81 (1972): 309.
28 Adams, "Moral Arguments for Theism," 158.
29 C. Stephen Layman, "God and the Moral Order," *Faith and Philosophy,* 23 (2006): 304–16.

Morality Does Not Depend on God

Graham Oppy

Study Questions

1. What does Oppy mean by "God"? What does he mean by "morality"?
2. What are the three ways in which morality might depend upon God? What four reasons might someone have for believing that morality could not depend upon God?

3. How does Oppy define "naturalism"? What does it entail with regard to God and the idea that morality depends upon God?

4. What is a possible world? Why does Oppy think that there is no possible world in which there are nonnatural entities or properties?

5. What are the differences between moral realism, moral skepticism, and moral anti-realism? Which view does Oppy hold?

6. How does Oppy respond to the claim that moral realism is inconsistent with evolutionary theory? How does he respond to Plantinga's argument that naturalism is inconsistent with evolutionary theory?

7. Why does Oppy think that moral facts are necessary truths that do not depend upon anything else?

8. Why does Oppy reject the possibility that morality is dependent upon God understood as a perfectly morally good person? What does he say about the idea that such a God helps humans know the content of morality?

9. How does the "analogical" view of God avoid the objection Oppy raised to the "perfectly morally good person" view of God? What problem does Oppy see with the analogical view of God?

Many theists believe that morality depends upon God in some way. Naturalists, however, have many and diverse reasons for thinking that morality does not depend upon God. I do not aim to give an exhaustive inventory of these reasons. Rather, I aim to give reasons that emerge from, or sit well with, the kind of naturalism that I accept. While some of the reasons that I give depend upon my naturalism, it is not clear to me that all of them do: even if you are not a naturalist, it may be that some of what I have to say will give you something to think about. I begin with some preliminary considerations that establish a framework for the subsequent discussion.

Preliminary Considerations

What one means when one says that *morality depends on God* turns on what one means by *God*, *morality*, and *depends*.

God

For the purposes of this discussion, I shall adopt a very inclusive conception of God. On that conception, to be God is to be the one and only god. And to be a god is to be a nonnatural being or force that has and exercises power over the natural world but that is not, in turn, under the power of any higher-ranking or more powerful nonnatural beings or forces. Setting aside all other relevant considerations, whether it could be reasonable for one to think that morality depends on God may turn on further details that figure in one's conception of God.

Morality

As noted by Bernard and Joshua Gert,[1] the term "morality" has two kinds of common uses. When used descriptively, the term "morality" refers to particular codes of conduct put forward by societies or groups, or accepted by individuals for their own behavior. If used normatively, the term "morality" refers to an informal public system of norms that, given specified conditions, would be endorsed by all suitably qualified persons. When a person claims that morality prohibits or requires a given action, it can be quite unclear whether "morality" refers to: (1) a guide to behavior that is put forward by a society to which the person may or may not belong; (2) a guide to behavior that is put forward by a group, to which the person may or may not belong; (3) a guide that someone—who may or may not be the person in question—regards as overriding and wants everyone else to adopt; or (4) a universal guide that all suitably placed persons would put forward for governing the behavior of all moral agents.

It is almost universally accepted that, in the descriptive sense, there are moralities distinct from systems of etiquette, laws, and religions. (These moralities are always concerned with minimizing harm to some (or all) human beings, but may also be concerned with other matters, such as loyalty, purity, and/or acceptance of authority.) However, some philosophers suppose that normative uses of "morality" fail to refer: there is no informal public system of norms that, given specified conditions, would be endorsed by all suitably qualified persons.

According to natural law theories of normative morality, any suitably qualified person in any society can know the general kinds of actions that normative morality prohibits, requires, discourages, encourages, and allows. *Theological* natural law theories maintain that God has implanted this capacity in all persons, but typically add that the exercise of the capacity may be disabled as one of the wages of sin.

Dependence

There are various ways in which it might be supposed that morality depends upon God. *First*, it might be supposed that the very existence of an informal public system of norms that, given specified conditions, would be endorsed by all suitably qualified persons, is entirely a result of divine providence: we would not live in conditions in which there is an appropriate informal public system of norms if God had not chosen for us to live in those conditions (call this the *Divine Providence View*). *Second*, it might be supposed that our knowledge of the content of morality depends upon God's having implanted in each of us a capacity to have that knowledge: we would not have moral knowledge if God had not given us the capacity to have moral knowledge (and, on some views, if divine grace did not undo the damage wrought by the wages of sin) (call this the *Divine Instruction View*). *Third*, it might be supposed that the very content of morality is determined by God: it would not be the case that our informal public system of norms has the content that it does if God had not decreed—or otherwise determined—that that informal public system of norms should have the content that it does (call this the *Divine Command View*).

Alternative Claims

Suppose that, for some determinate understanding of the claim that morality depends upon God, you reject that claim. Immediately, it follows that you hold that morality does not depend on God. But the position that you occupy may go well beyond mere maintenance of the claim that morality does not depend upon God. Perhaps, for example, you think that it could not be that morality depends upon God. One possible reason for adopting the view that it could not be that morality depends upon God is that you suppose that it could not be that God exists: if it could not be that God exists, then it could not be that morality depends upon God. A second possible reason for adopting the view that it could not be that morality depends upon God is that you suppose that, on the given determinate understanding of the claim that morality depends upon God, there is nothing to which the term "morality" refers: if there is nothing to which the term "morality" refers, then it could not be that morality depends upon God. A third possible reason for adopting the view that it could not be that morality depends upon God is that you suppose that, on the given determinate understanding of the claim that morality depends upon God, it could not be that there is anything that morality depends upon: if there could not be anything that morality depends upon then, in particular, it could not be that morality depends upon God. A fourth possible reason for adopting the view that it could not be that morality depends upon God is that you suppose that, on the given determinate understanding of the claim that morality depends upon God, while it is true that morality could depend upon something, it is not true that morality could depend upon *God*: if it is not true that morality could depend upon God, then it is true that morality could not depend upon God.

The Existence of God

I self-identify as a naturalist. "Naturalism" means very different things to different people. I take naturalism to be the view that there are none but natural entities involving none but natural properties. Since gods are nonnatural beings or forces (or powers or grounds), naturalism entails that there are no gods. Since to be God is to be the one and only god, naturalism entails that God does not exist. A fortiori, given my naturalism, there is nothing that depends upon God. In particular, then, it is not the case that morality depends upon God.

I hold an austere view of modality: I think that the range of what is possible is much narrower than most philosophers suppose. Philosophers typically think about modality—possibility and necessity—in terms of possible worlds. A possible world is a maximal possibility: a maximal possible way that things might be. The actual world—everything that there has been, is, and will be—is one possible world. Most of us think that things might have been different from how they actually are: for example, you might have had more siblings than you actually have. To say that there is at least one possible world in which you have more siblings than you actually have is just another way of saying that you could have had more siblings than you actually have. In general, for any proposition that p, it is possible that p just in case there is at least one possible world in which it is true that p; and it is necessary that p just in case in every possible world it is true that p. Many philosophers think that there is a vast range of possible worlds; many philosophers think that anything that you can coherently imagine is possible. I am not one of those philosophers; in comparison to others, I think that the range of possible worlds is quite narrow.

In my view, all possible worlds share a common initial history with the actual world, and diverge from the actual world only as a result of the outplaying of objective chances. If there are no objective chances, then there is just one possible world: the actual world. I think that there are objective chances; so I think that there are other possible worlds. If our world has an initial state—"the initial singularity"—then all possible worlds have that initial state: all possible worlds begin from the (same) initial singularity. However, if our world does not have an initial state, then all possible worlds share an infinite initial history with our world. Either way, given that our world contains none but natural entities with none but natural properties, and given that it is impossible for there to be a transition from a world state in which there are none but natural entities with none but natural properties to a world state in which there are some nonnatural entities with some nonnatural properties, there is no possible world in which there are nonnatural entities with nonnatural properties. So there are no possible worlds in which there are gods. So there is no possible world in which God exists. On my view of modality, it is impossible that God exists. Hence, on my view of modality, it is impossible that morality depends upon God.

I do not think that there is a knockdown argument in favor of my naturalistic worldview. Unsurprisingly, when I evaluate the merits of competing worldviews, I find that my naturalistic worldview comes out ahead. As I have said elsewhere,[2] it seems to me that my naturalistic worldview makes the best trade-off of simplicity against explanatory depth and breadth. However, this assessment is evidently controversial; I am happy to allow that we can reasonably agree to disagree about the doxastic virtues of competing worldviews. I am far more certain that there are no knockdown arguments in favor of competing worldviews; in particular, I have elsewhere argued at great length that there are no successful arguments in favor of the existence of God.[3]

Since what I have said to this point may be open to misunderstanding, I should emphasize that the theoretical weighing of theism and naturalism takes in considerations about morality. Comparison of a particular version of naturalism with a particular version of theism requires consideration of what they say about putative moral truth, putative moral knowledge, conscience, virtue, societal dysfunction, happiness, and so on. The judgment that God does not exist—and, so, the judgment that it is impossible that God exists—is not arrived at in advance of considerations about morality, and so cannot be taken to absolve naturalists of the need to pay attention to morality. The only point that I have been making here is that, since it is my all things considered judgment that it is impossible that God exists, it is also my all things considered judgment that it is impossible for morality to depend upon God.

The Existence of Morality

On the "descriptive" understanding of "morality," it is uncontroversial that "morality" refers to a set of empirical phenomena that includes, for example, manifestations of human capacities to exhibit sentiments like *remorse*, *sympathy*, and *resentment*, to deploy concepts like *goodness* and *fairness*, and to make normative judgments. Given this "descriptive" understanding of "morality," it is also uncontroversial that there can be systematic scientific investigation of the evolutionary origins and functions of our "moral" capacities.

On the "normative" understanding of "morality," it is controversial whether some moral judgments are representations of moral facts. According to *moral realists*, some of our moral judgments are representations of moral facts that obtain independently of our evaluative attitudes, and, in at least some cases, we have knowledge of those moral facts. However, according to *moral skeptics*, we are unable to obtain any knowledge of moral facts; and according to *moral anti-realists*, some other part of the moral realist position must be rejected. According to *moral error-theorists*, all primitive, positive moral judgments are false; according to *moral expressivists*, all moral judgments serve merely to express norms and attitudes rather than to represent an independent domain of moral facts; and, according to *moral subjectivists*, all moral truths are entirely functions of our evaluative attitudes.

I am a moral realist. I think that some of our moral judgments are representations of moral facts that hold independently of our evaluative attitudes, and that, in some of those cases, we know those moral facts. Consider, for example, the claim that *it is morally wrong to torture young children solely in order to ward off boredom*. I think that this claim is true, and that almost all human beings know that it is true.

Some philosophers hold that moral realism is inconsistent with naturalistic evolutionary theory. In their view, the fact that evolutionary influences have pervasively conditioned the contents of our moral thoughts provides a defeater for moral realism.[4] However, a plausible naturalistic moral realism *denies* that our evolutionary history *pervasively conditions* the contents of our moral thoughts.[5] Sure, we have an evolved capacity to form and employ normative concepts in our thinking and decision making, an evolved capacity that is present, in rudimentary form, in both human infants and chimpanzees. But our ability to grasp moral truths is also dependent upon our culturally enhanced capacities for autonomous moral reflection and reasoning—and this, in turn, is dependent upon our culturally enhanced general capacities for critical reasoning. There is no more reason to see pervasive evolutionary conditioning of the contents of our moral thoughts than there is to see pervasive evolutionary conditioning of our mathematical and scientific thought: but it is not very controversial to be a realist about some of our mathematical and scientific judgments.[6]

Some philosophers hold that naturalism is inconsistent with evolutionary theory. Notoriously, Alvin Plantinga[7] argues that we cannot rationally accept the conjunctive claim that naturalism is true and our cognitive faculties have come to be in the way proposed by contemporary evolutionary theory. In his view, there is a vanishingly small probability that our cognitive faculties are reliable—that is, produce a preponderance of true beliefs over false beliefs—*given* that naturalism is true and our cognitive faculties have come to be in the way proposed by contemporary evolutionary theory. However, if we suppose that most of our beliefs concern matters about which more or less all competent believers agree, then the probability in question is not vanishingly small: the evolved capacities that underwrite the judgments on which more or less all competent believers agree were evolutionarily successful precisely because those capacities track the truth. (Creatures that form true beliefs about the presence of predators in their immediate environment are more likely to pass on their genes than creatures that form false beliefs about the presence of predators in their immediate environment.) And if we suppose that most of our beliefs concern matters on which there is widespread disagreement, then it is simply not true that our cognitive faculties are reliable. In philosophy, religion, politics, and a host of other domains, there is no preponderant opinion: most philosophical beliefs are false; most religious beliefs are false; most political beliefs are false; etc. If it is very likely that our cognitive faculties produce a preponderance of true philosophical beliefs over false philosophical beliefs *given* that Plantinga's theism is true, then the correct conclusion to draw is that it is very likely that Plantinga's theism is false.[8]

The Independence of Morality

Suppose that, on the "normative" conception of "morality," things are as I suppose: there are "moral" facts. What should we suppose is the metaphysical status of these moral facts? In particular, should we suppose that there is something else upon which these moral facts depend?

I think not. Given that there are moral truths, the most plausible view is that those moral truths are necessary truths. If, as I suppose, it is true that it is morally wrong to torture children in order to ward off boredom, then it is necessarily true that it is morally wrong to torture children in order to ward off boredom. And if it is necessarily true that it is morally wrong to torture children in order to ward off boredom, then it is true *no matter what* that it is morally wrong to torture children in order to ward off boredom. But if it is true no matter what that it is morally wrong to torture children in order to ward off boredom, then there is nothing that the fact that it is morally wrong to torture children in order to ward off boredom depends upon. The claim that *there is nothing that the fact that it is morally wrong to torture children in order to ward off boredom depends upon* is a metaphysical claim.

If you believe that it is morally wrong to torture children in order to ward off boredom, then there will be countless valid derivations from claims to which you are committed, by the things that you believe, that have as their conclusion the claim that it is morally wrong to torture children in order to ward off boredom. If you want to say that the conclusion of a valid argument is "logically dependent" upon the premises of that argument, then it will be true that the claim that it is morally wrong to torture children in order to ward off boredom—like any other claim—is logically dependent upon other claims. But even if the claim that it is morally wrong to torture children in order to ward off boredom is logically dependent upon other claims, this goes no distance at all toward establishing that there is something that the fact that it is morally wrong to torture children in order to ward off boredom depends upon.

If you believe the claim that it is morally wrong to torture children in order to ward off boredom, it may well be that you inferred this claim from other claims that you believe. If you want to say that claims that you infer from other claims are "doxastically dependent" upon the claims from which they are inferred, then it will be true—at least for you—that the claim that it is morally wrong to torture children in order to ward off boredom is doxastically dependent upon other claims. But even if the claim that it is morally wrong to torture children in order to ward off boredom is doxastically dependent upon other claims (at least for you), this goes no distance at all toward establishing that there is something that the fact that it is morally wrong to torture children in order to ward off boredom depends upon.

If you are committed to the claim it is morally wrong to torture children in order to ward off boredom, it may be that this claim would not be an axiom in any most economical axiomatization of your (moral) beliefs and commitments. If you want to say that claims that would not be axioms in any most economical axiomatization of your (moral) beliefs and commitments are "epistemically dependent," then it will be true—at least for you—that the claim that it is morally wrong to torture children in order to ward off boredom is epistemically dependent (at least for you). But even if the claim that it is morally wrong to torture children in order to ward off boredom is epistemically dependent (at least for you), this goes no distance at all toward establishing that there is something that the fact that it is morally wrong to torture children in order to ward off boredom depends upon.

In order for it to be the case that there is something that the fact that it is morally wrong to torture children in order to ward off boredom depends upon, there must be something that makes a difference to the obtaining of this fact. But, if it is necessary that it is morally wrong to torture children in order to ward off boredom, then there cannot be anything that makes a difference to the obtaining of this fact: the fact obtains come what may. While there may be logical, doxastic, or epistemic dependence of the claim upon other claims, there cannot be metaphysical dependence of the fact upon other facts.

Many philosophers have claimed that the moral supervenes on the natural: there can be no variation in the moral without variation in the natural. This thought is readily vindicated if there is nothing that moral truth depends upon. While the application of particular evaluative moral terms to particular events and things depends both upon the necessary moral truths and the details of those particular events and things, the necessity of the moral truths ensures that the application of particular evaluative moral terms to particular events and things varies only as the particular events and things vary. (Compare with the application of mathematical terms to particular events and things. I have four oranges. I could have had five oranges. In the counterfactual circumstances in which I have five oranges, the necessary mathematical facts remain the same, but there is a change in the distribution of fruit. Hold fixed the distribution of fruit, and there can be no change in the correct application of the mathematical terms to the fruit.)

The Independence of Morality from God

I hold that it is impossible for morality—in either the descriptive or the normative sense—to depend upon God. So I hold that those who think that morality does depend upon God are necessarily mistaken. But it does not follow that I think that there is a contradiction in the beliefs of those who think that morality does depend upon God. Those who think that morality does depend upon God disagree with me not only about what is actual, but also about what is necessary and what is possible.

While I cannot provide a "counterfactual" consideration of the views of those who think that morality depends upon God—since I take it that counterfactuals with necessarily false antecedents are all trivially true—I can consider issues that I think would bother me were I a theist considering the claim that morality depends upon God.

Since there are many kinds of theism, there are many views to consider. What follows is both broad brush and impressionistic.

Some Christian theists hold that it is literally true that God is a perfectly morally good person. On this view, "moral goodness" picks out an attribute that is shared between God and human beings: God and human beings are morally good in exactly the same sense. Given that moral goodness is a property shared between the divine person and human persons, it is plausible to suppose that what makes it true that the divine person possesses this property is also what makes it true that human persons possess this property. But, if that's right, then it cannot be that God has a role to play in determining what it is for a person to be morally good. It cannot be, for example, that God's commands or decisions determine what is morally good because God is morally good *prior to* the giving of those commands or the making of those decisions. On this view, then, the content of morality is determined independently of God. Perhaps it might be said that, even if the content of morality is determined independently of God, God has a role to play in bringing it about that human beings know the content of morality. But that seems implausible. Given that the moral codes found in the foundational texts of all of the world's religions are based on in-group loyalty, hierarchical authority, rigidly enforced gender roles, and gratuitous regulations concerning sex and purity, those moral codes do not accord with contemporary deliverances of autonomous moral reflection, and so are not plausibly taken to be the deliverances of a morally perfect person. A morally perfect person simply would not be *for* tribalism, authoritarianism, out-group discrimination, rigid gender roles, etc. Perhaps it might be said that, even if it is not the case that God has a role to play in bringing it about that human beings know the content of morality, God took special measures to ensure that human beings have the capacity to arrive at moral knowledge through the exercise of autonomous moral reflection. But, as we have already observed, there is good reason to think that our possession of that capacity can be adequately explained in historical terms, adverting to a combination of biological evolution and cultural overlay: our capacity to arrive at mathematical knowledge and our capacity to arrive at moral knowledge fit into the very same explanatory framework. If it is literally true that God is a perfectly morally good person, then there is no significant way in which morality is especially dependent upon God.

Some Christian theists hold that God is simple and only describable in analogical terms. Because God is simple, God is ontologically sui generis: neither substance nor attribute, but something utterly beyond our familiar ontological categories. Because God is describable only in analogical terms, it is not true that God is a good, wise, powerful person, if "good," "wise," "powerful," and "person" are understood as they would be were we applying these terms to a human being. Rather—putting these two claims together—in the appropriate analogical sense of these terms, "God," "good," "wise," "powerful," "person," and so on, are just different ways of referring to the very same thing: God is identical to goodness, God is identical to wisdom, God is identical to power, etc. This view escapes the objection raised in the preceding paragraph that God is good in an analogical sense does not foreclose the possibility that God's commands or decisions determine what is literally morally good. However, the view is vulnerable to a different objection: namely, that it seems to make no sense to suppose that God is simple and only describable in analogical terms. It is uncontroversial that, taken literally, "good," "wise," "powerful," "creator," "savior," and "person" pick out very different members of very different ontological categories. What process of analogizing could possibly bring it about that, making use of that process of analogizing, we end up with a bunch of analogical terms that pick out the very same, ontologically sui generis, referent? (Perhaps it is worth noting that, when I listed the identities, I did not give the identity for "person." What would it be? God is identical to being a person? God is identical to a person? Even grammar resists the proposal that God is simple and describable only in analogical terms.)

I don't say that the kinds of considerations invoked in the preceding two paragraphs are a decisive strike against the claim that morality depends on God, even for the particular conceptions of God that have been considered. I have developed no explicit contradiction in either case. Some may think that explicit contradictions could be exposed with more careful and detailed work. I doubt that this is so. My reasons for thinking that morality does not depend on God have nothing to do with internal difficulties that arise for worldviews which maintain that morality does depend on God; rather, my reasons for thinking that morality does not depend upon God are grounded in, or that sit well with, the worldview that I accept, a worldview which I think is more theoretically virtuous than competing worldviews.

Notes

1 B. Gert and J. Gert, "The Definition of Morality," in *Stanford Encyclopedia of Philosophy*, http://plato.stanford.edu/entries/morality-definition/. See also: P. Kitcher, *The Ethical Project* (Cambridge: Harvard University Press, 2011).

2 G. Oppy, *The Best Argument against God* (New York: Palgrave Macmillan, 2013).

3 See, for example: G. Oppy, *Ontological Arguments and Belief in God* (New York: Cambridge University Press, 1996); G. Oppy, *Arguing about Gods* (New York: Cambridge University Press, 2006); and G. Oppy, *Describing Gods: An Investigation of Divine Attributes* (Cambridge: Cambridge University Press, 2014). For more arguments both for and against God's existence, see the essays by Joshua Rasmussen and Bruce Russell elsewhere in this volume.

4 See, for example, S. Street, "A Darwinian Dilemma for Realist Theories of Value," *Philosophical Studies*, 127 (2006): 109–66; and R. Joyce, *The Evolution of Morality* (Cambridge: MIT Press, 2006).

5 Contrast this view with the evolutionary account of morality defended by Michael Ruse elsewhere in this volume.

6 For the provocative—but I think plausible—suggestion that moral realism is in *better* standing than mathematical realism, see J. Clarke-Doane, "Morality and Mathematics: The Evolutionary Challenge," *Ethics*, 122 (2012): 313–40; and "Moral Epistemology: The Mathematics Analogy," *Noûs*, 48 (2014): 238–55. For further discussion of the arguments of Street and Joyce, see, for example, D. Copp, "Darwinian Skepticism about Moral Realism," *Philosophical Issues* 18 (2008): 186–206; and W. FitzPatrick, "Morality and Evolutionary Biology," in *Stanford Encyclopedia of Philosophy*, http://plato.stanford.edu/entries/morality-biology/#EvoBioDebMor.

7 A. Plantinga, *Where the Conflict Really Lies: Science, Religion and Naturalism* (Oxford: Oxford University Press, 2012).

8 For further discussion of Plantinga's argument, see, for example, M. Bergmann, and P. Kain, eds., *Challenges to Moral and Religious Belief: Disagreement and Evolution* (Oxford: Oxford University Press, 2014).

RESPONSES

Response to Flannagan

Graham Oppy

> **Study Questions**
>
> 1. According to Oppy, in what way is Flannagan's DCT "very narrow"? What problems might an "extended" version of Flannagan's DCT have?
> 2. On the most likely interpretation of "identity," how does Oppy suggest Flannagan's DCT be reformulated? What does this entail?
> 3. What concern does Oppy have with wrongness depending on commands from an appropriate authority? Why does he find "counterfactual" versions of this approach less objectionable?
> 4. How does Oppy respond to Flannagan's charge that secular metaethical theories have failed?
> 5. What is the problem that Oppy raises for the DCT in light of the observation that not all norms are moral norms?

Matthew Flannagan defines *Divine Command Theory* (DCT) as the view that *the property of moral wrongness is identical to the property of being contrary to God's command*. According to Flannagan, attempts to refute DCT have failed, and secular accounts of morality are subject to important skeptical challenges.

Problems for Flannagan's DCT

Flannagan's definition of DCT is very narrow: at most, it is an account of moral obligation and moral permission; it is plainly not an account of moral good or moral virtue. Other self-styled "divine command theories" have been far more ambitious. For example, Philip Quinn (1940–2004) maintains that *all* moral statuses are identical to divine actions.[1] More generally, as Murphy notes,[2] *teleological voluntarists* maintain that *some* range of evaluative statuses stand in *some* kinds of dependence relations to *some* kinds of divine actions or divine responses.

We might extend Flannagan's account to cover all evaluative statuses, or all normative statuses, or all moral statuses. However, if we extend it even so far as all moral statuses, then the objections he considers and dismisses—the "anything goes" objection, the "arbitrariness" objection, and the "vacuity" objection—all have genuine bite.[3]

We might alter Flannagan's account by replacing his identification relation with a causal relation, or an analytic relation, or a reductive relation that falls short of identity, or a relation of supervenience. As Murphy notes,[4] it remains a hotly contested question among contemporary theists whether to prefer an analytic relation to an identification relation.

We might modify Flannagan's account by replacing his divine acts of commanding with divine acts of willing or divine acts of antecedently intending. Again, as Murphy notes,[5] it remains a hotly contested question among contemporary theists which is the correct, or best, species of divine acts to be appealed to by teleological voluntarists.[6]

Flannagan's account relies on a claim about identity of properties. Philosophers divide on the question of what is required for two properties to be identical. Candidates include sameness of extension; necessary sameness of extension; sameness of encoding extension; sameness of analysis; sameness of conferral of causal/nomological powers; and sameness of semantic composition.[7] Since it is uncontroversial that the property of moral wrongness and the property of being contrary to God's command are not identical if identity of properties is determined by sameness of encoding extension, or sameness of analysis, or sameness of conferral of causal/nomological powers, or sameness of semantic composition, it seems reasonable to assume that Flannagan is supposing that necessary sameness of extension makes for identity of properties. But, if that's right, then his DCT can be properly reformulated as follows: *necessarily, for any x, x is wrong iff a necessarily existent, all-powerful, all-knowing, essentially loving and just, immaterial person who created and providentially orders the universe commands not x.*

Flannagan's account entails that, if there is no necessarily existent, all-powerful, all-knowing, essentially loving and just, immaterial person who created and providentially ordered the universe, then nothing is morally wrong. If, for example, Richard Swinburne is right, and there is merely a contingently existing, all-powerful, all-knowing, essentially loving and just, immaterial person who created and providentially ordered the universe, then, given Flannagan's account, it follows that nothing is—and nothing can be—morally wrong. In order to make room for disagreement about the nature of the being that issues the commands that determine what is wrong, we should consider a claim of the following form: *necessarily, for any x, x is morally wrong iff an appropriate authority commands not x.* Flannagan accepts this claim; he just has a particular view about what the appropriate authority could possibly be.

The claim that *necessarily, for any x, x is morally wrong iff an appropriate authority commands not x* entails that, in order for there to be moral wrongs, there must be commands that have been issued by an appropriate authority: whether some particular thing is wrong depends upon there having been a command from the appropriate authority against that thing. As Murphy notes,[8] commands are essentially communicative items: in order for one entity to give a command to another entity, there must be a communicative practice available to the one commanded in terms of which the one giving the command is able to formulate the command. Moreover, in order for one entity to have given a command to another entity, it must be that the second entity has registered the command from the first entity, and recognized it for the command that it is. Even many theists are skeptical that God has given us commands sufficient to exhaustively and accurately identify all of the moral wrongs.

If we are determined to stick with commands, then it seems that the best option at this point is to go counterfactual: *necessarily, for any x, x is morally wrong iff an appropriate authority would command not x.* And if we are prepared to accept some other kind of divine act, then we might go for a different counterfactual. Perhaps, for example: *necessarily, for any x, x is morally wrong iff an appropriate adviser would commend not x.* But, once we get to this point, we have reached an account of moral wrongness that it is possible for secular theorists to accept. While ideal adviser theory is not at all plausible as an account of the full range of moral statuses, it seems quite plausible that ideal adviser theory gives an acceptable account of moral obligation and moral permission: *necessarily, for any x, x is morally wrong iff an ideal adviser—that is, a fully informed, properly sensitive, fully virtuous, thoroughly good adviser—would counsel not x.*

Have Secular Theories Failed?

Flannagan says that secular metaethical theories face significant skeptical challenges. Many secular philosophers have agreed that it is hard to explain how moral judgments can be prescriptive ("objective," "categorical") and reason-giving ("overriding"). However, if we aim only to give an account of moral wrongness, and have complete freedom with respect to the rest of moral theorizing—as Flannagan supposes when he addresses attempted refutations of DCT—then these challenges have simply been set to one side. If there is a puzzle about how the (counterfactual) counsel of an ideal adviser—that is, a fully informed, properly sensitive, fully virtuous, thoroughly good adviser—would be prescriptive and reason-giving, then there is *exactly the same* puzzle about how the (counterfactual) counsel of God—a necessarily existent, all-powerful, all-knowing, essentially loving and just, immaterial person who created and providentially orders the universe—would be prescriptive and reason-giving.

Flannagan ends his discussion with the claim that his (secular) opponents are *required* to (a) show what's wrong with making morality dependent on God; and (b) show that better secular theories exist that aren't plagued by even more serious problems. I do not claim to have done either of these things; I do not recognize any requirement to try to do them. What I have argued is that there are secular variants of (the best version of) DCT that are no more problematic than it is. Since (the best version of) DCT is not, in any sense, a complete metaethical theory, mere endorsement of it does not entail that one has a position on which morality is dependent on God. For all that Flannagan has argued, endorsement of (the best version of) DCT may be no more than endorsement of the claim that the good is prior to the right. Moreover, mere endorsement of (the best version of) DCT says nothing about the ability of comprehensive theories that embed it to meet skeptical challenges about the allegedly prescriptive and reason-giving nature of morality.

One More Problem for Flannagan's DCT

In the preceding discussion, I have let various matters slip. I will conclude by mentioning one of these matters. There may be reasons to think that the claim that *the property of moral wrongness is identical to the property of being contrary to God's command* is wrong straight off the bat. In particular, one might wonder whether God can issue commands that have nothing at all to do with morality. It is a familiar observation that not all norms are moral norms: there are legal norms, linguistic norms, social norms, rational norms, and so forth. Suppose, for example, that, at a particular time, God commands particular Jews to obey the Roman Law. Suppose that Noam—one of the Jews in question—breaks the Roman Law, but does not otherwise violate any moral obligations in breaking the Roman Law. (Perhaps, for example, the parking meter for his merkabah expires just before his return.) While what Noam has done is *legally* wrong, it is not at all clear that what he has done is *morally* wrong, even though God has commanded him to obey the Roman Law. But, if what Noam has done is contrary to God's command and yet not morally wrong, then—prior to any other considerations—it cannot be that the property of moral wrongness is identical to the property of being contrary to God's command.

Notes

1 Philip Quinn, *Divine Commands and Moral Requirements* (Oxford: Oxford University Press, 1978).
2 Mark Murphy, "Theological Voluntarism," *Stanford Encyclopedia of Philosophy* https://plato.stanford.edu/entries/voluntarism-theological/.
3 See Edward Wierenga, "A Defensible Divine Command Theory," *Noûs* 17 (1983): 387–407. One way to see the "bite" is to note that we cannot explain God's goodness in terms of God's commands: it cannot be that God's being good is explained by God's self-command to be good.
4 Murphy, "Theological Voluntarism." Murphy provides explanation of "causation," "analyticity," "reduction," and "supervenience."
5 Ibid.
6 See, in particular, Linda Zagzebski, *Divine Motivation Theory* (Cambridge: Cambridge University Press, 2004).
7 See Francesco Orilia, and Chris Swoyer, "Properties," in *Stanford Encyclopedia of Philosophy,* https://plato.stanford.edu/entries/properties/#IdeCon. Note that Orilia and Swoyer explain sameness of extension; necessary sameness of extension; sameness of encoding extension; sameness of analysis; sameness of conferral of causal/nomological powers; and sameness of semantic composition.
8 Murphy, "Theological Voluntarism."

Response to Oppy

Matthew Flannagan

Study Questions

1. According to Flannagan, why does Oppy's version of the "vacuity objection" fail?

2. How is the divine command theory compatible with atheism and moral skepticism? Why is this point a problem for some of Oppy's reasons for thinking morality doesn't depend on God?

3. What is the equivocation that Flannagan seems to find in Oppy's argument that moral truths are necessary truths that don't depend on anything? Why might this be a problem?

4. What does Flannagan think is implausible about Oppy's claim that morality does not depend on anything?

5. What two problems does Flannagan have with the thesis (assuming Oppy holds it) that moral properties are irreducible?

In my main essay I defended two contentions. First, that attempts to refute a divine command theory of ethics have failed. Second, that secular accounts of morality are subject to skeptical challenges. Oppy doesn't address the second of these contentions. But he does address the first. Oppy identifies the "divine command view" as one determinate way morality might be said to depend upon God. He gives three considerations against such a view. One specifically against a divine command theory and two against the generic claim that morality depends on God.

The Vacuity Objection

Against a divine command theory, Oppy presses a version of what I called the "The Vacuity Objection." If God is essentially morally good, then "it cannot be . . . that God's commands or decisions determine what is morally good because God is morally good *prior to* the giving of those commands or the making of those decisions" (p. 114).

This objection fails to distinguish between two different senses of the word "good." When a divine command theorist says God is good, he means by this that God has certain *character traits*: God is loving, just, impartial, faithful, and so forth. However, when a divine command theorist says God's commands determine what is good, he means that the existence of *moral obligations* or *moral requirements* depends upon God.

The question of whether someone has certain character traits is distinct from the question of whether they have moral requirements. Consider a proponent of what Oppy calls a "moral error theory." Such a person could still, if he or she wanted, choose to live in accord with the norms of justice, and could choose to be a faithful, loving, and impartial person. What the person couldn't do was claim that there existed any moral obligation to live this way.[1]

This distinction removes the sting from Oppy's argument. God's commands determine what is good in the second sense. That is, God's commands determine the existence and content of moral requirements. This doesn't mean God's commands determine goodness in the first sense. His commands don't determine the existence of certain character traits. Consequently, God can have these character traits prior to giving any commands.

Atheism and Moral Skepticism

Oppy gives a further consideration as to why someone might think that morality doesn't depend on God. He or she might suppose that God doesn't exist.

Or the person might suppose that "on the given determinate understanding of the claim that morality depends upon God, there is nothing to which the term 'morality' refers" (p. 108). Oppy contends that, on either supposition, it follows that morality does not depend on God.

However, Mark Murphy has argued that a divine command theory is compatible with both atheism and moral skepticism.[2] He suggests that someone could accept that a divine command theory is the most plausible account of the nature of moral obligation, deny God exists, and conclude, therefore, that moral obligations do not exist, and embrace an error theory. This isn't merely a hypothetical possibility—both J. L. Mackie and Elizabeth Anscombe[3] have defended a position similar to this.

Richard Joyce explicates this possibility in more detail.[4] He explains that divine command theorists typically offer a two-stage argument. First, they analyze the concept of the morally obligatory, showing what features anything that answers this conceptual description must have. Second, they argue that the property of being commanded by God accommodates these features better than any alternative secular property.

Joyce spells out three replies an atheist could make in response: He or she could (i) deny that the property of being commanded by God accommodates these features better than any secular property. He or she could (ii) agree that God's commands do the best job of accounting for these features but come up with a secular property that also does a decent job. Or, (iii) he or she could agree that God's commands are the only property that does a decent job of accounting for these features and embrace an error theory. Joyce plums for (i). But the point is that (iii) is a theoretical option.

Necessary Moral Truths

Oppy's most interesting argument is that morality does not depend upon anything. It is "*necessarily* true that it is morally wrong to torture children to ward off boredom" (p. 112). However, necessary moral truths are true "no matter what." Consequently "there is nothing that the fact that it is morally wrong to torture children in order to ward off boredom depends upon."

There are two problems with this argument. First, *this argument equivocates*. Oppy states that there are necessary *moral truths*. But the phrase "moral truths" is ambiguous. As Russ Shafer-Landau shows, we may distinguish between "moral principles" and "moral facts."[5] A moral principle is "a conditional (an if-then claim). If certain conditions are met, then a certain moral verdict follows. . . . [I]f one kills, then one does wrong." By contrast, a moral fact is an "instance of goodness, or rightness, or virtue."

Consider, then, Oppy's claim that "moral truths are necessary truths" that hold "no matter what." If he is using the term "moral truth" to refer to moral principles, his claim seems plausible. Landau states that the principle, "If you torture another for fun, then that is wrong," is true "even if there are no people around to torture. It will continue to be true even after the human race is extinct." However, in this sense of the term "moral truth," the conclusion Oppy draws is compatible with a divine command theory. When a divine command theorist claims that moral truths depend upon God, he or she is saying that *moral facts* depend upon God. A divine command theory is an account of the *nature* of moral obligations. Divine command theorists typically contend that ethical *wrongness* is identical with the property of being contrary to God's commands. However, this is compatible with the conditional claim that *if* you torture another person for fun, *then it's* wrong. Presumably, a necessarily existent, all-powerful, all-knowing, essentially loving and just, immaterial person would prohibit torturing children for fun in any possible world in which it occurs.

For Oppy's argument to have a bite, then, the term "moral truths" must be used to refer to *moral facts*. He must be claiming that it's necessarily true that instances of rightness or wrongness exist. However, this is implausible. Moral wrongness is a property of certain kinds of human actions. For moral wrongness to exist agents must exist. Shafer-Landau explains: "Certainly there can be no moral facts prior to the appearance of humans (or beings relevantly like us). Before we arose, there were no instances of moral goodness or evil, since there wasn't anyone around who could satisfy the conditions set forth in the moral principles."

This brings me to the second problem with Oppy's argument. *The claim that morality does not depend on anything is implausible when one considers the kind of dependence that is at issue.* The postulated relationship between moral requirements and God's commands is one of identity; moral wrongness is identical with the property of being contrary to God's commands. It is implausible to suggest that moral properties aren't identical to *anything*. Oppy is a moral realist; he thinks moral requirements do exist in reality, and if they exist, there is surely something in reality that they are.

Irreducible Moral Properties?

Perhaps Oppy is alluding to the thesis that moral properties are irreducible and sui generis. They exist but aren't reducible to or identical with any other type of property, natural or supernatural. This thesis, however, is inapplicable in the context of our discussion.

First, Oppy self-identifies as a naturalist. *Naturalism* he defines as the thesis "that there are none but natural entities involving none but natural properties." Consequently, Oppy appears committed to claiming that moral properties are reducible to natural properties. So they can't be sui generis on his view.

Second, as a response to divine command theories, the thesis that moral properties are sui generis begs the question. The plausibility of the claim that moral properties are irreducible rests on the failure of attempts to reduce them. Divine command theories, however, are an attempt at a reduction. It is circular to object to an attempted reduction by assuming all such reductions will fail.[6]

Conclusion

I don't think Oppy has shown that morality doesn't depend on God. Despite his criticisms, a divine command theory remains a defensible metaethical theory, and he hasn't addressed the skeptical challenges that secular accounts face.

Notes

1. John L. Mackie makes this point in *Ethics: Inventing Right and Wrong* (Harmondsworth: Penguin Publishing, 1977), 16–17, 26–27.
2. Mark Murphy, "Theological Voluntarism," *Stanford Encyclopaedia of Philosophy*, available at https://plato.stanford.edu/entries/voluntarism-theological/ (accessed June 9, 2017), see section 1.2.
3. Elizabeth Anscombe, "Modern Moral Philosophy," *Philosophy,* 33:124 (1958): 1–16.
4. Richard Joyce, "Theistic Ethics and the Euthyphro Dilemma," *Journal of Religious Ethics,* 30 (2002): 68–69.
5. Russ Shafer-Landau, *Whatever Happened to Good and Evil?* (Oxford: Oxford University Press, 2003), 55–56.
6. See Gerald K. Harrison, "What Are Epistemic Reasons? A Divine Analysis," *Philosophia Christi,* 19:1 (2017): 23–36.

Questions for Reflection

1. What if it turned out that God's commands were arbitrary—that is, that God could just as well make rape and murder morally good? Would this be a devastating problem for the theist? Why?

2. How does Mark Linville define the DCT in chapter 12? How does this definition differ from how Flannagan defines it? What would Flannagan say to Linville?
3. Many atheists (e.g., J. L. Mackie, J. Sartre) have agreed that moral truths, if they exist, would depend upon God. Does this pose a problem for Oppy's view? Why? What might Oppy say to these anti-realist naturalists?
4. Oppy claims that he does not have to address most of the skeptical challenges to secular ethics head-on. Do you agree? Why?
5. If moral requirements are to be understood as divine commands, how do we *access* (learn, discover) those commands? Would your answer create a problem for Flannagan's view? Why?

4

Is Beauty in the Eye of the Beholder?

Beauty Is Relative

James Mock

Study Questions

1. According to Mock, how does Margolis "kill" strict nonrelativism?
2. According to Mock, what does Hume see as the proper role of the critic? What is the goal or purpose of the critic's activity?
3. Why does Hume think that the development of taste is valuable?
4. What is Dewey's view of the function of art? Why does he oppose the high-art/low-art distinction?
5. What shift in the aesthetic "center of attention" does Dewey make? What does Dewey consider the "actual work of art"?
6. What is the "scrutiny approach" to art criticism? What is the problem with this approach according to Wollheim?
7. According to Dewey, in what way is artistic response "relativized"? What, then, makes the difference between a good art product and a less good art product?
8. What is the cultural significance of art for Dewey?
9. Despite a "relativism of response," what leads to agreements in evaluation according to Santayana? What does he think accounts for the aesthetic effect of objects?
10. How does Mock sum up the relativistic and nonrelativistic aspects of his view?

In this essay, I defend a view of aesthetics I call *rational relativism*. I use "rational" relativism to mark it off from the standard undergraduate or "person in the street" variety, which simply claims that people have their own individual preferences in things artistic and that is, in brief, "it" for their entire approach to artworks. That tastes differ is an observation not new. Indeed, David Hume opens his 1757 essay "Of the Standard of Taste" with this very observation.[1]

However, Hume notes that there are better and less good responses that are changeable both for an individual and for a culture throughout his essay, pointing to the importance of reasoning in our responses rather than simply having a subjective emotional outburst. Hume does not propose simple truth claims. He says that we need to know many things about the world and an artwork to have anything approaching a full response and, more importantly, better responses to art will carry over into better responses in life. He notes that responses are relative to the age or life stage of the responding person, and very much holds that responses must change as the culture changes; a work that is considered good in one era may be a total failure in another after a culture has (hopefully) evolved toward greater civility. He also claims that the best critical opinions and responses will change as more is known about, or seen in, an artwork.[2]

I do not agree with those who have claimed that relativism fails because it produces contradictions, or incompatible truth values. In 1976 Joseph Margolis dispensed with the rigid truth-value arguments in his "Robust Relativism."[3] Among the many points raised, he pretty quickly kills strict nonrelativism by saying, "Grant only that a putatively relativistic set of judgments lacks truth-values (true and false) but takes values of other sorts or takes 'truth-values' other than true and false"[4] and the nonrelativistic approach has no support at all. Margolis closes his article with his thesis that art objects are culturally emergent. As he puts it about the familiar properties of art:

> Its internal purposiveness, its being assignable meanings . . ., forms, designs, styles, symbolic and representational functions, and the like all call for a sensitivity to cultural distinctions that cannot in any obvious way be directly accessible . . . to any cognitive faculty resembling sensory perception.[5]

It is clear that a culture can have a plurality of interpretations of the same artwork. As I find this in Hume, there can be better responses at a point in time, but not one single response for all time. I find significant similarities among the ideas of Hume and John Dewey, with important support in the works of Richard Wollheim (1923–2003) and George Santayana.

Hume's "Relativism"

Hume claims that there are pleasurable responses to actual properties of the "object" that elicits the response. The criteria for correctness of response are intersubjective and educable. If they were totally subjective, there would be no role for a teacher or critic, and if they were utterly objective, there would be no doubt about the applicability of an evaluation at all.[6]

We have response potentials that are normal for our sensory mechanisms. This collection of mechanisms may be fine-tuned, because we otherwise would never have tastes move beyond the simple, or childish, and this is very obviously not the way things work out in the real world. We are not going to discover one, infallible quality the presence of which is going to result in our claiming whatever it is that has the quality is beautiful. To discover beauty, all we really have to work with is our set of normal responses and the situations associated with them.

There is in Hume's scheme, no such thing as a single, sufficient condition for a correct attribution. We have sets of features, some beauty-making, some not, and they all are estimated in their particular context. The closest to a sufficient stimulus, "the florid and superficial,"[7] loses its hold on us as our taste evolves. As Hume states this, the thing our old, and possibly childish, taste valued "is rejected with disdain,"[8] or it is "rated at a much lower value."[9]

The proper role of the critic is to point out the important properties of any given work. As mentioned above, assuming a set of nonfaulty faculties, we can have our sensibilities more finely focused. The critic essentially says, "Attend to this!" and we should then have a starting point for moving into a fuller response to the work. For the critic to provide the essential guidance, Hume emphasizes, he or she must have a powerful sensitivity to the sort of art that is being estimated, a great deal of practice in this estimation process, and a lack of partisanship, or prejudice. Emphasizing the conceptual underpinnings of his theory, Hume says that "reason, if not an essential part of taste, is at least requisite to the operations of this latter faculty."[10] Hume, in other writings, does not have stagnation of critical opinion; critics must improve and evolve, otherwise the whole mechanism of response development would become circular, critics chosen because they agree with their predecessors.

As I mentioned earlier, Hume looks not for any one variety of beautiful feature to be always sufficient to make a work beautiful in its entirety, but for a variable collection of beauty- making features, the more the better. However, there are circumstances wherein the collection of beauties, regardless of how plentiful they may be, will be secondary to the correct evaluation of the work at hand as ugly. From era to era and from country to country, there are better and worse versions of moral behavior. Hume unambiguously observes that "where the ideas of morality and decency alter from one age to another, and where vicious manners are described, without being marked with the proper characters of blame and disapprobation; this must be allowed to disfigure the poem, and to be a real deformity."[11] No longer can one "relish the composition."[12] Hume, then, recognizes the problem of entering into alien moral perspectives, into endorsements of behaviors or into taking pleasure in phenomena derived from behaviors we find reprehensible.

The restraining mechanisms in issues of taste would require that there be correct knowledge of the specific type and category of an artwork, extensive experience with artworks of the sort being experienced, and so on to avoid overly subjective, or wildly person-on-the-street relativistic, responses. Individual sentiments are correctable not by rule, not by telling one to have a reaction, but by influences leading to subjective changes in responsiveness. We could condemn Alex in Anthony Burgess's (1917–1993) *A Clockwork Orange* because his rush of bloodthirsty sentiments and enthusiasm for mayhem, all associated with Beethoven's *Ninth Symphony*, are morally repellent, but we can also condemn him because his own sentimental response is an ignorant, uninformed, inappropriate response.

Carolyn Korsmeyer notes that Hume's justification for the development and the valuing of taste is its utility.[13] The person of refined taste is the person who has developed a balanced, calmly reflective character. The development of taste allows one to avoid the crazes to which an unsophisticated and hyperdeveloped sensitivity could lead. With good taste, one could proceed through life along a "more well-balanced" path.[14] Hume speaks precisely of this value in "Of the Delicacy of Taste and Passion." Developed taste strengthens the judgment, and as a result, "We shall form juster notions of life."[15] It will lead to a better life in society.

Dewey on Aesthetic Experience

I believe that Dewey's thoughts about art and the aesthetic experience are exceptionally apposite in any consideration of rational yet relative responses to artworks. The function of art, and the value and nature of the aesthetic experience, is centrally concerned with the removal of disorder and the provision of an ordered and consummate experience. As Dewey said, the function of art, even at its genesis, as a mere apprehension of rhythms found in nature, was "to introduce evident order into some phase of the confused observations and images of mankind."[16] The aesthetic enterprise is an ordering enterprise, a bringing to fulfillment of important but previously diffuse elements into a significant, life-enhancing whole.[17]

Dewey's theory expands the concept of the artwork itself as well as our understanding of aesthetic response in significant ways. These allow for an artwork that is therapeutic, that avoids the dichotomy between high-art and low-art, which has been so troubling in aesthetic speculation and has given rise to a disdain for aesthetic theorizing as inconsequential and elitist. Dewey presents the response to the artwork as one that is a function of our personal history and experience, all of which must be brought to bear on our experience of the work. This is in harmony with the ideas of such philosophers as Richard Wollheim. I shall close with the observation that the organic and complex response that Dewey wishes for in both the production of the art object and the response to the art object would be hailed by such critics of our media-saturated and cognitively fragmented world as Neil Postman (1931–2003).[18]

Dewey, who was opposed to dualisms wherever they were to be found, seeing in them impediments to thought, rejected the "high-art" "low-art" distinction and what I could call the museumification of artworks. The opening paragraphs in *Art as Experience* lament the production of lists of canonical objects and the accumulated historical prestige of such objects. As he says in his second paragraph: "When artistic objects are separated from both conditions of origin and operation in experience, a wall is built around them that renders almost opaque their general significance, with which esthetic theory deals."[19] Dewey sees a necessity in removing the dualism, art and not art. He wishes to restore, as he says, "continuity between the refined and intensified forms of experience that are works of art and the everyday events . . . that are universally recognized to constitute experience."[20] The removal to the museum or gallery and the establishment of the idea of the aesthetic as distinct from life is simply an error. These dichotomizing forces have "historically produced so many of the dislocations and divisions of modern life and thought that art could not escape their influence."[21] That speculation today involves closer analysis of the criteria for inclusion in the museum would, I suspect, irritate but not surprise him. What Dewey is after is an investigation of the living human as an organism in an environment, an analysis of how that organism relates to and develops in that environment, and the nature of what Abraham Maslow would call "peak experiences," which are for Dewey elicited most fully in the aesthetic response.

Not only does Dewey remove the high-art and low-art dichotomy, allowing that many art objects enable a fuller response than other art objects, but he also removes the dichotomy between artwork and spectator. The surprising development for those who are used to identification theorizing is that the work of art as such is not the object. That which was previously considered to be the stable and unchanging item of human productivity in the world is no longer the focus. Instead, the total interchange, the experience that is had by the human being in complex response to the object, becomes the center of attention. The key to Dewey's theory is given in the very title of his book, where we have art defined as experience. Experience is a specialized term in all of Dewey's philosophy, and requires a bit of elaboration here. In its simple formulation, experience is a culmination, a totality recognized by the person having the experience as being total and significant. Monroe Beardsley (1915–1985) says that Dewey's generalized description of the living being in nature "is now classic."[22]

> Direct experience comes from nature and man interacting with each other. In this interaction, human energy gathers, is released, dammed up, frustrated and victorious. There are rhythmic beats of want and fulfillment, pulses of doing and being withheld from doing.[23]

We have the person as a live creature interacting with and within an environment. In the ordinary course of interaction, things are experienced, but not in such a way as to run to a completion that is integrated and distinct from simple experiencing. As Dewey states it, "we have *an* experience when the material experienced runs its course to fulfillment. Then and then only is it integrated within and demarcated in the general stream of experience from other experiences."[24] This experience is not limited at all to the realm of art objects, but can be a response to many integrated interactions in the world. It is, as Beardsley terms it, "an experiential whole."[25] Beardsley claims that there are six basic components of the experience: it is complete; there is an internal drive rather than external compulsion; it has continuity; it is not shapeless; it is cumulative with "a sense of growing meaning conserved and accumulating toward an end that is felt as accomplishment of a process"[26]; and there is one dominant and pervasive quality. The dominant quality, styled emotional, is itself, as Dewey says, a quality "of a complex experience."[27]

There are many experiences possible for the living person, many moments of interaction that will run to their fulfillment to produce the emotional realization that one has had an integrated and meaningful experience. But the moments of interaction that come together and have the greatest significance, the most meaningful and integrated moments, are those that are the work of art. Dewey's thrust here is seen when he says of art that it can build "an integrated complex experience."[28] Normal perception is usually what Dewey refers to as object perception, a perception that is cut short when we experience recognition. Recognition allows us to use the object perceived "for customary purposes."[29] Dewey locates the importance of art when he says that "art operates by selecting those potencies in things by which an experience—any experience—has significance and value."[30] The producer of the art object is involved in a complex perceptual transaction with experience, which is worked through by the artist to a satisfactory conclusion. The details of Dewey's account of the artist are rich and complex, and for Dewey the art object has to be produced by a human being: natural formations are a different matter entirely. Enough so that Dewey claims that we have to perform a total reevaluation if we find that something previously aesthetically responded to is found to be a natural phenomenon. The art object Dewey refers to as the art product. The meanings and valuations, the emotional sense of completion, the enrichment, and pleasure involved in the human interaction collaborate to produce the art product. The human enlightenment that is elicited in the transaction with the art product, the experience of the perceiver, is the actual work of art.

In this transaction with the art product, we find the removal of another dualism. We do not have a work of art and a passive or minimally contributing spectator. Dewey insists that the experiential funding and history brought to the aesthetic experience by the participant is vital. This is not in any sense a passive interaction, and the art product is only stable in a presentational way. This introduces my earlier reference to Wollheim. In The *Mind and Its Depths*,[31] Wollheim gives a searching critique of what he calls the scrutiny approach to criticism. The scrutiny approach, which has been widely supported, argues for a self-limitation on what can be read, seen, or heard in a work. Wollheim claims that scrutiny, "the ideology of the New Criticism,"[32] while having an obvious appeal, is fundamentally flawed because it is based upon a fallacious theory of perception in general, and therefore "rests on an erroneous view of the role of perception in criticism."[33] The problem with the scrutiny approach is that it assumes that the critic "should utilize only what he has come to know through scrutinizing the work,"[34] but it "omits to say anything about what cognitive stock the critic may draw upon when he scrutinizes the work."[35] Wollheim is proposing a loosening of the approach, rather than a total rejection. He expands upon the role of cognition in perception and develops the position that there is no way around taking into consideration the evolving cognitive stock of the critic, which identifies and weights the elements of the work criticized. Wollheim, after careful presentation of an informed and competent critical evaluator, notes that "the process of understanding a work of art . . . is essentially experiential."[36]

The supporters of strict scrutiny "take a parsimonious view of the critic's cognitive stock"[37] because they fear arbitrary judgments. Wollheim rejects such worries. If the artwork is always returned to, and the interpretation is indeed constrained by, what is presented in the work itself, they are groundless. If one were not to recheck one's response by means of a return to the artwork, then there would be a problem. But, the important question for Wollheim is this: Does the "cognitive stock . . . so modify our perception that it allows us to perceive something in the work that we might otherwise overlook?"[38] If so, good. And I say that this is very much what Dewey is arguing for.

For Dewey, the response to the art product is enabled by the art product, but it is relativized to the mental funding and experiential history of the experiencer.

Not only do no two people have exactly the same experience stimulated by the art product, but the same person is also unlikely to have exactly the same experience twice. This is a simple acknowledgment of the evolution and shifting of our internal funding. None of us is identical with any other in terms of our experiences in the world, allowing, of course, that there are basic organic similarities: we do not have identical experiences. There are enough commonalities so that the producer and the experiencer are communicating, but the richness and application of the art product vary. Dewey gives much time and thought to the impossibility of apprehending the Parthenon as did an ancient Athenian, although there are common human responses and values to be experienced in interacting with it. Experience is interactive, and Dewey clearly says that this interaction of "the artistic product with the self . . . is not therefore twice alike for different persons. . . . It changes with the same person at different times as he brings something different to a work."[39] As Wollheim might say, Dewey indicates that simple perception theories fail because they do not "take into account that esthetic rhythm is a matter of perception and therefore includes whatever is attributed by the self in the active process of perceiving."[40] Indeed, the distinction for Dewey between the good art product and the less good art product has to do with the level of integration and depth of experience of the producer and the funding of the experiencer. Even the hold of simplistic products upon "the uncultivated shows that some order is desired in the stir of existence,"[41] and that the drive to order is natural. Again, in harmony with Wollheim, Dewey notes that "obtuseness in perception can never be made good by any amount of learning, however extensive, nor any command of abstract theory, however correct."[42]

The function and value of the aesthetic for Dewey is integrative. It is not only a private matter, but is of vast cultural significance. As Dewey says, "In the degree in which art exercises its office, it is also a remaking of the experiences of the community in the direction of greater order and unity."[43] This is a constant theme in his work. It is also a restorative theme when we look at concerns of those like Neil Postman, who, in his 1985 book *Amusing Ourselves to Death*, documents the fragmentation of consciousness and the decay of public discourse that is attendant upon the nonunified, disjointed nature of television in the late twentieth century. The nature of the medium has lent itself to entertainment's becoming "the supraideology of all discourse on television."[44] Postman sees both historical perspective and contextualization of information as having decayed in the public mind. I suspect that what we have is many experiences, but no unification. As conceived by Dewey, "Art that is faithful to the many potentialities of organization, centering about a variety of interests and purposes, that nature offers . . . may have not only a fullness but a wholeness and sanity."[45]

The development of art products that elicit the aesthetic response, the unification of strands of experience into meaningful experiences that fight the disorder and chaos that is the raw stuff of the world, and the removal of the false dichotomy that has led to art's isolation from life are of tremendous significance. Dewey said that "as long as art is the beauty parlor of civilization, neither art nor civilization is secure."[46] Art is restorative when properly considered and not quarantined. I see no real conflict between Hume and Dewey in this.

Santayana's Relativism of Response

I add a little bit from George Santayana's 1896 book *The Sense of Beauty*[47] to again reject simplistic relativism and to reinforce the value of rational, complex relativism and the importance of responses to artworks and the beautiful. Santayana maintains a "relativism of response," and does not deny that others may have the same response at the same or other times, but insists that social constraints conduce toward agreements in evaluation. Values carry over from life in the world and harmonize with one another in aesthetic contemplation. The harmonization and the response then carry over into responses of an aesthetic nature to life at large, not being limited to the category "artwork." Both Hume and Santayana believe that the development of responses to art and the exercise of those responses are practices essential for a rational life in the world.

Santayana rejected traditional philosophies of art as verbal games and exercises in triviality. Art as a category, he claimed, has technical facility and professional interests "on the practical side,"[48] and, on the other, the intellectual or luxurious pleasure that contemplation involves. Beauty is a good, a joy in the immediate, which is "possessed with wonder and . . . in that sense aesthetic."[49] Harmony is said to be the "principle of health, of justice, and of happiness."[50] The official arts may be rendered by fads and fashions superficial and useless and unworthy of attention, but the pleasure associated with the arts continues and can be found elsewhere. Indeed, "there will always be beauty, or a transport equivalent to the sense of beauty, in any high, contemplative moment."[51] We must all learn how to harmonize our interests and forge a wholeness of life that gives it character and quality. Beardsley says of Santayana's thoughts that "this rational pursuit of happiness is the life of reason,"[52] and the role of the aesthetic in this drive is the focus of Santayana's 1905 writing, *Reason in Art*. Santayana says that "as an instance of fully harmonized and rationally controlled pleasure, 'art in general is a rehearsal of rational living.'"[53] Santayana also says, in harmony with Hume, Margolis, Dewey, and Wollheim, that "the aesthetic effect of objects is always due to the total emotional vale of the consciousness in which they exist,"[54] and that perceiving consciousness is funded by a wealth of experiences, impulses, and predilections.

Relativism Is Not Insignificance: Closing Thoughts

Given the above, I say we are far away from the "person on the street" version of relativism and we have also significant reasons to care about "things artistic." That our responses are significantly shaped by our education and experiences does not at all mean that they are no different from "tastes" for such items as olives and anchovies, which I like and my wife despises. Olives and anchovies are only arguable from a merchant's perspective; they are a simple taste preference. The improvement of sensitivity and the tying together of life experiences and the recognitions of significance that are possible with evolving sensitivities to "things artistic" are simply more important than caring about olives. Again, as especially noted by Hume and Santayana, this sensitivity training should improve our responses to the emotions and reactions of not only ourselves (self-knowledge) but also of others; we should become more aware humans. And, importantly, lest anyone think that this is only a Western world and modernist approach, I must note Noel Carroll's very carefully worked out presentation of art as not only a cross-cultural phenomenon but also an obviously species-useful one. After a survey of the work of anthropologists, Carroll says,

> Art . . . is one of the most important cultural sites we have for training our powers for detecting the emotions and intentions of others. And in this regard it would appear to be unquestionably adaptive. For . . . [this] . . . is the cornerstone of human sociability—one modeled and refined by artworks.[55]

This may be relativized to individuals and to cultures and to eras, but it is not at all trivial. It is appropriate, I believe, to close with Carroll's claim that the skills developed in regard to emotional sensitivities are "indispensable for virtually every sort of human intercourse."[56]

Notes

1 David Hume, "Of the Standard of Taste," in *David Hume: Essays: Moral, Political, and Literary*, ed. Eugene F. Miller (Indianapolis: Liberty Fund, 1985).
2 I delve deeply into these points in my long article, "David Hume, 'Of the Standard of Taste,' and Aesthetic Theory," in *1650–1850: Ideas, Aesthetics, and Inquiries in the Early Modern Era*, vol. 12, ed. Kevin Cope (New York: AMS Press, 2006), 125–45.

3. Joseph Margolis, "Robust Relativism," *Journal of Aesthetics and Art Criticism*, 35 (1976), 37–46. Reprinted in *Philosophy Looks at the Arts*, ed. Joseph Margolis (Philadelphia: Temple University press, 1977).
4. Margolis, *Philosophy Looks at the Arts*, 387.
5. Ibid., 398.
6. This section on David Hume derives, in parts directly, from my "Response to 'Hume and the Ethics of Taste,'" *Southwest Philosophy Review,* 30:2 (2014): 37–39.
7. Hume, "Of the Standard of Taste," 238.
8. Ibid., 238.
9. Ibid.
10. Ibid., 240.
11. Ibid., 246.
12. Ibid.
13. Carolyn Korsmeyer, "Hume and the Foundations of Taste," *Journal of Aesthetics and Art Criticism,* 35 (1976): 211.
14. Ibid.
15. David Hume, "Of the Delicacy of Taste and Passion," in Eugene F. Miller, *David Hume: Essays: Moral, Political, and Literary*, 6.
16. John Dewey, *Art as Experience* (New York: G.P. Putnam's Sons, 1958), 148.
17. This section on John Dewey derives, in parts directly, from my "Comment on David Hildebrand's 'Art Is Not Entertainment: John Dewey's Pragmatist Defense of an Aesthetic Distinction,'" *Southwest Philosophy Review*, 31:2 (2015): 67–71.
18. Neil Postman, *Amusing Ourselves to Death: Public Discourse in the Age of Show Business* (New York: Penguin Books, 1985).
19. Dewey, *Art as Experience*, 3.
20. Ibid.
21. Ibid., 6.
22. Monroe C. Beardsley, *Aesthetics from Classical Greece to the Present: A Short History* (New York: Macmillan, 1966), 335.
23. Dewey, quoted in Ibid., 335.
24. Dewey, *Art as Experience*, 35.
25. Beardsley, *Aesthetics from Classical Greece to the Present*, 336.
26. Ibid.
27. Dewey, quoted in Ibid., 337.
28. Dewey, *Art as Experience*, 171.
29. Ibid., 177.
30. Ibid., 185.
31. Richard Wollheim, *The Mind and Its Depths* (Cambridge: Harvard University Press, 1993).

32 Ibid., 133.
33 Ibid.
34 Ibid., 135.
35 Ibid.
36 Ibid., 142.
37 Ibid., 143.
38 Ibid.
39 Dewey, *Art as Experience*, 331.
40 Ibid., 162.
41 Ibid., 169.
42 Ibid., 298.
43 Ibid., 81.
44 Postman, *Amusing Ourselves to Death*, 87.
45 Dewey, *Art as Experience*, 321.
46 Ibid., 344.
47 George Santayana, *The Sense of Beauty: Being the Outlines of Aesthetic Theory* (New York: The Modern Library, 1955).
48 George Santayana, in *The Philosophy of George Santayana*, Library of Living Philosophers, vol. 2, ed. Paul Arthur Schlipp (Chicago: Open Court Press, 1971), 20.
49 Santayana, in Ibid., 20.
50 Santayana, in Ibid.
51 Santayana, in Ibid.
52 Beardsley, *Aesthetics from Classical Greece to the Present*, 329.
53 Ibid., 332.
54 Santayana, *Sense of Beauty*, 230.
55 Noel Carroll, "Art and Human Nature," *Journal of Aesthetics and Art Criticism*, 62 (2004): 101.
56 Ibid.

Beauty Is Objective

Carol S. Gould

Study Questions

1. What does Gould mean when she says that beauty is objective?

2. What are the "subjectivity" and "reductive" arguments against the objectivity of beauty? How does Gould respond to them?

3. How does cultural relativity pose a threat to objectivism? What observations does Gould make that undermine this threat?
4. How do Descartes and Hume set the stage for the contemporary dispute between aesthetic objectivists and subjectivists?
5. How, according to the objectivist, might aesthetic disagreements be settled? How does Gould illustrate this process?
6. What is the distinction between the aesthetic and the erotic? Why is this distinction important?
7. Why, according to Gould, does objectivism not require that beauty exist independently of humans?
8. What is the importance of disinterestedness in aesthetic evaluation?
9. What is the institutional theory of art? How is it, along with other contemporary views, unkind to objectivism? What new developments, however, are "bringing beauty back from exile"?
10. According to Gould, how may one discern objective beauty in mathematics? How does beauty in mathematics illuminate beauty in art?

When we say that a poem or painting is beautiful, we are making a value judgment. Many people insist that value judgments are simply a matter of subjective opinion because we find value in things that we find pleasurable or that serve our interests. Contrary to popular opinion, at least *some* judgments of beauty, despite being value judgments, are objectively true. Let us stipulate that by describing beauty as objective, we mean that people can, in principle, give reasons for, or justify, their assessments, reasons that should be accepted or rejected by others. Notice that "objectivity" can be either a metaphysical concept or an epistemic one. Although I think beauty has a type of reality, the limitations of space do not permit me to defend that in detail. I am primarily making the case that claims about beauty can be true or false, claims that when adequately justified should be accepted as such—by all reasonable and sensitive people.

Assaults on Objectivism

We apply the term "beauty" to many types of things and in different domains: natural phenomena, artworks, perfumes, assemblages of food, and other things we perceive with our senses, as well as mathematical proofs, and even ideas. Beauty is an aesthetic concept, one among others,[1] and inseparable from a certain kind of pleasurable experience. Even before people begin to philosophize (perhaps by taking a philosophy course), many take a stand on beauty, believing that objectivity about beauty is impossible, precisely *because* we sense beauty through individual, subjective experiences. This does not defeat the objectivity of beauty. After all, we perceive the color blue through subjective experience; but all people (with normal vision) who see the same blue object will not disagree that the object is blue. But in some, indeed, many, cases, not all people feel pleasure from a particular thing. One person feels pleasure in bucolic nature and thus sees it as beautiful, while others may agree with the French eighteenth-century rococo painter François Boucher (1703–1770), who said that "nature is too green and poorly lit."

In the Western tradition, for instance, one criterion for finding something visually beautiful is symmetry. The eighteenth-century philosopher Frances Hutcheson (1694–1747) contends that beauty involves a certain relation of a thing's parts to the whole—a balance of uniformity and variety that gives the viewer aesthetic pleasure, very much like the harmony in a musical work. While one might object that objectivism sounds reductive in that it reduces beauty to a relation between parts of a whole (or to whatever other criteria one might offer as a standard for justification), this would not defeat objectivism. If someone asks you why you love a particular person, you may offer reasons, but that does not entail that your reasons exhaustively explain why you love this person. If you say that you love them because of their sparkling wit, you are not reducing love to the appreciation of wit, or to anything else. Yet your reason might be sufficient to satisfy your interlocutor. Similarly, if you say that a particular musical work is beautiful because of the unusual and complex texture of its orchestral tone color, you are not reducing beauty to a work's having a certain combination of timbres. But you are providing a legitimate reason for finding the musical work beautiful. So neither the reductive argument, nor the subjectivity argument undermines the objectivity of beauty.

Others assail objectivism because of cultural relativity among standards of beauty and the vastly different criteria for judging beauty. Thus, they aver, beauty is embedded in cultural standards determined by political power structures, economics, religion, and language. For example, traditional Japanese aesthetics prizes *asymmetry* of structure (in architecture and picture space). The early-twentieth-century Japanese philosopher Kuki Shuzo (1888–1941) draws invidious comparisons between the French aesthetic, with its love of decoration and symmetry, and the spare suggestiveness of Japanese aesthetic taste.[2] One might conclude that beauty, or what gives one pleasure, must be a matter of cultural preference. Cultural relativism about beauty poses a serious threat to objectivism.

Languages differ vastly, as we know. Noam Chomsky, however, tells us that all languages share the same deep grammar. Just as languages differ, but share an underlying deep grammar, perhaps different cultural views of beauty share some underlying structural element, as some have argued. The celebrated composer and pianist Leonard Bernstein (1918–1990), in a series of lectures at Harvard,[3] applied Chomsky's linguistic theory to music, concluding that at the root of all musical languages lay certain musical universals and aesthetic universals. Yet aesthetic differences persist across cultures.

Consider, however, the *golden ratio*, which seems to be at the foundation of an uncanny multiplicity of things people consider beautiful—across cultures and throughout history. Literature abounds with this ratio: 1:1.618033988.... The number 1.1618033988, referred to as "phi," is found in nature, artworks in Renaissance and Western art, as well as in a wide range of Asian art over the centuries.[4] It seems to be the foundation of architectural design (even dating back to Stonehenge, and famously, the Pyramids of Giza and the Parthenon), contemporary graphic design, and now, of course, in designer faces promised by some cosmetic surgeons. In music, too, composers have used and do use the golden ratio.[5] Strikingly, beautiful things in nature exhibit the golden ratio, and their repeated patterns instantiate the Fibonacci series that we find in the ratio itself.[6] This casts doubt on subjectivism.

Some Historical Background to the Dispute

The dispute between aesthetic objectivists and subjectivists is a storied and vibrant one, going back at least to Plato's debates with the Sophists, the itinerant teachers who taught young Greek men various subjects, with the core of their education consisting of rigorous training in rhetoric. Rhetorical agility was essential to social mobility, because it would help a citizen persuade anyone of anything, even the soundness of an egregiously unsound argument. According to the Sophists, all truth is a matter of convention, or, "man is the measure of all things," as Protagoras (481–411BC) famously puts it.[7] For the Sophists, there are no wrong judgments about beauty, just as there are no wrong ethical judgments. The Sophists would grant, however, that some judgments are more culturally adaptive than others.

The debate over beauty heats up when we get to the eighteenth century, in which philosophers find themselves in a post-Cartesian world. Now that Descartes (1596–1650) has established the essential subjectivity of all of our claims about the world we perceive (in contrast to claims about the realm of logic and mathematics), philosophers must struggle with the question of what truly exists apart from one's particular subjective experience. Although Descartes shows no interest in questions of aesthetic value, he formulates and probes the question of how the human subject can justify knowing anything apart from the tableau of its own internal experience. However misguided or glib one may think Descartes's deus ex machina solution to the problem of empirical knowledge is, it is hard to deny that he established a new paradigm for examining reality. David Hume's empiricist system is a response to Descartes's problem. If we want to justify any belief, Hume argues, we must do so only with reference to sense perception and introspection. If you claim your laptop is real, Hume contends, you are claiming that you have a set of consistent, predictable sense experiences—because you are directly acquainted with only your sense experiences of the laptop. Hume basically adopts a principle of acquaintance, according to which you can admit the existence of only what you experience directly in sense experience or introspection. When you admire your laptop's design as beautiful, to what experiences are you referring other than the visual sense data of its design elements? What do you mean when you refer to "beauty"? Although Hume analyzes the material world in terms of perceptual phenomena, he does believe that empirical statements have truth-value. If you claim to have seen a living sphinx at the zoo, Hume's system would allow for your judgment to be false. Hume points to aesthetic pleasure as the ground for our judgments of beauty, or our aesthetic judgments more generally. So, why should we not conclude that the subjectivity of pleasure does not give us a good reason for rejecting the objectivity of beauty, just as the subjectivity of sense perception does not require us to reject the objectivity of the empirical world?

Resolving Aesthetic Disagreements

Imagine Kim saying to her friend Jesse, "Gustav Klimt's (1862–1918) *Portrait of Adele Bloch-Bauer I* is beautiful." Jesse disagrees. Can this claim be true or false independently of their personal opinions? Can Kim, who thinks it is true, resolve their disagreement about the painting by invoking evidence? The objectivist would reply in the affirmative. The subjectivist denies that such resolutions are possible. Would it be a waste of her time for Kim to try to convince Jesse that it is beautiful? The subjectivist would find Kim's efforts as fruitless as if she were trying to convince Jesse that cucumbers taste better than ice cream. Most subjectivists would grant that you could convince her that cucumbers are 96 percent water, as long as you give her adequate reasons based on empirical evidence described in terms of the currently accepted scientific paradigm. Is one's judgment about the Klimt more like the one about the deliciousness of cucumbers or the one about their water content? It is hard to adjudicate between these conflicting aesthetic judgments. According to the objectivist who agrees with Kim about the painting's beauty, Jesse, who denies the beauty of *Portrait of Adele Bloch-Bauer I*, is simply wrong and has no taste. Kim, unlike Jesse, has a trained eye. Kim cannot fault Jesse, however, for disliking cucumbers, Kim's favorite food.

Aesthetic Criteria

For the objectivist, you can appeal to criteria to settle the disagreement. Some judgments of taste have more epistemic value than others. Kim might point to the complexity of texture, the luminosity of the surface, the visionary use of abstraction that blends Adele's likeness into the design, so that Klimt captures her spirit that radiates into the world as her portrait does into the glittering surface of the painting. Kim could also show Jesse how Klimt's painting shows an advance in the historical development of European painting, while showing his understanding of his predecessors and his place among them. He reportedly was influenced by the flat-surfaced, radiant mosaics at Ravenna. Kim could explain to Jesse how *Portrait of Adele* shows that Klimt saw in the mosaics exactly what makes them aesthetically striking. Klimt, with his original, artistic technique, shows us, the spectators, something new about the mosaics, while also revealing Adele's remarkable personality. His use of abstraction and flatness of surface (like that of Cezanne, Picasso, and others) is avant-garde, but utterly different from his French contemporaries, and Klimt thus takes abstraction in a new direction.

Both Hume and, slightly later, Kant (who assigns to beauty a certain *type* of reality) would advise Jesse to take as authoritative the judgments of an informed critic, which Kim herself seems to be. Similarly, a person with a trained ear may evaluate as beautiful a commercially unsuccessful performance of a Brahms string quartet or a rap performance. According to Hume and others, such training allows one to hear, for example, interesting rhythmic pattern, timbre, phrasing, harmonies, and intonation. So we should not assume they are flops because they are unpopular.

The Aesthetic versus the Erotic

Before exploring the debate further, we must get clear on an important distinction about beauty that arises from our frequent use of the term "beauty" and its cognates to describe people—in fact, perhaps the most common use of the term in ordinary parlance. Before knowing about philosophical reasons, let us consider the issue from our experience in everyday life, the close observation of which usually leads us to think philosophically.

In the 2017 film *Paris Can Wait,* the female protagonist notices the beauty of mundane details of sense experiences. She savors colors and textures, devouring the lush beauty of flowers, fabrics, people, and artworks, all of which she photographs incessantly in even their minute details. Her gourmet companion on a road trip from Cannes to Paris takes extraordinary delight in the flavors of food and has an expertise in all matters culinary. As they travel through Southern France, he teaches her to appreciate the complexity and harmony of flavors, and she helps him to appreciate the splendor of the visual details that she so hungrily photographs. The film also shows the unfolding of a flirtation and then deeper understanding between the two characters; yet their mutual attraction is *not* mutual aesthetic appreciation, but, rather, an amorous attraction. His perception of her as a beautiful woman is not an aesthetic experience.

The film shows us an important ambiguity in the notion of beauty. Beauty is inseparable from pleasurable experience. We apply it in contexts both aesthetic and erotic. Because we so often overlook this ambiguity, it is easy to think that beauty is purely a function of the prism through which each of us sees the world, a matter of individual attraction. The twentieth-century art historian Kenneth Clark (1903–1983) confuses the erotic and aesthetic notions in his study of the nude,[8] where he contends that in order to have aesthetic merit, a nude must be erotically stirring. In contrast, the now-canonical aesthetic formalist Clive Bell (1881–1964), explicitly distinguishes aesthetic value (which he calls "significant form") from beauty,[9] precisely because of the erotic connotation of "beauty." Aesthetic appreciation, Bell tells us, has nothing to do with erotic desire. Aesthetic experience, for Bell, is separate from ordinary life and one's concerns and one's own practical interests and emotions, an unpopular view among many philosophers and art theorists.

In this, Bell shows himself to be a descendant of the eighteenth-century aesthetic perception theorists, as well as Kant, and, even more so, the nineteenth-century philosopher Arthur Schopenhauer (1788–1860).[10] They attach great importance to disinterested, as opposed to interested, attention, a notion to which we shall return shortly. First, notice that as we discuss beauty, we wander into discussing art and artworks. Until recently, most debates about beauty in the field of aesthetics have centered on the nature and evaluation of artworks. Artworks are artifacts, that is, entities made by human beings. But we perceive beauty in things other than artworks, some not created by human beings, as noted earlier. It is worth asking whether the existence of beauty requires human perception, or even human existence. If so, one might argue, then objectivism must be wrong, because objectivism presumes the existence of aesthetic universals. For the philosopher Plato,[11] however, beauty is inherent in the structure of reality itself and therefore is ontologically independent of human beings. Plato notwithstanding, objectivism about beauty does not *require* that beauty exist independently of human beings, any more than science requires that scientific facts exist independently of human perception. Science, itself, requires human existence, because (to put it simplistically) science is a human practice. If human beings did not observe and describe material objects, scientific statements about the universe would not, strictly speaking, have any truth-value or even existence. Harkening back to the old question—if a tree falls in the forest and no one is there to hear it, does it still make a sound?—an objectivist could consistently reply either "no" or "yes." The phenomenon of sound, for example, is a function of human faculties. But the conditions for sound, arguably, would exist with or without a human perceiver. Although time does not allow us to probe this further, let us say that the conditions for beauty could exist, even if no human beings were there to appreciate it. For instance, the posited *conditions* (light waves, molecular structures of surfaces, etc.) could exist that give rise to the vibrant colors of a sunset, even though human perceivers must exist in order to see colors as vibrant and to experience vibrant colors as beautiful.

Disinterestedness

Many who analyze the idea of aesthetic experience describe it as *disinterested*, requiring us to put all practical interests, personal desires, and prejudices aside. Suppose that Ms. X owns a valuable painting. In order to appreciate it aesthetically, to enjoy its beauty, she must be able to observe it without any thought of its market value or any pleasure in its being one of her financial assets. Or, suppose Mr. Y enters a gallery where he gasps upon seeing an unfamiliar painting. He finds himself transfixed by its visual power and luminescence. As soon as he feels a desire to own this painting, he no longer views it with disinterested attention and thus turns away from the painting's beauty. To speak in Kantian terms, he is viewing it as a means to an end.

Arguably, then, in order to apprehend beauty, one must be willing to experience it with disinterestedness. But that is just one component of aesthetic perception, as traditionally construed. As the mid-twentieth-century aesthetician Jerome Stolnitz famously describes it, aesthetic perception is disinterested, sympathetic, and actively attentive.[12] Stolnitz's analysis is akin to the Japanese Zen notion of the aesthetic, which governs the principles of many Japanese artistic traditions. More recently, Thomas Hilgers[13] cogently analyzes disinterestedness in the context of its historical tradition. Hilgers also *defends* it against the many who have indicted its importance in contemporary philosophical and artistic practice. Since the early twentieth century, many philosophers and artists have vigorously rejected the concept, be it explicitly through philosophical arguments or implicitly by engaging in new artistic practices. Such artistic developments would include, to use a couple of Hilgers's examples, theatrical conventions that require audience participation in the live drama and works by performance artists, such as Marina Abramović, whose work requires audience involvement. Philosophically, both analytic and so-called Continental philosophers have variously challenged the notion of disinterestedness.[14] Conversely, Plato acknowledges the possibility of disinterestedness, but implores us to avoid it, most famously in Book 10 of his *Republic*. An ethically pure (literary) artwork, he argues, is aesthetically boring. Plato worries that too often a good artwork overtakes us with its beauty and other positive aesthetic properties, leaving us unable to probe the work's morality. Thus, he grants the existence of beauty in artworks, but judges it morally dangerous.

Some have charged that the experience of beauty is a function of one's sociocultural environment and prejudices, that beauty cannot be a timeless, universal concept. The objectivist may reply that a viewer might need to learn about the artwork's sociocultural origin in order to observe the work disinterestedly and thus to experience its beauty. That is, some people may not be able to apprehend beauty without information about the historical-cultural context of a work or the artist's beliefs. For example, Chris Offili's 1996 *Holy Virgin Mary* ignited the rage of then New York City Mayor, Rudy Giuliani, who reacted to the sentiments of many vocal New York Catholics. He tried to censor the painting and close down "Sensation," a traveling exhibition from the Saatchi collection on display at the Brooklyn Museum of Art in 1999. Offili's painting includes, among other materials, two blobs of elephant dung and shows the virgin surrounded not by cherubim, but, rather, tiny images of derrieres and female genitalia. What Offili's enemies did not realize was that Offili, who was himself serious about Catholicism, had grown up with a complex religious heritage that allowed him to see certain biological materials and symbols as holy. His remarkable work expresses religious awe and displays the artist's desire to enrich and take his place in the Western art historical tradition. A spectator does not *have* to know these facts—but Offili's antagonists could not appreciate the beauty of Offili's work, let alone its artistic meaning, because they were unwilling to hold in abeyance their religious worldview, which blinded them to the aesthetic properties of the work. It is not *necessary* to understand either Offili's artistic achievements or the complexity of his cultural roots in order to appreciate its beauty, although such knowledge would prepare an adversary to observe his *Holy Virgin Mary* with a disinterested, aesthetic perception. Whether this observer would appreciate its artistic meaning is another story.

The Contemporary Scene

In the twentieth century, the notion of aesthetic experience and its attendant concept of beauty came under assault by philosophers of art, notably, by

George Dickie, first in his attack on the aesthetic attitude as a myth and then in his formulation of the *institutional theory of art*. According to the institutional theory, an artifact gains its status as an artwork if it is "offered as a candidate for appreciation by a member of the artworld." That is, something is an artwork, according to Dickie, in virtue of the institutional status of the person who presents it as worthy of attention. In Dickie's early formulation of the theory, he avers that a chimpanzee's painting gains an aesthetic standing if someone in the institution of the artworld believes that it merits a spectator's attention, that a spectator might find it beautiful. In this case, the chimp's painting becomes the artwork of the person of institutional standing who displays it. Even though the chimp made the painting, he is not the artist. The painting becomes an artwork through the gesture of the person offering it for appreciation. This resonates in the aesthetics of the French sociologist (and public intellectual) Pierre Bourdieu (1930–2002), who agrees that an aesthetic judgment gains its credibility by the social capital of persons who belong to a network that tacitly establishes standards of beauty and aesthetic merit, more generally, such as critics, curators, etc.[15]

Philosophers in the positivist tradition, dismiss all aesthetic claims as meaningless, on the ground that there exist no possible observations that could validate them. Many other philosophers, too, have rejected the objectivity of beauty because of their discomfort with its possible metaphysical commitments. More radically, neo-pragmatists, poststructuralists, feminists, and Marxist theorists indict judgments of beauty as grounded in cultural biases or the preferences of those high in the socioeconomic hierarchy whose interests such value judgments serve. On their view, the issue about beauty is not simply about the metaphysical or aesthetic implications, but also about the social, economic, and ethical implications of these judgments. The debate then becomes about social and economic justice and the political consequences of objectivism. Artists, too, have been unkind to beauty. For instance, Dadaists such as Marcel Duchamp (1887–1968) and Man Ray (1890–1976), conceptual artists such as Allan Kaprow (1927–2006), and neo-conceptual artists such as Jenny Holzer, separate beauty from art. Marcel Duchamp, who is unfortunately best known for his *Fountain*, rather than his prodigious oeuvre of expressive, formally inventive works, once said that when he created *Fountain* during his Dadaist period, he wanted to use materials to which he was aesthetically indifferent.

In the last two decades, however, more theorists and artists have been bringing beauty back from exile through changes in the artworld and a broadening of philosophical attention. This is an enormously complex matter, but we should note that in the Western artworld, purely conceptual art has grown stale. Artists are seeking new forms of expression. New technologies and media, as well as globalization, have allowed artists to focus on beauty anew. Moreover, artists have not been immune to the passion surrounding environmental concerns, which has led many to shift their artistic eye (or ear) to nature and natural beauty. While environmentalism has elicited a new appreciation for the beauty in nature, both philosophers and artists express a keen urgency to preserve it. Thus, we are witnessing burgeoning fields of environmental aesthetics and environmental ethics. Globalization has allowed for a cross-fertilization of the non-Western and Western sensibilities, thus impelling many Western artists to respond to the acceptance of beauty in, for instance, traditional Asian or African cultures. A contemporary artist might express their own visions of beauty by incorporating ancient techniques or genres into their own work. For instance, French watercolorist Varvara Bracho has a new series (*Nine Muses, or Daughters of the Memory*) strongly influenced by the colors and forms of the Japanese landscape where she recently spent six months. Her aim is purely visual rather than conceptual.

As for philosophy, aesthetics replies to the artworld.[16] The artistic quest for beauty requires philosophers to reexamine the epistemological and ontological status of beauty. Philosophy, too, has become less provincial in that philosophers, especially in aesthetics, feel unconstrained by such bifurcations as non-Western/Western and Analytic/Continental. Also, instead of separating the aesthetic from everyday life, many philosophers (and artists) are expanding the range of the aesthetic so as to include everyday life.

Beauty in Art

As for the question of whether good art must be beautiful, that is a different question from whether beauty is real. Let us note that even *if* beauty and other aesthetic properties are not essential to art, or good art, it does not follow that beauty is not real, nor does it follow that we cannot make objective aesthetic judgments about other things. In the domain of mathematics and logic, a proof can be beautiful. Mathematicians and logicians often evaluate proofs on aesthetic grounds. An argument that is taut, concise, elegant, and clearly structured can be beautiful. There are properties of proofs and theories that elicit a response to them as beautiful. If I do not understand why mathematicians find a given proof beautiful, a mathematician could explain to me how the proof meets aesthetic criteria of elegance and conciseness. All being well, the mathematician could help me directly experience the proof's beauty. Judgments of beauty arise from a certain pleasure, aesthetic pleasure. When you see the elegance of a proof, your pleasure may not be a sensory pleasure, but it is pleasure nonetheless. Moreover, this pleasure is independent of your personal interests and practical needs. The beauty of a mathematical proof is not in "the eye of the beholder."[17] Some, however, might be right in saying that even aesthetic pleasure in mathematics has a bodily aspect. This does not weaken our objectivist argument.

If beauty can be objective in mathematics and logic, then it may be objective in other dimensions, as it arguably is. In fact, mathematical beauty can illuminate beauty in other kinds of things. We take pleasure in the beauty of a well-wrought, imaginative sentence, with an unexpected, but precise choice of words and an economic structure both in the sentence and in the work itself. Such pleasure straddles the sensory and nonsensory experiential realms. Words conjure images in our sensory imaginations, whereas the structure pleases us more conceptually. A sentence of Nabokov, George Eliot, Plato, or Chekhov can bring powerful aesthetic gratification. What we appreciate in an argument is just one element that we also find in great literature, and not only in the work's sentences. A work as a whole may have an elegant or taut structure. Many writers aim to express emotional complexity with the conciseness that Chekhov achieves in some of his short stories. A reader might object to the ideas in Chekhov, say his nihilism or cynicism; but by taking a disinterested stance, s/he can appreciate its spare elegance that draws us to its beauty. The difference between beauty in mathematics and beauty in art is that in artworks, the span of aesthetic criteria is broader, based more in sense perception, and less predictable. We may judge a painting as beautiful based on a pleasingly unexpected use of color and another based on a breathtaking intricacy of design.

Conclusion

Objectivism about beauty, however unfashionable, is defensible. In our examination of objectivism, we covered a wide swathe of territory. Although we cannot do so here, the next task is to investigate the nature of beauty. It may have something to do with the relation among parts of a whole—or conditions of that sort may be neither necessary nor sufficient. Let us conclude with the assurance that we have good reason to accept objectivism and that it can point us in exciting new philosophical directions.

Notes

1 The distinguished aesthetician Monroe C. Beardsley argues cogently that we must avoid conflating "beauty" with "aesthetic value," the latter being a broader term. See his *Aesthetics: Problems in the Philosophy of Criticism*, 2nd ed. (Indianapolis and Cambridge: Hackett Publishing, 1981), 505–9.

2 Hiroshi Nara, *The Structure of Detachment: The Aesthetic Vision of Kuki Shûzô*, with a translation of *Iki no Kôzô* and essays by J. Thomas Riner and Jon Mark Mikkelson (Honolulu: University of Hawai'i Press, 2004).

3 Leonard Bernstein, *The Unanswered Question* (Cambridge: Harvard University Press, 1976).

4 See, for example, http://www.presentationzen.com/presentationzen/2005/08/from_wabisabit.html.

5 See, for example, https://www.theguardian.com/music/2009/oct/15/fibonacci-golden-ratio.

6 Literature abounds on the Fibonacci Sequence. For a helpful, nontechnical treatment, see Mario Livio's *The Golden Ratio: The Story of Phi, the World's Most Astonishing Number* (New York: Broadway Books, 2002).

7 Protagoras was one of the few Sophists whom Plato respected. He was professionally accomplished and one of the richest men in Greece. To understand Protagoras's sophisticated version of relativism about value judgments and truth, more generally, see Plato's dialogue, *Protagoras*, in which the eponymous character gives Socrates a run for his money.

8 Kenneth Clark, *The Nude: A Study in Ideal Form* (Princeton: Princeton University Press, 1956, 1984).

9 Clive Bell, *Art* (New York: Frederick A. Stokes Company, 1913).

10 Schopenhauer expounds his aesthetics in most of his writings. See especially his major work, *The World as Will and Representation*, trans. E. F. J. Payne, 3rd edition, 2 vols. (Dover, NY, 1966). For a good translation of Kant's primary treatment of Aesthetics, see his *Critique of the Power of Judgment*, ed. Paul Guyer, trans. Paul Guyer and Eric Matthews (Cambridge and New York: Cambridge University Press, 2000).

11 Plato's articulates most explicitly and famously his "Platonic" theory of Beauty in his *Symposium*. For one of several excellent translations, see Plato, *Symposium*, trans. Christopher Gill (London: Penguin, 2003).

12 Jerome Stolnitz, *Aesthetics and the Philosophy of Art Criticism* (Boston: Houghton Mifflin, 1960), 29–42.

13 Thomas Hilgers, *Aesthetic Disinterestedness: Art, Experience, and the Self* (New York and London: Routledge, 2017).

14 George Dickie, *Art and the Aesthetic: An Institutional Analysis* (Ithaca, NY: Cornell University Press, 1974).

15 See Bourdieu's *Distinction: A Social Critique of the Judgment of Taste*, trans. Richard Nice, with a new introduction by Tony Bennett (London and New York: Routledge, 2010).

16 While many aestheticians discuss this, it is perhaps most eloquently explained by Arthur Danto in his now-classic essay, "The Artworld," *Journal of Philosophy*, 61 (1964): 571–84.

17 This claim is not unprecedented: Two notable examples are Bertrand Russell, *Mysticism and Logic* (New York: Dover Publications, 2004); and Eddy Zemach, *Real Beauty* (University Park: Penn State University, 2004).

RESPONSES

Response to Mock

Carol S. Gould

Study Questions

1. What danger does Gould see in naïve relativism?

2. What is the "flaw" that Margolis sees in the anti-relativist's argument? How does Gould respond to Margolis?

3. Why does Gould criticize Mock's sympathy for Margolis's idea of "cultural emergence"?

4. Why does Gould think that Hume's and Dewey's views are inconsistent? How does this pose a problem for Mock?

Professor Mock defends his version of Rational Relativism. In discussing beauty and aesthetic value, he restricts himself to aesthetic judgments about artworks. He contrasts Rational Relativism with what we might call "naïve relativism," a pre-reflective view that beauty is a matter of individual choice. The naïve relativist would balk at the idea of refined taste or critical expertise, because each one of us is the final authority on what we like or what gives us pleasure. Mock sets out to defend a relativism that, unlike naïve relativism, allows for the crucial distinction between cultivated aesthetic responses and uneducated ones. The distinction can be exploited for nefarious purposes, such as censorship. In the former Soviet Union, for example, the state sanctioned only art that could speak to the aesthetically unsophisticated person, one either unfamiliar with artistic practice and expert critical responses or intuitively insensitive. Thus, the government censored works of many fine artists (notably Shostakovich) and destroyed their lives. Naïve relativism appeals to those who feel that artistic expertise is elitist. But a view's being elitist does not entail it is false. Mock, like other, more sophisticated relativists and unlike naïve relativists, aspires to accommodate the tension between the subjectivity of our aesthetic responses and the clear critical expertise exhibited by those with a cultivated eye, ear, or nose. At the same time, he wants to allow for a plurality of critical responses to a work.

Mock's argument rests on a systematic review of important philosophers whose views he analyzes as versions of aesthetic relativism. He defends his thesis by pointing to tenets of the aesthetic theories of Joseph Margolis, John

Dewey, David Hume, and Richard Wollheim. With the exception of Margolis, whose relativism is indeed robust, the other three express less vigorous relativisms. First, he relies on Margolis's philosophically sophisticated rebuttal of a standard argument against relativism (especially of the subjectivist variety). He goes on to claim that Hume and Dewey put forth similar relativist theories. We must consider first then whether the relativisms of Hume and Dewey are mutually consistent.

Mock's discussion raises many questions, which the limitations of space do not allow me to develop in depth. Let us focus on these two key matters: First, let us ask whether Mock adequately defends the strength of Margolis's response to that standard anti-relativist ("truth-value") argument. Next, let us ask whether Mock is justified in classifying Hume and Dewey as similar.

Mock's (Mis)Appropriation of Margolis

Margolis describes weaker versions of relativism than his own as "uninteresting." Margolis would consider, I suspect, Hume and Dewey as espousing types of weaker relativism. Mock rightly indicates that one objection to relativism is that it would allow for contradictory claims to be equally acceptable. For example, both of the following would be indisputable:

(1) Bernini's *David* is aesthetically magnificent.

(2) It is false that Bernini's *David* is aesthetically magnificent.

If Ted believes (1) and Mario believes (2), according to the relativist, they are both right. For the relativist, both statements are unassailable, which, according to the anti-relativist, is logically impossible. Margolis avers that the anti-relativist argument is logically valid. But, he continues, it rests on a flawed view of truth-value as bivalent. So, aesthetic claims such as (1) and (2) might be neither true nor false, for there are other possible truth values. For example, a claim can be *probable*. Given that probability can be a truth-value, it is possible that (1) and (2) are equally probable. Thus, Margolis concludes, they would not be contradictory.

It is not clear that Margolis's objection, however brilliant, "quickly kills" this anti-relativist argument, as Mock alleges. For neither Margolis nor Mock explains what it means for an *aesthetic* claim to be probable. We know what it means for an empirical hypothesis to be probable (e.g., "Two Tylenol tablets will cure my headache"). But an aesthetic judgment is *not* an empirical hypothesis. Therefore, whatever else one might think of the anti-relativist truth-value argument, or, for that matter, Robust Relativism, Margolis's assault on the truth-value argument is not lethal.

Margolis begins his article, "Robust Relativism," by presenting the truth-value anti-relativist argument presumably because it has such wide intuitive appeal that he has to dispense with it early. Had Mock probed Margolis's rebuttal further, he might not have dismissed it so cavalierly. As Mock then points out, Margolis describes artworks as "culturally emergent." Margolis's well-known idea of cultural emergence need not be unique to relativism. That is, someone *could* consistently believe in both the objectivity of beauty and the cultural emergence of artworks. The concept of an artwork is logically independent of beauty. Many artworks derive their importance in the artworld from properties other than beauty. A good example of this is the twelve-tone music that emerged in the early twentieth century. Few deny it is important, yet many deny it is beautiful. Margolis argues that the artwork's identity, *qua* artwork, blossoms within a given cultural ecology. That would not preclude its being beautiful. Its material, artistic identity shifts as the winds of culture turn through history, or contemporaneously, to different points on the globe.

Mock's Inconsistent Appeal to Hume and Dewey

Mock does not exactly argue for his Rational Relativism. Rather, he invokes the theories of two widely respected figures in aesthetics, Hume and Dewey, who, he believes, see eye to eye. He explicates their respective views in order to explain and defend his "rational relativism." Let us *assume* that this appeal to Hume and Dewey is a legitimate argumentative strategy. We then must consider whether Hume and Dewey agree on their core ideas. If not, does that put Mock's theory on shaky ground?

With regard to the two philosophers, their views arguably *are* inconsistent. Hume's aesthetic theory, unlike Dewey's, is not clearly relativist, although one would expect it to be given Hume's epistemology and ontology. Let us examine their differences.

There is much scholarly debate on Hume's aesthetics, especially over Hume's commitment to aesthetic relativism. Mock reminds us of Hume's well-known contention that some aesthetic judgments carry more authority than others. Those with experience, sensitivity, cultural understanding, and knowledge of a given area of art can guide those with less experience, knowledge, or sensitivity. Hume would say that a person well-acquainted with, appreciative of, or well-versed in, abstract expressionist painting would be better qualified to judge the aesthetic merits of a particular work than would someone unfamiliar with the genre. The mid-century critic Clement Greenberg (1909–1994) championed the artistry of Jackson Pollack (1912–1956) (and others) against those who dismissed Pollack's paintings as incompetent—those who had no understanding of the ideas and evolution of Western painting, let alone nonrepresentational art. According to Hume, Greenberg's judgment carries weight, and Greenberg's success in advancing public acceptance of abstract art adds to the heft of his authority.

Hume allows that in different cultures and at different historical moments within the same culture, to quote Mock, "there is no such thing as a single, sufficient condition.... We have sets of features, some beauty-making, some not" (p. 129). Yet one need not be an aesthetic relativist to grant that there is no sufficient condition for judging a work to be beautiful, nor that some attributions of beauty (or other aesthetic properties) may well be relative to a given sociocultural moment. Mock also underscores Hume's concern with the relation between moral and aesthetic judgments. Here, too, one need not be a relativist to wrestle with *aesthetic moralism*, the idea that an artwork's moral value is relevant to its aesthetic value. If Hume's aesthetic theory is a form of relativism, it is one diluted by his allowing for beauty-making features, his moralism, and his defense of the authoritative critic.

Dewey, Mock indicates, abhors elitism, the idea of the authoritative critic, the high/low-art distinction, and, indeed, even the distinctions we make among art forms themselves. Dewey realizes that some people, through openness and exposure to the world, develop a discriminating awareness. Dewey would applaud the current emphasis on everyday aesthetics and the elasticity in the notion of aesthetic experience. While both Hume and Dewey ground their aesthetics in pleasure, they analyze aesthetic pleasure differently. For Dewey, our experience of art merges with an object to create the work itself. An artwork is largely constituted by what he sees as a continual "rhythmic" experience that organizes a Heraclitean flow of experience. The work (or "product") changes the experiencing person. For Dewey, the artist, too, both makes and experiences the work as she makes it, internally editing her experience as she proceeds. The artist's engagement with new technologies is another facet of creativity.

Art is *poiêsis*, in the Classical Greek sense, both for the maker and the spectator. On Dewey's account, an artwork (or product) differs, as Mock points out, from person to person. This would necessarily be the case given that the artwork is constituted by the dynamic interaction between a self and the product. One can nonetheless make assertions about an artwork, and the assertions will have truth values. Both Matt and India may experience the same product; but they will experience different artworks. If India has more artistic experience, can she discuss it with greater authority than Matt, if, as Dewey has it, they are experiencing different things? (In fairness, Dewey does try to accommodate objectivity in criticism, and he would say that India could help Matt evolve aesthetically.) This implication of Dewey's theory, then, would be inconsistent with Hume's aesthetics.

Where does this leave Mock's interesting Rational Relativism? One might be confused by his account in its current form. As he describes it in some places, the theory teeters close to objectivism. Also, his Rational Relativism would be stronger, were he to argue forcefully for its tenets.

Response to Gould

James Mock

Study Questions

1. How does Mock respond to Gould's assertion that there are claims about beauty "that when adequately justified should be accepted . . . by all reasonable and sensitive people"?
2. What point does Mock make in using Pollock's paintings in response to Gould's discussion of objective patterns like the Fibonacci series?
3. What concern does Mock have regarding the ugly in art?
4. In what way does Mock find agreement with Gould's concern for disinterestedness?
5. How does Mock qualify Gould's presentation of Dickie's theory of art?
6. What response does Mock make to Gould's claim to find objective beauty in mathematics?

I find myself in agreement with many points raised by Professor Gould, but I continue in my disagreement with strong objectivism. This said, I find myself in a quandary as to how to write my objections in so short a response. Gould says that she thinks that "beauty has a type of reality," but "the limitations of space do not permit me to defend that in detail" (p. 139). Just so, I cannot fully critique it here. So, the best way to respond to her paper is to simply mention points of agreement and disagreement.

Miscellaneous Agreements and Quibbles

Gould says that "claims about beauty can be true or false, claims that when adequately justified should be accepted as such—by all reasonable and sensitive people" (Ibid.). My first response is to note the problem of sorting out who is reasonable, and who is sensitive. As I discussed this in my main essay, I agree with David Hume that this is an important requirement, but very few are going to fall into the reasonable and sensitive group without natural endowments of an unusual order, and experience and training in the art form that is being evaluated. (My father was seriously tone deaf, and my father-in-law is red-green color blind. Music with a heavy beat worked for my father in a way that I can't really understand, and my father-in-law is hopelessly at sea with abstract expressionist paintings.) Gould, of course, notes that we are assuming normal vision when looking at and agreeing on blues, but this relativizes with age and person: I have lost a surprising amount of color acuity with age, and my hearing is deteriorating, and thus my responses to paintings and music are changing. There is also the psychological feature that we miscalculate our response-state, assuming that our tastes become stable at a time in our lives.[1] Blue is blue unless I have something to add to the perception.

As with color, we have a non-aesthetic, brute feature to which the perceiver adds or contributes, thus producing the aesthetic evaluation. My personal knowledge, and actually irreducible personal taste, is very much going to determine how I respond to the non-aesthetic properties of "something." When Gould moves from blue to nature, things get more complex, and I would argue in accord with Allen Carlson that our fullest responses to nature require vast knowledge or what I will simply call a scientific grasp of nature.[2]

On criteria and symmetry, the eighteenth-century theorists before Hume were trying to find rules, or trigger-stimuli, that would assure the correct attribution of the term beauty. Gould is simply correct that the presentation of one feature doesn't warrant a correct and full explanation. Hume went for a weighing of elements, and Kant declared that there are no rules of taste. However, when she says that a musical work is beautiful because of the "unusual and complex texture of its orchestral tone color" (p. 140), I say that much ear-training is needed for perception of this feature.

I can quibble about speaking of music as language. Roger Scruton, among many others, claims that music and language have similarities, but are seriously not identical.[3] Also, yes, there are musical differences between cultures, but also within, as we find with twentieth-century atonal music which hasn't had much public acceptance but which has been a success with many in the avant-garde music world.

On built-in reactions, such as the Fibonacci series, yes, like blue, there are such things, but my favorite example is Jackson Pollock paintings. Pollock paintings have been studied and present an astonishing number of fractal patterns, to which we respond (if we attend to the painting), but his color sense adds to the patterning and results in the aesthetic response as such.

Another quibble is to add to the perfectly correct presentation of the Sophists and matters of convention that they recognized the utter necessity of understanding and following the customs of any country they visited. There may be "no wrong ethical judgments" in theory, but there are in practice.

I agree happily with Gould on Kim and Jesse regarding expert opinion, and training in the history of art and sensitivity improvement. And I like *Paris Can Wait* as an example, but I worry about beauty and pleasure, which I would like to see more on. There is a long-running discussion on the ugly in art, famously associated with the work of Jerome Stolnitz who presented an overview of the use of the term "beauty" and the opening up of the term "to make room for ugliness within the realm of aesthetic value."[4] This has led to the long-standing question: What do we do with "beautifully" crafted paintings of objectively ugly scenes, such as my favorite, Titian's (1490–1576) *Flaying of Marsyas*?[5] This is a question going back to Aristotle. And what do we do with fabulously well-crafted films, such as Leni Riefenstahl's (1902–2003) *Triumph of the Will* promoting Nazi ideals: Do we evaluate it as morally repellent but beautifully made?

I will dig in my heels and object to conditions for beauty with no humans to perceive it. Yes, there may be light waves, et al, but if there are no humans, there simply can't be claims about anything at all, much less anything having to do with appreciation.

Kant, Dickie, and Mathematics

On disinterested appreciation and the work of Kant, I offer this from one of my articles:[6] Theories derived from the work of Kant hold that an aesthetic response to a work of art is radically disinterested. George Dickie, in *Evaluating Art*, says that "the disinterestedness of beauty is achieved by isolating the experience of beauty from any anticipated future benefit, and in doing this the beautiful object is isolated from anything else it stands in relation to, including anything it might represent."[7] The work becomes a relationless object. We are not to be "concerned with the real existence" of the "thing," but "only with the present object in experience independent of its relations to other things."[8] If one is going to have disinterest as a component of one's response, I cannot argue against Gould's statement that "the objectivist may reply that a viewer might need to learn about the artwork's socio-cultural origin in order to observe the work disinterestedly and thus to experience its beauty" (p. 146). One has to be well informed, which I see as being in harmony with Hume and the others noted in my main essay.

On the contemporary scene, and the evaluations drawing on the work of George Dickie, I just wish to add a touch. As Gould nicely has it, the "thing," whatever it is, is identified as an artwork courtesy of an artworld person presenting it as such. The presenter must have official standing for this to work. Then, I wish to emphasize, the spectator has to operate on faith that the person who has identified the "thing" as an artwork knows what he or she is doing, so that we have correct identification. Then there are a couple of other important stages. One: after the "thing" has been identified, there is the question of whether or not the artwork is a good example of its type of artwork. Then we get to the purely personal evaluation: yes, it's an artwork, yes, it is a good example of its type, but do I like it? Here we may agree on the first two points, yet really dislike the artwork.

With nature, as I noted earlier, so too with mathematics and logic. Knowing more allows for recognition and appreciation. My graduate school housemate was a doctoral student in computer science, and my other close friends were in physics and mathematics. We talked about the beauty of proofs quite a lot, and they did their best to explain what it was that struck them as beautiful. I can't say that I ever really "got it," because I would have needed to be at the dissertation stage to follow their analysis. My closest friend's dissertation was, literally, an equation, with background text and a projection of future usefulness in artificial intelligence programming. I looked at it with as little comprehension as "the man on the street" looking at an abstract expressionist painting (I adore many abstract expressionist paintings!).

Conclusion

I think that Professor Gould and I agree on quite a bit, although we have a disagreement about simple objectivism. We are in harmony regarding the knowledge needed to appreciate an artwork, and my formulation of Rational Relativism strikes me as, at base, something that she might agree with, as I can happily agree with her clear recognition that cognition is needed for appreciation. We might bicker about additive features, but perchance not.

What I can say with no reservations is that this has been a delightful project and has been good for my lifelong search for clarity on the topic of beauty.

Notes

1 Harvard psychologist Daniel Gilbert produced a very large-sized study of people's notion of when their tastes stabilize, or when they as persons stabilize. Gilbert and colleagues speak about people recognizing that their tastes and values have changed as they have aged, but they regarded their present as a watershed moment at which they have finally become the person they will be for the rest of their lives. This is a pervasive belief, called "the end of history illusion." People are, quite simply, wrong in this, and the illusion leads to what are often called suboptimal decisions. There is a Ted Talk on this, and many references. I offer this short *Guardian* web sample: https://www.theguardian.com/lifeandstyle/2013/jan/19/change-your-life.

2 For example, one of many of his works developing this theory is: Allen Carlson, "Appreciation of the Natural Environment," *Journal of Aesthetics and Art Criticism*, 37 (1979): 267.
3 Roger Scruton, *The Aesthetics of Music* (New York: Oxford University Press, 1997), 171–210.
4 Jerome Stolnitz, "'Beauty': Some Stages in the History of an Idea," *Journal of the History of Ideas*, 22:2 (1961): 193.
5 This was also Iris Murdoch's favorite painting, as in: Dan Piepenbring, *Paris Review* (July 15, 2015), available at https://www.The parisreview.org/blog/2015/07/15/iris-murdochs-favorite-painting/.
6 James Mock, "David Hume, 'Of the Standard of Taste,' and Aesthetic Theory," in *1650–1850: Ideas, Aesthetics, and Inquiries in the Early Modern Era*, ed. Kevin Cope (New York: AMA Press, 2006), 125–45.
7 George Dickie, *Evaluating Art* (Philadelphia: Temple University Press, 1988), 150–53.
8 Ibid., 28.

Questions for Reflection

1. Has Mock appropriately understood Hume as a "rational relativist"? Why?
2. Do you agree with Gould that claims about beauty can be objectively true or false? Why?
3. Do you think that beauty could exist if humans did not exist? Why?
4. What role, if any, do professional art critics have in judging the aesthetic value of an art work? Do their judgments have authority? Why?

5

What Is the Meaning of Life?

The Meaning of Life Is Found in God

Douglas Groothuis

> **Study Questions**
>
> 1. What are the various kinds of meaning? What sense of "meaning" is most relevant to the question of life's meaning?
> 2. How does Groothuis define theism? What are the three areas of enquiry that he discusses and how does theism provide meaning in each area?
> 3. How does Groothuis define atheism? What seems to be the implication of atheism for meaning in life? Why?
> 4. What does Groothuis think of Sartre's attempt to avoid nihilism by allowing each person to define his or her own meaning?
> 5. What is the "is-ought" problem? Why does Groothuis think it is especially acute for the atheist?
> 6. What three problems does Groothuis raise for the idea that survival is the ultimate value for human beings?
> 7. What are the two forms in which Groothuis summarizes his argument? Which form actually reflects Groothuis's own view of reality?

Can there be meaning in life and death without God, without a supernatural creator, designer, lawgiver, judge, and savior? Can life be worth living if living has no design, purpose, or destiny? These are the central questions of this essay. But, first, what is meaning and why should we be mindful of it?

The Meaning of "Meaning"

What does the word *meaning* mean? What does it signify? To answer the question of whether God is necessary for life to have meaning, we ought to be clear on definitions.[1] The semantic range of *meaning* is broad. Meaning means many things. We can speak of the meaning of a word, such as the word *meaning* or the word *absurdity*. This is the definition of how a word is used in various settings in light of its author's intended meaning.[2] We may ask of the *meaning* of a sentence. That is, what is this sentence doing as a sentence? If it is ambiguous, we must disambiguate it to find its *meaning*.

Texts or books are interpreted to find (if possible) their *meaning*. For example, what is the essential thematic meaning of *Moby Dick* or the book of Job? One can ask for the original *meaning* of the American Constitution. This query takes up the question of what the authors meant to convey in their documents. Or, we consider how symbols relate to a proposition or set of propositions. That is, what does the symbol of the Cross *mean* with respect to Christianity's teachings? Or what is the meaning of the symbol of the crescent with respect to Islam's teachings?

Meaning may refer to a mind-independent (objective) state of reality or to a mind-dependent (subjective) state. If I say, "My dog Sunny means so much to me," I am referring to a particular canine that exists apart from my mind (objective); but the *meaning* of Sunny is unique to me; it is subjective. Sunny does not mean the world (or anything) to those who know nothing about Sunny or who (worse yet) have never seen a dog. The Rosetta stone may "mean the world" to an Egyptologist, but what she cares about is its *objective meaning*, because the decoding of the Rosetta stone provided a key for translating ancient Egyptian and Greek texts. Perhaps Sunny has mind-independent meaning as well.

Humans can *get meaning wrong* by misinterpreting something—a text, a facial expression, a religious symbol, or a political movement. Philosophers often argue about the proper interpretation of a philosopher's work, such as the meaning of Kant's epistemology or the meaning of Aristotle's view of logic. When we speak of the *proper interpretation* or the *most likely interpretation*, we do not mean that *anything goes*, since so many things go wrong. Errors abound and there is work to be done in resolving them.

It seems evident that if we can misinterpret a work of literature or a religious text, we could, likewise, misinterpret the meaning of existence itself; that is, we could get reality wrong. Few will argue against the truth-claim that Adolf Hitler got reality wrong in horrendous and long-lasting ways by virtue of his Nazism—thinking, for example, that Jews were less than human. In another way, those afflicted by eating disorders get reality wrong by abusing their bodies through bizarre eating patterns.

But the concept of *meaning* expands far beyond what I have so far discussed. A perennial topic is that of "the meaning of life" or "the meaning of everything." Under this topic, one might ask, "What does it all mean?" In this sense, meaning concerns what, if any, *lasting significance* one's life has; or what, if any *enduring, objective value* attaches to my life or way of life. Human beings often want to know whether or not their lives fit into a larger and coherent picture and whether or not the moral values they live by are more than mere human opinion. I argue that atheism offers neither.

Consider the cosmic. Is there an objective meaning to the universe and to our individual lives as dwellers in this cosmos? The idea of meaning adds something to the mere fact or idea of existence. For any positive thing to have meaning, it must exist; but do existing things have meaning? We readily admit that characters in a novel, say *The Brothers Karamazov*, play a role and have a meaning with respect to the plot, which is the humanly intended meaning and structure of the novel. But what if there is no plot for the universe, history, and humanity? Can there still be meaning?

Having addressed the nature of meaning in various senses, let us now consider how theism and atheism fare on giving meaning to existence. Contrasting these two worldviews should clarify the case on both sides.

Theism and Meaning

Monotheism can be understood to include Judaism, Christianity, and Islam. However, I will only address the broad Judeo-Christian version of monotheism, since Islam differs so radically from the two religions that it claims to replace. The Eastern family of religions—Hinduism, Buddhism, and Daoism—will be outside of our purview as well.[3] Monotheism (or theism), as I address it, is the claim that

> the cosmos is created and sustained by a perfect and personal being (God), who transcends it, superintends its history as its Author, and who will bring it into final scrutiny (judgment and restoration) in the future. Being perfect means that God is omnipotent, omniscient, omnipresent, and omnibenevolent. God can and does work miracles and inspires Scriptures to guide his human creatures, who bear his image and have, therefore, incomparable value. Thus, all of life has objective meaning which is grounded in the character and plan of God.[4]

When I say "God" (or "theism") in what follows, I mean the description just given. How, then, might theism give meaning to life? There are three principal areas: ontology, teleology, and axiology, which are all closely linked.

The theistic doctrine of creation affirms that an unlimited and personal agent brought the universe into existence at some time in the past, such that its very *ontology* (i.e., its being and nature) is divinely intended. According to the book of Genesis when God completed his creation, he deemed it "very good." Further, the narrator affirms that God created each thing according to its "kind." This need not necessarily map onto any biological category, but, rather, indicates that God created essences or natures that demarcate the ontology of members of this kind. The Apostle Paul also mentions this idea of various kinds of "flesh" in his discussion of the resurrection of the dead.[5] Thus, theistic ontology claims that God produced the entire system of finite things, persons, and processes according to his own nature. Creation is grounded in its Creator, for both its origination and continuation. Our being is not an accident, nor did it come about through an impersonal necessity. We are designed creatures with a purpose.

Given this ordered *ontology*—based on the creative design of a personal God—kinds of entities have a particular *teleology* (purpose or direction) based on their own natures and in relation to the being, design, and value of other entities. To illustrate, consider the human heart. The nature of a heart is a biological pump. The purpose of a heart is to pump blood throughout the body. It could not fulfill its purpose independently of its nature. A liver is not a pump; thus, it could not fulfill the purpose of a pump, although a liver has its own nature and purpose which functions in conjunction with the heart and the rest of the human body. Any medical professional assumes a teleology of the human body, whatever else he or she believes. Moreover, the human person in its entirety is made to "glorify God and enjoy him forever," in the words of the Westminster Catechism.

On this theistic ontology, the creation has an intrinsic meaning. Nothing is "just there, and that's all," as Bertrand Russell claimed for the universe in his debate with Fredrick Copleston (1907–1994) in 1948.[6] It was put there by someone who knew what to do with his creation. According to theism, human beings, for example, thrive when they act consistently with their God-intended nature. Thus, a divinely grounded *axiology* (study of value) finds good metaphysical company with *ontology* and *teleology*.

For example, humans, as made in God's image, were created to represent God and to develop his creation. This understanding has many implications, one of which is that it gives dignity and value to work. Sweat is good and has its rewards. Humans, as they are able, ought to develop and care for creation through activities that yield desirable results for which they receive due payment. For one seeking meaning, work should not be escaped or minimized, but embraced for one's own and the common good.[7] These facts also imply a moral responsibility, which the Apostle Paul captured in his advice for a lazy Christian, "We gave you this rule: 'The one who is unwilling to work shall not eat.'"[8]

Sexuality finds its place on this worldview as well. Since human beings are either male or female, they have somewhat different natures—at least regarding sexuality. Their biology and anatomy serves as the basis for their sexuality. Against current trends, one cannot choose a gender by identifying as X or Y. Humans are identified by God as being male or female and, as such, find their meaning and purpose therein. Jesus affirms the Genesis teaching that gender is fixed and that it grounds appropriate relationships. Responding to a question about divorce, Jesus said:

> Haven't you read . . . that at the beginning the Creator "made them male and female," and said, "For this reason a man will leave his father and mother and be united to his wife, and the two will become one flesh"? So they are no longer two, but one flesh. Therefore what God has joined together, let no one separate.[9]

Since the Judeo-Christian tradition forms the backbone of Western civilization, one could go on, but one more example will suffice: human rights.[10] The idea of universal human rights is not universal. It arose in the Judeo-Christian West, although it is not unique to that culture now. As the Hebrew Bible states, humans are unique in their divine origin and, therefore, should not be murdered. When Cain murdered Abel, his blood cried out from the ground for justice (Gen. 4). The seventh commandment is blunt, "You shall not murder." The basis of this injunction is the dignity and worth of human beings. The more a culture violates this law, the less it will flourish. The heritage of theism's claim on human rights is no better illustrated than in *The Declaration of Independence* (1776).

> We hold these truths to be self-evident, that all men are created equal, that they are endowed by their Creator with certain unalienable Rights, that among these are Life, Liberty and the pursuit of Happiness.

I have argued that monotheism, because of its ontology and teleology, grounds meaning in the areas of work, sexuality, and human rights. Further, death is not the end of God's creatures, so the meaning of life is not exhausted by one's mortality.[11] Of course, one could go on, but it is time to consider if atheism can give meaning to life.

Atheism and Meaning

What is atheism? "A-theism" is a negative term. Indeed, it negates (or should negate) all things necessarily dependent on a god or gods. There are various versions of atheism, but they all can affirm the following, which parallels the structure of the definition of monotheism given above.

> The cosmos is the entirety of existence. This leaves no room for God, gods, or sacred states. There is no Author of the universe, and, thus, no plot. Thus, the cosmos was not created. It has either existed forever or came into being out of nothing without a cause. The original entities and processes of this entirely material universe are undesigned and achieve no preset goals. Design only emerges from the brute facts of the universe when sentient entities are capable of designing things. History has no culmination and the fate of the universe—on the best present theories of physics—is the elimination of all available energy, which spells the end of all life.

In *What Does it All Mean?* Thomas Nagel concludes that while it may "take the wind out of our sails," we should acknowledge that "life may be not only meaningless, but absurd."[12] Nagel does not develop the ethical, political, or psychological implications of such an approach (which suggest nihilism, the idea that life is utterly meaningless), but he believes a thinking and mature person must learn to live with the implications, whatever they may be. He makes this judgment only after rejecting theism.

Frederick Nietzsche insisted that atheism be brought dead to rights. Speaking about British moralists who tried to keep Christian morality without God, Nietzsche observes:

> When one gives up the Christian faith, one pulls the right to Christian morality out from under one's feet . . . . Christianity is a system, a *whole* view of things thought out together. By breaking one main concept out of it, the faith in God, one breaks the whole: nothing necessary remains in one's hands. Christian morality . . . has truth only if God is the truth—it stands and falls with faith in God.[13]

Atheism, for Nietzsche, should not smuggle in ideas only justified by Christianity. Atheism must deny all the meaning and morality that is only supported by a Christian worldview. Few if any have stated the core of atheism better than Bertrand Russell in his much-anthologized essay, "A Free Man's Worship":

> That Man is the product of causes which had no prevision of the end they were achieving; that his origin, his growth, his hopes and fears, his loves and his beliefs, are but the outcome of accidental collocations of atoms; that no fire, no heroism, no intensity of thought and feeling, can preserve an individual life beyond the grave; that all the labours of the ages, all the devotion, all the inspiration, all the noonday brightness of human genius,

> are destined to extinction in the vast death of the solar system, and that the whole temple of Man's achievement must inevitably be buried beneath the debris of a universe in ruins—all these things, if not quite beyond dispute, are yet so nearly certain, that no philosophy which rejects them can hope to stand. Only within the scaffolding of these truths, only on the firm foundation of unyielding despair, can the soul's habitation henceforth be safely built.

Few have Russell's rhetorical gifts, but the man was also one of the first analytic philosophers and a mathematician. He, I claim, knew where atheism led and he followed it. An author and influential director of many films, Woody Allen is an atheist who emphasizes the ephemerality of value.

> I firmly believe . . . that life is meaningless. This is because every 100 years, there's a big flush, and everybody in the world is gone. And there's a new group of people. And that gets flushed, and there's a new group of people. And this goes on and on interminably—and I don't want to upset you—toward no particular end, no rhyme or reason.
>
> And the universe, as you know from the best of physicists, is coming apart, and eventually there will be nothing, absolutely nothing. All the great works of Shakespeare, and Beethoven, and Da Vinci, all that will be gone.

For Allen, if something of seemingly great value will be destroyed for no reason, then life is meaningless. If meaning only lasts as long as there are those to feel or recognize it, then when death overtakes all, all meaning will be lost. Given his premises, the logic follows a cruel necessity.

Despite this dismal tale told by atheists, are there options for atheists to find meaning in life nonetheless? For Jean-Paul Sartre (1905–1980), there is no given meaning, since there is no God to give it; however, people can create meaning freely. He writes in *Existentialism and Human Emotions*:

> Atheistic existentialism . . . states that if God does not exist, there is at least one being in whom existence precedes essence, a being who exists before he can be defined by any concept, and that this being is man, or, as Heidegger says, human reality. What is meant here by saying that existence precedes essence? It means that, first of all, man exists, turns up, appears on the scene, and, only afterwards, defines himself.[14]

This implies, for Sartre, that humans have no essence, no nature, because there is no God to give it. However, he attempts to avoid the nihilism of objective meaninglessness by asserting the individual as the meaning-maker. Human beings have no God-given essence (and thus no teleology), but each person may define himself as he wishes without appeal to a transcendent moral standard. He starts with the subjective, which is a radical freedom. Sartre wants to avoid pure relativism by saying that each person must choose for the whole human race and, somehow, respect the subjectivity of other meaning-makers. Further, one must not exercise bad faith by blaming one's choices on outside forces or inner urges.

But can Sartre, or similar existentialists, climb out of the pit of cosmic meaninglessness on the basis of human subjectivity? I think not. For Sartre, humans are free in a vacuum. They have no compass and no direction, spare that of freedom, which could lead anywhere. The human "I am" of freedom (which Sartre calls the "for-itself") has no metaphysical foundation, since it mysteriously emerged from the world of impersonal necessity (which Sartre calls "the in-itself"). However, the concept of personal freedom emerging from an impersonal necessity is less than compelling. Sartre cannot appeal to God giving humans freedom. He must rely on an unaided nature wholly unsuitable for such a metaphysical bestowal. Perhaps Sartre (or a Sartrean) could say that human subjectivity popped into existence out of nothing, but this beggars both reason and imagination, since out of nothing, nothing comes (*ex nihilo nihil fit*).

As Sartre puts it, we can appeal to no "heaven of ideas," since there is no God and no heaven. The problem centers on the *is-ought problem*. Atheism is committed to philosophical materialism—all that exists is matter specified by certain natural laws. Many atheists (although not existentialists) put great stock in science, which they understand in a materialistic sense.[15] However, scientific investigation can explain what *is* (to some extent), but it cannot tell us what *ought* to be. It can give us knowledge about how to achieve certain ends, but it cannot *justify* those ends themselves by science. We *can* freeze human embryos, but *should* we? A sociologist may tell us what most Americans think is morally right, but no sociologist (or any other scientist, hard or soft) can, on the basis of her descriptions alone, tell us whether the consensus is morally right.

Perhaps C. S. Lewis (1898–1963) put it best:

> From propositions about fact alone no practical conclusion can ever be drawn. . . . The Innovator [one who attempts to create values] is trying to get a conclusion in the imperative mood out of premises in the indicative mood: and though he continues trying to all eternity he cannot succeed, for the thing is impossible.[16]

The well-known new atheist, Sam Harris, argues in *The Moral Landscape* that morality can be determined apart from religion and on the basis of science alone. It is obvious from the first chapter that Harris has cheated by assuming that certain states of being are better than others. Once this has been determined—that the good life includes a healthy environment, etc.—then science can lend a hand. On what basis can Harris privilege some states of affairs over others? Nothing in chemistry, biology, physics, sociology, psychology, or anthropology can tell him that.[17]

At this point, an atheist might say that *survival* is the ultimate value for human beings, since Darwinian evolution shows that beings strive to survive, but only the strongest survive. This grounds meaning and morality. Therefore, we must work and will to survive. However, three problems present themselves here.[18] First, we deem many activities as meaningful and valuable quite apart from any relation to our own or to others continued survival or procreation. When I visit the Denver Art Museum, I do so for enjoyment and, if I attend with a friend, for friendship. This activity might have survival value, but that is far from my mind or my friend's mind. Its survival value would be only incidental. The *meaning* we find in art has nothing to do with survival.

Second, to reduce meaning and morality to mere survival value hardly gives any objective value to life. One may preserve one's life by any number of immoral ways, such as aspiring to be part of a master race, as did Hitler. Further, what meaning could suffering have when one must die, even die a premature death? As German psychiatrist and holocaust survivor Viktor Frankl (1905–1997) said in relation to the suffering in a concentration camp:

> The question that beset me was, "Has all this suffering around us a meaning?" For, if not then ultimately there is no meaning in survival; for a life whose meaning depends upon such happenstance—whether one escapes or not—ultimately would not be worth living at all.[19]

Third, the is-ought problem still remains. Simply from describing the pattern of evolution, one cannot derive any imperative to survive. That would have to come from elsewhere, but there is no *elsewhere* for the atheist. The material world exhausts the possibilities, which exhausts materialism. However, the insurmountable chasm between is and ought did not stop Darwin from speaking of "favored races" and predicting that "lesser races" would succumb to the greater ones. This mentality fueled the eugenics movement, and Hitler's philosophy cannot be understood apart from social Darwinism.[20] While nature alone cannot give moral guidance, it offers a compelling model to emulate if one prizes survival above all things.

Other possibilities for finding meaning in a godless world may be pursued, but I do not see how they could succeed. Atheist philosophy professor, Alex Rosenberg, agrees. He finds no meaning at all and bites the metaphysical bullet, advising that since life is meaningless, drugs may be necessary: "So, what should we scientistic [atheist] folks do when overcome by *Welschmertz* (world-weariness)? Take two of whatever neuro-pharmacology prescribes."[21] Rosenberg advises this since nothing in his worldview could bring one out of such a depression. If so, then atheism gives no consolation or inspiration to the troubled soul.[22] In fact, he defends nihilism as an implication of atheism, since there is no purpose of the universe and no meaning of life. Thus he answers his own question: "*What is the difference between right and wrong, good and bad?* There is no moral difference between them."[23]

No God, No Meaning

To sum up: objectively grounded meaning in life is based on ontology, teleology, and axiology. Atheism's ontology is little more than "stuff happens"; it provides no teleology; it lacks any objectively grounded moral standard (or axiology) for living well.[24] Theism, on the contrary, offers a God-given ontology, a providential purpose to history, and an objective value based on God himself and on that which God gives to his creation.

I will put my argument in two simple forms. First, the atheist should reckon the following modus ponens argument to be sound:

1. If there is no God, there is no meaning.

2. There is no God.

3. Therefore, there is no meaning.

Or consider the following modus tollens argument, one I have not stated outright, but which has been whispering on the sidelines.

1. If atheism is true, there is no objective meaning.

2. There is objective meaning.

3. Therefore, atheism is false.

Although my argument is complete, one may wonder why atheists often insist that life has meaning when their worldview cannot support it. Those atheists, who are not nihilists, often defend the idea that since they find some things subjectively meaningful (in one way or another), their atheism is irrelevant to meaning.

Theism, however, proffers another explanation. Since God has imbued the world with meaning and made mortals to experience some of that meaning, even if an atheist denies God, he or she can still taste something of God's good creation—even though they deny the source of the meaning. In other words, as Nietzsche might put it, many atheists are living on stolen capital.

Notes

1. For some of the technical issues concerning meaning (but not in the meaning of life sense), see *The Cambridge Dictionary of Philosophy*, 2nd ed, s.v. "Meaning" (New York: Cambridge University Press, 1999).
2. See E. D. Hirsh, *Validity in Interpretation* (New Haven, CT: Yale University Press, 1967).
3. These religions deny the reality of the God of monotheism through pantheism, polytheism, or atheism (in some forms of Buddhism). They, like secular atheism, deny the existence of a personal and providential being who gives life meaning.
4. Both Jews and Christians will agree with this statement, although Christians are quick to add that God is triune and has incarnated in Jesus Christ. These claims have profoundly meaningful entailments for human flourishing, but cannot be addressed here.
5. See 1 Corinthians 15.
6. Bertrand Russell and Fredrick Copleston, "A Debate on the Existence of God," in *The Existence of God*, ed. John Hick (New York: Macmillan, 1964), 175.
7. See Timothy Keller with Katherine Leery Alsdorf, *Every Good Endeavor: Connecting Your Work to God's Work* (New York: Penguin, 2014).
8. 1 Thessalonians 3:10.
9. Matthew 19:4–6.
10. See the many works of Rodney Stark on this, such as *The Victory of Reason: How Christianity Led to Freedom, Capitalism, and Western Success* (New York: Random House, 2005).
11. For the Christian understanding of immortality, see 1 Corinthians 15.
12. Thomas Nagel, *What Does It All Mean?* (New York: Oxford University Press, 1987), 101.
13. Frederick Nietzsche, "Twilight of the Idols," in *The Portable Nietzsche*, ed. and trans., Walter Kaufmann (New York: Viking, 1968), 515–16.
14. Jean-Paul Sartre, *Existentialism and Human Emotions*, trans. Bernard Frechtman (New York: The Philosophical Library, 1957). 15.
15. On this spurious view of science, see Douglas Groothuis, *Christian Apologetics: A Comprehensive Case for Biblical Faith* (Downers Grove, IL: InterVarsity Press, 2011), 300–305.
16. C. S. Lewis, *Abolition of Man* (New York: Macmillan Publishers, 1955), 43–44.
17. See the debate between Harris and William Lane Craig, https://www.youtube.com/watch?v=ynMm9coeWBY.
18. I do not here address the logical and evidential failings of Darwinian evolution as a sufficient explanation for the entire biosphere. But see Douglas Groothuis, *Christian Apologetics*, chap. 13.
19. Viktor Frankl, *Man's Search for Meaning* (New York: Pocket Books, 1973), 183.
20. See Jerry Bergman, *Hitler and the Nazi Darwinian Worldview: How the Nazi Eugenic Crusade for a Superior Race Caused the Greatest Holocaust in*

21 Alex Rosenberg, *The Atheist's Guide to Reality: Enjoying Life Without Illusions* (New York: W. W. Norton Company, 2011), 282.
22 I am not condemning the use of mood altering prescription drugs or saying that if one believes in God, there is no need for them.
23 Rosenberg, *The Atheist's Guide to Reality*, 3.
24 Some atheists hold to *atheistic moral realism*. This is the view that objective morality exists but are not grounded or located in any physical substance or quality. It is a kind of Platonism about moral truths. Even if this view were true, the atheistic worldview still lacks a divinely- given value to life and is barren of teleology. Thus, it could not provide meaning to life. For more on atheistic moral realism, see my, *Christian Apologetics,* 357–63.

The Meaning of Life Can Be Found without God

Christine Vitrano

Study Questions

1. What are the various categories and subcategories into which answers to the question of life's meaning can be divided? Which view does Vitrano defend?

2. How does Vitrano understand the general concept of a meaningful life? What view of happiness does she adopt?

3. How does Vitrano summarize Camus's interpretation of the Myth of Sisyphus and his view of the meaning of life? What problems does she have with Camus's view?

4. What are the two alternative versions of the Sisyphus story that Richard Taylor tells? What kind of meaning can Sisyphus's life have on each of these versions of the story?

5. Why does Vitrano (along with Taylor) think that the kind of meaning Sisyphus has in the first of Taylor's versions is inadequate? What does she think is the key to living a meaningful life?

6. What is the serious objection to which Taylor's view is vulnerable? How does Vitrano modify Taylor's view to avoid this problem?

7. What objection might the objectivist make to Vitrano's view? What is Wolf's version of this objection? What does Vitrano think is the weakness in Wolf's view?

When I enrolled in my first philosophy course, I had no experience with the subject, but I assumed one topic we would spend time discussing was the meaning of life. Although we learned quite a bit about the nature of reality and knowledge, theories of right and wrong, and even a bit of logic, the meaning of life never once came up. The closest we came to the topic was a discussion of the ancient ethicists and the pursuit of happiness. I would later learn that questions about the meaningfulness or significance of our lives are largely absent from the classic literature. These questions only started receiving serious philosophical attention from contemporary philosophers fairly recently.

However, despite the lack of historical attention, philosophers today are engaged in a lively debate over the meaning of life. Broadly speaking, one can divide the terrain into two large categories: those who view the meaning of life as dependent on God (theistic approaches) and those who deny that God is necessary for life to be meaningful (nontheistic alternatives). One can then further subdivide the category of nontheistic alternatives into two groups, those who appeal to the objective value or worthiness of one's activities to anchor judgments of meaning (objectivist theories) and those who deny the need for such values (subjectivist theories). For our purposes, I will consider all approaches that appeal to some kind of objective value as objectivist, even if they also include subjective elements like happiness or pleasure. Thus, objective and subjective theories will comprise two mutually exclusive and exhaustive groups. My goal here is to defend the nontheistic view that the meaning of life can be found using an entirely subjectivist framework.

I will begin with a brief discussion of the concept of meaning, distinguishing it from other values, such as morality and happiness, and isolating the distinct way in which it implies that a life is good. Then I will introduce a subjectivist account from Richard Taylor (1919–2003), who defends the view that meaning is something internal to us, arising from our attitudes toward the things we do. Put simply, Taylor's view implies that if we are enmeshed in our lives such that we enjoy our daily routines and are happy, our lives are meaningful. Although I find Taylor's account persuasive, it is vulnerable to an objection. After raising this objection, I will suggest a modification to his theory that I will argue provides the best explanation for how life can be meaningful without invoking the existence of God. Next, I consider how an objectivist might object to my theory, and I use Susan Wolf's view to illustrate objectivism. I will then discuss several problems with Wolf's view, concluding that the most plausible account of meaning eschews all reliance on objective values and focuses solely on subjectivity, or more specifically on the subject's happiness and engagement in her life.

The Concept of Meaning

Let us begin with a question: What do we mean when we say that a particular life is meaningful? Common sense tells us that meaningful lives are important or significant, or that they matter in some sense. Susan Wolf describes questions about meaningfulness as the kinds of questions one asks on her "death bed" or at the end of life, when one reflects back on all she has accomplished. Wolf suggests that one might wonder whether her life has been meaningful even if she is confident that it has been happy or morally good. Thus, meaning picks out a distinct domain of value or way in which one's life can be good, which is independent of both happiness and morality.[1]

Robert Audi describes a life as meaningful "*in relation to the good*, for instance by *either* being good or contributing significantly to something else that is good."[2] That is, "a life is meaningful on the basis of the good that is realized *in* it or the good created *by* it."[3] Therefore, to say that a life is meaningful is to commend that life, for it implies that a person's life is good in some respect. As Thaddeus Metz explains, "When people ask what, if anything, makes an individual's life meaningful they are generally asking something to the effect of what it might be about life that is worthy of great pride or admiration, or how one can make one's existence estimable apart from making it well off or fulfilling moral obligations."[4]

Most theorists would agree that meaning is a kind of value that good lives can have, and some theorists include meaning as one component of a person's well-being or "the good life." Despite their disagreements, all theories of meaningfulness try to provide the conditions that must be met in order for a life to count as meaningful. Put succinctly by Metz, "A conception of life's meaning is a theory of what makes a life meaningful. It is a general, fundamental, and systematic account of the conditions that constitute a significant existence."[5]

Since happiness will play a key role in both the subjectivist and objectivist theories of meaning we shall consider, it is worth pausing briefly to discuss the nature and value of happiness. Unfortunately, there is just as much disagreement within the happiness literature as there is within the meaning of life literature over precisely how we should define this concept. Interestingly, the debate about happiness mirrors the debate about meaningfulness with theorists favoring both subjective and objective conceptions of happiness. Delving into that debate would take us too far afield, so for the sake of simplicity, I am going to offer what I find to be the most plausible conception of happiness, which best captures the way in which we use the word today.[6]

According to the "life satisfaction view," happiness is a mental state of satisfaction, which implies that one is pleased with her life or views it favorably.

Happiness, on this view, represents a distinct domain of value that implies nothing about how good one's life is morally or prudentially. So it is entirely possible that one will be happy doing things that are not good for herself (such as abusing drugs) or that are not good for others (such as engaging in an extramarital affair). But as long as the subject is satisfied with her life, she will be happy, regardless of the actual material conditions of that life.

The life satisfaction view implies that there will be a huge range of possible lives that make people happy, given the diversity in people's tastes and inclinations. It follows that what makes one person happy may make another miserable, so the only way to evaluate a person's happiness is to find out how she feels about the conditions of her life. If she is satisfied, that is the only necessary condition that must be met to ensure her happiness, assuming she is not lying and understands the meaning of the word. Therefore, our third-party opinions about the sources of her happiness or the conditions of her life are irrelevant, and no immediate contradiction arises when we imagine a happy pauper, a happy hermit, or a happy immoralist, for all will be happy if they are satisfied with their lives.

A Subjectivist Account of Meaning

Richard Taylor does not begin with an account of what makes life meaningful, for he observes that this is a difficult question, which inspires very different intuitions in people. Instead, he starts with an example we can all agree typifies a meaningless existence, the ancient myth of Sisyphus.[7] Sisyphus is condemned by the gods to a life of sheer futility: he is doomed, for all eternity, to repeatedly roll a rock up a hill only to watch it roll back down again. When we reflect on the fate of Sisyphus, it is interesting to observe that our repulsion at the thought of living his life has nothing to do with the difficulty or painfulness of his task, for carrying a rock up a hill is not particularly labor-intensive or challenging. Rather, it is the sheer monotony and boredom that we imagine Sisyphus must feel as he repeats the same pointless action over and over again, with no end in sight.

Before examining Taylor's view, let us first look at how Albert Camus (1913–1960) uses this ancient myth to discuss the meaning of life.[8] Camus studies Sisyphus during his pause at the top of the hill, when the rock has rolled back down and Sisyphus is fully aware that he must go retrieve it. Camus refers to this moment as Sisyphus's hour of consciousness, for he can harbor no delusions about his life and its absurdity. Camus argues, "The lucidity that was to constitute his torture at the same time crowns his victory," because "there is no fate that cannot be surmounted by scorn."[9] Camus refers to Sisyphus as "the absurd hero," because he is constantly confronted with the meaninglessness of his own existence, yet he manages to summon up the will to carry on.[10]

Camus believes that our lives were just as absurd and meaningless as the life of Sisyphus, though few of us acknowledge this fact, choosing instead to remain asleep while living out of habit. Sisyphus is constantly confronted with his own absurdity, but Camus suggests this gives his life an air of nobility, and he says we must imagine Sisyphus to be happy. For Camus, Sisyphus is happy because he fully embraces the absurdity of his life. Sisyphus accepts his fate, and chooses to carry on with his pointless task.

Camus believes that we are also better-off shedding our delusions about the value of our lives and acknowledging their absurdity, for "everything begins with consciousness and nothing is worth anything except through it."[11] Recognizing that our lives are meaningless is painful, but Camus argues that we should reject suicide and face the truth with an attitude of defiance and scorn. If we choose to continue living in the face of absurdity, we, like Sisyphus, have a "will conjured up out of nothing" and this makes our lives exceptional.[12] According to Camus, acknowledging the truth can make us conscious of our true freedom and provide us with a real passion for living.

Although Camus describes Sisyphus's defiance in the face of his own absurdity as noble, many find this conclusion difficult to accept. First, it is not clear why we should view Sisyphus as a hero, when he is being *forced* to roll those rocks up the hill. Why is his action admirable, when he appears to have no other choice? It is also unclear why we must imagine Sisyphus to be happy. If happiness is equivalent to life satisfaction, why should we believe that Sisyphus is satisfied with his life? Furthermore, how can the negative emotions of scorn and defiance lead one to view life positively or favorably? Sisyphus continues to roll rocks, but he doesn't really have any other options—this is his punishment. Resigning himself to his fate, even if Sisyphus believes that he deserves this punishment, seems to be quite different from actually being happy with one's life.

Finally, many people reject Camus's conclusion about the absurdity of our own lives. Of course, there is a lot of debate about *why* our lives are meaningful, but few theorists would accept that *all* of our lives are no different from the life of Sisyphus. Camus's conclusion diverges greatly from our commonsense intuitions about the meaning of our lives. If our lives were tedious and absurd, why bother getting out of bed each morning? Why continue living at all? And if Camus really thought *his* life was meaningless, why would he bother writing this essay? One might worry that actually accepting the absurdity of life would *not* inspire one to conjure up a will out of nothing and develop a passion for living, but, instead, lead one to despair. For absurdity would imply that it truly does not matter whether one lives or dies, and that is not a conclusion most people would be willing to accept.

Richard Taylor also draws a parallel between our lives and the life of Sisyphus, but he reaches a positive conclusion about the meaning of our lives, which I believe better resonates with our commonsense intuitions. Taylor presents two versions of the Sisyphus myth. In the first one, we are to imagine that instead of rolling back down the hill, the rock remains at the top where it, along with many other rocks, is assembled into a beautiful temple. Sisyphus plays no part in the construction of this temple, for his role is the same as in the original scenario, to simply roll rocks up the hill. Nor does Sisyphus's emotional state change, for he doesn't take any interest in the creation of the temple, and he still views his task as boring and pointless. However, instead of the rock rolling back down, his labor does have a purpose, for the rock is used (along with other rocks) to build a beautiful temple.

The important question is whether this change alters the meaning of Sisyphus's life. An objectivist might argue that Sisyphus's life is now meaningful because he is involved (even if only indirectly) in the creation of something that is objectively valuable. The fact that his labor is no longer futile, because there is a significant purpose to his actions, is sufficient for conferring some meaning on his life. These reflections suggest that one way to increase the meaningfulness of our lives is to partake in activities that are themselves valuable.

However, Taylor also presents a second version of the Sisyphus example for us to consider. In this version, although Sisyphus is condemned to the same endless task of rolling a rock up a hill, the gods have also implanted in him a strange and irrational impulse to compulsively roll rocks up hills. Although externally identical, the change renders Sisyphus internally different, for rather than feeling dejected and bored by his actions, Sisyphus now feels excited and deeply engaged in his task. We can imagine that each time the rock rolls back down the hill, Sisyphus is overcome by a strong desire to race back down and retrieve the rock, and he is filled with excitement about doing it all over again. Instead of feeling hopeless and dejected, we must now envision Sisyphus as happy, because he is able to satisfy his strongest desire all day, every day, for all eternity.

As an outside observer, you might not find Sisyphus's life attractive, and you might have a hard time understanding how anyone could enjoy such a futile task. But it is important to remember that his impulse or desire to roll rocks is irrational; it doesn't have to make sense to us. What is important is that Sisyphus loves his life, regardless of how we feel about it.

So how does this change affect the meaning of Sisyphus's life? I would argue (along with Taylor) that Sisyphus's life is now meaningful, for he is able to do what he most enjoys, forever. How many of us are fortunate enough to pursue what we love without distraction? Many people choose jobs that provide financial security but are not personally fulfilling, leaving them with little time to do what they actually enjoy. When I consider the life of Sisyphus in this version, I find his life no longer inspires pity, and it could even be described as enviable.

Returning to the debate between subjectivists and objectivists, we can use these two fictional scenarios to test our intuitions about the source of meaning in our actual lives. In the first version, Sisyphus feels internally dejected and bored, but his labor results in the creation of something valuable, a beautiful temple. In the second scenario, his labor has no external value, for he is just pushing a rock up a hill, but his internal perspective has changed. He now feels deeply engaged in his task, and is happy with his life.

If we grant that both versions of the story alter the meaning of Sisyphus's life, one externally and one internally, which one reflects the kind of meaning we strive to have in our own lives? One might be tempted to choose the first version, where Sisyphus's labor helps to create the beautiful temple, for one might argue that it better represents our actual lives, which most of us believe do have a purpose. Surely, our accomplishments have some kind of worth or value, unlike the futile pursuit of Sisyphus in the original scenario.

I disagree, however, for I am skeptical as to whether the external value of our accomplishments is sufficient to make our lives meaningful. Consider how Sisyphus must feel about his life in the first scenario: if he truly doesn't care about the creation of the temple, he would feel dejected and hopeless, and I imagine him hating every second of that journey up the hill, knowing he is condemned to repeat this task over and over again. I would judge Sisyphus's life as wasted if he spends all his time doing something he deplores, even if that work amounts to something *other* people value. A person's life should feel meaningful to the person living that life, and even if we all agree that Sisyphus is doing something significant, if he takes no joy in the task, then his life has been wasted.

Reflecting on our own accomplishments, Taylor also raises the problem of their lack of permanence. Although our personal achievements seem important to us right now, over time, their significance will fade and they will be viewed as less impressive. Even great works of art, music, literature, and architecture eventually get old, and receive less attention as newer, more exciting creations emerge. Most of us will not even accomplish anything as significant as a great work of art or literature, for we are likely to spend a lot of our time raising families and trying to provide for their future. Taylor suggests the next generation will build new monuments, create new masterpieces, and as our culture progresses, even the greatest accomplishments will be forgotten, or worse, viewed as trivial and insignificant. As Taylor explains, "The picture of Sisyphus is the picture of existence of the individual man, great or unknown, of nations, of the race of men, and of the very life of the world."[13]

Although Taylor agrees with Camus that when viewed externally, our lives do resemble the life of Sisyphus, he rejects the conclusion that our lives are absurd, arguing, instead, for the kind of internal meaning found in the second scenario. Thus, the key to living a meaningful life is to pursue projects you find deeply engaging and that make you happy. Don't worry about what you manage to accomplish (from an external perspective), because it is not important as long as you are happy with your life.

Although I believe that the meaning of life must be found internally, Taylor's account is vulnerable to one serious objection. The problem arises when we imagine someone who is happy doing terribly immoral things, like torturing and mutilating innocent people. If this person deeply enjoys harming others, his sadistic acts would contribute to the meaning of his life on Taylor's view.

I should note that the question of whether an evil or immoral person can have a meaningful life is a point of contention among theorists. For instance, Harry Frankfurt offers an account of meaning similar to Taylor's, for he argues that "devoting oneself to what one loves suffices to make one's life meaningful, regardless of the inherent or objective character of the objects that are loved."[14] Frankfurt, like Taylor, places no constraint on the nature of what is loved, and he allows for the possibility that even Nazism might offer its leaders a "complex, exhilarating, and rewarding life."[15]

I am willing to grant the *happiness* of evil and immoral people, but I do not agree that they are living *meaningful* lives, mainly because I find it implausible to describe a morally depraved life as good or commendable. Thus, to avoid this implication, I suggest including one additional requirement to Taylor's theory of meaning. We can say that a life is meaningful if one is happy, and her happiness does not violate our commonsense understanding of what it means to live a morally decent life. I will rely on our ordinary intuitions about morality to determine which acts are impermissible, but the general idea is that your happiness cannot involve the deliberate infliction of pain and suffering on others, for that would clearly violate our moral norms and our commonsense understanding of decency. The upshot is that as long as one's happiness is not morally objectionable, engagement in one's life (regardless of what one chooses to pursue) is sufficient for making that life meaningful.[16]

The Objectivist's Reply

Now that we have seen how the subjectivist can ascribe meaning to a person's life without invoking God, we must consider a potential objection to this view. The objectivist might argue that happiness, even if achieved in morally acceptable ways, is not sufficient for meaningfulness, because this view places no other constraint on the kinds of activities one may pursue. That is to say, my subjectivist account is too permissive, for it allows almost anything (even rolling rocks up a hill) to count as meaningful so long as the person performing that task is happy. The objectivist might agree that being happy or deeply enmeshed in one's life is necessary for meaningfulness, but not sufficient. And the objectivist might appeal to truly admirable people, such as Gandhi, Mother Theresa, or Albert Einstein, to illustrate real meaningfulness because their achievements were so significant.

As an alternative to the kind of subjectivist theory I have proposed, the objectivist might offer a hybrid view that incorporates both subjective and objective elements, such as that offered by Susan Wolf. According to Wolf, a person's life is meaningful if she is actively engaged in projects of worth. Just being actively engaged in one's projects and activities is not sufficient for meaningfulness. Those projects themselves must also be objectively valuable, such that their worth is at least partly independent of one's own preference or enjoyment. Wolf admits that she has "neither a philosophical theory of what objective value is nor a substantive theory about what has this sort of value."[17] She relies mainly on our commonsense intuitions about which activities are worthy.

To illustrate the distinction between worthy and worthless activities, she offers the following examples of valuable activities: moral and intellectual accomplishments, relationships with friends and relatives, and aesthetic enterprises. In contrast, she describes crossword puzzles, sitcoms, computer games, eating chocolate, and doing aerobics as "not the sorts of things that make life worth living."[18] Wolf also offers the following examples to illustrate meaninglessness: the person who collects rubber bands, memorizes the dictionary, makes handwritten copies of *War and Peace*, "the corporate lawyer who sacrifices her private life and health for success along the professional ladder, the devotee of a religious cult" or "the pig farmer who buys more land to grow more corn to feed more pigs."[19]

Wolf's theory implies that a life will not be meaningful if it fails to meet either of her two conditions. So, if a person doesn't care about her daily routines and activities, and she is entirely indifferent toward her projects and goals, then her life will fail to be meaningful, even if what she is doing or accomplishing is important and valuable. Wolf, Taylor, and I all agree on this condition. However, for Wolf, even if a person is passionate about her projects, and looks forward to each new day with enthusiasm and joy, "if the objects of her involvement are utterly worthless,"[20] that person's life will fail to be meaningful.

The main difference between Wolf's view and the one I favor is her reliance on objective value. However, this is the weakest part of Wolf's theory. Wolf fails to provide us with any kind of theory of objective value, leaving us without a principled way of determining which sorts of activities and projects are worthy, and which are a waste of time. In the absence of an actual theory of objective value, her lists of worthy and worthless activities are entirely unjustified. Wolf seems to assume that our pre-theoretic intuitions about value will be sufficiently robust and universally shared, such that they can anchor judgments about meaning, but I do not believe this assumption is warranted. Just look at the different choices people make about how to spend their time. What one person finds gripping and exciting, another deems to be a pointless waste of time. But, if there is such fundamental disagreement over which activities have merit, how can we rely on our intuitions to issue judgments about meaning? If each person simply defers to her own preferences, how is this a reflection of objective value?

Further inconsistencies can be found within Wolf's own examples of worthy and worthless activities. For instance, why include intellectual and aesthetic pursuits as worthy, but exclude computer games and crossword puzzles? Crossword puzzles are intellectually challenging, and many computer games have genuine aesthetic value. Wolf's list also betrays a bias toward the intellect, which is not surprising given that she is a professional philosopher. But what reason do we have for not finding value in challenging oneself physically? What do we say about the value of running a marathon or playing a sport competitively? But if Wolf is willing to include challenging physical activities like these, then why exclude aerobics?

The problems with Wolf's view all stem from her reliance on the concept of objective value, while failing to provide us with a formal theory detailing exactly what this value is. Her attempt at appealing to our commonsense intuitions is unsuccessful because there isn't universal agreement about which activities are worthwhile, and, therefore, we have no way of issuing stable judgments about meaning. However, if we remove this problematic element from Wolf's view, we are essentially left with meaningfulness as subjective attractiveness, which is the view I have been defending all along.

Conclusion

We have considered two different approaches to the meaning of life that do not rely on the existence of God: one that embraces objective values and one that relies solely on our subjectivity. Given the problems associated with the concept of objective value, I believe we ought to adopt a purely subjective account of meaningfulness that identifies it with being happy with one's life. The value or worthiness of what we choose to do is irrelevant, for it is our happiness that determines whether our lives have been meaningful. Put simply, if we are fortunate enough to find something that we love and that deeply engages us, and we aren't doing anything morally wrong in the process, then our lives are meaningful. So go out there and enjoy life!

Notes

1. Susan Wolf, "Happiness and Meaning: Two Aspects of the Good Life," *Social Philosophy and Policy,* 14 (1997): 207–22.
2. Robert Audi, "Intrinsic Value and Meaningful Life," *Philosophical Papers,* 34 (2005): 343.
3. Ibid.
4. Thaddeus Metz, "Baier and Cottingham on the Meaning of Life," *Disputatio,* 1 (2005): 255.
5. Thaddeus Metz, "The Concept of a Meaningful Life," *American Philosophical Quarterly* 38 (2001): 138.
6. I offer a full defense of the life satisfaction view and critical analysis of other dominant theories of happiness in *The Nature and Value of Happiness* (Boulder, CO: Westview Press, 2014).
7. Richard Taylor, "The Meaning of Life," in *The Meaning of Life*, 3rd ed., ed. E. D. Klemke and Steven M. Cahn (New York: Oxford University Press, 2008), 134–42.
8. Albert Camus, "The Myth of Sisyphus," in *Ethics: History, Theory and Contemporary Issues*, 6th ed., ed. Steven M. Cahn and Peter Markie (New York: Oxford University Press, 2016), 465–73.
9. Ibid., 472.
10. Ibid.
11. Ibid., 467.
12. Ibid., 468.
13. Ibid., 139.
14. Steven M. Cahn and Christine Vitrano, *Happiness and Goodness: Philosophical Reflections on Living Well* (New York: Columbia University Press, 2015), 5–6.
15. Ibid., 20.
16. For a further defense of this view, see *Happiness and Goodness: Philosophical Reflections on Living Well.*
17. Wolf, "Happiness and Meaning," 209.
18. Ibid., 210.
19. Ibid.
20. Ibid., 211.

RESPONSES

Response to Groothuis

Christine Vitrano

> **Study Questions**
>
> 1. Why does Vitrano think that Groothuis is guilty of attacking a straw man?
> 2. What middle ground does Vitrano defend between theism and nihilism?
> 3. Besides purpose and morality, what else does theism provide for believers? How does Vitrano use this point to challenge Groothuis's view of life's meaning?

Douglas Groothuis considers the question of whether life can be worth living if there is no supernatural creator, and he concludes that an atheistic worldview cannot support meaning in life. I shall discuss two problems with Groothuis's argument. First, he seems to be committing a fallacy by assuming there are only two positions—belief in God (and hence, meaningfulness in life) and atheistic nihilism (which views life as meaningless and absurd). But he overlooks the possibility that one can remain agnostic with respect to the existence of God, but not endorse nihilism or absurdity. I shall argue that Groothuis's arguments against atheistic nihilism do not challenge the view I put forth regarding meaning, and thus do not support the conclusion that belief in God is necessary for living a meaningful life.

My second objection centers on the question of whether belief in God is sufficient for living a meaningful life, and I shall argue that theism is compelling as a theory of meaning mainly because it tacitly assumes the theist is both happy and moral. But in the absence of these two conditions, I shall argue that belief in God alone is *not* actually sufficient for living a meaningful life.

Groothuis's Argument

Let us begin with a brief recap of Groothuis's argument for why theism leads to a meaningful life. According to Groothuis, there are three principal areas in which theism supports meaning: ontology, teleology, and axiology. Put briefly, the theist believes that a perfect God created the cosmos, and human beings were designed with a purpose. Thus, our existence is not accidental, and our lives are not unimportant. Rather, human beings possess intrinsic value, and are governed by a divinely grounded moral code that tells us how to live. Based on these three considerations—ontology, teleology and axiology—Groothuis concludes that belief in God is *sufficient* for providing an objectively grounded meaning in life.

Groothuis then considers whether theism is also *necessary* for meaning, or whether one could live a meaningful life without the belief in God. To answer this question, he considers the opposite of theism, atheism, which he describes as denying the existence of God as author of the universe. Groothuis characterizes atheism as entailing nihilism, or the view that life is meaningless and absurd. He cites Nietzsche, who argues that atheism commits one to denying all the meaning and morality that depends on a Christian worldview, and he suggests that the atheist's materialism can only tell us what *is*, not what *ought* to be. The atheist, therefore, lacks an objectively grounded moral standard by which to live, and Groothuis concludes with the following modus ponens argument: If there is no God, there is no meaning. There is no God. Therefore, there is no meaning.

In sum, Groothius has argued that belief in God is both *necessary* and *sufficient* for living a meaningful life. Theism is sufficient, because of its ontology, teleology, and axiology; and it is necessary, because the worldview presupposed by atheism is nihilistic and cannot support meaning.

Theism Not Necessary for Meaning

Groothuis's argument that theism is necessary for a meaningful life is fallacious for two reasons. First, *he is attacking a straw man*. Atheistic existentialists like those cited by Groothuis are all too happy to conclude that life is meaningless—so arguing that their worldview cannot support meaning does not really prove anything these theorists have not already stated themselves.

Second, *he assumes that there are only two positions relevant to this debate about meaning: theism and atheistic nihilism*. But the fact that one does not anchor one's theory of value in the existence of God does not necessarily commit one to nihilism, subjectivism, or relativism. Virtue theories and Kantian deontology appeal to human nature and our rationality to ground moral judgments. Consequentialist moral theories appeal to some conception of the good, such as pleasure in utilitarianism, to anchor moral judgments about which acts are morally right. In all of these cases, moral judgments are objectively determined and categorically binding; they are neither subjective nor relativistic, yet they do not rely on the existence of God. Groothuis seems to assume that if one is not a devout theist, one must be an atheistic nihilist, but surely this overlooks the vast middle ground that occurs between these two extreme positions.

To recap, I have not yet challenged Groothuis's claim that theism is sufficient for meaning in life, but I have argued that he has failed to prove that belief in God is necessary for meaningfulness, because he has overlooked the possibility that one can deny nihilism and absurdity without relying on God to anchor one's value judgments. Thus, all Groothuis has shown is that atheistic nihilism implies that life is meaningless, but this should come as no surprise to anyone who has read the existentialist literature, much of which openly declares that life is absurd. More importantly, his arguments do not challenge the view I put forward, which is that life is meaningful if one is achieving happiness in morally acceptable ways.

Theism Not Sufficient for Meaning

Now I would like to question whether belief in God is sufficient for living a meaningful life. Theism is supposed to ground objective meaning by providing one with an ontology, teleology, and axiology. That is, theism explains to the believer why she is here, what her purpose is, and how she should pursue it. To start with axiology, theism prescribes moral rules by which to live, and I agree with Groothuis that living a morally decent life is an important part of living a meaningful one. But I would also point out that for many believers, theism is an important source of happiness. For example, faith in God can promote resilience by providing people with the inner strength to cope with misfortunes and tragedies, and it also offers hope of an afterlife of eternal happiness.

If we agree with Groothuis that many theists are living meaningful lives, the question is whether it is the belief in God that makes their lives meaningful, or the happiness and sense of moral purpose that their religion provides. If it is solely the belief in God, then we should be able to take away both the happiness and moral goodness, and still consider the theist's life meaningful. But if we remove these elements, and we lose the meaning, then it was the happiness and moral goodness that were driving our judgments about meaning, and the theism (by itself) would not be sufficient for living a meaningful life.

To answer this question, let us engage in a thought experiment: consider a person who believes in God, but is neither happy nor moral. Imagine a person who receives no solace or comfort from her religious belief, and, instead, is filled with fear and hatred. This person believes her religion is under attack and she must arm herself to defend her freedom. She also believes the end of the world is near, and that she, as a true believer, is fighting a war against all the nonbelievers. As she becomes increasingly agitated and isolated, she eventually decides she must take matters into her own hands to carry out God's plan. So she arms herself and commits mass murder at a Planned Parenthood clinic, killing many innocent women and children before being killed by police.

The question is: How should we judge the meaning of this woman's life? Should we commend her actions by calling them meaningful simply because she believed in God and thought she was carrying out his divine plan? If I were to read about this person in the newspaper, I would view her life as a tragic waste—a waste of both her own life and the lives of the innocent people she murdered. To say that her life was meaningful would imply that it was good, but I don't see how we can commend her life when she was so consumed by hatred, fear, and paranoia that she committed an atrocity.

This reasoning suggests that theism alone is *not* sufficient for meaning. I believe for many people, belief in God is a source of both happiness and moral goodness, and this is why we generally judge the lives of theists favorably, deeming them meaningful. But what this thought experiment shows is that what is actually driving our intuitions about meaning is *not* the theism so much as what the religious belief provides, namely, happiness and a sense of morality. But living a happy, morally decent life is the view of meaning I have been defending all along.

Response to Vitrano

Douglas Groothuis

Study Questions

1. How does Groothuis summarize Vitrano's argument? With what points does he agree? What does he see as the crucial flaw in her argument?
2. What dilemma does Vitrano face according to Groothuis?
3. What irony does Groothuis find in Vitrano's critique of Wolf?
4. How does Groothuis summarize his case against Vitrano?

Professor Vitrano's essay is lucid, well informed, and carefully developed. She works thoroughly through the possibilities of finding meaning without God, rejecting several proposals and settling on her own.

Atheism, as she sees it, has two options for meaning. The *objectivist* account of meaning appeals to values beyond the valuation of any subjects. Someone's life can be meaningful or meaningless according to extra-personal criteria. According to atheism, God is not the source of this meaning. The *subjectivist* account anchors meaning only in the individual subject and eschews objective standards or sources for meaning.

Vitrano's Argument

I take this to be her essential positive argument (with my responses in italics):

1. An atheist account of meaning in life can be either objectivist or subjectivist. *This, indeed, exhausts the alternatives.*

2. The subjectivist account better suits atheism. *I agree since it is difficult to find any objective meaning if there is no objective meaning-maker—that is, God as the source and giver of meaning to his world and to humans.*

3. Meaning for the subjectivist is found in "life satisfaction."

4. The subjectivist account, however, is subject to the charge of justifying *anything* the subject takes as meaningful, even odious philosophies such as Nazism. *I agree with this as well and add that the mass murderer, Ted Bundy, held to such a view. The philosopher Max Stirner took atheism to this nihilistic end as well.*

5. It's not the case that *anything* the subject takes as meaningful can be justified. *I could not agree more.*

6. Because of (4) and (5), subjects should not take as meaningful anything that is hurtful to others. *By so doing, she believes she has offered a justified subjectivist theory of meaning. I quote her in full:*

   > I am willing to grant the happiness of evil and immoral people, but I do not agree that they are living meaningful lives, mainly because I find it implausible to describe a morally depraved life as good or commendable. Thus, to avoid this implication, I suggest including one additional requirement. . . . We can say that a life is meaningful if one is happy, and her happiness does not violate our common sense understanding of what it means to live a morally decent life. I will rely on our ordinary intuitions about morality to determine which acts are impermissible, but the general idea is that your happiness cannot

involve the deliberate infliction of pain and suffering on others, for that would clearly violate our moral norms and our common sense understanding of decency. The upshot is that as long as one's happiness is not morally objectionable, engagement in one's life (regardless of what one chooses to pursue) is sufficient for making that life meaningful. (p. 178)

Vitrano's Dilemma

The argument is clear enough. However, her attempt to rescue her theory by ruling out evil actions is unsuccessful for a simple reason. There is no justification for eliminating cruel actions from a purely subjectivist theory of meaning. "Common sense understanding of decency," as she puts it, counts for nothing. Her own theory disallows it. However, we know intuitively, for example, that *torturing the innocent for pleasure is always wrong*. Yet this principle cannot be binding on everyone everywhere on a *subjectivist* account of meaning. There may be some intersubjective agreement on this principle, but it is not universal if even one subject disagrees. Even if the principle were held universally by all subjects, it would remain merely subjective, having no normative force on *any* subject. If Vitrano's principle must apply to all subjects, then it is precisely *objective*, not merely *subjective*. But this is precisely what she denies.

If any subject finds torturing the innocent for pleasure subjectively meaningful such that it gives "life satisfaction," then that judgment is unimpeachable by anyone else's merely subjective response. Perhaps a short dialogue will help explain.

> Ted: I find tormenting animals quite satisfying.
> Vinny: What?
> Ted: After years of trying to find meaning, I have found that this activity gives me satisfaction.
> Vinny: That is abominable!
> Ted: Why?
> Vinny: You are inflicting unnecessary pain on sentient beings.
> Ted: Duh. I know that. That is why I do it.
> Vinny: No one should do that. Find a legitimate source of meaning, such as volunteering at an animal shelter.
> Ted: That does not give me meaning. I hate animals. Vinny, are you an atheist?
> Vinny: Yes.

Ted: So what is this "legitimate source of meaning" if it is not God's plan for how we should act?

Vinny: No, God is not the standard. However, we cannot allow for pleasures and meaning of your sort!

Ted: Says who?

Vinny: Says any right-minded atheist with a qualified subjectivist account of meaning.

Ted: You are begging the question: If it all comes down to you, the subject, to make meaning, how can you tell me what to do? You would need the kind of objective standard that you have eliminated in principle.

Vinny: I am keeping my dogs away from you, Ted.

Vinny and Vitrano face an irreconcilable dilemma:

A. If Vinny grants Ted's "life satisfaction" as legitimate, then he cannot rule out any behavior, including animal torture; and, thus, he becomes a nihilist.

B. If Vinny denies Ted's "life satisfaction" as illegitimate and wrong, he cannot remain a subjectivist. He must grant either atheistic objectivism or some other form of objectivism.

Vitrano's subjectivist account of meaning fails Vinny. Her theory provides no criterion with which to trump Ted's. Even if Vinny holds his belief strongly and dedicates his life to preventing cruelty to animals, by volunteering for and financially supporting the Humane Society, his judgment has no normative force on Ted's life. It is merely subjective.

There is irony in Vitrano's proviso (6). In addressing Susan Wolf's objectivist nontheistic account of meaning, Vitrano chides Wolf for not having a sure source or standard for objective meaning. Wolf is too fuzzy. Vitrano also takes exception to the examples Wolf gives of meaningful and meaningless pursuits in life. Perhaps a video game has value that Wolf neglects and is not meaningless, as she thinks. In other words, who is to say what is meaningless or meaningful? Wolf is an intellectual, so she favors cognitive activities and achievements. But why should that matter?

Vitrano is hoist by her own petard. If she disallows Wolf any appeal to any objective standard in judging what is meaningful in pursuing happiness, then she, too, is denied an appeal to an objective standard. At least Wolf overtly appeals to the existence of an objective standard even if her account of it is fuzzy. Vitrano denies any objective standard at all, but then illicitly invokes it to censure what some consider "life satisfying" experiences. She cannot have it both ways, as far as I can tell.

Conclusion

Given my evaluation of Vitrano's argument, I can restate my objections simply:

1. A subjectivist account of meaning, the *life satisfaction view*, seems to leads to nihilism, since subjective experiences of meaning exhaust the field of meaning. They are uncorrectable.

2. The attempt to exclude nihilism by restricting what counts as legitimate life satisfaction fails, because there is no basis for making such judgments on a subjectivist view of meaning.

3. If, as Vitrano claims, nihilism is false, her life satisfaction view of meaning is false as well.

4. Therefore, to escape nihilism and find a coherent and cogent sense of meaning, one must look for an objective source and standard of meaning.

I cannot comment in detail on atheistic objectivism here.[1] However, my initial essay argued that traditional monotheism grounds objective meaning in the existence and character of an infinite and personal God. God gives the universe a teleological structure and commends ways of being commensurate with his own character and the nature of creation. Herein one may find a "life satisfaction" with moral meaning, existential significance, a philosophy and psychology of suffering,[2] and divine approval in this life and the next.[3]

Notes

1. See Douglas Groothuis, *Christian Apologetics: A Comprehensive Case for Biblical Faith* (Downers Grove, IL: InterVarsity Press, 2011), 357–60.
2. See Douglas Groothuis, *Walking through Twilight: A Wife's Illness—A Philosopher's Lament* (Downers Grove, IL: InterVarsity Press 2017).
3. See J. P. Moreland, "God and the Meaning of Life," in *Scaling the Secular City* (Grand Rapids, MI: Baker Books, 1987).

Questions for Reflection

1. Some philosophers have argued that for God to give human beings purpose would be condescending or degrading, to treat people as gadgets or even slaves. Could Groothuis respond to such an objection? How?

2. Is Groothuis correct that Vitrano's reliance on objective morality is inconsistent with her subjectivist account of meaning? How might Vitrano respond?
3. What response, if any, could Groothuis make to Vitrano's example of the unhappy murderous theist?
4. Both Groothuis and Vitrano reject the atheistic objectivist account of life's meaning. What reasons might they have for this? Can this view be defended? If so, how?

Essay Suggestions

A. Imagine that you and a group of about fifty other people—men and women—were stranded on a remote island with no hope of rescue in the near future. And suppose that everyone's survival depends upon the cooperative efforts of each person. What's more, since you expect to be there for many years, you are concerned about more than just survival; you are also concerned about *flourishing*—being as happy and well-off as conditions allow. Write an essay in which you list about 10 rules or principles that you believe everyone on the island should follow in order to survive and flourish. Explain why you think these rules are the right ones, and whether or not your rationale comports better with Ruse's relativistic view of ethics or Beckwith's objectivist view.

B. In the short story, "Those Who Walk Away from Omelas," Ursula K. LeGuin weaves a tale about a utopian city called Omelas whose citizens enjoy completely happy, rewarding lives. There's just one catch. The happiness they enjoy mysteriously depends upon the suffering of a child who is kept in a filthy, lonely dungeon beneath the city. Most of the citizens, when they learn about the child's suffering, manage to go on with their lives and put the child out of their minds. Some, however, decide to quietly leave Omelas, never to return. Write a paper in which you explain whether or not you would walk away from Omelas and which moral theory—utilitarianism, the respect for persons ethic, or some other theory—best accounts for your decision. Be sure to explain also why other moral theories do not deal adequately with your decision.

C. Consider the question, "Why be moral?" The question concerns what reasons there are, if any, to accept the dictates of morality (as opposed to other considerations such as self-interest) as binding on our choices and behavior. Write an essay answering this question in light of the debate over God and morality. If God exists, would there be an adequate answer to the question? If so, what is it? If not, why? If God does not exist, can the question still be answered? If so, how?

D. In the Bible, God is portrayed as sometimes commanding people to do things that we would ordinarily see as immoral. For example, God commands the patriarch Abraham to sacrifice his son Isaac as a burnt offering (Gen. 22:1-19). Write an essay arguing that such a command, if true, either is or is not consistent with the divine command theory as developed by Flannagan.

E. Write a paper in which you compare two famous artworks of the same genre (e.g., two paintings or two sculptures). Based upon your considered opinion on whether or not aesthetic qualities like beauty are objective or relative, argue for or against the claim that one artwork is better than the other.

F. Suppose that you and a friend observe a colorful sunset. You remark that the sunset is beautiful. Your friend disagrees. She sincerely says it's ugly. (If you like, you can reverse who says what.) Write a paper in which you argue either that you are both correct (thus defending a form of aesthetic relativism), or that your friend is wrong in her judgment about the sunset and why (thus defending aesthetic objectivism).

G. Write a paper in which you describe the life of a person that you know or someone you have heard of that you are confident leads a meaningful life. Explain what it is about that person's life or about reality (e.g., whether or not God exists or there is life after death) that you believe makes that person's life meaningful. Explain also why you think an alternative view of meaning would not account for the meaningfulness of that life.

For Further Reading

Ethics—Moral Relativism, Normative Ethics, God and Ethics

Beckwith, Francis J., and Gregory Koukl. *Relativism: Feet Firmly Planted in Mid-Air.* Grand Rapids: Baker, 1998.

Budziszewski, J. *Written on the Heart: The Case for Natural Law.* Downers Grove, IL: InterVarsity Press, 1997.

Joyce, Richard. *The Evolution of Morality.* Cambridge, MA: MIT Press, 2007.

Loftin, R. Keith. *God and Morality: Four Views.* Downers Grove, IL: InterVarsity, 2012.

Moser, Paul K., and Thomas L. Carson. *Moral Relativism: A Reader.* Oxford: Oxford University Press, 2000.

Pojman, Louis P., and James Fieser. *Ethics: Discovering Right and Wrong.* 8th ed. Belmont, CA: Wadsworth, 2016.

Shafer-Landau, Russ. *Ethical Theory: An Anthology.* 2nd ed. Malden, MA: Wiley-Blackwell, 2012.

Aesthetics

Cahn, Steven M., and Aaron Meskin, eds. *Aesthetics: A Comprehensive Anthology.* Malden, MA: Blackwell, 2007.

Carroll, Noël. *Philosophy of Art: A Contemporary Introduction.* New York: Routledge, 1999.

Neill, Alex, and Aaron Ridley, eds. *Arguing about Art: Contemporary Philosophical Debates.* 3rd ed. New York: Routledge, 2007.

The Meaning of Life

Seachris, Joshua, ed. *Exploring the Meaning of Life: An Anthology and Guide.* Malden, MA: Wiley-Blackwell, 2012.

Seachris, Joshua, and Stewart Goetz. *God and Meaning: New Essays.* New York: Bloomsbury, 2016.

Wolf, Susan. *Meaning in Life and Why It Matters.* Princeton, NJ: Princeton University Press, 2012.

PART TWO

Problems in Political Philosophy

Introduction to Part Two

Steven B. Cowan

Part Two is concerned with philosophical problems related to the nature and justification of civil government. This is the domain of *political philosophy*, a special branch of value theory. Some of the oldest and most valued philosophical books are devoted to matters of political philosophy. Plato, while seeking to address the question "Why be moral?" in his *Republic*, spends most of its pages discussing the nature, organization, and citizenry of the ideal state. Plato's pupil, Aristotle (384–322 BC), in his *Politics*, argued that humans are by nature social beings, and so naturally join together to form communities and, ultimately, city-states. Thus, human beings are essentially "political animals." The Christian philosopher, St. Augustine (354–430), discusses political philosophy in his massive *City of God*, especially dealing with questions concerning the relation of church and state. And down through the centuries since, many other important philosophers—Aquinas, Machiavelli (1469–1527), John Calvin (1509–1564), Thomas Hobbes (1588–1679), John Locke (1632–1704), Jean-Jacques Rousseau (1712–1778), Karl Marx (1818–1883), etc.—have written treatises on political theory and political issues that have had a significant and lasting impact on society.

There are lots of questions that arise in political philosophy. One concerns the *form of civil government*. There are lots of options:

- Monarchy—rule by one sovereign individual; usually hereditary
- Oligarchy—rule by a small group of "qualified" people. There are different options for who counts as the most qualified:
    - Aristocracy—rule by the nobility (those of elite or noble birth)
    - Timocracy—rule by the honorable or celebrated
    - Plutocracy—rule by the wealthy
    - Technocracy—rule by technical experts or the educated
    - Theocracy—literally "rule by God," but practically rule by a religious elite/priesthood
- Democracy—rule by the majority

There are variations on all the main types of government. Democracy, for example, can be a *pure democracy* in which decisions are made by a simple majority vote of the citizens; or a *representative democracy* in which the citizens elect certain people to represent them in the government (e.g., a parliament or congress); or a *constitutional democracy* (like the United States) in which the will of the majority is constrained by constitutionally guaranteed rights that all citizens enjoy.

As important as it may be, the question of the form of government will not be debated in this volume. There are other issues in political philosophy that are more fundamental and perhaps more relevant in today's world. So, instead, we will explore the following three problems: (1) the justification of civil government, (2) the question of distributive justice, and (3) the ethics of war.

The Justification of Government

Few people, in historical memory, have lived outside the scope or authority of some civil government. Almost everyone has been subject to a king, or a governor, or a tribal council, or a legislative assembly, or a military dictator. But why? Why do we have government in the first place? Of course, there are cases in which one person or a group of people subjugate others against their will, and that explains why *those* people have government—it is forcefully imposed on them. In situations like that, many of us would think that such government is unjustified. Yet, many of the same people would still claim that government per se *is* justified. Most people today (at least in the West) do not live under self-proclaimed dictatorships. We live under government that is, in some sense, *chosen* by us. We think that government—*our* government— has legitimate authority. But what is the basis of that authority? What makes the government's authority legitimate? The question is all the more pressing because all of us admit, as noted above, that some government authority is *il*legitimate.

In previous centuries, when monarchy was the most common form of government, some defenders of monarchy would have justified it by appeal to *the divine right of kings*. Note the words of the New Testament book of Romans:

> Every person is to be in subjection to the governing authorities. For there is no authority except from God, and those which exist are established by God. Therefore whoever resists authority has opposed the ordinance of God; and they who have opposed will receive condemnation upon themselves. (Rom. 13:1-2, NASB)

Since the kings in these earlier centuries were the authorities "which exist," their rule had the highest endorsement possible: God! Who could argue with that?

Nobody today accepts the divine right of kings. Much more common today is the *social contract theory* devised initially by Thomas Hobbes (1588–1679) and further developed by John Locke (1632–1704). The latter's version of the theory was co-opted by Thomas Jefferson (1743–1826) in his drafting of the American *Declaration of Independence*, the most well-known portion of which reads:

> We hold these truths to be self-evident, that all men are created equal, that they are endowed by their Creator with certain unalienable rights, that among these are life, liberty and the pursuit of happiness. That to secure these rights, governments are instituted among men, deriving their just powers from the consent of the governed.

The last sentence of this quote explains where, on the social contract theory, government gets its legitimate authority: *from the consent of the governed*. That same sentence tells us why people would (or should) consent to government: *to secure their God-given natural rights*, the rights mentioned in the first sentence.

Many interpreters of Locke's theory believe that it justifies, at best, a *minimal state*. This means a small government whose sole responsibility is to secure (make safe, protect) our natural rights, especially our right to liberty. This minimal state perspective is called *libertarianism* (not to be confused with the metaphysical view on free will that goes by the same name—see *Problems in Epistemology and Metaphysics*, Chapter 9). However, some philosophers who accept something like the social contract theory—or who otherwise believe that government can have legitimate authority—think that the state can and should have more power than the minimal state view allows. This view, called *welfare liberalism* (or just liberalism), allows that government can exercise power (including raising and redistributing taxes) to promote the common good of all citizens and the well-being of the society as a whole.

Yet other philosophers argue that government authority can never be legitimate. This view is called *anarchism*. The anarchist believes that there should be no civil government, that government is, in fact, immoral. Why? Well, the essence of government is *coercive force*—government, whether minimal or maximal, is given (or takes) a monopoly on the use of force in society, and uses that force to *enforce* its will, its laws, on the people. And this is true whether the people consent to the laws or not. The anarchist holds that this monopoly on coercive force is both dangerous and unfair.

Roderick Long (Auburn University) makes the case for anarchism in Chapter 6. The heart of Long's case is his challenge to the assumption that the services government provides—laws, a justice system, a military, aid to the poor, etc.—are best provided by a civil government with a monopoly on coercive force. He argues that private contractors and organizations can provide all of these services at least as well as government and without the danger of the government's misuse of its monopoly power. Moreover, he challenges the notion that government is based on consent. Few people explicitly consent to government at all, and some actually withhold consent—what gives government legitimate authority over them? Long also argues that government tends to favor the interests of the wealthy at the expense of the less fortunate, while a free market under anarchism creates a much more even playing field.

Alex Tuckness (Iowa State University) takes up the cause of civil government. Appealing to the arguments of John Locke and the twentieth-century libertarian Robert Nozick (1938–2002), he argues that the insecurities of the state of nature justify at least a minimal state. He is skeptical of the anarchist confidence in private contractors to protect our basic natural rights. Further, Tuckness claims that there are important public goods (e.g., education) that should be available to people regardless of their ability to pay. These, along with other social benefits, justify a nonminimal state. Additionally, even if one is convinced that government per se is illegitimate, Tuckness argues that one should agree that we need government if for no other reason than that there are *other* governments in the world that would pose a threat to an anarchist society.

Distributive Justice

Consider Joe, a hardworking blue-collar guy who struggles to make a living to provide for his family. Let's say that his employer pays him $1,000 per week. Friday comes and Joe gets his paycheck for $700. What gives? Well, *Joe* gives . . . taxes! No doubt some of the money the government takes in taxes from Joe goes to pay for things that benefit Joe: the army and navy, the local police and fire departments, the roads that Joe uses to drive from home to his workplace, the postal service, and so on. Yet, a significant amount of the taxes collected does not benefit Joe. Some of that money is transferred to other citizens for their personal use, and some of it is transferred to pay for things that Joe believes to be immoral.

Consider Cecille, a young single mother whose husband has deserted her. Cecille got married and got pregnant right out of high school. She has few marketable skills. The only job she can get is stocking shelves at a local supermarket, but to keep that job she has to pay for childcare for her two-year-old son, and the job barely pays enough to put food on the table and keep the lights on. Some of Joe's tax money pays for Cecille's childcare and some of it is given directly to her in the form of food stamps.

Now consider Roger. He is a doctor who performs abortions at the local Planned Parenthood facility. Some of Joe's tax money goes to keep the lights on at that facility so that Roger can provide his services to women who have an unplanned and unwanted pregnancy.

Joe thinks that he should not have to help pay for Cecille's needs and for Roger's services. Those people didn't earn the money, he did. And Joe is staunchly pro-life; he believes that abortion (except when the mother's life is in real jeopardy) is morally wrong. So he thinks that some of his money is being used to support evil. What's more, about half of that $300 that the government takes from Joe's paycheck would be just enough for Joe to get his daughter into a nearby private school so that she would not have to attend the second-rate public school in Joe's neighborhood.

Of course, on the other side of the equation, we should consider that without Joe's (and every other taxpayer's) money, Cecille would have trouble buying enough food for her and her son, and she would likely have to quit her job due to a lack of childcare. And, without Roger's services, many desperate women would be burdened with unwanted pregnancies.

This case involving Joe, Cecille, and Roger, underscores the problem of *distributive justice*. Broadly, the question here is: What is a just distribution of the wealth produced within a society? And closely related is the question: What role, if any, does the government have in establishing and maintaining a just distribution of wealth? As with every philosophical problem, there are multiple viewpoints. First, there is *socialism*, the view that a just distribution of wealth is a completely equal distribution of wealth. This is based on the socialist principle that equity of persons is the highest social ideal. Thus, the socialist advocates that government redistributes wealth to achieve the economic equality of all citizens. Second is *welfare liberalism,* which sees a just distribution of wealth as one that balances individual liberty with the welfare of all citizens. Thus, the welfare liberal advocates *some* redistribution of wealth to ensure that everyone has enough to meet their basic needs. Lastly, *libertarianism* claims that a just distribution of wealth is whatever distribution results from a free and fair market. Since personal liberty is the highest social ideal, there should be no government redistribution of wealth.

Chapter 7 begins with Jon Mandle (University at Albany-SUNY) advocating the cause of Cecille by defending a welfare liberal approach to distributive justice (he calls it "egalitarianism"). Mandle notes that libertarian theories of distributive justice such as Nozick's presuppose a particular view of property rights and then ask what, if any, government "redistribution" of wealth would be morally justifiable. As Mandle sees it, the correct approach to distributive justice is to back up a step and ask what *system of property rights* itself would be more just. In contrast to a libertarian system, he understands a *progressive* system of property rights as one that would not see the money given to Cecille (and perhaps Roger) as a redistribution at all, but as *her property*. Appealing to the ideas of John Rawls (1921–2002) and other liberal philosophers, Mandle then argues that any justifiable system of property rights must protect the core needs and interests of every person in society. The progressive system of property rights succeeds in this regard, the libertarian system does not.

The libertarian view of distributive justice is defended by Jan Narveson (University of Waterloo). He thinks it misleading to speak of the *re*distribution of wealth. Such language would suggest absurdly that when a person creates, through his own labor and ingenuity, some valuable commodity, his creation is a "distribution." With this in mind, the real question in the debate has to do with "the moral status of the creation of what has economic value." Does the government have the right to forcibly take some of what another person has created and give it to others? Alternatively, does the government have the right to "redistribute" the wealth acquired by someone through a fair and voluntary exchange with others? Narveson thinks the answer to these questions is *no*. There is, he argues, a natural and strong connection between productive effort and possession of the results. The call for redistribution wrongly assumes that there is no such connection or that the wealth thus acquired was acquired unjustly. As for the poor and the need for "public goods" like education and roads, such things are best left to voluntary private institutions.

The Ethics of War

Soldiering has been called "the second oldest profession."[1] This is a figurative way of recognizing that war has been a constant reality among human beings. Why there has been war is a question subject to considerable debate, and no doubt there are multiple causes: greed, envy, revenge, desperate need for resources, etc. Whatever the cause, war is a horrible thing. It is the source of untold destruction, waste, death, and human anguish. This immediately leads us to the ethical question: Can war ever be morally justified? Or, since it is generally left to civil governments to wage war, the question may be rephrased in terms of political philosophy: When, if ever, may the government justly wage war?

Probably no one today gives the *amoralist* answer: *Anytime it pleases for any reason it pleases*. This position assumes that the government is not constrained by moral considerations. Such a position is, of course, highly implausible and would likely require a defense of some extreme form of moral relativism (see Chapter 11).

Many people do hold a view at the opposite end of the moral spectrum, however. *Pacifism*, as usually understood, is the view that *war is never morally justified*. This position is often grounded in a belief that violence in general is always immoral, even in self-defense. Some pacifists may grant that *some* violence may be justified, but hold that the level of violence entailed by war far exceeds what may be justifiable in other circumstances. Pacifism is often (but not always) based on religious principles such as the teachings of Jesus to "turn the other cheek." But whether it is religiously based or not, pacifists commonly argue that the best way to respond to military aggression is to utilize forms of nonviolent resistance. Violence, they believe, only begets more violence.

Striving to capture a middle ground between amoralism and pacifism is the *just war theory*. According to its advocates, *the government may sometimes wage war under specified conditions*. Chief among these conditions is that there must be a just cause for going to war. Traditionally, just war theorists contend that the only just cause is self-defense against actual or impending foreign aggression. There are also restrictions on the kinds of weapons that may be used and what people may be intentionally targeted.

In Chapter 8, Andrew Alexandra (University of Melbourne) defends what we might call *practical pacifism*. He does not argue that war is *intrinsically* wrong as the traditional pacifist would, but, rather, that war is never the best political policy since there are better, nonviolent ways of responding to military aggression. He begins by defending, among others, the moral principle that violence in general is only justifiable if it's the only feasible way to avoid a greater evil. Applied to the question of war, it too is justifiable only if it's the only feasible way for a government to avoid a greater evil. Alexandra argues, however, that war is *not* the only feasible way to avoid a greater evil. He cites examples of cases in which nonviolent civil resistance has been effective against violent aggression. Moreover, he argues that the normal practice of nations preparing and arming for war actually makes a nation less secure: by causing other nations to engage in an arms race in response to what they see as a threat, and by creating powerful military establishments that pose an internal threat of political usurpation.

Nathan Cartagena (Baylor University) makes a case for the just war theory. After clarifying precisely the relevant senses of the terms "war" and "government," Cartagena presents two case studies that illustrate legitimate reasons why government may sometimes wage war. The first is the Austro-Hungarian attack on Serbia that initiated the First World War. The second is the NATO intervention in Bosnia to stop the Serbian genocide of Muslims and

Croats. These examples suggest that governments may justly wage war: (1) in response to unjust foreign aggression against its own nation, and (2) to stop or prevent egregious injustices elsewhere. Cartagena then explains in detail the criteria that must be met for a war to be just under three headings. First, the *jus ad bellum* (criteria for justly *going to* war), which includes the just causes noted above, right intention, and others. Second, the *jus in bello* (criteria for just conduct *during* war) such as noncombatant immunity and proportionality. Finally, the *jus post bellum* (criteria for justice *after* war) which consists in actualizing the right intention for war.

Note

1 The title of *oldest* profession has always gone to prostitution.

6

Do We Need Government?

We Do Not Need Government

Roderick T. Long

Study Questions

1. What are the two special privileges that government claims for itself?
2. What three arguments are given for the idea that government is based on the consent of the governed? How does Long respond to these arguments?
3. According to Long, what moral problems are perpetrated or created by government?
4. How, according to Long, does anarchism alleviate the problems associated with capitalism?
5. What problems does Long point out with Hobbes's defense of government? Why is Long not moved by the example of Somalian anarchy?
6. What were Locke's reasons for preferring government over anarchy? How does Long respond?
7. Why does Nozick think that government is inevitable? What is his "risk" argument? Why does Long think that Nozick's arguments fail?
8. Why is Long not worried about the poor under anarchy?

Governments provide us with many useful services, including streets, schools, post offices—the list goes on and on. Most distinctively, governments provide laws and regulations to protect people's rights and interests, and to enable people to coordinate their plans; a justice system to adjudicate disputes, secure compliance, and restrain wrongdoers; and a military defense to ward off invaders. What kind of crazy person would want to abolish government?

Well, the mere fact that, under present circumstances, a given institution provides valuable services is no proof that it is the best institution to provide them. After all, in past centuries Roman emperors and feudal lords provided some of those services, but that's no argument for going back to having Roman emperors or feudal lords. If you're unjustly incarcerated in a prison camp, the guards will probably do you the admittedly desirable service of bringing you daily meals, but you might well prefer to get out of the prison camp and make other arrangements for your sustenance.

A government is a special kind of institution, distinguished from other institutions by two special privileges it claims for itself. (I'm using "government" here to mean the institution of the state. The term is also sometimes used more narrowly, like "administration" or "regime," to mean whichever political group is currently in charge of the state, but that's not how I'm using it here.) First, governments claim a *monopoly power* over a given territory (or, sometimes, a given population). That is, they not only provide the aforementioned services, but they also forbid competitors to offer the same services within that territory (or to that population). A government may, admittedly, permit competitors to offer alternatives to *some* of its services, such as schools or roads (though it typically reserves the right to regulate those alternatives quite strictly); but in its most central operations—legislation, courts, police, armed forces—it allows very little competition. To be sure, there are private arbitrators, private security guards, and the like; but in any conflict with the state's versions of those services, the private providers are required to yield.

The relationship between government officials and private citizens is thus one of a fundamental *inequality of power*. A police officer has the right to arrest you if he thinks you've committed a crime; you don't have a right to arrest a police officer if you think he's committed a crime. A judge can issue a warrant authorizing people to break into your house; you can't issue a warrant authorizing people to break into the judge's house. (Yes, under a democratic government you can vote for actions against government officials, but this is hardly a comparable degree of power; imagine how powerless a police officer would feel if he had to get the consent of millions of other people before arresting somebody?)

Second, unlike ordinary service providers, governments do not obtain their revenue through voluntary contracts with their customers; instead, the government simply *takes* your money, without permission, in the form of "taxes" (something governments call "theft" when someone else does it), and then gives you in return whatever bundle of services it decides you should have. Maybe a majority of voters consented to those taxes and that bundle, but that's little comfort to any minority who may have opposed these measures. A government, then, claims for itself and its agents an exemption from the ordinary moral rules that the rest of us are expected to obey.

Is Government Based on Consent?

It is sometimes argued that the unequal privileges that define a government's relation to its citizens are ones that those citizens have really consented to. One argument, going back to Plato,[1] is that by continuing to reside within the territory of a government and accepting the benefit of its protection, one has consented to obey its laws. But the argument is dubious. If we had *already established* that the government's claim of authority over its supposed territory is legitimate, then it might make sense to say that by staying in the territory, you implicitly agree to be bound by its laws, just as in visiting someone's house you implicitly agree to the house rules ("no smoking," say). But the legitimacy of the government's authority over that territory is what the argument is trying to *establish*, so it would be circular to start off simply assuming it. As for accepting benefits, if in most cases the state *forbids* us to seek those benefits from competing providers, how much gratitude can it really demand for the benefits it provides us?

Another argument one sometimes hears is that citizens consent to the government's actions by *voting*. But at most, only those in the majority count as having consented; what about the minority who were outvoted? If one says they, too, have consented simply by participating in the voting system, what do they have to do in order *not* to consent? After all, if they don't vote at all, they're likely to be told that as nonvoters they have no right to complain! Consent isn't worth much if nothing you do counts as non-consent.[2] In any case, citizens often vote simply in self-defense, to prevent other voters from imposing on them some candidate or policy they detest; thus they vote for the option they find least objectionable, but might well prefer not to have to choose among *those* options at all.[3] And given the infinitesimal impact that any one vote has on the final outcome, voters seldom have much incentive to become informed or active on the issues (unlike special-interest lobbyists, who have more individual impact on the political process, and so much greater incentive to become informed and active). Economist David Friedman writes:

> You can compare 1968 Fords, Chryslers, and Volkswagens, but nobody will ever be able to compare the Nixon administration of 1968 with the Humphrey and Wallace administrations of the same year. It is as if we had only Fords from 1920 to 1928, Chryslers from 1928 to 1936, and then had

to decide what firm would make a better car for the next four years. . . . Imagine buying cars the way we buy governments. Ten thousand people would get together and agree to vote, each for the car he preferred. Whichever car won, each of the ten thousand would have to buy it. It would not pay any of us to make any serious effort to find out which car was best; whatever I decide, my car is being picked for me by the other members of the group.[4]

It's sometimes pointed out that since rulers are generally outnumbered by those they rule, a government's power must rest on popular acquiescence rather than greater coercive might.[5] Does this mean that government necessarily rests on the consent of the governed? Not at all. Even if a large minority of people would like to defy the government, so long as the majority obeys and supports that government, the minority may be afraid to resist. For that matter, even if those who'd like to resist are a *majority*, each individual in that majority may be afraid to make the first move, not knowing whether enough others will follow suit.

Moral Problems with Government

Moreover, even if it were true that people do generally consent to government, we can still ask whether they *should*. From a *deontological* ethical standpoint (one that takes the standard of morally right action to be conformity with inherently binding principles, such as respect for persons as ends in themselves), allowing one group of people, calling itself the government, to claim monopoly privileges for themselves that are denied to ordinary people seems suspect. And from a *consequentialist* ethical standpoint (one that takes the standard of morally right action to be good consequences), monopolies are objectionable because they are notoriously beset by both incentival and informational perversities. When a firm's customers are forbidden to switch to a competitor, the firm's managers have little incentive to keep prices low or quality high, or to refrain from abusing power; that's monopoly's *incentival* perversity. And even if the firm's managers are well-meaning, without competition it's hard for them to get reliable feedback on the quality of their services; that's monopoly's *informational* perversity.

Nor are these perversities minor matters of inefficiency. We're all familiar with devastating stories about abusive behavior by police officers, often racially motivated; if only communities victimized by police could fire their police departments and sign up with a competitor! Still more alarmingly, political scientist R. J. Rummel (1932–2014) estimates that during the last century, governments murdered 262 million (innocent, noncombatant) people—a vastly greater number than victims of ordinary homicide.[6] When institutions make abuse of power easier, the results can be horrific. People sometimes say that only a hopeless optimist about human nature could favor a society without government; but, in fact, it's precisely skepticism about humans' ability to be trusted with power that tells in favor of *anarchy*—which means not the absence of *order* or the absence of *rules*, but the absence of *government* (and, more broadly, any form of coercive domination).

Less dramatic than mass murder, but still devastating, is the impact that governments have on the economic lives of their citizens. Even in democracies, as noted earlier, ordinary people seldom have the kind of influence over the political process that special interests have; hence it's no surprise that even under the least objectionable governments, economic rewards tend to be skewed toward an influential elite.

The economic form that prevails in most modern societies is *capitalism*. Capitalism is sometimes equated with private property and free-market competition, but strictly speaking it means something much more specific: namely, the concentration of ownership of the means of production (land, factories, capital equipment, intellectual property) in a small number of hands—the capitalist class—leaving the majority no means of survival except by performing wage labor for the capitalists.

Now within the anarchist movement, there are many who assume that private property and free-market competition inevitably *lead* to capitalism. Some of these anarchists, rejecting capitalism as an oppressive system of domination, are thereby led to view free markets with hostility; others, embracing free markets as a realm of individual choice, are thereby led to embrace capitalism as well. But there is a third tradition in anarchism, one whose viewpoint is represented by the present essay, according to which free markets and capitalism are *at odds*, so that the best way to combat capitalism is to promote free markets. (Thus the third group has more affinity with the first two groups than the latter have with each other.)

When one person or firm discovers a profitable technique, it gives other people or firms an incentive to imitate that success; hence, so long as competition is not impeded, the first firm cannot reap high profits for long, as competitors will bid prices down. Hence, vast concentrations and inequalities of wealth tend to be *prevented* and/or *eroded* by market competition. The capitalist class did not gain its position by free-market means, nor does it maintain it by such means; careful analysis reveals in nearly every case the role of government in stifling competition to prop up a wealthy elite with bailouts, subsidies, enclosure, eminent domain, and other forms of corporate welfare—while bureaucratic requirements such as licensure, zoning, and minimum wage laws make entrepreneurship prohibitively costly for the least affluent.[7]

In the United States, most of the land west of the Mississippi is owned either by state, federal, and local governments or by favored private firms to whom governments granted rights to land they had never homesteaded by occupying it or laboring on it; if you want to see the government creating artificial scarcity, look no further. And it's no accident that governments behave this way; it's their nature to respond to concentrated interests at the expense of dispersed ones.

It's sometimes said that domination of the economy by a small number of large firms is only to be expected in a free market, because larger companies are more efficient. But while increased size brings certain efficiencies, it brings inefficiencies as well, since larger firms, having their internal operations more insulated from market feedback, exhibit some of the perversities of socialist central planning. At a certain point the inefficiencies ("diseconomies of scale") tend to outweigh the efficiencies ("economies of scale"), which would put a natural stop to increased firm size, were it not for government interventions that enable firms to reap the benefits of increased size while passing the costs along to the public (as when government funding of highways forces taxpayers to shoulder part of the shipping costs of big-box stores; long-distance trucking is responsible for the lion's share of wear and tear to the highway infrastructure, but shipping companies do not bear a similar proportion of the tax burden).

In addition to empowering the rich at the expense of the poor, governments also empower the intolerant at the expense of the tolerant. For most intolerant people, intolerance is a luxury good; they may favor repressive policies toward religious and sexual minorities or nonviolent drug users, for example, but in most cases they're not going to be willing to pay extra for the enforcement of such laws. However, when all that the intolerant people have to do to enact their favored policies is to pull a lever in a voting booth, rather than pay a hefty extra monthly premium to have private security providers snooping on their neighbors, one can expect a higher amount of intolerant legislation.

Hobbes's Defense of Government

For philosophers, the most famous defense of government is by the seventeenth-century philosopher Thomas Hobbes, in his book *Leviathan*.[8] Hobbes argued that the only reason it's ever rational to trust other people to behave cooperatively toward you is if either (a) they've proven themselves trustworthy in the past, or (b) you know they'll be punished by the government if they don't behave cooperatively. If there were no government, then (b) would not apply, and you'd be left with (a). But given (a), you have no reason to cooperate with me unless I cooperate first, and I likewise have no reason to cooperate with you unless you cooperate first; hence, even if everyone wants to be cooperative, it's not rational for anyone to make the *first move* toward cooperation, and so unless there's a government, people will be unable to cooperate, and social chaos will result.

The most obvious problem with this argument is that establishing a government is itself a project that requires cooperation; so, if cooperation were impossible without government already on the scene, governments could never have arisen in the first place—yet here they are. Moreover, contra Hobbes, contemporary work in game theory suggests that making the first move toward cooperation is more likely to be beneficial than harmful, whether or not government is present.[9] An updated version of Hobbes's argument suggests that social cooperation is a *public good*—that is, a good there's no way to exclude people from using, even if they haven't contributed to producing or maintaining it—and that the consequent incentive to undercontribute can be corrected only by having government *force* people to contribute. This may sound convincing in theory; but in fact, so-called public goods have regularly been provided throughout history with little or no top-down compulsion.[10] Those who stand to benefit from the provision of these goods generally have a greater incentive to figure out noncoercive strategies for funding them than do ivory-tower theorists loftily declaring such funding impossible.

Theories like Hobbes's seem to fall under the spell of thinking of government as some kind of external force *constraining* society to be orderly and cooperative.[11] But the existence of government *consists* in social interaction. It is human cooperation that makes government possible, not vice versa. Recall the earlier point that since the ruled outnumber their rulers, no government can operate without popular acquiescence; this itself shows that government presupposes cooperation rather than being its prerequisite.[12]

Hobbesian-minded critics of anarchism nowadays often point to the undesirable living conditions in stateless Somalia as evidence that life without government is violent and chaotic. But as bad as conditions in Somalia during its period without government may have been, empirical research shows that conditions were *even worse* in Somalia during the period that it had a government, and likewise have been even worse in neighboring states similar to Somalia but with governments.[13] There's room for debate on what the chief causes of Somalia's difficulties have been, but anarchy does not seem to be the culprit; on the contrary, anarchy seems to have made things somewhat better. Indeed, economist Peter Leeson has argued that whatever one may think of the prospects for anarchist reform in the most economically developed countries, anarchy would be an unambiguous improvement for most third-world countries, given their history of extreme governmental corruption.[14]

Locke's Defense of Government

Among philosophers, the second most famous defense of government is probably that of Hobbes's younger contemporary, John Locke, in his *Second Treatise of Government*.[15] Locke was more optimistic about life without government than Hobbes was; he figured that most people would manage to cooperate with one another most of the time. Nevertheless, he thought government was necessary in order to provide a known and settled body of law with adequate powers of enforcement; and he also thought that requiring individuals to delegate their right of private reprisal to a central authority was the only way to avoid the bias involved in allowing people to be the judges in their own cases.

Unfortunately for this argument, there now exists a massive literature on how private, bottom-up systems of law and dispute resolution can function, and historically have functioned, quite reliably, either without government or in spite of government, and have succeeded in providing uniform, predictable standards and adequate incentives for compliance.[16] Indeed, in a number of cases these private legal systems were developed precisely because those in charge of the prevailing governmental systems had failed (owing to lack of incentive, given their monopoly status) to provide sufficient uniformity and predictability. Similar proposals have been offered for private military defense,[17] sometimes coupled with strategies for mass civil disobedience in case of invasion.[18] And certainly the anarchist militias in the Spanish Civil War seem to have been quite militarily effective, despite their rejection of traditional military hierarchy and deference.[19] (Admittedly, the anarchists *lost* that particular conflict, but the traditionally organized government military lost, too.)

As for the worry about anarchy requiring people to be judges in their own cases, Locke seems to have fallen into a *fallacy of composition* here—that is, the kind of mistake one would make if one were to infer from the premise "every person has someone who is his father," to the conclusion "there is someone who is the father of every person." Locke's analogous mistake is inferring from "everyone needs to submit their disputes to a neutral arbitration institution," to "there needs to be a (single, monopolistic) neutral arbitration institution to which everyone submits their disputes." Nothing in Locke's concern about bias rules out the possibility of competing arbitration institutions; on the contrary, one had *better* have competing arbitration institutions, since otherwise the single monopoly institution will always be a judge in its own case, should any disputes arise between private individuals and *it*.

Locke favors a constitutional government of divided powers, and hopes that they will check and balance each other. This is certainly an improvement over

Hobbes, who thought all governmental decision making should be maximally unified, in a single person if possible. But when the number of branches in a Lockean government is fixed by law, there is little one can do if the branches start colluding with each other. One might think of anarchism as improving on Locke in the same way that Locke improves on Hobbes: under anarchy, there is *free entry* into the checks-and-balances industry, so that if existing agencies start colluding, a new agency can form (without permission from the old ones) and constrain it from without, ideally by attracting customers away.[20]

Nozick's Defense of Government

Another famous defense of government is that of the twentieth-century American libertarian philosopher Robert Nozick, in his book, *Anarchy, State, and Utopia*.[21] Nozick argues as follows: if there are multiple competing security agencies, they will sometimes come into conflict; and if they do, they will resolve their disputes either through violence or through arbitration. If the agencies are equally matched, they will end up carving out distinct turfs and will become territorial monopolies; if they are not equally matched, the winner will wipe out or absorb the loser and become a territorial monopoly. If they, instead, resolve their disputes through arbitration, then the ongoing networks of arbitration agreements among agencies will come to constitute a single legal system for the whole area, and thus will likewise become a territorial monopoly. Hence, government is inevitable. Moreover, a security agency's developing into a territorial monopoly is also morally permissible, since an agency has the right to protect its customers by banning other agencies whose enforcement procedures might put its own customers at risk.

Is Nozick right? Well, to begin with, competing security providers seem likely to choose arbitration over violence in most instances, because violence is the more expensive option, and competing firms—unlike governments—lack the ability to prevent their customers from switching to a cheaper competitor. (Since security firms are non-territorial, one can switch to a different one just like switching to a different phone service provider, without the expense and difficulty of having to leave the territory; it is governments' captive customer base that makes them able to indulge their preferences for violence—though even rival governments cooperate far more often than Hobbesian arguments would seem to predict.) And the development of arbitration agreements among different agencies does seem to make possible the development of something like a shared legal framework.

But does that network of security agencies constitute a territorial monopoly? Only if it forbids free entry by newcomer firms. And would it be able to forbid such entry? Current members of the network might try to form a cartel to exclude newcomers; but cartels are notoriously unstable without government force to back them up—since while members of the cartel have a *collective* incentive to maintain the cartel, each has an *individual* incentive to break it in order to reap the economic benefit of (temporarily) exclusive trade with the newcomer.[22] As for Nozick's risk argument, it's hard to see how one agency could be justified in banning its competitors just because their procedures *might* be risky; surely a higher standard of proof is requisite.

What about the Poor?

Many on the left look to government as a protector of the poor and a bulwark against corporate interests, and see those on the right, with their free-market rhetoric, as attempting to dismantle the one institution that best safeguards the less affluent. (Rhetoric aside, the idea that most on the right have any actual interest in decreasing government intrusiveness and empowering markets—as opposed to further empowering a specific wealthy subset of market actors—is hard to square with the actual behavior of right-wing administrations.) But as we've seen, the wealthy are the chief beneficiaries of government intervention, just as the poor would be the chief beneficiaries of government's abolition. Historically, the whole regulatory state apparatus touted as protecting the poor against the rich, and workers against employers, was actually advocated and lobbied for by the corporate elite who understood that these regulations would at last hand them the kind of cartelized economy they'd been unable to achieve without government intervention.[23] To be sure, government welfare programs are currently indispensable for many people; but governments historically *made* these programs indispensable by driving out of business a thriving ecology of mutual-aid networks among the less affluent.[24]

Some may worry that in a world where security provision is a service for which customers must pay, those without means will be left without legal protection. But first, with government no longer around to prop up capital concentration and massive wealth inequality, far fewer people would be without means. And second, there would certainly be firms that offered security services for free to indigent clients. How do we know? Because there *already* are thousands of public-interest organizations offering pro bono legal services—organizations that depend in large part on charitable contributions. If such organizations can find funding even under present circumstances, how much more funding would be available in the more egalitarian and prosperous society that the abolition of government would bring?

Conclusion

In 1792, Thomas Paine (1737–1809)—drawing on his own experience in the American colonies during the Revolution, when there were "no established forms of government," and yet "order and harmony were preserved as inviolate as in any country in Europe"—observed that most of the "order which reigns among mankind" is "not the effect of government," but, rather, "has its origin in the principles of society and the natural constitution of man," and so not only "existed prior to government," but "would exist if the formality of government was abolished."

> In fine, society performs for itself almost everything which is ascribed to government. . . . Formal government makes but a small part of civilised life; and when even the best that human wisdom can devise is established, it is a thing more in name and idea than in fact. It is to the great and fundamental principles of society and civilization—to the common usage universally consented to, and mutually and reciprocally maintained—to the unceasing circulation of interest, which, passing through its million channels, invigorates the whole mass of civilised man—it is to these things, infinitely more than to anything which even the best instituted government can perform, that the safety and prosperity of the individual and of the whole depends.[25]

Paine didn't draw the conclusion that government should be abolished; but he should have, since he knew not only how unnecessary government is but also how dangerous it is. (It was Paine, after all, who cynically observed that "taxes were not raised to carry on wars," but rather "wars were raised to carry on taxes.")[26] Government doesn't create social cooperation; on the contrary, it's a parasite on social cooperation. *We* create social cooperation—you, and I, and our neighbors, and our neighbors' neighbors, as well as people on the internet ten thousand miles away, every day—without government compulsion, often in spite of government compulsion. Government couldn't exist unless we were cooperating, anarchically. Government couldn't fund anything unless we were producing, anarchically, the wealth it then expropriates as taxes.

The British anarchist Colin Ward (1924–2010) once described anarchy as "a mode of human organisation" that "operates side by side with, and in spite of, the dominant authoritarian trends of our society," so that "an anarchist society, a society which organises itself without authority, is always in existence, like a seed beneath the snow," waiting for us to uncover it.[27] Why not grab a shovel?

Notes

1. Plato, *Crito*, 53–57.
2. Herbert Spencer, *Social Statics: Or, The Conditions Essential to Happiness Specified, and the First of Them Developed* (London: John Chapman, 1851), 211–12.
3. Lysander Spooner, *No Treason No. VI: The Constitution of No Authority* (Boston: Lysander Spooner. 1870).
4. David Friedman, *The Machinery of Freedom: Guide to a Radical Capitalism*, 2nd ed. (LaSalle: Open Court, 1989), 131–32.
5. David Hume, "Of the First Principles of Government," in *Essays: Moral, Political, and Literary* (Indianapolis: Liberty Fund, 1985), 32–36; cf. Étienne de la Boétie, *The Politics of Obedience: The Discourse of Voluntary Servitude*, trans. Harry Kurz (Montreal: Black Rose, 2003); and William Godwin, *An Enquiry Concerning Political Justice* (Oxford: Oxford University Press, 2013).
6. R. J. Rummel, *Death by Government: Genocide and Mass Murder Since 1900* (New Brunswick, NJ: Transaction Publishers, 1997).
7. For the many ways in which government interference with the market props up capitalism, empowering the rich while keeping the poor in poverty, see Kevin A. Carson, *Studies in Mutualist Political Economy* (North Charleston, SC: BookSurge, 2007); *Organization Theory: A Libertarian Perspective* (North Charleston, SC: BookSurge, 2008); *The Homebrew Industrial Revolution: A Low-Overhead Manifesto* (North Charleston, SC: BookSurge, 2010); *The Desktop Regulatory State: The Countervailing Power of Individuals and Networks* (Auburn, AL: Center for a Stateless Society, 2016); Gary Chartier, *The Conscience of an Anarchist: Why It's Time to Say Good-Bye to the State and Build a Free Society* (Baltimore, MD: Cobden Press, 2011); Gary Chartier and Charles W. Johnson, eds., *Markets Not Capitalism: Individualist Anarchism Against Bosses, Inequality, Corporate Power, and Structural Poverty* (London: Minor Compositions, 2011); Roderick T. Long, "Left-Libertarianism, Market Anarchism, Class Conflict and Historical Theories of Distributive Justice," *Griffith Law Review*, 21:2 (2012): 413–31; Mary J. Ruwart, *Healing Our World: The Compassion of Libertarianism*, 4th ed. (Kalamazoo, MI: SunStar Press, 2015); and James Tuttle, ed., *Free Markets & Capitalism? Do Free Markets Always Produce a Corporate Economy?* (Auburn, AL: Center for a Stateless Society, 2016).
8. Thomas Hobbes, *Leviathan*, ed. C. B. Macpherson (London: Penguin, 1985).
9. Robert Axelrod, *The Evolution of Cooperation* (New York: Basic Books, 1984).
10. Tyler Cowen, ed., *Public Goods and Market Failures: A Critical Examination* (New Brunswick, NJ: Transaction Publishers, 1992); Elinor Ostrom, *Governing the Commons: The Evolution of Institutions for Collective Action* (Cambridge:

Cambridge University Press, 1990); and David T. Beito, Peter Gordon, and Alexander Tabarrok, eds., *The Voluntary City: Choice, Community, and Civil Society* (Oakland, CA: Independent Institute, 2009); cf. David Schmidtz, *The Limits of Government: An Essay on the Public Goods Argument* (Boulder, CO: Westview Press, 1991).

11 Roderick T. Long, "Rule-Following, Praxeology, and Anarchy," *New Perspectives on Political Economy,* 2:1 (2006): 36–46; and "Market Anarchism as Constitutionalism," in *Anarchism/Minarchism: Is a Government Part of a Free Country?*, eds. Roderick T. Long and Tibor R. Machan (New York: Routledge, 2016), 133–54.

12 Godwin, *Enquiry*, 65.

13 Benjamin Powell, Ryan Ford, and Alex Nowrasteh, "Somalia After State Collapse: Chaos or Improvement?" *Journal of Economic Behavior and Organization,* 67 (2008): 657–70; Peter T. Leeson, *Anarchy Unbound: Why Self-Governance Works Better Than You Think* (Cambridge: Cambridge University Press, 2014).

14 Leeson, *Anarchy Unbound.*

15 John Locke, *Second Treatise of Government*, ed. C. B. Macpherson (Indianapolis: Hackett, 1980).

16 Some of the most important sources, both historical and theoretical, on nongovernmental provision of systems of law and dispute resolution are: Terry L. Anderson and Peter J. Hill, *The Not So Wild, Wild West: Property Rights on the Frontier* (Stanford: Stanford University Press, 2004); Aviezer Tucker and Gian Piero de Bellis, eds., *Panarchy: Political Theories of Non-Territorial States* (New York: Routledge, 2015); Randy E. Barnett, *The Structure of Liberty: Justice and the Rule of Law*, 2nd ed. (Oxford: Oxford University Press, 2014); Beito, Gordon, and Tabarrok, *Voluntary City*; Tom W. Bell, "Polycentric Law," *Humane Studies Review,* 7:1 (Winter 1992): osf1.gmu.edu/~ihs/w91issues.html; Bruce L. Benson, *The Enterprise of Law: Justice Without the State* (San Francisco: Pacific Research Institute, 1990); Gary Chartier, *Anarchy and Legal Order: Law and Politics for a Stateless Society* (Cambridge: Cambridge University Press, 2014); Robert C. Ellickson, *Order Without Law: How Neighbors Settle Disputes* (Cambridge, MA: Harvard University Press, 2005); Friedman, *Machinery of Freedom*; Friedrich A. Hayek, *Law, Legislation and Liberty: A New Statement of the Liberal Principles of Justice and Political Economy*, rev. ed. (New York: Routledge, 2012); Michael Huemer, *The Problem of Political Authority: An Examination of the Right to Coerce and the Duty to Obey* (New York: Palgrave Macmillan, 2012); Long and Machan, *Anarchism/Minarchism*; Murray N. Rothbard, *Power and Market: Government and the Economy*, 2nd ed. (Kansas City: Sheed Andrews and McMeel, 1977); *The Ethics of Liberty*, 2nd ed. (New York: New York University Press, 2003); *For a New Liberty: The Libertarian Manifesto*, 2nd ed. (Auburn, AL: Mises Institute, 2006); Edward P. Stringham, ed., *Anarchy, State, and Public Choice* (Cheltenham, UK: Edward Elgar, 2006); *Anarchy and the Law: The Political Economy of Choice* (New Brunswick, NJ: Transaction Publishers, 2007); *Private Governance: Creating Order in Economic and Social Life* (Oxford: Oxford University Press, 2015); and William C. Wooldridge, *Uncle Sam, The Monopoly Man* (New Rochelle, NY: Arlington House, 1970).

17 Hans-Hermann Hoppe, ed., *The Myth of National Defense: Essays on the Theory and History of Security Production* (Auburn, AL: Mises Institute. 2003).

18 Bryan Caplan, "The Literature of Nonviolent Resistance and Civilian-Based Defense," *Humane Studies Review,* 9:1 (Summer 1994), econfaculty.gmu.edu/bcaplan/nonviolent.pdf.

19 Robert J. Alexander, *The Anarchists in the Spanish Civil War,* 2 vols. (London: Janus Publishing, 1999).

20 Long, "Market Anarchism as Constitutionalism."

21 Robert Nozick, *Anarchy, State, and Utopia* (New York: Basic Books, 1974).

22 Bryan Caplan and Edward P. Stringham, "Networks, Law, and the Paradox of Cooperation," in Stringham, *Anarchy and the Law,* 295–314; cf. Roderick T. Long, "Toward a Libertarian Theory of Class," *Social Philosophy and Policy,* 15:2 (Summer 1998): 303–49.

23 Gabriel Kolko, *The Triumph of Conservatism: A Reinterpretation of American History, 1900–1916* (New York: Free Press. 1963); *Railroads and Regulation, 1877–1916* (Westport: Greenwood, 1977); Butler Shaffer, *In Restraint of Trade: The Business Campaign Against Competition, 1918–1938* (Auburn, AL: Mises Institute, 2011); James Weinstein, *The Corporate Ideal in the Liberal State, 1900–1918* (New York: Farrar Straus & Giroux, 1971).

24 David T. Beito, *From Mutual Aid to the Welfare State: Fraternal Societies and Social Services* (Chapel Hill: UNC Press, 2000); P. Gosden, *Self-Help: Voluntary Associations in 19th Century Britain* (London: Batsford Press, 1973); David Green, *Reinventing Civil Society: The Rediscovery of Welfare Without Politics* (London: IEA: 1993).

25 Thomas Paine, *Rights of Man,* ed. Ronald Herder (Mineola, NY: Dover Publications, 1999), 107–8.

26 Ibid., 38.

27 Colin Ward, *Anarchy in Action* (London: Freedom Press, 1982).

We Need Some Government

Alex Tuckness

Study Questions

1. What is Tuckness's central thesis?

2. How does Tuckness define government? How does he clarify the definition?

3. What are the three "inconveniences" that justify government according to Locke? How does Tuckness respond to the objection that people don't actually consent to government?

4. How does Nozick envision a state coming into being? In what way does his view parallel Locke's?

5. What are "public goods"? How might such goods serve to justify a non-minimal state?

6. What is Rawls's view of the role of government? What objection would the anarchist raise to Rawls's view? How does Tuckness respond?

7. Why does Tuckness think that the monopoly power of government is a good thing?

8. Even if one thinks that government is illegitimate, what practical reason does Tuckness give for having government anyway?

Dissatisfaction with government is very common, both on the right and on the left. On the right, many are still captivated by the words of Ronald Reagan (1911–2004), "Government is not the solution to our problem; government is the problem."[1] More than a century earlier, Henry David Thoreau (1817–1862), whom we might today call a member of the radical Left, opened his famous essay *Civil Disobedience* with these words:

> "That government is best which governs least"; and I should like to see it acted up to more rapidly and systematically. Carried out, it finally amounts to this, which also I believe—"That government is best which governs not at all"; and when men are prepared for it, that will be the kind of government which they will have.[2]

Some think that government is an inefficient monopoly that gets in the way of free enterprise while for others, like Thoreau, it is an agent of nationalist oppression. Some people think it is both. Governments have certainly been responsible for many injustices, but is it better to try to improve governments to make them more just or should we just get rid of them? This essay will argue for the former: that despite the flaws and imperfections, we need government and that without it our lives would be worse, our liberty less secure, and societies less just.

Before making the case that it is better to improve governments than to try to abolish them, it will be helpful to define our terms. By a "government" I mean an entity that is regarded as having the exclusive power to legislate for the residents of a defined territory, to enforce those laws through coercive means, and to tax those who live in its territory in order to pay for its operations. Governments may do much more than this, but if an entity does all three of these things, I will call it a government. For simplicity we will assume that there is only one government per territory (thus if there is a national government we will set aside the case for provincial, state, and local governments) and will set to the side, for now, questions of international law.

A few clarifications about the definition are in order. The exclusive power to legislate, enforce the law, and collect taxes differentiates the state from a private organization. A private organization may have rules for its members, collect dues or fees from its members, and even enforce sanctions against its members. The difference is that one can renounce one's affiliation with the private organization without needing to leave a particular territory. Once one does so, one is no longer under the private organization's jurisdiction.

Second, in saying that governments have the power to legislate, we are not saying that anything a government does is therefore just and legitimate. For many years a particularly brutal form of slavery was legal in the United States. Endorsing governments does not mean endorsing everything governments do for the same reason that endorsing free enterprise does not mean endorsing the human rights violations committed by corporations.

Third, saying we need government does not mean that in every instance government is better than anarchy. Thomas Hobbes seems to have thought this, but it seems implausible. There is no reason to deny that a particularly brutal government which is able, because of its power and organization, to execute massive evil very efficiently could sometimes be worse than no government at all. Similarly, it is not a sufficient argument against anarchy to point to isolated examples where anarchy actually does turn into the war of all against all that Hobbes feared. We are looking for a generalization that holds true in the majority of cases, but not necessarily in all cases.

With these clarifications in mind, we are now in a position to examine arguments in favor of government. One complication is that people often envision very different things when they think of government. The structure of this paper takes this into account by linking different arguments for government to different conceptions of government. The first set of arguments assumes governments of a fairly limited nature—the sort of minimalist state that protects people from theft, assault, fraud, breach of contract, and similar acts, but does not, for example, engage in economic redistribution, fund public schools, or subsidize health care for the poor. The minimalist arguments are important because they show why even libertarians who believe in very limited government think that government is superior to anarchy. The second set of arguments describes the benefits that might come from having a government that does engage in economic redistribution and that uses its taxation power to promote the public good. These arguments will show additional advantages for government compared to anarchy. The final set of arguments are based on nonideal theory: even if you are unpersuaded by the first two lines of arguments, one may need government given that one lives in a world where governments are prominent.

A Minimalist Government Is Better than Anarchy

We begin by looking at arguments for why a minimalist government is better than anarchy. One important historical source for this argument is John Locke who argued in the *Two Treatises of Government* that there are three main "inconveniences" to living in what he called a "state of nature," that is, in the absence of government.[3] Locke believed that we had moral rights and duties even in the absence of government, but that these are often ambiguous. Even if we grant, for example, that a person who has spent the afternoon fishing from an unowned lake has a right to the fish she caught, there will be ambiguities that can lead to conflict. If she normally fishes from the same spot each day, does she have a right to that spot? If she leaves the fish for a long time, are they available for someone else to take? If so, after how long? What should the penalty be for stealing fish? In the absence of an authoritative interpreter, these ambiguities will lead to frequent conflicts and quite possibly violence as people try to enforce their rights on each other.

Second, Locke noted that the above problem is made much worse by the fact that people are systematically biased toward their own cause. We make excuses to minimize our own wrongdoing but are outraged by those who wrong us. In the absence of government, each person may try to enforce her own rights, but this makes each person judge in her own case. This is likely to lead to a vicious cycle. You punish me for something and I either think I didn't do anything wrong or that your punishment is excessive. I now feel justified in punishing you since your wrongful punishment was, I think, an assault. You, however, think the original punishment was justified and view my retaliation as unprovoked aggression, thus warranting more punishment. And thus the cycle continues.

Third, even if there were no ambiguity, and even if people were not biased in enforcing their rights, there is no guarantee in the state of nature that the wronged party would be able to successfully enforce her rights. In the state of nature, the stronger party would win, and there is no reason to think that the wronged party will be systematically stronger than the party in the wrong.

The solution to these problems is the creation of a government with the power to legislate, judge disputes, and enforce its judgments. Locke sees this as a huge improvement over "self-help" justice in the absence of government. One objection to Locke can be set aside. Locke is often interpreted as claiming that government is the result of a contract where people get together and promise to obey the government in order to avoid these inconveniences. The objection is that this is implausible as a description of either how governments came to be or why people now have an obligation to obey the government (few people actually make a free and conscious promise to obey the government). The objection can be set aside because our question is not about the specific grounds for obeying the government but whether it is a good idea to have government. Our focus is on Locke's arguments for the superiority of government to anarchy rather than whether consent is the explanation for the moral obligation to obey the government. The main point is captured well by Thomas Jefferson in the *Declaration of Independence* when he states: "to secure these rights, Governments are instituted among men." Government is not the source of our right to either life or liberty, but it is needed to make those rights secure.

Locke's argument, taken this way, is actually similar to the position of another philosopher, David Hume.[4] Hume would have agreed with the basic claim that by providing greater stability and predictability, governments are a major improvement over anarchy. However we got them (whether through a contract or in some other way), the important thing is that since we are better-off with them, we should keep and respect them (at least under normal circumstances—both Locke and Hume agreed that under certain conditions an unjust government could be overthrown).

Robert Nozick in the twentieth century followed some aspects of Locke's approach.[5] He, too, assumes we have basic rights to acquire property and live our lives as we see fit so long as we do not harm others. He further notes that, in the absence of government, trying to enforce these rights will be very inconvenient. What would people do? He asks if it's possible to imagine a state coming into being in a way that would not violate the rights of people.

He thinks it could in roughly this way: because of the insecurity in the state of nature, people would hire protection agencies. These protection agencies would protect members from attack and collect damages from the attackers. If there is conflict between two members of the same agency, the agency would arbitrate the dispute and award damages as appropriate. If there is conflict between members of different agencies, they would have to find some way to settle the dispute, ranging from negotiation to violent conflict. Nozick thinks that in a competitive market the larger and more powerful protection agencies would have the advantage over the smaller ones. In negotiating, their greater size and power would allow them to get more favorable terms. The more people who belong to the same association, the more conflicts can be settled internally, lowering the cost. The result would be that over time, the competitors would be driven out of business leaving just one protective agency.

From Nozick's perspective, this remaining protective agency would be a de facto monopoly and, in practice, a state, albeit a minimal one. Space will not permit going into all the complexities in his account of how this plays out. For our present purposes, notice that Nozick's argument is parallel to Locke's in this sense: both think that we are much better-off with a single monopoly that adjudicates disputes and has the power to enforce its judgments than we are in a situation of either individual self-help or competing protection agencies of comparable strength. Competing protection agencies would struggle with the same problems that individuals in the state of nature do, albeit to a lesser extent: they would not all have the same legal rules; in cases of conflict, each of the agencies would likely be biased in favor of paying members over nonmembers; smaller agencies would be at a disadvantage in enforcing their claims even if the claim was valid. A minimal state with a monopoly on law enforcement in a given territory would be an improvement over this situation.

A Nonminimalist Government Is Better than Anarchy

So far we have discussed the advantages of having a state that performs a limited but very important set of functions: protecting people from violence, creating rules for how people acquire and transfer property, and adjudicating disputes and awarding compensation to those who have been wronged. But in practice, most of us think of governments as doing much more than this. Governments often build parks and set zoning regulations; they set environmental standards and building codes; they help fund health care and provide assistance to those in poverty. In this section we discuss the rationale for why having a nonminimalist government is better than having no government at all.

One important role governments play is helping to provide what economists call "public goods." Public goods are goods that provide benefits where it is difficult or impossible to exclude those who want to enjoy the benefit without paying their fair share. In a sense, we have already seen this in the previous section. A minimalist state would defend its members from external attack. Consider what would happen if contributions for national defense were based on a "fee for service" instead of a mandatory tax. If territorially based groups exist, then there is no way to defend the people on the exterior of a territory without also defending the people on the interior. In order to defend Minnesota against a Canadian invasion, one must also defend Iowa and Missouri. There would thus be a significant incentive for people to be "free riders," enjoying the benefits without paying for them. Where it is impossible to exclude some who benefit, the resulting good will be undersupplied if we simply leave things to the market.

This basic problem applies to many things, not just national defense. Consider parks: one could put gates and fences around parks and charge admission to them (some parks operate in this way), but there are downsides to this approach. The fences might decrease the appeal of the park. Moreover, there are people who benefit without entering. An apartment overlooking the park may be more valuable because the park is there even though the apartment owner never enters the park. In the case of public schools, the primary beneficiaries are students, so one could charge them fees. This is not the only group of beneficiaries, though. A highly educated population provides benefits to society as a whole in addition to the benefits to individual students. In the absence of a tax system, things like education and parks would be underfunded. Governments can solve public goods problems, coordination problems, and other forms of market failure.[6]

The above examples point us toward a different justification for a more extensive state, namely that there are certain goods and opportunities that we may think should be available to citizens regardless of their ability to pay. In the absence of the state, individuals would only have access to whatever they can gain in trade (including trading their labor) or what others give them. In the absence of government, inequality of wealth would likely be even more extreme than it already is. Even if we imagine a completely equal and equitable initial distribution of wealth, those who are more successful than others will use a portion of their excess wealth to give their children advantages. Governments can provide things like universal public education to ensure that all people have access to at least basic education and a reasonable chance for success in life, even if they have the misfortune of being born into families that are unable to afford school tuition.

One influential philosopher, John Rawls, would say that the issue is not the inequality per se, but the unfairness.[7] He would argue that we should view the members of society as partners in a cooperative venture who should fairly divide up the proceeds of that venture. Rawls's argument, very roughly, was that we should imagine what distribution of rights, opportunities, and resources people would choose if they didn't know what place they would occupy in society (rich or poor, healthy or sick, and so on). Rawls's contention is that many of the things that give people advantages over other people in life are not deserved (you don't deserve your innate abilities, or the family you were born into, or the quality of the schools that happened to be available to you). Governments provide a way to reshape the structure of society so that opportunities are more fairly distributed.

One objection to this argument is that it presupposes the very thing that is under debate. Rawls is already assuming the existence of something like a state with people who are already a part of a community. Those people then debate about fair terms of cooperation. The anarchist would here object that whether people should be thought of as members of these sorts of communities is precisely the question. If we deny the initial premise (that people begin as members of cooperative communities), Rawls's conclusion may not follow.

One possible response could be adapted from Immanuel Kant. Kant recognized that in the absence of government people would still interact with each other and come into conflict with each other. In such a case we can contrast two different ways of resolving the conflict: self-help and lawful arbitration by government. What if one of the parties, being stronger and thus likely to prevail under self-help, refuses arbitration? Kant would argue that as a matter of justice it is right to compel the parties to enter into a political relationship so that they can resolve their differences lawfully.[8] The argument we can extract from this would be that anarchists are no more entitled to the presumption that people start off in a nonpolitical state than their opponents are entitled to the assumption that we are already in a political state. Neither side has a greater burden of proof than the other. Instead, we should ask which way of settling disputes will be fairer and more just. Kant thought that civil government was a more just way of settling disputes than self-help.

A third advantage of a nonminimalist government is the opportunities it provides for democratic engagement. In a nonminimalist state, citizens can have the opportunity to deliberate about the public good and to subject the basic structures of society to democratic scrutiny. They can shape their world as citizens and not merely as consumers. In the absence of government even more of our lives would be shaped by the aggregated preferences of people functioning as consumers. Aristotle argued that human beings are political animals and that we cannot reach our full potential if we lack opportunities to deliberate with others about the public good.[9] To be sure, actual governments fall short of this idealistic picture, but even with its imperfections government provides opportunities for citizens to shape the world in which they live through their participation in the democratic process.

Here is one practical example of why this is important: *monopolies*. One of the arguments sometimes used against government is precisely that the government has a monopoly on things like tax collection and law enforcement and that we would be better-off if there were competition: multiple firms offering different packages for different fees. In other words, monopolies are bad, and the government is a monopoly. We have already seen that one of the arguments in favor of government is that this is one area where monopoly may actually be better than competition: better one police force than 20 police forces trying to work in the same geographic area.

Suppose one is not persuaded by this argument and thinks that the government is not an example of a so-called "natural monopoly" (a sphere of life were monopoly is superior to competition), and that governments use their monopoly power to exploit their citizens. This raises the question: Why did governments arise if they are inefficient? One explanation would be that an organization can gain enough power to give itself an advantage over its rivals, drive them out of business, and then extract huge profits once the rivals are out of the way. Competitors may be unable to enter the market either because the start-up costs are prohibitive or because the monopolist can undersell at a loss and run them out of business. Perhaps this is what happened with governments: once a group gains enough military power it can run the competitors out of business, so to speak, in a given territory.

If we accept this, it certainly portrays government in an unflattering light, but it also gives us reason to believe that large corporations would, in the absence of government, also become exploitative monopolies. Here government provides a solution: governments have the authority to break up monopolies so that there is greater competition. The threat of doing so can also help deter exploitative behavior by large companies since they know exploitative behavior could lead to antitrust action. While the government is itself a monopoly, it can be organized on democratic principles so that its power is used according to the will of its citizens. Better one democratically controlled monopoly regulating the others than exploitation by a number of private monopolies. In the absence of government, the fate of companies is determined by our uncoordinated actions as consumers, but with government we can decide these questions as citizens. The place of monopolies is ultimately a political question that should be settled by governments through a democratic process, not an economic question to be decided by individual purchasing decisions.

Government Is Needed, Given that Governments Are Already Widespread

So far we have seen two different arguments for government, the first arguing for the advantages of a minimalist state over anarchy and the second arguing for the advantages of a nonminimalist state over anarchy. The success of either argument would give us a good reason to prefer government to anarchy. Suppose, however, that a person is unconvinced by any of the arguments listed above. Is there a different type of argument for government available? There is, but it differs from the above in that it relies more heavily on nonideal theory.

There are different ways of answering the question "what do we need?" You could start by imagining a perfectly just world filled with perfectly just people and then imagine what we would need in such a world. Some things we now take for granted, like locks, would be unnecessary. In a world of perfectly just people, no one would try to steal from me or enter my home without permission. This is not, however, a particularly helpful way of deciding what we need since it is so radically different from the world we actually do live in.

We could modify the exercise by, in the philosopher Jean-Jacques Rousseau's words, "taking men as they are, and laws as they can be."[10] Here we assume that human nature is more or less as it actually is and ask what laws (or perhaps the anarchist would say absence of laws) would be best given the sort of beings we are. This approach can also recognize that our character may be shaped in important ways by the sort of society we live in. The arguments we have looked at so far are roughly of this type: they assume human nature as it is and thus consider the fact that some people will commit crimes, that those with power may exploit it, and so on.

Nonetheless, one might still find this inadequate as a framework. We do not, after all, actually live in a world with the best laws (or the absence of laws if that is best). A third way of asking what we need is to ask what we need given the actual laws and institutions that surround us. Suppose I find myself living under the authority of a government in a territorial state but, unconvinced by the arguments above, think the government illegitimate and that people would be better-off if governments everywhere were abolished. Granting all of that, we can still ask the question, "Would we be better-off without our government given that other nations are still going to have them?" In other words, even if we were to grant that in the best of all possible worlds, taking human nature as it is, there would not be government, we might still need government because we live in a world of governments. If we successfully convinced enough people in our nation to disband our government and move to a state of anarchy, we might be at risk from the governments that surround us.

There are several reasons to think this might be true. First, governments have advantages over nongovernments in being able to defend their citizens from attack. The ability to coordinate military action and efforts thus gives citizens of a state greater protection from attack than citizens without a state would have. Second, because the international system is state-based, citizens who have a government have a much easier time negotiating with foreign countries on things like the environment, trade, and immigration. In the absence of government, collective decisions on these issues would be difficult or impossible. With government, one can more easily negotiate a treaty with another country. Third, participation in the state system makes it easier for citizens to influence the international legal regime as a whole. In addition to trade and immigration agreements between particular countries, there are also larger international legal frameworks that help regulate areas such as the protection of human rights. States play a large role in determining these international legal regimes.

Conclusion

In many parts of the world, people are very frustrated with government. This is often justified as governments are very imperfect entities run by very imperfect people. Nonetheless, the contention in this essay is that things could be worse, in fact much worse, without them. Having a government with the ability to enforce the law and arbitrate disputes places us on a more stable footing for protecting people's rights and maintaining public order. Governments can help solve collective action problems by providing public goods that would be underprovided in the absence of government. Governments can contribute to the fairness of society by offsetting some of the impact luck would otherwise have on how people's lives go. Governments can provide the opportunity for citizens to engage in democratic self-rule and to deliberate with their fellow citizens about the public good. Governments can regulate and even break up monopolies. Governments are also an important source of protection and influence in a world where governments are already common.

The underlying assumption in this essay is that the criterion for whether we need government is whether we are, on the whole, better-off with it than without it. In this sense the essay follows Hume, although others have used similar criteria. This is a better test than whether we can prove that without exception every person is better-off with something than without it. Surely there are some individuals who might be better-off under anarchy, but it is similarly true that some people will be better-off under government. Unless we have assumed that one form of organization has a higher burden of proof than the other, something we have denied above, there is no reason that one person has the right to insist on anarchy if the rest of the world would be better-off without it, or vice versa. Instead, it is better to ask whether, on the whole, people are better-off with government than without it. That is how we know whether or not we need it. Even acknowledging government's imperfections, our lives are much better-off with it than without it.

Notes

1 Ronald Reagan, First Inaugural Address, 1981.
2 Thoreau's essay can be found at: http://xroads.virginia.edu/~hyper2/thoreau/civil.html (accessed November 15, 2016).
3 John Locke, *Two Treatises of Government*, Student ed., ed. Peter Laslett (Cambridge: Cambridge University Press, 1988), 350–53, 59. For a more contemporary statement of many of the same themes, see Christopher Heath Wellman and A. John Simmons, *Is There a Duty to Obey the Law?*, For and Against (Cambridge: Cambridge University Press, 2005), 5–12.

4. David Hume, *Political Essays*, ed. Knud Haakonssen (Cambridge: Cambridge University Press, 1994), 186–201.
5. Robert Nozick, *Anarchy, State, and Utopia* (New York: Basic Books, 1974).
6. Gregory S. Kavka, "Why Even Morally Perfect People Would Need Government," in *For and against the State: New Philosophical Readings*, ed. John T. Sanders and Jan Narveson (New York: Rowman and Littlefield, 1996), 45.
7. John Rawls, *A Theory of Justice*, Rev. ed. (Cambridge, MA: Belknap Press of Harvard Univeristy Press, 1999).
8. Immanuel Kant, *Kant: Political Writings*, ed. Hans Siegbert Reiss, 2nd, enl. ed. (Cambridge: Cambridge University Press, 1991), 98.
9. Aristotle, *The Politics,* trans. C. D. C. Reeve (Indianapolis: Hackett, 1998), 1252a24–1253b38.
10. Jean-Jacques Rousseau, *The Social Contract and Other Later Political Writings*, ed. Victor Gourevitch (Cambridge: Cambridge University Press, 1997), 41.

RESPONSES

Response to Long

Alex Tuckness

> **Study Questions**
>
> 1. What evidence does Tuckness offer against the idea that the rich need government to oppress the poor?
> 2. Why is Tuckness dubious of Long's view that without government there would be a competitive non-geographical market for protective services?
> 3. Why does Tuckness think that the poor would likely have little or no legal protection under anarchy?
> 4. How does Tuckness respond to Long's claim that the nonminimal state makes the poor worse-off?
> 5. What danger does Tuckness see with monopolies under anarchy? What danger is there in being the first to abolish government?

In my initial essay, I defended three claims: that minimal government is better than anarchy, that nonminimal government is better still, and that we have reason to choose the state given the fact that other people will be organized in states. If any one of these claims succeeds, we have reason to choose government over anarchy. Since Long's version of anarchy is a market-based one that has many commonalities with a minimal state, most of my response here will be defending the first claim. A minimal state, like anarchy, would not include the corporate welfare that Long detests. A minimal state would do a better job than private, for-profit protection agencies at protecting people's basic rights under anarchy. I will more briefly defend my second and third claims about the benefits of nonminimal states and the dangers of abolishing government unilaterally in a world where governments are still a powerful force.

Contra Private Protection Agencies

Long thinks that governments are inefficient monopolies and that the services they provide (primarily promulgating and enforcing rules and arbitrating disputes) could be performed by private companies that are not monopolies. Instead, people could switch protection agencies as easily as they switch cell-phone plans. There are several problems with this position. First, Long gives the impression that the rich need government in order to oppress the poor. This is false. Slavery is still a major problem in the world, with some estimates putting the number of people in slavery over 20 million. In many countries slavery is illegal and exists in spite of the state rather than because of it. Modern slavery tends to flourish either where the state is weak and unable to protect people from predators, or in parts of the economy that provide illegal goods and services and operate outside the protections of the government (the illegal sex trade, for example). Slavery is often a profitable management practice in labor-intensive industries where it is relatively easy to coerce workers and avoid government interference.[1] It is sometimes profitable to hire thugs to intimidate captive workers. Poor workers lack both resources and opportunities to organize and are unable to hire their own protection agency to help them. Where states are weak, predators flourish. How much more would predators flourish in their absence?

A second problem with Long's argument is his overconfidence that what would emerge in the absence of government is a competitive market for legal protection in which people can easily change protection agencies. There are good reasons to think that there would be economic advantages for protection agencies that are geographically based. It would be more obvious which rules apply where, there would be fewer conflicts where one had to negotiate with a competing agency, and the agency's resources could be deployed in a much smaller area. Agencies might well acquire continuous blocks of territory and allow only members of their association to live there. Even now, the rich often have a tendency to live either in upscale apartments with additional security or in expensive neighborhoods that the poor cannot afford. In the absence of government, "gated communities" would likely have much more effective defenses against outsiders than they do at present. Unlike cell-phone plans, your choice might be geographically determined.

In addition to the advantages of geographic concentration, there are also advantages of scale. If disputes between agencies are settled by negotiation apart from government, a more powerful agency can credibly threaten a less powerful one into accepting a settlement that favors the former. This gives people more incentive to sign on with the powerful agency, which can get them better settlements, reinforcing the cycle. The economics of anarchy lead to large, geographically based agencies that have monopolies within their districts. We would then be stuck with entities that are still monopolies but which operate more like for-profit companies than democratically controlled states. This is important because states can use taxation to fund the protection of rights for those who cannot afford it. For example, a disabled person who lacks economically viable skills to trade on the market would be unable to purchase protection. Taxation can insure resources for that person.

Perhaps these people's rights will still be protected because enough people will make charitable donations to fund the premiums of those who cannot afford them. Long reasons that if attorneys already provide pro bono legal services without the government forcing them to, people in general would contribute even more if the stakes were higher and the poor risked not just lack of legal counsel but the complete absence of legal protection. This is a questionable assumption. The amount of money needed to provide full protection for the poor would be extensive. We are not just talking about needing a few more attorneys but paying for police protection, a whole court system, a penal system, and more. In other words, generosity would need to increase very dramatically.

Would people contribute more generously because there was more need? There is good reason to doubt that generosity levels are simply correlated with either ability to give or the degree of need. Right now there are hundreds of millions of people in the world living in extreme poverty, experiencing malnutrition and at risk of starvation. There are also hundreds of millions of people in the world with plenty of disposable cash to help them, and yet the problem persists. Why? One explanation is that generosity is significantly related to how connected we feel to those to whom we give. One study found that rich people give a smaller percentage of their income to the poor than the poor do and that one of the most important variables for the rich is how much interaction they have with the poor. One theory is that the rich are less generous because they are more isolated from the poor in terms of where they live, work, etc.[2] The wealthy would have even more reason to live in gated communities under anarchy than they do now as it would be an efficient way to buy extra protection.

Moreover, people are much more willing to fund programs for the poor who are members of their state than for foreigners. Even if governments often rely on "imagined communities," the sense of shared identity that governments foster increases people's willingness to contribute on behalf of fellow group members. Under anarchy, the rich neighborhood and the poor neighborhood nearby would not have a common political identity to unite them, decreasing the interest of the rich in helping the poor. While other types of identity (religious identity, for example) can motivate generosity, because inequality often tracks with both family and neighborhood, the anarchist society could well be one where the rich feel very little connection to those in poverty around them. We thus have reason to doubt that anarchy could protect people from predation as well as states can and thus reason to affirm my first claim, that a minimal state would be better than anarchy.

The Nonminimal State and the Problem of Other States Redux

I now want to reiterate my second claim, that a nonminimal state is better still. Long thinks that governments, in fact, make the poor worse-off by funding corporate welfare, enforcing minimum wage laws, and stifling competition. I would agree that corporate welfare is a problem, but changing these policies is a better option than eliminating government. In the same way that large protection agencies could use their bargaining power exploitatively, so, too, could employers exploit workers in the absence of minimum wage laws. Moreover, the reasons given earlier for doubting there would be enough charity to fund the protection premiums for the poor give us similar reasons to doubt that enough people will pay for the food, shelter, healthcare, and education of others. These tax-funded services that governments provide are real benefits for those who otherwise would be deprived.

Governments also benefit us by breaking up private monopolies. Better one monopoly (government) subject to democratic control than lots of private monopolies extracting huge premiums and using violence to protect their monopolies. For the same reasons that the powerful will use violence to sustain debt slavery and human trafficking, it will often be profitable to hire mercenaries to prevent competitors from breaking up a profitable monopoly. Again, we see that illegal enterprises that operate without government protection readily use violence to help secure their profits. It is untrue that monopolies can only thrive with government backing.

Lastly, we should remember that there is no realistic way to simultaneously abolish all governments in the world. Given that fact, the people who abolish government first will find their security very precarious as they are surrounded by geographically based states with standing armies and the power to tax to fund those armies. The absence of government is not a peaceful utopia, but people subject to the predation of other forms of power.

Notes

1. Andrew Crane, "Modern Slavery as a Management Practice: Exploring the Conditions and Capabilities of Human Exploitation," *Academy of Management Review*, 38:1 (2013): 49–69.
2. See https://www.theatlantic.com/magazine/archive/2013/04/why-the-rich-dont-give/309254/.

Response to Tuckness

Roderick T. Long

Study Questions

1. What assumptions are made by Locke's and Nozick's arguments for government that Long challenges?
2. Why does Long think that public goods problems do not require government solutions?
3. How does Long respond to Tuckness's arguments for the necessity of government to provide military defense?
4. What problem does Long have with Rawls's solution to economic inequalities?
5. Why does Long think that the statist, not the anarchist, shoulders the burden of proof?
6. Why does Long think that the state is a threat rather than a benefit to public deliberation?
7. How does Long respond to Tuckness's arguments for the benefits and inevitability of a government monopoly?

Some of Alex Tuckness's arguments for the necessity of government are ones I've already addressed in my main essay, while others are new. I'll make some quick points on both.

Locke and Nozick

Locke assumes without argument that only a *monopoly* institution can supply such desiderata as third-party arbitration, organized enforcement, and a known and settled body of law. But today there exists a vast literature (see previous citations) on how all three of those desiderata have regularly been supplied by competitive, polycentric legal systems. Tuckness likewise asserts that under anarchy, there are just "two ways" of resolving conflicts, "self-help and lawful arbitration by government"—ignoring the long tradition of lawful but *nongovernmental* arbitration. Historically, much of existing state law actually arose under non-state systems and was only subsequently co-opted by the state;[1] indeed, Adam Smith famously attributes the "admirable constitution" of the English court system to its competitive origins.[2]

As Tuckness notes, Nozick's argument assumes that in a competitive market, larger protection agencies would have an advantage over smaller ones. But, as I've argued, beyond a certain point increased firm size becomes a liability rather than an asset in a competitive market, and can be sustained only with government assistance.

Public Goods and Military Defense

Tuckness points to state intervention as the only solution to public goods problems. But, if markets could not solve such problems, radio broadcasts would be impossible, since listeners can receive these whether or not they pay for them. Historically, private roads and parks have often been opened to the public without charge, as a strategy for increasing the owners' property values; and so on (see previous citations). Public goods problems (unlike the public-choice problems associated with state provision) are usually self-solving, since they create incentives for entrepreneurs to figure out how to provide such goods. In fact, governments spend much of their time attempting to *suppress* bottom-up, grassroots efforts to provide public goods like education, day care, and aid to the homeless.

With regard to military defense, Tuckness notes that one cannot defend Minnesota without (to some extent) defending Iowa. Yet, it is equally true that one cannot defend, *for example,* Austria without (to some extent) defending Switzerland; hence, if Tuckness is right, the only solution is not just government but *world* government. Yet, successful defense does happen without world government. In any case, the role of non-territorially based tactics (such as cyberattacks) in military planning is increasing.

Even if, ideally, no governments would be necessary, Tuckness argues, so long as our own nation is surrounded by *other* nations with governments, we may need a government (a) to provide military defense against aggression by other governments, and (b) to negotiate with other countries on such matters as "environment, trade, and immigration" (p. 227). Point (a) I've addressed previously; as for point (b), such negotiations are typically agreements among exploiters over how best to manage the exploited, and so from an anarchist perspective are not something to encourage. In any case, anarchist activism aims at worldwide transformation, not just at reforms in one's own country.

Fairness and Equality

Tuckness cites Rawls's concern that the products of social cooperation be distributed *fairly*, in such a way that economic inequalities are minimized except when they benefit the least advantaged. Suppose Rawls is right. Still, Rawls assumes without argument that only *government* can achieve this desideratum. Tuckness likewise asserts that under anarchy, "inequality of wealth would likely be even more extreme than it already is" (p. 224). But see my previous essay for the evidence that it is the nature of government to promote economic inequality, while competitive markets promote equality.

Tuckness anticipates a different reply from the anarchist: that by starting from a description of human beings as members of cooperative communities, Rawls is illegitimately taking for granted the existence and legitimacy of the state. But no anarchist is going to raise this objection, because no anarchist thinks of cooperative communities as implying or requiring states in the first place. On the contrary, for anarchists the state is a parasite on cooperative communities, not an enabler of them. (Rawls also offers no argument for his assumption that cooperative communities correspond in any interesting way to the territories of nation-states; in the real world, cooperation does not stop at national borders.)

Burden of Proof

Tuckness maintains that there are no grounds for an initial presumption either in favor of or against a state; that is, neither the anarchist nor the statist has the burden of proof. But it seems plausible to suppose that there is a presumption in favor of *equality of rights*; that is, anyone who maintains that people should have *un*equal rights must shoulder the burden of proof. Given that the state, as a monopoly, by definition involves an inequality of rights while anarchy does not, the initial burden of proof must always lie with those who advocate the state.

Public Deliberation

A further benefit of the state, Tuckness tells us, is that it allows citizens to "deliberate about the public good" and "subject the basic structures of society to democratic scrutiny" (p. 225). But why should a centralized, coercive structure be needed for this? As Don Lavoie (1951–2001) notes:

> The force of public opinion, like that of markets, is not best conceived as a concentrated will representing the public, but as the *distributed* influence of political discourses throughout society. These open discourses are our

eyes on the polity, and the attempt to resolve their differences into a single political will embodied in a monopoly institution destroys our political vision.[3]

A conversation that is destined to end with the stronger party *forcing* its judgment on the weaker seems a poor model for public deliberation.

Benefits and/or Inevitability of Monopoly

Sometimes monopoly is better than competition, Tuckness says; "better one police force than 20 police forces trying to work in the same geographic area" (p. 225). Try telling that to minority communities victimized by police brutality; the ability to switch to a different service provider would be a welcome check on such abuse. Competition is a restraint on power.

Incidentally, there was a time when it was assumed that monopoly in *religion* was better than competition. Indeed, if a medieval European could join our present conversation, he would have little trouble being convinced of the practicability of competing *legal* jurisdictions within the same territory, since such competition would have been a feature of his daily life.[4] But the notion of competing *religious* denominations coexisting peacefully within the same territory would have struck him as a bizarre pipe dream. One reason the later European wars of religion were so intractable is that as religious diversity increased, it was still taken for granted that every country had to have a single dominant religion that would be imposed on society generally, and so, of course, each faction wanted its own religion to be the one chosen. We should beware of the parochial tendency to treat a given industry as inevitably monopolistic merely because it has been monopolistic in our own time and place.

But, Tuckness asks, "why did governments arise if they are inefficient?" The answer, he suggests, is that there is a natural tendency for exploitative monopolies to arise. Hence, even if the state is somewhat less than angelic, it may be needed as a necessary constraint on the tendency of *other* institutions, such as large corporations, to develop into exploitative monopolies, especially since the state can be "organized on democratic principles" to ensure that "its power is used according to the will of its citizens"—a more effective remedy, Tuckness suggests, than leaving societal regulation up to "individual purchasing decisions" (p. 226).

But there are sound theoretical reasons for thinking that subjecting the state to democratic constraints is impossible. Governments don't check corporate power, they reinforce it. Governments magnify the power of the wealthy;

since state actors are controlling other people's money rather than their own, the amount that special interests have to spend to get their favored projects funded is only a fraction of their full cost. The less affluent, by contrast, are a dispersed and distracted constituency that cannot hope to compete with corporate lobbyists. Butler Shaffer once defined (political) democracy as "the illusion that my wife and I, combined, have twice the political influence of David Rockefeller."[5] In a competitive market, the path to wealth is success in serving the public; under a state, the path to wealth is political privilege. Hence, a state can never be as democratic as a market. (Moreover, market activity is not just a matter of "individual purchasing decisions"; organized cooperative action is a market phenomenon, too.)

As for the argument that states must be inevitable because they're here, we need to beware of historical myopia. Two and a half centuries ago, nearly all of the world's economically advanced nations were monarchies, and it was generally assumed that monarchy's prevalence was to be explained by its superiority to other systems of government such as democracy. (I'm talking about monarchies where the monarch exercises considerable personal power, not in-name-only monarchies like present-day Britain or Sweden, which are, in fact, representative democracies whose "monarchs" perform a primarily ceremonial function.) Yet, despite monarchy's apparent success, it was, in fact, an institution on the verge of serious decline. The growth of modern communication technology, with its flatter, decentralized network structure, bypassing traditional hierarchies, suggests that the writing may be on the wall for the state as well.

Notes

1 See, for example, John Hasnas, "The Obviousness of Anarchy," in *Anarchism/Minarchism: Is a Government Part of a Free Country?*, ed. Roderick T. Long and Tibor R. Machan (New York: Routledge, 2016), 111–31; Bruce L. Benson, "The Spontaneous Evolution of Commercial Law," *Southern Economic Journal*, 55 (1989): 644–61.

2 Adam Smith, *An Inquiry into the Nature and Causes of the Wealth of Nations*, vol. 2, ed. R. H. Campbell and A. S. Skinner (Indianapolis: Liberty Fund, 1981), V.i.b, 720.

3 Don Lavoie, "Democracy, Markets, and the Legal Order: Notes on the Nature of Politics in a Radically Liberal Society," *Social Philosophy & Policy*, 10:2 (Summer 1993): 103–20.

4 Harold J. Berman, *Law and Revolution: The Formation of the Western Legal Tradition* (Cambridge, MA: Harvard University Press, 1983), 10.

5 Butler Shaffer, "On the Receiving End of Democracy," LewRockwell.com (October 29, 2009), https://www.lewrockwell.com/2009/10/butler-shaffer/what-the-taliban-actually-think/.

Questions for Reflection

1. Long argues that government authority is not based on the consent of the governed as is often thought. Why is this a problem? Can the "consent view" be justified in a way Long doesn't consider? Is there a way to legitimize government authority apart from consent?
2. Long believes that the poor would be better-off under anarchy while Tuckness thinks they would be worse-off. Which view do you think is closer to the truth? Why?
3. Is Tuckness correct that Long's private protection agencies would eventually turn into geographical monopolies? Why? How, if at all, could Long respond to Tuckness's concerns?
4. Tuckness believes that government is the only way to prevent exploitative economic monopolies. Long claims that government is not necessary to prevent such monopolies and is, in fact, more dangerous. Whose view is correct? Why?

7

Should Wealth Be Redistributed?

Wealth Should Be Redistributed

Jon Mandle

Study Questions

1. What is the difference between egalitarians and libertarians on the distribution of wealth? What three points does Mandle seek to establish?

2. What conclusions does Nozick draw from his "Wilt Chamberlain" example? What ambiguity does Mandle notice in the concept of "redistribution" that might question Nozick's conclusions?

3. What two systems of property does Mandle contrast? What is Wilt Chamberlain entitled to under each system?

4. What is a "moralized" account of liberty? How might such an account make the libertarian system of property rights circular?

5. What is Jan Narveson's non-moralized account of liberty? What problem does it have according to Mandle? Why is he not convinced by Narveson's response to this problem?

6. What do all liberal theories of justice require in order to protect fundamental interests? Given these requirements, what is the problem with the libertarian system?

7. What apparent inconsistency does Mandle see in Nozick's theory? What conclusion does Mandle draw from this?

8. How is the shift in orientation from outcomes to input useful according to Mandle?
9. What is the difference between "ideal theory" and "nonideal theory"? What is the place of each in discussions of distributive justice?

Egalitarians characteristically hold that wealth should be redistributed in order to achieve some kind of distributional equality. In contrast, libertarians, because of their understanding of property rights and liberty, typically oppose the redistribution of wealth. In this chapter, I will defend egalitarianism, but as will become clear, the statement "wealth should be redistributed" does not adequately capture the kind of egalitarianism that I will defend or what I take to be the core disagreement between egalitarians and libertarians. In addition to defending egalitarianism, I will try to establish three main points. First, the debate between egalitarians and libertarians is not best understood as a disagreement over when property rights can be violated in the name of equality. Instead, it is a dispute concerning which scheme of property rights is justified in the first place. Second, while libertarians sometimes argue that only their principles respect liberty, this is so only on a "moralized" conception of liberty, and because there are different moralized conceptions of liberty, by itself this cannot decide the case between a libertarian and egalitarian system. And third, it is misleading to say that egalitarians are in favor of maintaining a certain fixed pattern of distribution while libertarians are opposed to it.

When understood one way, and stated this abstractly—"*sometimes* wealth should be redistributed"—the claim is not controversial. Libertarians who profess to oppose redistribution do not oppose *all* state-enforced transfers of goods from one person to another. They may, for example, oppose redistribution for the purpose of increasing people's level of well-being or equalizing it. But if one individual had possession of another's property, libertarians would typically support state action to forcibly return it to the rightful owner, although they would be unlikely to call this "redistribution." It is also obvious that nobody supports *all* forms of redistribution—whatever that could mean. If an existing distribution of wealth is already just, it should not be redistributed. The real disagreement between egalitarians and libertarians is not best presented as being either for or against redistribution. Rather, it concerns when an existing distribution of property is just and when it is not. So we must ask: Which principles should we use to determine when a distribution is just and when it is not?

Nozick's Libertarian Theory

One approach to answering this question is to attempt to identify a particular pattern to which the distribution of property (or wealth) must continuously conform in order to be just. For example, we might say that all property should be distributed equally or, alternatively, that it should be distributed in whatever way would result in equal levels of well-being. On such a theory, any deviation from the correct pattern would be unjust. Robert Nozick argued against such theories in his 1974 defense of libertarianism, *Anarchy, State, and Utopia*.[1] In his celebrated "Wilt Chamberlain" example, Nozick asserts that any "patterned principle" of justice will conflict with individual liberty, and this, he suggests, shows that all such conceptions of justice are misguided. Suppose, he argues, that the distribution of wealth in some society conforms to one's favored patterned principle of distributive justice. For simplicity, consider the principle that requires an equal distribution of wealth, and suppose that a society satisfies this requirement. As individuals make decisions concerning how to spend their money in order to satisfy their various preferences and desires, that distribution will change in unpredictable ways. In Nozick's example, many people pay to watch Wilt Chamberlain play basketball, and this results in an unequal distribution of wealth as Chamberlain reaps his reward for his rare and valuable skills. "Any favored pattern would be transformed into one unfavored by the principle, by people choosing to act in various ways," Nozick writes. The only way to maintain a fixed pattern would be to "continually interfere to stop people from transferring resources as they wish to, or continually (or periodically) [to] interfere to take from some persons resources that others for some reason chose to transfer to them" (p. 163). Therefore, "patterned principles of distributive justice necessitate *re*distributive activities" (p. 168, emphasis in original). According to this argument, no patterned principle of justice is acceptable because the continuous redistribution that would be required to maintain any pattern would interfere with individual liberty. And to repeat: this conclusion is supposed to hold for *any* pattern of distribution, not only strict equality. Instead of relying on a distributive pattern to specify the requirements of justice, Nozick holds that an ideal theory of justice must be limited to specifying the procedures by which individuals can justly acquire and transfer property.[2] Economic justice, on this view, is strictly independent of any concerns for limiting inequality or ensuring a minimal share of goods for all.

Nozick makes his example vivid by having us imagine that spectators deposit part of their admission fee directly into a box marked for Chamberlain. Once that has been done, the only way to reestablish an equal distribution would be for the state to forcibly confiscate some of it (perhaps through a tax system) and to redistribute it to those who have less. For Nozick, this redistribution would be unjust since it would violate either Chamberlain's property rights (taking what is rightfully his) or the property rights of the spectators (who would be unable to freely transfer their property to him). But consider now a variation of Nozick's story, and suppose that Chamberlain's team employs a pickpocket who lifts the wallets of the spectators while they are distracted by Chamberlain's great play and places the wallets in his box. When, at the end of the night, the outraged spectators demand their wallets back, they are demanding that the state forcibly transfer possession of the wallets from Chamberlain to them. However, it would seem fatuous to say they were demanding a "redistribution" of wealth. On the contrary, they would say that they were simply demanding the return to them of what was rightfully theirs—the physical location of their wallets is irrelevant. Nozick agrees: "Returning stolen money or compensating for violations of rights are *not* redistributive reasons" (p. 27). This points to an ambiguity in the concept of "redistribution." Redistribution is not a mere change in location or physical possession. Rather, to properly call something a "redistribution" seems to require a change in what people *rightfully* possess, and to complete a rough definition, let us add that redistribution also must be enforced by the state and must be independent of individual consent. Nozick believes that in his original example, it is perfectly obvious that Chamberlain *is* rightfully entitled to whatever people have put in his box. After all, they consented to the transfers, unlike in the pickpocket example. They successfully transferred their property to him when they freely put it in his box with the intention that he acquire it.

But *have* the spectators succeeded in transferring their property rights to Chamberlain? This question can be understood either as a question about the just procedures for transferring property rights or as a question about the content of the property rights themselves. Nozick says that a theory of justice requires principles for the just transfer of property, but here it might be more useful to think of this as a question about the content of the property rights themselves. When one (rightfully) owns property, this gives one the right to do various things with that property. Sometimes it is said that one has a right to do whatever one wants with one's property, but this is obviously false. Nozick himself points out that "my property rights in my knife allow me to leave it where I will, but not in your chest" (p. 171). We need some way of distinguishing what a property right entitles one to do from what one may not do. Some libertarians insist that the only thing that can limit what one can do with one's property are the property rights of others. They would understand Nozick's knifing you in the chest as impermissible because it violates your property right to your own body. Non-libertarians may say that there are additional limitations on what one may do with one's property that are not grounded solely in the property rights of others. We need not resolve this dispute here because both sides agree that we need some way of specifying what property rights entitle one to do, and in particular whether they entitle the spectators to transfer their property to Chamberlain.

Two Systems of Property

It is possible to specify an internally consistent system of property rights that entitles the spectators to transfer their (full) property rights to anyone they choose, as Nozick assumes. Call such a scheme a *libertarian system of property*. But other systems are also possible. For example, consider the system that grants to property owners all of the rights of the libertarian system, with the following exception: when transferring property rights to another person, the value of that property is taxed at a rate of 10 percent, with the tax being transferred to the least-advantaged members of society. Call this a *progressive system of property*, with the understanding that this is only an example and it is not necessarily the system I will ultimately defend. Compared to the libertarian system, under the progressive system property owners are limited in what they can do with their property—they cannot transfer 100 percent of its value to a person of their choosing. But notice that this limitation comes from the property rights that others (the least advantaged) have under this same system. If Chamberlain lived in a society with the progressive system of property, he would *not* be entitled to the full value of what the spectators put into his box. The spectators would have succeeded in transferring only 90 percent of the value to him, while the least-advantaged members of society would have a property right in the other 10 percent. As we have seen, it does not matter where the money is physically located. The only relevant question is who is rightfully entitled to it. If, under the progressive system, Chamberlain kept everything put in his box, he would be violating the property rights of the least advantaged, no less than if he kept what the pickpocket had placed in his box. If it is misleading to say that the pickpocket victims are demanding redistribution, then it is also misleading to say that the least advantaged are demanding redistribution. Whether a particular transfer is something one has a right to do, and whether a state-enforced transfer is properly understood as the enforcement of or the violation of property rights, depends on which scheme of property rights is just.

Which System Is More Just?

How do we decide whether the libertarian or the progressive system of property is more just? Libertarians often argue that regardless of the possible distributive inequalities that their system might produce, it is just because only it respects liberty, which they understand to be the absence of external constraints. For this argument to work, our understanding of liberty must not beg the question and assume that we already know which system of property rights is just. Although Nozick doesn't technically talk about "liberty," we can construct an argument derived from his approach.[3] Consider a case in which the action of one person, A, limits the options available to another person, B. Does A's action restrict B's liberty? Nozick answers that this "depends upon whether these others [A] had the right to act as they did" (p. 262).[4] If A had the right to act in a way that limits B's options, then there is no restriction on B's liberty, and, consequently, no injustice. Call this a *moralized* account of liberty, since a person's liberty, and therefore what would restrict her liberty, depends on a prior account of rights. The problem is that libertarians typically take *property* rights to be fundamental, and this makes their argument circular. To see this more clearly, note that the progressive system of property defines a different system of rights, so it would have its own corresponding conception of moralized liberty. The libertarian and progressive systems disagree about what rights individuals have, so they disagree about what would restrict a person's liberty. Each system protects its own moralized version of liberty better than the other, so by itself this cannot decide the case between them.

Consider, then, a non-moralized account of liberty, for example that of Jan Narveson. He begins by stating that libertarianism "is the doctrine that the only relevant consideration in political matters is individual liberty."[5] He then emphasizes that one's liberty is not restricted just because someone else fails to help one achieve one's ends. The relevant baseline for judging whether there is a restriction on one's liberty, he claims, is what one would be able to do without the intervention of another. A restricts B's liberty only if "A [brings] it about that B is unable to do what B would otherwise be able to do even without A's assistance."[6] This is a *non-moralized* account of liberty because it does not depend on the rights of A or B, but only on the counterfactual of what B would be able to do in the absence of A. The problem is that when liberty is understood in this way, *all* systems of property, including the libertarian one, restrict liberty. Imagine the case in which we have no property rights at all. In such a state of nature, both A and B are each at liberty to pick and eat an apple that they find. Since B can do this without the assistance of A, if A prevents B from doing so by grabbing the apple out of B's hands, A restricts B's liberty. Now suppose that in a society with a libertarian system of property rights, A (properly) claims that the tree and its apples are on his property. Seeing B pick an apple from his tree, he calls the police who arrest B for trespassing and take the apple from his hand and turn it over to A. This is no less a restriction on B's liberty than it was in the state of nature, since once again A's action is preventing B from doing something that she could have done without A's assistance. The property system itself—more specifically, A's property right as recognized by and enforced by that system—is restricting B's liberty. To be sure, the system of property is at the same time *protecting* A's ability to exercise his liberty, since it is protecting A's ability to do something he could do without B's assistance—namely, pick and eat the apple. The introduction of any system of property rights would restrict some non-moralized liberties and enhance others.

Narveson is not unaware of the problem. He wants to argue that A can acquire a property right to some previously unowned land, for example, without violating the liberty of B and therefore that such a property claim would not be unjust. However, on the non-moralized view, when A claims a property right, he manifestly *does* restrict B's liberty since he prevents B from doing something she otherwise could have done—namely, use the land without A's assistance. To avoid this implication, Narveson subtly shifts to a moralized view of liberty: "People may, then, take what they please, so long as what they take . . . does not adversely affect the rights that people already have. That my acquisition of a given plot thereby disenables you from having that plot is true enough, but nothing to the point since you *had no right to that plot*, any more than I did."[7] Narveson seems to concede that the property claim does restrict B's liberty—it "disenables" her—but he denies that this is relevant for justice. There is a difference, he tells us, between *restricting* a liberty and *violating* a liberty: "If the liberty restricted is not one to which we have a right, then its restriction is not a violation."[8] In effect, this is to introduce a restricted class of liberties—those to which we have a right—and to hold that justice is only concerned with these moralized liberties. How do we identify the liberties to which we have a right? We cannot simply assume that libertarian rights identify the liberties that justice protects, because that is exactly what the defender of progressive rights disputes. We would need an independent moral argument to identify our rights. To his credit, Narveson does provide such an argument, claiming that the introduction of a libertarian system of property rights would benefit everyone (or at least not harm anyone), and that this justifies it. I cannot examine this argument here, but I simply make two points. First, such an argument based on assessments of costs and benefits abandons the libertarian claim that liberty is "the only relevant consideration in political matters."[9] And second, and more importantly, if we concede that everyone would benefit from the libertarian system (compared to a state of nature with no property rights at all), it is equally true that everyone would benefit from the egalitarian system of property. We remain at a stalemate between the libertarian and the progressive system.

Libertarians often aim to establish strong property rights by arguing that they would exist even outside of political society, in a suitably understood state of nature. The idea is that if there are natural property rights, then justice will require that political societies respect those rights. Those who make such arguments are correct that states should not have complete discretion in choosing a system of property. But constraints on state action need not come from a conception of pre-political rights. Instead, we can consider directly which state actions and institutions are, and which are not, justified. This casts the justification of property in a new light. Whatever property rights (if any) we might think exist in the state of nature, the crucial fact is that in political society the state is called on to enforce a system of property rights.[10] We can simply bypass the question of property rights in the state of nature and ask directly what the state is justified in enforcing.

The Liberal Argument

Many liberal theories approach questions of this kind by considering which principles or institutions could be justified to all reasonable persons who would be subjected to their coercive imposition. John Rawls, for example, addresses this question by considering the choice from the "original position," while T. M. Scanlon asks which principles individuals could reasonably reject, and Jeremy Waldron holds that "Liberals demand that the social order should in principle be capable of explaining itself at the tribunal of each person's understanding."[11] Details aside, these approaches agree that an adequate justification for a coercively imposed institution can be given only when the institution protects the core needs and interests of each person subjected to it. An institution that violated or prevented an individual from protecting his or her own fundamental interests could not be justified to that individual, at least when a superior alternative is possible.

Liberals disagree about precisely which institutions would receive the strongest justification on this approach. Arguably, there are many systems of property rights that would be likely to protect our fundamental interests. If so, then although they may not all be equally just, they all would meet the threshold of legitimacy—that is, their enforcement would be justifiable—if chosen through a democratic political mechanism. Rawls endorses particular principles of justice, but he recognizes that there are other potentially legitimate rivals. While these alternatives differ in their details, they all protect fundamental interests, and so they all require: (1) protection of basic rights and liberties; (2) assigning special priority to those rights and liberties; and (3) "measures ensuring for all citizens adequate all-purpose means to make effective use of their freedoms."[12] Our focus is on the last of these requirements, which, once again, can be interpreted in different ways. If individuals can reasonably demand institutions that protect, under the first principle, their religious liberty and freedom of association, for example, they can also demand economic institutions that provide protection against a catastrophic loss of resources since such a loss would render the protections of the first principle empty. Rawls himself holds that this requirement goes far beyond the necessities for merely biological existence and includes the resources necessary to be able to participate fully in society as an equal citizen. But all liberal theories agree that a system that failed to ensure that all individuals receive adequate resources to satisfy their basic needs would be unjust (at least when such a guarantee would be available under a different system). As Corey Brettschneider puts the point: "No satisfactory justification could be given to anyone who falls below the threshold established by a set of basic welfare rights."[13] The libertarian system provides no such assurance, so it cannot justifiably be enforced on all when a superior system is possible. The progressive system mentioned earlier does not explicitly guarantee that none would fall below that threshold, but such an outcome seems far less likely than under the libertarian system, and to that extent the progressive system is more just.

Comparing systems of property rights based on their likely consequences in this way may appear antithetical to the libertarian approach, and it certainly conflicts with much of Nozick's rhetoric. In the Chamberlain example, Nozick assumes, in effect, that the spectators have an unlimited right to transfer their wealth to Chamberlain regardless of the distributive consequences. However, at a crucial moment in his argument, he holds that the content of the property rights themselves are determined in part by the consequences of their use. Nozick holds that the initial acquisition of property is limited by the "Lockean proviso" which requires that the acquisition not (materially) worsen the situation of others. He adds: this restriction also "constrains later actions. If my appropriating all of a certain substance violates the Lockean proviso, then so does my appropriating some and purchasing all the rest from others who obtained it without otherwise violating the Lockean proviso" (p. 179). So, for example, if all of the water rights in an area are held by various people, they may *not* then transfer all of their rights to a single individual. And crucially, Nozick says, this restriction is not an external limitation on rights, but is "internal to the theory of property itself, to its theory of acquisition and appropriation" (pp. 180–181). They don't have the right to make such transfers. This restriction does not require violating anyone's property rights in the name of some more fundamental moral consideration, but, rather, is relevant to defining which property rights people have in the first place. Contrary to the impression giving in the Chamberlain example, therefore, Nozick holds that property rights do not entitle one to transfer ownership without limitation. Furthermore, and strikingly, these limitations are grounded in the unacceptable distributive consequences that would result from allowing unlimited rights of transfer. The progressive scheme confers on property owners a different set of rights and prohibitions based on different consequences than those that concern Nozick, but in this sense it is not different in kind.

Recall that the targets of Nozick's Chamberlain argument were all theories that required that a particular pattern of distribution (such as equality) be maintained at all times. The progressive system of property rights is not like that. It follows Rawls in holding that

> a distribution cannot be judged in isolation from the system of which it is the outcome or from what individuals have done in good faith in the light of established expectations. If it is asked in the abstract whether one distribution of a given stock of things to definite individuals with known desires and preferences is better than another, then there is simply no answer to this question.[14]

Once a just institutional structure is in place, individuals may exercise their specified property rights in pursuit of their permissible ends, and "the distribution that results will be just (or at least not unjust) whatever it is."[15] The key, of course, is to specify correctly exactly what the property rights entitle one to do. The choice of one scheme of property rights over another does require that we look at the likely distributive consequences and choose a scheme that is likely to ensure that everyone's fundamental interests are satisfied and protected. Rawls advocates an institutional scheme in which the least-advantaged position does as well as possible, but as mentioned earlier, he holds that other schemes may also be legitimate, even if not as fully just. But once such a legitimate scheme is in place, justice requires that we enforce the specific property rights to which individuals come to be entitled. Nozick is right that individuals' specific property entitlements, and therefore the specific distributive outcome, will be largely unpredictable because they will be determined by the free choices that they and others make against the background of that system of property rights. But he is wrong when he suggests that distributive consequences are irrelevant to determining property rights, and even he concedes the point with regard to the Lockean proviso.

Economic and Social Justice

When we think of distributive justice as *procedural* in this way, our primary focus shifts away from the *outcomes* of the procedures specified by the economic institutions and toward the *inputs*, that is, the conditions under which individuals enter social and economic interactions.[16] To be sure, the outputs of the economic system at one point in time become inputs to the system in the future. Still, this shift in orientation is useful. For one thing, it helps bring out the point of economic justice, which is not to achieve some pattern of distribution for its own sake. Rather, it is to put each individual in a position to secure and protect their fundamental interests. This perspective also allows us to integrate the concern for distributive justice with the broader requirements of social justice. In addition to economic resources, individuals need political and civil rights, education, and fair opportunities, and the principles of justice governing these can be given a unified defense. This, in turn, helps to rebut the charge that the concern for economic justice is motivated by envy rather than the goal of equal citizenship. This perspective also helps to clarify the difference between welfare-state capitalism and what Rawls, following James Meade (1907–1995), calls a "property-owning democracy."[17] For Rawls, the goal of economic justice is not simply to ensure that "none should fall below a decent minimum standard of life," as welfare-state capitalism requires.[18] Rather, a property-owning democracy achieves distributive justice,

> not by the redistribution of income to those with less at the end of each period, so to speak, but rather by ensuring the widespread ownership of productive assets and human capital (that is, education and trained skills) at the beginning of each period, all this against a background of fair equality of opportunity. The intent is not simply to assist those who lose out through accident or misfortune (although that must be done), but rather to put all citizens in a position to manage their own affairs on a footing of a suitable degree of social and economic equality.[19]

For Rawls, economic institutions, and the property rights that they recognize, must be designed to ensure that everyone's fundamental interests are satisfied so that everyone can participate fully in social institutions as an equal. Only those institutions can be justified to all.

The argument rehearsed above for a progressive system of property rights is quite abstract. It depends on specifying our fundamental interests and then determining which institutions would best secure them. The earlier specification of a progressive system with a 10 percent tax was obviously a gross simplification. Which economic institutions and policies—including property rights, tax schedules, health, safety, and labor regulations, zoning restrictions, etc.—would best secure everyone's fundamental interests will vary in different circumstances and will be subject to reasonable disagreement. Democratic societies should have considerable, although not unlimited, discretion in the design of their economic institutions and policies. Furthermore, this entire argument has been conducted at the level of "ideal theory" since I have not considered what would be an appropriate response to past or ongoing injustice. I agree with Rawls that investigating ideal theory can help us identify and understand injustices where existing institutions depart from the ideal, but also that this is only a first step to identifying the correct response to injustice:

> Obviously the problems of partial compliance theory are the pressing and urgent matters. These are the things that we are faced with in everyday life. The reason for beginning with ideal theory is that it provides, I believe, the only basis for the systematic grasp of these more pressing problems.[20]

When existing systems of property are unjust, ideal theory helps us identify the broad direction of reforms but not the specific steps required.

Nonideal theory addresses the proper response to past and ongoing injustice. Here the case for some type of "redistribution" is apparently strong. Nozick recognizes this problem, and so in addition to his principles of initial acquisition and transfer, he asserts that we also need principles of rectification (although, as noted above, he denies that these are properly called "redistributive"). He holds that when an injustice occurs, the ideal response would be to transfer the property to the individual who *would* have acquired it (or would have been likely to acquire it) if the injustice had not occurred. But this hypothetical will often exceed our knowledge and may even be indeterminate in principle. In the face of such uncertainty, he suggests that a patterned principle may have a role: "Perhaps it is best to view some patterned principles of distributive justice as rough rules of thumb meant to approximate the general results of applying the principle of rectification of injustice" (pp. 230–231). In fact, alluding to Rawls's "difference principle," Nozick speculates that lacking detailed historical information about past injustices, "a *rough* rule of thumb for rectifying injustices might seem to be the following: organize society so as to maximize the position of whatever group ends up least well-off in the society" (Nozick, p. 231).

Conclusion

I have defended a broadly egalitarian theory of economic justice: a just society would have economic institutions and recognize a system of property rights that protected people's fundamental interests. As a matter of nonideal theory, the effort to address past injustices and to transition to a just system would, no doubt, involve transferring some goods from some individuals to others. In one sense this may be "redistributive," but this would be done in order to correct the effects of an unjust system, and this makes it analogous to the actions that would fall under Nozick's principles of rectification. As a matter of ideal theory, a progressive system would not engage in "redistribution" but merely in the enforcement of property rights once they have been properly specified. From the point of view of a libertarian system, this will appear to be redistributive; but equally, the libertarian system will appear to be redistributive from the progressive point of view. The choice between these schemes cannot be made by determining which is "redistributive." Rather, it requires that we consider which institutional scheme can be justified to all, and this depends in part on their likely distributive consequences.[21]

Notes

1. Robert Nozick, *Anarchy, State, and Utopia* (New York: Basic Books, 1974), see especially pp. 150–64. References to this work will be cited parenthetically in the text.
2. In addition to principles of just acquisition and transfer, Nozick recognizes the need for a principle of rectification to be applied when the other principles are violated. We will return to this point.
3. Instead of asking whether a person has liberty, Nozick focuses on whether an action is voluntary, and whether limitations on available opportunities render an action nonvoluntary. To simplify the exposition, we can say that a person has had their liberty violated if the actions of another person renders their action nonvoluntary.
4. See the discussion in G. A. Cohen, "Justice, Freedom, and Market Transactions," in *Self-Ownership, Freedom, and Equality* (Cambridge University Press, 1995), 59–60; and Jon Mandle, *Rawls's Justice as Fairness: An Introduction* (Cambridge, 2009), 187–92.
5. Jan Narveson, *The Libertarian Idea* (Philadelphia: Temple University Press, 1988), 7.
6. Ibid., 30.
7. Ibid., 85.
8. Ibid., 63.
9. This is most clear in Narveson's justification of the acquisition of unowned property. Narveson defends A's appropriation of unowned by focusing not on liberty but on levels of well-being: "A has not *harmed* B; he has not worsened B's situation." B's liberty, which was restricted, if not violated, is irrelevant to determining whether B's rights were violated. See Jan Narveson, "Liberty, Property, and Welfare Rights: Brettschneider's Argument," *Libertarian Papers*, 5:2 (2013), the quote is from p. 207.
10. Many people have emphasized this point, including Corey Brettschneider, "Public Justification and the Right to Private Property," in *Property Owning Democracy: Rawls and Beyond*, eds. Martin O'Neill and Thad Williamson (Malden, MA: Wiley-Blackwell, 2012), 58.

11. John Rawls, *A Theory of Justice*, revised edition (Cambridge: Harvard University Press, 1999); T. M. Scanlon, *What We Owe to Each Other* (Cambridge: Harvard University Press, 1998); Jeremy Waldron, *Liberal Rights* (Cambridge: Cambridge University Press, 1993), 61. For a brief overview of the original position, see Samuel Freeman, "Original Position," *Stanford Encyclopedia of Philosophy*, https://plato.stanford.edu/entries/original-position/ (accessed April 13, 2017).
12. John Rawls, "The Idea of Public Reason Revisited," in *Political Liberalism*, expanded edition (New York: Columbia University Press, 2005), 450.
13. Brettschneider, "Public Justification and the Right to Private Property," 61.
14. Rawls, *A Theory of Justice*, 76.
15. Ibid., 267.
16. Some theorists call this orientation "pre-distribution" rather than redistribution. See Martin O'Neill and Thad Williamson, "The Promise of Pre-distribution," http://www.policy-network.net/pno_detail.aspx?ID=4262&title=The+promise+of+pre-distribution (accessed January 16, 2017).
17. John Rawls, *Justice as Fairness: A Restatement* (Harvard University Press, 2001), 135–40. For the history of this idea, see Ben Jackson, "Property-Owning Democracy: A Short Introduction," in *Property-Owning Democracy: Rawls and Beyond* .
18. Rawls, *Justice as Fairness*, 139.
19. Ibid., 139.
20. Ibid., 8.
21. Thanks to Corey Brettschneider, Steve Cowan, David Reidy, Sarah Robert-Cady, and Ariel Zylberman for comments and suggestions.

Wealth Should Not Be Redistributed

Jan Narveson

Study Questions

1. What is the relevant sense of "redistribution" that libertarians find objectionable? Why might "distribution" and "redistribution" not be the most accurate terms for what is being discussed in this debate?

2. What, according to Bastiat, has economic value? How and why do people engage in economic exchange?

3. How might the libertarian deal with the problem of the poor? In what ways might the redistributionist create a moral claim on producers to give to the poor? How does Narveson respond to these proposals?

4. How does Narveson respond to the argument that the maker of X is not entitled to X? What about the argument that the poor contribute an equal share with the rich?

5. What does Narveson have to say about government "paternalism"?

6. What problem does Narveson have with government funding for "public goods"? How does he respond to the objections that (a) we need government to prod us to do what is right; and (b) if we don't like a proposal, we can vote against it?

7. Why does Narveson think that the redistributionist, not the libertarian, is truly guilty of immorality? How does he respond to the "bleeding heart" libertarians?

8. What is the libertarian alternative to the welfare state?

The Kind of Redistribution That's Relevant

The proposition we are discussing here needs a bit of definition. First, the word "should" here has a specific connotation when used in reference to "redistribution." In one sense, when you spend your money in any one way rather than another, you are thereby "redistributing" it—a different set of people wind up with that money than was previously the case, or than what would otherwise be the case. And sometimes, the people who end up with it do so because you simply gave it to them, as in leaving your house to your daughter. No reasonable person opposes "redistribution" in that sense. Our question is whether things—especially income and wealth—"should" be done something with in the sense that people should have no choice but to have that done with it, after they have earned it in the usual legitimate ways, as in wages for work, or returns on investments. Thus, when the government passes laws the effect of which is to move wealth, involuntarily, from some people to others, then we have redistribution of the kind we are interested in here. It is that sense of "redistribution" which is the object of many thinkers' disapproval—especially those called "libertarians."

Next, "redistributed" is a bit of a term of art in social philosophy these days. Ordinarily, to say that something is redistributed is to imply that it was previously "distributed" in some sense. But we need to think about that way of characterizing the situation. If we object to redistribution, it must evidently be supposed, then, that there is some kind of priority to the initial "distribution"— else how could one rationally be against doing it all over again? But what would give it that priority if, after all, the original "distribution" was just one more distribution of things, or money or wealth, with nothing special about it? ("The Lord giveth, and the Lord taketh away; blessed be the name of the Lord!" [Holy Bible, book of Job 1:21] Do we want to say that about the state, too? If we put it like that, it's hard to see how we could coherently object to redistribution.)

At this point, at least some of a philosophically relevant story on this subject needs to be told. In fact, the word "distributed" as a description of the situation existing before the "redistribution" being contemplated, is one to which there is reason to take exception. For in the situation ex ante, things aren't exactly "distributed" at all, really. "Distribution" suggests some sort of central headquarters that says where this is to go and where that is to go, and so on, and then that central headquarters takes steps to get it to the intended new destinations—pretty much how the Soviet Union was supposed to have worked back in its heyday. The reason for objecting to what is called "redistribution" lies in the fact that what there is in the first place is not a "distribution" in that sense, but, rather, roughly speaking, things like plain hard work (in most cases), or good luck in coming upon some valuable thing, or ingenuity expended in the course of creating the things in question (which is really more hard work, though requiring less muscle.) All of those terminate not in somebody giving something to somebody—that is, transferring its ownership or its possession from one person, A, to another person, B—but rather, in somebody coming to have something that he or she did not have before, and to have it by one or another endeavor of his or her own. Or, in the case where luck is a factor, in some bon chance of *her* own—it was she who stumbled upon it, not I, and so it's hers, not mine. Or, it was you who figured out how to make such a thing, or who actually did make it, not I. And so on. In short, the connection between the valued thing in question and the person who initially has it is direct and personal, rather than a function of some equation being manipulated by somebody, or of buttons being pushed by somebody. What theorists these days call "initial acquisition" is, generally speaking, not so much "acquisition" as creation. Those who speak of "acquisition" especially have in mind natural things—pieces of land, or fruit taken from trees that just grow on their own, or perhaps minerals taken from the ground. Yet all of those, too, require certain individuals being there and doing the work—"taking possession" by activities of their own, rather than standing there and collecting goodies falling from the sky upon them.

And so when someone proposes to "redistribute" it, there is at least a suggestion of violation of persons. In saying this, however, I pick up on the other aspect of "redistribution," namely that we are supposing that what is so-called is mandatory, forcible redistribution. Uniformed men come along and take the stuff into their hands, delivering it to that central distributor: they don't ask for it—they just take it. That's what we're talking about. The Tax Man may not actually enter your house, but if you don't send off the check, someone will come to your door, and you will have to do as he says or suffer severe consequences. Under this latter description, it surely sounds a lot more objectionable than the innocuous-sounding word "redistribution."

By contrast, consider a genuine case of "redistribution" of my first kind: for things to change hands as a result of voluntary transactions or acts of friendly gift-giving is another matter entirely. We do this all the time, after all. Among the members of families, for example, or in circles of friends, or in charitable organizations, and in many other ways, we part with some valuable things and perhaps receive others, often in the hope of making a profit, but also often just because we like the people we give them to, and because they enjoy or need the things we buy. No problem here: this is the stuff of life, and a great deal of it, too. And once again, we have to point out, forcible redistribution by the state would cut into those friendly activities, too, quite possibly severely. If you take half of my fortune, there's that much less for me to give to my favorite symphony orchestra, or niece, or whatever other set of persons I think are deserving of my assistance, whatever it may be. And then the question is: Why do you—the distributor—get to override my judgments on these matters, in regard to what to do with my things—my wealth, my possessions, my manuscripts? How does someone else have that authority over me—the person who is responsible for the very existence of the valued things in question?

The Case against Redistribution

Our question, again in philosophical language, is thus the moral status of the creation of what has economic value. But what is economic value, in particular? To this, I think, the French philosopher/economist/journalist/gentleman farmer Frederic Bastiat (1801–1850) gives the fundamental and correct answer: what has economic value is not "goods," just like that, but more generally services.[1] A is willing to "pay" something to B if B performs a particular service for A that A wants B to do. Quite often, to be sure, the service will consist in transferring possession of some objects to A, as at the grocery store. But often it will consist not in transferring an object but doing a service in a narrower sense: attending to A's illness if B is a doctor, for example; or performing a violin concerto; or advising A about investment strategy; or participating in the design of some sophisticated piece of software. In those cases, pretty much nothing in the way of material objects passes from one person to another, apart from the odd sandwich or piece of notepaper. (But what does get "transferred" in the way of music or software ideas may be very valuable, indeed.)

How much will A pay? Notice that paying for something is also doing a service: if B desires money, which most of us do, then transferring to B possession of some of A's money does B a desired service. The amount A will pay is based on A's perception of the relative value to A of B's particular service, as compared with alternatives. The alternatives might consist of doing something himself without any transaction, or buying something else, or putting the money back in the piggy bank—it's all up to the individual with the money or with whatever else he or she proposes to trade for it.

If someone discovers the idea of the plan for an invention, say, and is able to put it into manufacture or sell it to someone who does and who will bring it to the attention and availability of consumers, that will do a useful service to millions of people—and this inventor just might end up making a great deal of money. It happens. If B is a really good racing car driver and millions of people are interested in watching him drive, he may be paid a great deal of money for this. (The best current Formula One drivers are earning many millions of dollars per year. Those not quite so good may actually be paying for the privilege of driving one.) And so on. In all these cases, the parties to the exchange participate voluntarily: each is trying to pursue his or her interests—no one forces the parties to make the exchanges in question. We do things for each other, to each other's benefit.

The people who buy this service, then, in whatever way they do (by buying a ticket to the race, or by buying advertised items on the TV broadcast, etc.), do so voluntarily. They like what they see and are willing to pay the proposed price—otherwise, they would not avail themselves of that service (for example, the many people not interested in races do not buy tickets to them.)

As Robert Nozick plausibly argued,[2] it is hard to see how one could complain about this, since both parties get what they want, and third parties are not affected (though to be sure, sometimes they are, and when that is so, it is important to get their approval as well.) On the other hand, if authorities come along and prevent one or both from making the transactions in question, then it surely looks as if they do have a complaint. Their preferred ways of living have been to that extent disrupted.

Now, why should that matter? It is easy to see why it matters to those particular people. They are acting on their interests, fulfilling those interests in what they see to be good ways. They are living their lives. Persons' interests are part of them. Along with their bodies and the rest of their souls, interests define the person: this is what they do, what they want, and thus what guides their choices.

The Poor

One major claim of redistributionists concerns the "poor." They hold that those who do well by exchanging the various services they are able to perform ought to accept a reduction in their incomes for the sake of those who do not do so well. What, if anything, might persuade those high-income-earners of this? Notice how the question is put. It isn't that we get to assume a superior attitude and just tell the rich that their superior wealth is morally tainted, or whatever (though it often seems that way). Rather, the more rational redistributionist argues that if we are all to be acting together in this world, then each of us should be ready to agree on our terms of acting thus.

And how could we reach such agreement—practical agreement, after all—other than on the basis of each person's interests, which are what make them tick? Of course, they may have moral ideas (often primitive ones) or even moral principles in there somewhere, too. But (a) would everybody have the same ones, when they differ so much about everything else? As we know, certainly not. And what do we do, then, about the ones who do differ? And (b) what about those who appear to have none at all? In these latter cases, we need some way of persuading them, with good arguments, that this or that is the way we should all be going. That is, we "need" that way if we are to claim that we are proceeding rationally, respecting everyone's reason rather than just trampling over people.

So how do we do that? The brief answer is by contemplating interaction among all these people. Each of us has some considerable power to affect the lives of those around us, and they have the power to affect ours. If I make use of my power by trying to exact what I want, by force, from the others, then they'll respond by using their probably pretty much equal power to prevent me from succeeding, or they'll turn tables and elect to try to exploit me as I try to exploit them. In the large, this is a lose-lose proposition. On the other hand, how about using our powers to create values that others may choose when they can? And how do they persuade us to part with those valued things? Surely the best way is by proposing to do services for us in return, sufficiently valuable to induce our favorable response. And if neither of us has anything to offer? Then at least we can agree to leave each other in peace, to get on with our lives as best we can.

Doing this last may not always be easy, but, at least on the face of it, it is always possible. We can draw boundaries, for example, and then each remain within the territory that is ours, asking permission whenever we want to use someone else's. And of course, we can plead for assistance. It is often likely to be forthcoming. We are all mortal, and vulnerable, and we can often be of help to each other. You help me, I help you! That is the flip side of: You don't hit me, I don't hit you.

Now the problem with the "redistributionist" becomes clear: Person A has created something of value; person B has not, or at any rate not enough to attract the favorable attention of A. Suppose that B now claims to be (and perhaps really is) in need. A can agree that B has a perfect right to ask for his assistance—words are (usually) cheap. But the redistributionist alleges that B doesn't need to ask: by right, says our hypothetical theorist, his needs create a moral claim upon A. Well, if they, indeed, do, then how do they create that claim? Unfortunately, the hypothetical theorist has no good answer. He can proclaim that, after all, we are all equal. That may be a charming slogan, but it has one serious problem: we manifestly are not equal, and especially so in the respects most relevant to the situation here, namely, the ability to create what will sustain our lives. If the theorist holds, instead, that this is a basic moral equality, what is to prevent A from telling him to either explain this in ways that make sense to him, or just dry up? Unfortunately, redistributionists by and large do neither. And they need to do better, else they have no case.

On the other hand, there is a case for general peace. But general peace does not consist in some people depriving others of what they have made, and even of proclaiming a right to do that on top of it. Just the opposite: this is likely to generate war as the relative "haves" defend their possessions. To be general, the peace must be enjoyed by all—the rich as well as the poor. Peace is when we are all safe from the predations of all others. It is not, however, when we are all safe from droughts, storms, lightning strokes, and so on. It is when we are safe from each other. But your being compelled to feed me is not just a matter of "safety." After all, you (we are supposing) had nothing to do with my unhappy situation. On the contrary, by working and inventing, etc., you have probably made my life better already than it would otherwise have been. How does that generate a case for compelling you to do still more?

If this is to be seriously disputed, one of two major changes in basic ideas will be needed. Either it must be argued that the maker of X is not entitled thereby to X; or, it must be argued that, contrary to appearances, the poor do, in fact, contribute an equal share with the rich (or, at any rate, with those among the rich who we think are "self-made"). Neither looks very promising. And they are extreme. Of course we may, if we wish, adopt the Marxian slogan ("From each according to his ability; to each according to his need!") as a personal maxim: the highly productive are certainly welcome to share their output with all and sundry if they wish. The question is not that. It is whether we, the rest of us, get to compel the highly productive to do that. That is far from obvious. Either of the two claims would, if established, be sufficient to establish our right to do that. So they are clearly relevant. But they are not, to put it mildly, clearly right. The connection between productive effort and capability, and possession of the results, is natural and strong. We work that we may eat, and if we work extraordinarily effectively, we eat extraordinarily well. Indeed, the use of our products is usually the point of production—consumption by the producer is part or most of the point of productive action. If you sever the connection, you demotivate the producer. For many people, the question "Why work if you don't thereby get to eat?" is decisive. They won't work in order that others may eat, and especially not that they eat well. Or at least, they won't work nearly as much or as well.

Turning to the other issue, here the problem is that empirically it is really obvious that we are not all equally productive. Many do not contribute, and among those, many could not contribute, to the making of good X. The number of people who could contribute significantly to fundamental physical theory is miniscule—a few handfuls in the world. The rest of us can only stand by and admire, if, indeed, we have any idea what they are doing. If those who can do nothing to make X nevertheless contribute to the making of Y, and if Y is valued, then exchange becomes relevant, and the benefits of the division of labor set in. But here is where the two issues interact. May not a given participant judge the proposed terms of exchange and decide whether what is offered in return for his or her products is worth it? That's normal in market exchanges, after all. And if one concludes it is not, doesn't one's right extend to turning down the offer and awaiting a better one? To deny this is to curtail human freedom. And how do you justify that? Why does one person's utility override another's freedom?

The view that the state knows better than we what to do with our lives goes under the name "paternalism"—treating us adults as if we were children. When we consider what sort of people the state typically consists of, most of us would view with incredulity the claim that they know better than we how to run our lives. Do you really think your prime minister or president, or the members of their cabinets, have the wisdom and discernment to tell us how we should live? I doubt it!

All of us, these days, do, indeed, consult experts on many matters: financial, medical, legal, agricultural, you name it. But those experts do not have the power to tell us what to do. Instead, they are purveyors of advice, which we are free to reject. That is not so with our governments. Their pronouncements are not advice. They are orders. We do what they say, or else! Surely we should ask: Is that any way to run a society?

Public Goods

There is a special set of subcases that is generally appealed to by defenders of government programs. These concern "public goods": goods that are "public" in the sense, first, that they are supposed to be of benefit to people at large, to the public, rather than just some few particular individuals. And secondly, they have the peculiar and very important property that you can't apportion the benefits to those who pay for them. Examples include such things as roads, public transportation, parks, and the like. With public goods, some people can "free ride"—get the benefit without paying. And the people who do pay (with their money or their work) end up not getting nearly the benefits they have created.

For example, in my town, the local government recently decided to build an "LRT" (Light Rail Transit), supposedly because this would provide efficient transportation to vast numbers of people (who don't yet inhabit our rather small urban area). During the years when this proposal was being vetted by members of the relevant government, one argument was especially effective: that—what do you know!—most (about two-thirds) of the very substantial cost (a billion dollars, at least) would be picked up by the Province of Ontario and the Government of Canada. So, the 34.5 million Canadians who do not live in my city would be paying most of the cost for a railroad system that would only benefit a few people living here. Critics, meanwhile, demonstrated that the existing bus system was well able to transport the expected numbers at about the same level of efficiency. The LRT in this city is a "public bad"—it inflicts costs on all and benefits only very few. I suggest that that is a very typical case of "supply of public goods" by governments, composed as they are of ambitious people wanting to be identified with "projects for the good of the people." In the process, as I've noted, the Will of the People—famed in democratic theory—was thoroughly ignored, and their pocket books invaded well into the fairly far future, for something few wanted or would benefit from, in lieu of available well-working alternatives.

But the case against redistribution doesn't rest only on glaring bad examples, however numerous. Rather, it rests on typical, quite normal examples. Little that governments do, indeed, does not involve taking from some people to give to others, with an expectation that by and large there are more losers than winners in the process. After all, if all the premises that are invoked to justify it were true—if we all really did benefit from the imposed expenditure—then why would it have to be extracted from us? Surely we would voluntarily buy things and systems with those lovely properties. If Light Rail Transit could be profitable, we would not need taxed money to form the capital for it: some people could make a profit by providing the capital and planning themselves. Government imposes on us precisely because those properties are, in fact, very rarely if ever possessed by very many of the things they do.

It might be suggested that we don't voluntarily do what we know is right because we are not very good, morally speaking, and we need government to prod us into doing the right thing. If you think that, you thereby reject the entire basis of liberalism. And, of course, you have the question of, who does know what is right—and if we did know who, how would we be sure that our political system would get him into office? Plato's Guardians seem to have been a self-selected elite—as it must be, because who else could have enough wisdom to identify, and then install in the appropriate places of power, those Right People? Who, as the classic question puts it, guards the Guardian? Questions like that have plagued political Platonism since the beginning.

It would be silly to say that we should never be guided by anyone else's judgment. We pay doctors, financial advisers, and many more to do things that we think they will do better than we could. But there's all the difference between being free to select our advisers, and someone else making those decisions without consulting the persons for whom the decisions are made. It might be responded that we do, after all, have the vote. But then the same question arises: if you disagree with the majority's (or more likely, the smallish plurality's) view, you have no recourse. Your weight is 1/N where N is the number of voters in the relevant constituency—a vanishingly small amount, as compared with the 1/1 weight that your judgment has in the case of you. We do far better at buying groceries, or selecting charities to support, than the majority does in buying for us.

The argument here has two different aspects, which we should now separate:

(1) On the one hand, there is an argument about the efficacy, even perhaps the rationality, of the kind of collective decision making that what we are calling redistribution involves.

(2) On the other, there is a question of principle here. If your own judgment is to be regarded as fundamental and to be protected, in all matters, then that includes the disposal of your income or other assets in the direction of the needy.

People vary. Almost all of us are positively disposed toward the poor and needy: we wish them well. But perhaps not nearly so many are ready to contribute really substantial amounts for their support if that were to prove necessary. Critics will thus accuse the libertarian, who insists on our liberty in all matters other than those that would inflict undeserved costs on others, of being coldhearted, selfish, and no doubt immoral.

Morality is the central issue here. If, as libertarians claim, we have the fundamental right to use ourselves and thus our resources as we direct, then it is the critic whose advocacy of exacting support for the poor by forcible extraction from the better-off who stands convicted of immorality. And who has the better morality? I think the libertarians do! The "case" for redistribution rests entirely on sheer assertion and feeling. The libertarian's case against it rests on rational analysis.

In so saying, I take issue with many in the ranks of those who today account themselves as libertarians. These are "bleeding heart" libertarians, who profess more sympathy with at least parts of the welfare state. The difficulty with their position on the face of it is that it's hard to see how we can defend any clearly redistributive policies on purely libertarian premises. But there is some common ground. Especially, there are serious questions about public goods. These are the goods that don't track easily to the free interactions of individuals on the market. If everyone benefits but no one is forced to pay, will we have such benefits? A common answer is "No," with the implication that we will need to resort to political agency, with its powers of compulsion, to provide them.

Then the question is whether welfare can be understood as a public good, and the trouble is that it surely seems not to be. If Jones is sick, or his skills become useless in the prevailing technological circumstances, how do we all benefit from maintaining him despite his problems? Of course, it's easy to see why his employer would want to be sure that Jones had good health insurance; but otherwise, it is hard to see that there is any good answer to this, except for the benefit of seeing our fellows happy rather than miserable (or in the extreme, alive rather than dead.) And while this latter is a benefit to most of us—well, the trouble is that it's only "most of" us. In many parts of the world, where many people hate our guts, quite likely it isn't viewed as a benefit at all, but rather as an occasion to cheer!

The Alternative to the Welfare State

Libertarians hold that everything in society should be done with the consent of all who are affected. Business transactions—hated by so many "liberals" these days—normally have this property. Both parties in their own view benefit from the deal, and usually outsiders are not affected. That is, not unless you claim that being on the downside of an "inequality" is an effect. But what is the "effect"? It is that their sense of envy is dissatisfied. Suppose I make $10,000 and you and Ed make a deal which makes each of you $100,000, doing nothing for me (I don't perhaps buy the goods they make). Am I now "harmed"? I still have my $10,000, after all. And if my outrage at being left out is counted as a "harm" to me, then what about all those fanatical proponents of religion X, who take offense at the rest of us insisting on remaining with our previous religions? Those who invoke such arguments have long since abandoned liberty as their guide.

Meanwhile, it would be possible to form associations of those who want to help life for the poor. Indeed, it is widely done already. America and Canada are well equipped with care institutions, which are willing to take in the needy and provide them with clean beds and wholesome meals. And the money saved from the taxes that would no longer be imposed to support typically inefficient welfare agencies would be available for possible investment as well as charitable work. Those who think this impossible underestimate the warmth and generosity of their fellows. But there's no underestimating the spirit of rent-seeking, which hovers over all proposals to exert coercion against people who don't agree with the planners' idea of "public charity."

Notes

1 Frederic Bastiat, "On Value," in *Economic Harmonies*, trans. W. Hayden Boyers (Irvington-on-Hudson: Foundation for Economic Education, 1996), 99–155.
2 Robert Nozick, *Anarchy, State, and Utopia* (New York: Basic Books, 1974), chap. 6.

RESPONSES

Response to Mandle

Jan Narveson

Study Questions

1. How does Narveson respond to Mandle's claim that the real issue concerns the correct system of property rights?
2. How does Narveson clarify his view of liberty? What does he think Mandle fails to see?
3. What do libertarians believe to be the only rightful interferences with liberty? Why does this pose a problem for redistributionists like Mandle?
4. According to Narveson, what does Mandle ignore in his criticism of "initial appropriation"?
5. Why does Narveson think that a Rawlsian system of distributive justice is incoherent?
6. How does Narveson reply to Mandle's claim that everyone would benefit from an egalitarian system of property?

Professor Mandle's paper is interesting and involved, and deserves much more discussion than we are allowed here. But he makes three main points to which I will reply.

Redistribution *Is* the Issue

First, Mandle claims that the issue before us is not properly one of when it is justified to interfere with property rights, but, rather, what the correct system of rights is in the first place—thus, as he supposes, opening the door to alternatives.

Quick reply: Of course, what we want to know is the correct principle of property rights; but then, if there is a correct system, and there is some government initiative in which its requirements are impugned, it will be reasonable to describe that initiative as involving "redistribution." Naturally, I think that the sort of measures Mandle favors are describable in this way.

Liberty Is a Moral Issue

Second, Mandle claims that despite my professions, I employ a "moralized conception of liberty," and, indeed, that I go contrary to my proclamation that the only thing that should count in politics is liberty.

My response here is denial, along with the needed clarification (as in "a philosopher is a person who, when he or she gets in trouble, makes a distinction!"). Mandle's discussion mainly depends on an endnote (note 9), in which he makes this remark: "Narveson defends A's appropriation of unowned [items] by focusing not on liberty but on levels of well-being," [saying, for example] "A has not harmed B; he has not worsened B's situation." Mandle infers: "B's liberty, which was restricted, if not violated, is irrelevant to determining whether B's rights were violated."

The sentence by me which he quotes talks about harming and worsening. These are things people do to each other. But B's liberty in relation to A consists in the absence of harmings, or worsenings, of B's situation by A if B doesn't do what A wants him to. It is impossible to talk about liberty otherwise: it has to do with interventions or their lack. The defense of the libertarian view of initial appropriation is that if A does not deprive B of anything—does not proceed by visiting or threatening B with some sort of harms or deprivations in the process of appropriating—then we should award the status of property (rightful possession) to A. Each person acts to achieve some envisaged good for himself (or that of selected others, such as loved ones). But it is not from some impersonal interest in promoting or maximizing good that we come up with principles of justice: it is, rather, from an interest in enabling all of us individuals to get on with our lives, which requires being free from the impositions—the imposed harms—of others. In other words, our interest in our liberty.

Mandle fails to see that distinguishing between A's picking of the apple and B's picking it on the basis of who got to it first is not arbitrary, but fundamental and essential. It is relevant because, if A already has it and B comes along and takes it from A, then B has harmed A, and so curtailed A's liberty. (A wanted to pick and eat the apple; B forcibly prevents A from doing so. Of course, if B had been first, then that would not have been an imposition on A.) As Hume observed long ago, trying to award rights on the basis of equality or virtue leads to chaos. But prohibiting violence, such as by those who "arrive" too late to get the first apples, is the way of peace, and thus to a just and productive society.

When I say that bad systems "lead to chaos" or the like, do I mean to deny that liberty is "the only relevant consideration in political matters"? No. Firstly, remember that these are political contexts. In civil life, we generally aren't pushing people around, whereas in politics we always are. As I have written previously, principles about right and wrong always deny liberty to some and award it to others. The only question is, Whose liberty do we restrict, and why? Libertarians hold that rightful interferences with liberty are preventions of the liberty to interfere with, destroy, etc., the liberty of others. These others have to have "rightful," legitimate liberties in the relevant contexts, of course. What makes them so? In libertarians' views, it is that the activities they are doing or proposing are, in turn, harmless: they involve only voluntary relations with others. A doesn't push B around; but B does push A or C around. Good political institutions are so by virtue of preventing B from doing the "pushing" in question—from promoting his own good by worsening the situations of others, in Gauthier's elegant formulation.[1] That is, it is those who contravene the liberty of others whose liberty to do that is to be denied, not those whose activities are harmless (i.e., that do not so contravene the liberties of further parties). Redistributionists like Mandle, however, do favor engaging in such contraventions, namely, on those who work and produce without doing so at the expense of others. That is the basis of libertarian opposition to what is very reasonably referred to as "redistribution."

When governments propose to provide goods and opportunities to some on the sort of grounds Mandle advocates, such as "need" or "disadvantage," they thereby violate this voluntariness. The taxes they impose for helping B are imposed on A, who has no choice. In the hardware store, or the stock market, or in charitable endeavors, all the participants act on their own volitions, buying, selling, or giving as seems best to them. But not in governmental interventions. Those are coercive. Are those coercions justified? In my view, only when their purpose is to prevent (or perhaps punish) the coercions of others. But Mandle thinks ordinary productive people may be coerced—robbed, as many would put it—solely in order to benefit selected others.

In his criticism of "initial appropriation," Mandle pays no attention to what we libertarians insist is central: production, or creation, of what is valuable. The fact that somebody makes the goods doesn't seem to interest him. But libertarians think that factor is crucial: it is the basis of that maker's claim to own (i.e., to be held to have the right to determine the further "distribution" of) the things in question, rather than persons who contributed nothing to its production but would still like to have the benefits of it.

Contra Rawlsianism

Mandle's third claim is that we can coherently proceed along Rawlsian-type lines, in which there is a "progressive system of property"—for example, one in which property owners have libertarian rights, except that 10 percent of the sales are transferred to the "least advantaged members of society." We libertarians think that such systems are (a) incoherent, and (b) especially unfounded. Let me explain why.

When Mandle calls the 10 percent rule a "system," he apparently means that it is a logically possible piece of legislation. But that isn't what we're talking about here. We are talking about fundamental principles, and these should underpin legislation rather than simply being possible examples of it. So the question is, Where would be the conceptual underpinnings of such an arbitrary idea? If it's Rawls, then the reader should be aware that Rawls's idea, as found in his Second Principle of Justice, has a huge problem.[2] His idea is that goods should be distributed "to the greatest benefit of the least advantaged." Question: Always? Without qualification? If so, his principle would entail pure equality: if anybody has less than anybody and redistribution is possible, then it would be called for by this understanding of the principle.

But that isn't what he wants. He thinks inequalities are possibly justifiable (as do we all). What would "justicize" them? Rawls's answer is: incentive. If the worse-off can have more because the better-off create still more, why not pay them more to get it? Well, with what further restrictions? Is it, "so long as there is any sort of benefit to any of the 'less advantaged'?" If so, that's the free market, for such transactions are always to mutual benefit, with the further libertarian restriction, of course, that others are not to be worsened in the process. But this does not compel the better-off to continually supply the worse-off with free stuff.[3] The point is that Rawls has no clear principle of distribution apart from the libertarian one. And neither, I submit, does Mandle.

Both Rawls and I claim that the principle of justice (as Mandle notes) should benefit everyone. To my claim that libertarianism and only libertarianism does this, Mandle makes a twofold reply. "First," he says, "such an argument . . . abandons the libertarian claim that liberty is 'the only relevant consideration in political matters'" (p. 246). I have already shown above that this first claim is wrong.

"Second," Mandle says, "if we concede that everyone would benefit from the libertarian system (compared to a state of nature with no property rights at all), it is equally true that everyone would benefit from the egalitarian system of property" (Ibid.). That would, indeed, be definitive—but it is not true! For an egalitarian "system of property" necessarily requires violence against the more productive, and that does not "benefit" them. Obviously, it harms them. You'd have to find some way of claiming that commencing to labor on hitherto unowned bits of stuff somehow harms (i.e., interferes with the liberty of) those who are thereby rendered unable to use that stuff—which after all is then the owned property thus acquired—and attempts to do that are incoherent. As Locke pointed out, if you try to universalize that as a complaint, you end up with nobody being allowed to use anything, and we all starve to death. That's equality, perhaps, but not quite what Mandle or Rawls wants!

A more careful reading, then, shows that Mandle's criticisms are baseless. Coerced redistribution still looks unjust.

Notes

1. David Gauthier, *Morals by Agreement* (New York: Oxford, 1986), 203–5.
2. John Rawls, *A Theory of Justice* (Cambridge: Harvard University Press, 1971), 302.
3. For more, see Jan Narveson, "A Puzzle about Economic Justice in Rawls's Theory," *Social Theory and Practice*, 4:1 (Fall 1976): 1–28.

Response to Narveson

Jon Mandle

Study Questions

1. What does Narveson wrongly take for granted according to Mandle?
2. What does Mandle think that justice requires regarding the question of property rights? Why?
3. What questions or problems does Mandle raise for Narveson's claim that there is a natural connection between production and ownership?
4. What criticisms does Mandle make of Narveson's "contract model" of property rights?
5. According to Mandle, what is the proper perspective from which to compare systems of property rights? Why does he think this perspective is just?

Jan Narveson and I agree that not all changes in ownership count as redistribution in the relevant sense. We also agree that the relevant conception of redistribution involves a change in ownership that is enforced by the state and is independent of the consent of the individuals involved. But Narveson seems to believe that the moral issue of redistribution is best addressed by asking when the violation of one person's property rights is justified by some external purpose, such as increasing another person's utility. His answer, roughly, is that such violations are rarely if ever justified, since they all involve restricting the property owner's freedom. This approach takes for granted that we know what rights a person has when he or she owns some property, since only then can we know whether a tax, for example, violates those rights. In contrast, I believe that the most productive philosophical engagement occurs not in determining whether some particular tax or public expenditure is just, efficient, or prudent, but, rather, in determining what system of property rights is justified in the first place.

Not Just One Possible System

There is not just one natural or obvious system of property rights that is best for all times and places. In fact, for any given society, there are typically many possible systems of property rights that could potentially be legitimate. Therefore, justice requires that there be a political process, itself legitimate, to authoritatively select from among these possibilities for a society. Narveson apparently disagrees and seems to suggest that there is no real problem in determining how property rights are generated or their content. In most cases, at least, he thinks that there is a natural relationship between production and ownership that doesn't require further exploration: "The connection between productive effort and capability, and possession of the results, is natural and strong" (p. 259).[1] But to use one of his examples: What are the rights of someone who "discovers the idea of the plan for an invention . . . that will do a useful service to millions of people" (p. 257)? A society must choose not only whether to recognize intellectual property, but also many other issues, such as: What types of knowledge are subject to such ownership? What legal form does it take? How long does such ownership last? What, if anything, must be done to protect such ownership? Is there mandatory licensing, and if so, at what rate? Are there exceptions for fair use? The specification of property rights in physical objects, in real property (land), and in legal tender, all raise distinct but analogous questions—for example: What risks does ownership allow one to impose on others? How extensive are the air rights over one's land or mineral rights below? May one create or destroy banknotes? And to what systems of taxation are all of these forms of property subject? Morality does not dictate a single answer to these (and innumerable other) questions for all times and places. At the philosophical level, the most we can do is to identify the considerations that are relevant to the political process that must answer these questions for a given society.

Narveson suggests that recognizing property rights serves as an incentive to production and innovation: "If you sever the connection, you demotivate the producer" (p. 259). This is often true, although not always, and is a relevant consideration when a society considers which system of property rights to recognize. But patents, for example, need not last forever in order to serve as incentives, and there are considerations other than productive efficiency that a society should take into account. To repeat Nozick's example, if a system of property rights makes it likely (or even possible) that one person may come to own all of the water rights in a community, this tells strongly against that system of property. Similarly, if a system of property is likely to result in vast wealth for a few individuals and the impoverishment of the majority, this, too, is an important reason to reject that system of rights.

How Do We Decide?

How should a society decide, through its political mechanism, which system of property rights to recognize and enforce? Narveson suggests a contract model in which an adequate justification of a system of property requires that it serve the rational self-interest of each individual. In other words, a system is justified only if it benefits everyone. But what is the relevant baseline from which to judge each individual's gains or losses, and therefore the rational acceptability of a proposal? Sometimes Narveson seems to argue that the recognition of property rights is beneficial for everyone compared to there being no property at all, while at other times he suggests that we compare alternatives to the current de facto system of property. The problem with the former is that there are many different systems of property rights that would satisfy this requirement—some will be highly inegalitarian while others will be much more egalitarian—and he gives us no method for choosing from among them. The problem with the latter is that it risks codifying existing injustice, as an example will illustrate.

The Emancipation Proclamation of 1863, and the 13th Amendment, adopted in 1865, represented radical changes in the scheme of property rights in the United States. No longer were property rights in other persons to be recognized. There was also a possibility of further redistributive changes during Reconstruction. Who would own the land that had been the property of white plantation owners but worked by slaves? In January 1865, General Sherman issued Special Order 15, which, as historian Eric Foner describes, set aside "the Sea Islands and a portion of the low country rice coast south of Charleston, extending thirty miles inland, for the exclusive settlement of blacks. Each family would receive forty acres of land, and Sherman later provided that the army could assist them with the loan of mules."[2] And in July 1865, without telling President Johnson, Oliver Howard, the Commissioner of the Freedmen's Bureau, "issued Circular 13, which instructed Bureau agents to 'set aside' forty-acre tracts for the freedmen as rapidly as possible."[3]

This order conflicted with the spirit, if not the letter, of President Johnson's Amnesty Proclamation of May 29, 1865.[4] Johnson "soon directed Howard to rescind his order," and "in the end the amount of land that came into the possession of blacks proved to be miniscule."[5] Writing in 1935, W. E. B. Du Bois (1868–1963) pointed out: "Again and again, crudely but logically, the Negroes expressed their right to the land and the deep importance of this right . . . for 250 years the Negroes had worked on this land, and by every analogy in history, when they were emancipated the land ought to have belonged in large part to the workers."[6] Against this, however, he observed, there was a "deep repugnance on the part of Northerners to confiscating individual property."[7] Without resolving what exactly justice would have required, I will simply observe that the redistribution of land would not have served the plantation owners' interests relative to the existing distribution. Yet, that fact is surely not morally decisive. If an existing distribution is unjust, justice may very well require a redistribution that does not benefit everyone.

When we focus on whether a scheme of property rights is just, the question of whether some individual act of state enforcement counts as a redistribution or not fades in importance. What matters is the selection of the particular system of property rights that the state will enforce—including entitlements, limitations, tax rates, answers to the questions listed above, and much else. I agree with Narveson that this system must recognize the interests of all citizens and, in some sense, be justifiable to them. But this justification cannot take for granted the existing distribution of wealth. We need a baseline that is itself just. Since the selection of a system of property is a collective political decision, the proper perspective from which to compare alternative schemes is a hypothetical one in which all citizens are political equals. A system of property rights that predictably leads to the violation or neglect of the basic interests of some citizens simply cannot be justified to those individuals, whoever they are. The reform of an unjust system and the transition to a just one will, no doubt, involve redistribution (relative to the previous system), and the demands of justice may be contrary to the self-interest of those who profited unjustly from the previous regime. Once a just system of property is in place, however, the normal role of the state will be to enforce each individual's rights and thereby allow individuals to freely pursue their goals in ways that are compatible with others doing the same.

Notes

1 By "possession" Narveson must mean not merely physical possession but rightful possession, or property.

2 Eric Foner, *Reconstruction: America's Unfinished Revolution, 1863–1877*, updated edition (New York: Harper Perennial, 2014), 70.
3 Ibid., 159.
4 Ibid., 183.
5 Ibid., 159, 161.
6 W. E. B. Du Bois, *Black Reconstruction in America 1860–1880* (New York: The Free Press, 1998, first published in 1935), 368.
7 Ibid., 601.

Questions for Reflection

1. Mandle seems to deny that property rights are natural rights—that is, he seems to hold that property rights are created and defined by social or political institutions. Would you agree? Why?
2. How would you respond to Nozick's "Wilt Chamberlain" case? Is he entitled to all the money that people put in the basket for him or not? Why?
3. Mandle favors Rawls's view of distributive justice that seeks to make sure that the institutions and policies adopted by a society do not have harmful consequences for its least-advantaged members. Narveson favors Nozick's view that focuses on whether or not the initial acquisition of property is just or not. Which approach do you think is morally better? Why?
4. Narveson thinks that government-enforced redistribution of wealth is tantamount to stealing. Is he right? Why?
5. What do you think is the best way to care for the needs of the poor—the libertarian voluntary approach or the liberal government welfare approach? Why?

8

When May the Government Wage War?

The Government Should Never Wage War

Andrew Alexandra

> ### Study Questions
>
> 1. What three moral precepts underlie Alexandra's argument against war? What follows from these precepts? What factual question does the debate over war hinge on?
>
> 2. Why, according to Alexandra, is violence a bad thing? What conditions must be met in order to justify the use of violence?
>
> 3. What special demands do the conditions for the use of violence place on those who may be attacked?
>
> 4. How does war amplify the badness of violence?
>
> 5. What are the two legitimate functions of armies? Which function is primary? Why?
>
> 6. What policy regarding war do modern nations adopt? According to Alexandra, what is the only way this policy can be justified? Why do modern nations think it is justified?
>
> 7. What evidence does Alexandra provide for the effectiveness of civil resistance over military defense?
>
> 8. What is the "Security Dilemma"? How does a policy of civil resistance apparently resolve the dilemma?

9. How, according to Alexandra, do powerful militaries subvert a nation's political integrity? What threat do such militaries pose to their nation's own people?

The government should never wage war. Not only should it never wage war, but it should also never be *able* to wage war. It should remove its capacity to do so by destroying its stockpile of weapons and disbanding its armed forces, and put in their place a system of organized nonviolence—civil resistance—to deter and resist potential invasion.

Accustomed as we are to thinking that our security depends on the existence of powerful armed forces, those claims might seem implausible, fanciful, or even ridiculous. They are presented here, however, as conclusions of an argument whose premises consist only of broadly accepted moral precepts and well-supported appeals to matters of fact. If that argument is cogent, then those who accept these premises should, at the very least, be prepared to take seriously the thought that our government should never wage war. The next two paragraphs provide the skeleton of my argument; the sections that follow put flesh on the bones of that skeleton.

Three moral precepts underpin my argument: firstly, that violence is a bad thing; secondly, that violence can nevertheless be justified if, and only if, it is the only feasible way to avoid some greater evil; and finally, that the government has a duty to protect the territorial and political integrity of the state over which it has authority. So far, I think, so uncontroversial. It follows from these precepts that if we can equip ourselves with effective nonviolent means to avoid the evils that would justify the use of violence absent such means, then we should do so. So, if the territorial and political integrity of the state can be protected by civil resistance, the government should adopt it as the system of national defense, and do away with its capacity and willingness to wage war.

Resolving the disagreement between those who think that the state should do away with its capacity to wage war and those who don't thus hinges on the answer to a factual question: Can civil resistance protect the state? Attention to the historical record, and reflection on the theoretical basis of civil resistance, justify a positive answer to that question; civil resistance is probably at least as effective as armed force. Moreover, relying on armed forces for security actually increases the risks from which those forces are supposed to protect us. They contribute to the militarization of the international sphere, making it increasingly unstable, and they can be—and often have been—used to usurp or undermine democratic control of the government. Civil resistance, on the other hand, will help demilitarize the international sphere, and can itself be democratically structured.

The Morality of Violence

War is a form of violence and violence is a bad thing. It causes pain, fear, and anger in its victims and distress to those who witness it. Targets of violence often respond in kind, setting off an escalating struggle, the outcome of which is unpredictable and may be radically disproportionate to the original wrong. Violent antagonists see each other merely as obstacles to be overcome, rather than as rational beings with whom disagreements can be resolved through reason and mutual compromise. Who prevails depends on relative strength and cunning, not on who (if anyone) is in the right. And the aftermath of such struggles is often destruction, trauma, hatred, and remorse. Violence, then, is both bad in itself, in its denial of our nature as rational, cooperative beings, and bad in its consequences.

Since violence is a bad thing, the less of it there is, the better. Some thinkers, such as Leo Tolstoy (1828–1910), have seen violence as so bad that its use could never be justified. Most of us think, however, that the badness of violence does not mean that we could never be, or never actually are, justified in using it. We think, for example, that we are entitled to use violence if it is necessary to prevent being bashed or raped, as are others who come to our aid. In such cases, violence does not stop being bad; it becomes the lesser of two evils. Because it remains bad we need to justify its use—to show that certain conditions hold that permit us to do things which are normally forbidden. The most important of these conditions are just cause, proportionality, last resort, and necessity. Let me briefly explain them.

A person has a *just cause* for the use of violence when some important right of theirs, such as the right to bodily integrity, has been, or is about to be, violated. The amount of violence they may use, however, must be *proportionate* to the potential harm that would be done to them if they did not successfully defend their right—we are not justified in stabbing someone to prevent them pinching us, for example.

The *last resort* condition requires us to take active steps to avoid the need for violence. It may be, for example, that the person who is threatening us mistakenly thinks we are threatening *them*, and convincing them that we have no malicious intent is sufficient to remove the threat. (Note that "last resort" should not be taken literally here. It means that we should explore feasible, reasonable alternatives to violence, not every possible alternative, no matter how unlikely to succeed or costly they may be.)

Necessity permits us to use violence only if there is no other way of achieving our just cause. If we can simply lock a door, or run away, to prevent being harmed, we should do so. It also requires that we use violence only to the point where doing so will achieve that cause. We might be justified in punching someone if that is necessary to stop an attack—but not to go on punching them after they have lost consciousness, say.

Finally, we should note that these conditions are individually necessary—if any one of them does not hold, the use of violence is not justified—and jointly sufficient—if they all hold then a person has a right to use violence.

When all the above conditions apply, an attacker becomes liable to have violence used against them by those they have attacked, and by others who come to their aid. In those circumstances, the attacker has no legitimate complaint if violence is used against them—they have not been wronged. However, this does not mean that the defender, or those on whose behalf they are acting, are immune to moral criticism.

Looking more closely at the conditions of last resort and necessity, outlined above, will help us understand the basis of such criticism. Both conditions make demands on the person attacked: *necessity*, that they use violence only if they have no other effective option available; *last resort*, that they take reasonable steps to generate such options. Last resort has a kind of logical priority over necessity. A course of action is not in itself necessary (or not); rather, it is necessary relative to other available options to achieve a goal. Those options can expand or contract, or become more or less feasible, and as they do so, a course of action that was necessary to achieve a goal may no longer be so (or vice versa). Last resort asks us not simply to take as given the options available to us to respond to a threat, especially if the use of violence is the only effective response we can make, but to actively seek to expand those options. We must do this, and include the further options (if such there be) in our considerations, before we can decide if the use of violence is really necessary.

The last resort condition is motivated by the idea that since violence remains bad, even when it is the lesser of two evils, we have a responsibility to reduce or avoid it if we can, consistent with addressing the worse evil. That responsibility applies when we are deciding how to act on particular occasions—when we are attacked, or an attack appears imminent, for instance. But it also applies to the plans we make about future action. It is often more efficient and economical to adopt a policy to act in a standardized way whenever a regularly recurring situation arises rather than having to decide anew on each occasion. In order to carry out that policy, we may have to adopt particular types of equipment, training, and so on, choices that will constrain and guide our future actions. Given the presumption against violence, the requirements of last resort and necessity apply to the choice of a policy to use violence. We are justified in making that choice only if there is no less violent policy available to us to deal with some serious problem, and only if we are satisfied that we cannot make such a policy available.

Moreover, if we fail to adopt a nonviolent policy when we could have, we are at fault if we find ourselves in a situation where we have to use violence, even where we are justified in using violence in that situation. It is one thing to decide that someone's action is justified in the circumstances they face; it is another to decide whether they, or those on whose behalf they are acting, have some responsibility for creating those circumstances or allowing them to continue. Consider a police officer who becomes involved in an increasingly acrimonious dispute with a large man. Eventually the man picks up a large stone and rushes at the officer who, fearing for her life, fatally shoots him. The officer was justified in shooting: she did so to defend herself against an unprovoked attack (a just cause); doing so was proportionate to the harm she would have otherwise suffered; since she had no other way of defending herself it was a last resort and it was necessary. She did not act wrongly in shooting her attacker: he forced her to choose between his life and hers, thereby making himself liable to the violence that protected her life. However, suppose it turns out that the police force to which the officer belongs does not provide training in the method of "verbal judo," which helps police to de-escalate potentially hostile confrontations, and only equips their police with revolvers, not less lethal weapons. Police officers predictably face potentially violent situations, so police forces have a duty to adopt policies which will reduce the likelihood that that potential will be realized, such as providing training in methods of conflict resolution. Though the officer was justified in her use of violence, the police force is blameworthy for the policies they instituted.

The Morality of War

War involves violent conflict between states, typically prosecuted by well trained and armed militaries, supported by the resources of the peoples in whose name they are fighting. Its organized nature amplifies the inherent badness of violence. Propaganda fosters hatred and dehumanization of "the enemy," while modern weapons systems inflict immense amounts of physical and psychological harm on individuals, many of them innocent, and devastate the natural and built environment. As with many violent conflicts, the course of a war is unpredictable, often spinning out of the control of the antagonists, with harmful consequences rippling far into the future. And victory (if there is one) reflects strength, not justice.

Since war is a form of violence, what holds of the morality of violence in general, holds of the morality of war in particular. Since violence is, in itself, bad, so is war. Nevertheless, just as the presumption against the use of violence can be defeated on particular occasions, when the conditions outlined earlier apply, so can the presumption against war, with the relevant defeating conditions suitably adjusted to reflect that war is undertaken by political groups. (This way of thinking about when war is justified is rooted in the tradition of just war theory, originally systematized by Aquinas in the thirteenth century.) And since the presumption against violence obliges us to try to find and use nonviolent or minimally violent ways of dealing with threats, so governments have an obligation to try to find ways to deal with potential threats to their territorial and political integrity without going to war.

Members of the international community have, in fact, taken important steps to make serious disputes between states less likely, and to diminish the attractiveness of using military force to resolve disputes which do arise. This has been accomplished through the development of instruments for consultation, arbitration, and adjudication, both on a state-to-state basis, and as part of the function of supranational bodies such as the World Court and the United Nations. The prohibition of aggressive war after the Second World War, expressed in the Charter of the United Nations, was a major step in this process. And the legal prohibition on "weapons of mass destruction" (chemical and nuclear weapons) has helped reduce the potential for harm when war does occur.

Nevertheless, all modern states retain the capacity to make war, manning and equipping large standing armies, developing contingency plans for their deployment, and so on. Given the prohibition on aggressive war those armies have two legitimate functions: in the first place, to maintain peace by deterring other states from using military force; and, if deterrence fails, to resist that force and restore peace. The deterrent function must be primary: a fully effective army would never have to fire a shot in anger. But to be effective, it has to be demonstrably willing and able to use military force—to wage war. And, of course, that willingness is all too often translated into action.

Modern states thus adopt willingness to wage war as a policy, equipping themselves with armed force as the tool to implement it. Given the presumption against violence and war, that policy can be justified only if there is no viable alternative policy which does not rely on a readiness to use violence as a means to national security. Typically, in making decisions about policy, governments have to choose between options, and in doing so take into account a range of different, and often competing, kinds of considerations as they apply to those options—including cost (broadly understood), efficiency (the ratio of cost to benefit), distribution of costs and benefits, public opinion, the fit with other policies and values, and so on. So, one option might be preferable to the others because it is the most effective; another attractive because it is only slightly less effective, but far cheaper, and so on. In the process of choosing among options, however, effectiveness must be the first thing considered: only if an option reaches some threshold of effectiveness is it worth evaluating how it compares with other options. Most of the discourse around the morality of national defense simply presumes—takes as self-evident—that civil resistance is so far below the threshold of effectiveness that it cannot be a serious contender as a policy for national defense. If so, armed defense satisfies the conditions of last resort and necessity by default—there simply is no other way of defending the state in the face of violent invasion.

Civil Resistance Is Effective

However, it is not self-evident that civil resistance is ineffective. Indeed, there is good reason to think that it is highly effective. Over the past century political activists have successfully deployed a wide range of nonviolent tactics against violent opposition. Grouped under the headings of "protest and persuasion" (such as demonstrations and renunciation of honors), "non-cooperation" (such as civil disobedience and strikes), and "interventions" (such as sit-ins, creation of alternative institutions, and counterfeiting), these tactics have been of primary importance in such successful struggles against oppression or invasion as the overthrow of the Iranian shah in the late 1970s, the removal of the Marcos dictatorship in the Philippines in the 1980s, and the eventually successful struggle of the East Timorese to remove the Indonesian invaders in the 1990s. (Note that there is no question that in all these case, the opponent against which nonviolence was used was determined, capable, and ruthless.)

These successes show that civil resistance can be effective against violent opposition. Its superiority to violence is indicated by the analysis of large-scale political struggles, including against foreign occupation, undertaken by American social scientists Erica Chenoweth and Maria J. Stephan,[1] who showed that nonviolent campaigns have been significantly more effective than violent ones in achieving both short- and long-term goals. There are a number of reasons for this. For one, violence tends to entrench and amplify existing hostility, turning opponents into enemies, while nonviolence holds open the possibility of fruitful dialogue, compromise, and persuasion. Moreover, success in political struggles is strongly correlated with high levels of participation by members of a society. This is true for both violent and nonviolent campaigns, but it is generally easier and less costly to participate in nonviolent campaigns, and, so, easier for such campaigns to obtain high levels of participation. Unlike military defense, successful civil resistance is nonhierarchical and decentralized in structure. This makes it less vulnerable to the loss of centralized authority, and encourages responsiveness and innovation at the local level. Mass participation makes it difficult for an occupier to gain the civilian cooperation without which continued occupation is neither possible nor attractive. Think, for example, of how easy it is for a technologically sophisticated workforce to sabotage modern economies (a form of resistance important in the overthrow of the shah of Iran, for example). And, of course, civil resistance is being made more potent by developments in media technology, especially the internet and social media, which facilitate communication between members and with the rest of the world. Note, too, that the successes of civil resistance campaigns occurred despite their emerging only in the face of violent suppression—imagine how formidable civil resistance would be if it were organized and equipped, with governmental support, before it was needed.

Attention to the historical evidence indicates that, on the grounds of effectiveness alone, the government should disband its armed forces and replace them with a properly organized system of civil resistance. And given the presumption against violence, even if nonviolent resistance is only as effective as military force it is preferable on moral grounds. Furthermore, there are at least three other reasons to think that organized nonviolent resistance is superior to military force on both pragmatic and moral grounds.

Dehorning Dilemmas

Firstly, the current international security system, where each state tries to make itself secure by force of arms, actually makes all states less secure. Political scientists have dubbed this apparently paradoxical situation "The Security Dilemma." The dilemma arises because national planning for military security standardly relies on the premise that while the offensive intentions of potential foes are opaque and changeable, their offensive capacities are apparent. Each state then develops its own military capacity, not according to its assessment of the intentions of other states, but, rather, according to its assessment of the capacities of other states with which it might find itself in conflict—even if it is currently enjoying friendly relations with those states. Since most weapons systems can be used for both defensive and offensive purposes, as a state increases its own capacity, then by parity of reasoning the states which it sees as potential enemies, see *it* as presenting an increased threat to *their* security, requiring a corresponding growth in their military strength. Hence the apparently implacable logic of the "arms race," leading to the development and installation of more and more fearsome weapons systems, to the point where we have the capacity to destroy all human life many times over. Increasing militarization itself makes the international system more unstable, with fear of preemption drawing states into military conflict, and those conflicts becoming more destructive.

The horns of the dilemma on which each state is supposedly caught are then, on the one hand, continuing to increase its military capabilities, with the undesirable consequences pointed to earlier, or, on the other hand, not doing so, leaving itself vulnerable to conquest or domination. Corresponding to the two horns of the dilemma, there are two requirements for a state to escape the dilemma: to demonstrate that it had no capacity for aggression, thereby removing the possibility of being seen by other states as a threat that needed to be neutralized; and constructing an effective system of defense that could deter and resist potential invaders.

A state that relies only on civil resistance obviously satisfies the first requirement, removing the possibility that other states would attack it out of fear of its aggressive intentions. And since, as discussed above, it can effectively resist attacks from potential usurpers, it will also deter them. Such a state at the same time comes to possess an effective form of national defense, removes a potential cause of conflict, and starts the process of ratcheting down the destructive potential of the international system.

There is another, perhaps less noticed, dilemma inherent in governments' use of armed forces to protect the territorial and political integrity of their state: increasing the power of those forces enhances its territorial security, but at the same time subverts its political integrity. Modern armies are well-coordinated organizations with vastly more coercive power than any other in a society, with the consequent potential for usurping political power—the very thing they are supposed to prevent. And that potential is consistently realized: coups are the single most important proximate cause of the downfall of democratic governments (and non-democracies are even more prone to coups). According to a recent paper, "By one count, three out of every four failures of democracy are the result of a successful coup d'état."[2]

Even where armies do not themselves usurp political authority, their coercive power can be misused by political authority against the people *they* are supposed to be serving; that is, they can be a tool of political oppression and injustice within a state as well as outside it.

Replacing the armed forces with organized civil resistance removes both of these threats to a state's political integrity. Instead, by its very nature—involving mass participation, and decentralized, nonhierarchical organization—civil resistance exemplifies and reinforces the democratic values which we look to a defense system to protect.

Conclusion

Since a—perhaps *the*—fundamental duty of government is to ensure the security of both the citizens and the state as a whole, the policies that it puts in place to discharge this duty are of first importance. I have in effect presented two broad kinds of considerations in favor of the claim that the government of a state should adopt a policy of civil resistance to discharge that duty, rather than one of armed force. The first points out that there is a presumption against the use of violence, and so a presumption against a policy that relies on the use of violence. That presumption can be defeated if certain conditions, particularly those of last resort and necessity, are satisfied. Since we have good reason to think that civil resistance is an effective way of protecting the state, a policy of armed force is not necessary, and since it is not necessary, it is not justified. Secondly, even if the idea that there is a presumption against violence is rejected (as it is, for example, by some "realists" about international relations), civil resistance is, all things considered, preferable to armed force. Although the lack of any substantial government- sponsored system of civil defense makes comparison with armed force somewhat speculative, we have reason to think that civil defense is at least as effective as armed force, and superior in other ways. It defuses the "Security Dilemma," removes the possibility of the armed forces themselves taking over power or being used as an instrument of oppression by the powers-that-be, and is more consonant with democratic values.

Two final points. Firstly, to say that civil defense is superior to armed force as a method for national defense does not mean that it will always be effective. Neither is armed force. Secondly, a government that continues to rely on armed force may find that it has to go to war as the only way to protect the state. In effect, it is making the best of a bad situation. It is blameworthy, not for making that choice, but for helping create a situation where it has no other choice.

A government that thinks seriously about the morality of violence and its duty to protect the state should never wage war because it should have done away with its capacity to wage war, and replaced it with a morally and practically superior alternative.

Notes

1 Erica Chenoweth, and Maria J. Stephan, *Why Civil Resistance Works: The Strategic Logic of Nonviolent Conflict* (New York: Columbia University Press, 2011).

2 Hein Goemans, and Nikolay Marinov, "Coups and Democracy," *British Journal of Political Science*, 44 (2014): 799–825.

The Government May Sometimes Wage War

Nathan L. Cartagena

Study Questions

1. How does Cartagena understand the concept of "war"? What examples does he use to clarify this concept?

2. What is meant by "government"? What does a government's just rule require?

3. What are the options facing a nation like Serbia when attacked by another nation? Which option does Cartagena believe is consistent with a government's duty to protect its society? Why?

4. How does the notion of the common good justify a government waging war even if not attacked? What example does Cartagena use to illustrate this argument?

5. What are the five criteria that regulate a government's actions before waging war (*jus ad bellum*)?

6. What are the two criteria that regulate conduct during war (*jus in bello*)?

7. What is the criterion of justice for conduct after a war ends (*jus post bellum*)?

"I am sick and tired of war," Union General William T. Sherman declared, reflecting on a war in which approximately 620,000 soldiers and 50,000 civilians died. "It is only those who have neither fired a shot nor heard the shrieks and groans of the wounded," he added, "who cry aloud for blood, for vengeance, for desolation. *War is hell*."[1] Sherman's grim estimate of war is not unique. Nearly 600 years before the American Civil War, the Christian scholar Thomas Aquinas wrote: "[T]he practices of war contain the most unrest, and so hinder the spirit from contemplation of divine things and from the praise of God and prayer for the people."[2] Aquinas contends that war can fundamentally dehumanize people, severely damaging their abilities to love God and neighbor. Many endorse Aquinas's general claim—war can fundamentally dehumanize people—without endorsing his specific theological commitments. The Greek poet Homer (c. 750 BC), for example, powerfully captures war's dehumanizing effects in the *Iliad*'s depiction of Achilles's descent to madness after the death of his cousin. And the contemporary secular psychiatrist Jonathan Shay uses this portrait to explain the psychological wounds of Vietnam veterans.[3]

Given war's brutality and dehumanizing-tendency, may governments ever wage it? In this chapter, I argue that despite its brutal and deforming effects, governments may *sometimes* wage war. I do so in three parts. First, I clarify some concepts my arguments employ. Second, I provide two arguments for why governments may *sometimes* wage war. Third, I discuss criteria that must be met when governments do so.

Clarifying Concepts

I am arguing that governments may *sometimes* wage war. So, let me clarify two concepts: "war" and "government."

We use the word "war" in several different ways. For instance, we say that war is an armed conflict between two or more societies. The First World War and the Second World War are clear examples of this sense of war. Yet we also call conflicts that are not between two or more societies, wars. The war on drugs, the war on terror, and the war on illiteracy—these "wars" involve one or more societies attempting to combat a social or ideological problem, not another society. Furthermore, we metaphorically say competitions are wars. We speak of sporting events and political races as "warzones" in which participants "go to war" or "take up arms." But we do not mean that Michael Jordan literally "went to war" against the opposing basketball team, or that President Trump really "took up arms" against the other presidential candidates. Instead, we use the language of war in an extended sense to illuminate aspects of these competitions. So, we regularly say war is: (1) armed conflict between two or more societies; (2) a conflict against a social or ideological problem, but not a society; and (3) a metaphor for competitions.

In this essay, I use war in the first sense. I am arguing that governments may *sometimes* wage war, where "war" refers to armed conflict between one or more societies. Here "society" is a broad category that includes tribes, countries, and empires. I also intend "society" to include guerrilla groups (e.g., the Revolutionary Armed Forces of Columbia), dissenting sides in a civil war (e.g., the Confederate States of America), and terrorist organizations (e.g., al-Qaeda). Hence, on my view, although the United States *cannot* literally wage war against drugs, it *can* do so against guerrilla groups or terrorist organizations selling them.

I wish to clarify three additional aspects of what I mean by "war." First, war is a practice under human control. As a practice, wars receive their structure and aims from their participants. Put another way, societies do not simply wage war; they wage particular kinds of war. Consider, for example, the Second Boer War (1899–1902) between the British regular army and the opposing joint force of the Transvaal Republic and Orange Free State. Before fighting, both sides agreed to combat terms. And given these terms, each side cared for the other's prisoners and wounded, observed the practices of parlay and truce, and refrained from targeting civilians. Each side also refused to ask the Zulus for assistance. Zulu warriors did not observe such combat terms, but regularly slaughtered prisoners and wounded, and killed or enslaved the defeated party's women and children. For the Zulus, victory in war gave the victor complete rule over the defeated. But whereas the Zulus saw war as an endeavor to annihilate an enemy and acted accordingly, the participants in the Second Boer War did not. They thought war had a different aim—a mutual, lasting peace for all involved.[4] They also assumed such peace was incompatible with unrestrained combat, enslavement, and annihilation, and endorsed rules of war prohibiting these things. Whether they abided by these rules was up to them—it was under their control. In this instance, both sides mostly did.

Second, like other practices under human control, *war changes*. "War" does not refer to a static event recurring throughout human history; it refers to a constantly changing mode of human interaction. Three historic examples make this clear.

In the Heroic Age, tribal societies primarily fought hero-centered wars consisting of battles between two tribal representatives. Everyone else watched them fight. Furthermore, everyone expected victors to fight without mercy—killing their fallen opponents, plundering their armor and weapons, and displaying their bodies during their victory-celebration.

Another form of war appeared with the decline of the Roman Empire and the emergence of Christendom: medieval chivalry. Influenced by Augustine's teachings on just war, societies in this era waged war with knights who endorsed a code of chivalry depicting them as defenders of the helpless who were not to fight—let alone kill—someone below their station. And as city-siege tactics improved, these societies implemented the "The Peace of God" rule prohibiting warfare in certain locations (e.g., farms) and against certain people (e.g., farmers and their families).[5] Similarly, some societies prohibited the use of particular weapons in war (e.g., crossbows). This context fostered crusades *and* extremely limited wars—in 1127, a yearlong war involving 1,000 knights ended with five casualties, four of which were the result of accidents.[6]

A third form of war developed after the decline of Christendom and the establishment of modern states: total war. Two features distinguish total war: (1) a greatly enhanced destructive capacity and (2) the willingness to attack civilians to attain victory. The industrial revolution (~1760–1840) fostered the first feature. Its machine-based manufacturing mass-produced high-quality rifles and artillery, increased the availability of money and men, and supported the growth of railroads that efficiently transported these things to the battlefield. And as these things entered battles in increasing numbers, so too did an enormously enhanced capacity to destroy. The second feature of total war arose as societies increasingly began to see "destruction of the enemy" as the goal of war. A quotation from Francis Lieber (1798–1872)—author of the 1863 "General Orders No. 100," which outlines a formal code to regulate military conduct—shows this transition. Lieber wrote: "If destruction of the enemy is my object, it is not only right, but my duty, to resort to the most destructive means."[7]

A Lieberian view of the goal of war and the enhanced capacity for destruction actualizing it in battle produced the first total war—the American Civil War (1861–1865). After several years of fighting with strategic captures and maneuvers against the Confederate army, Union Generals Grant, Sherman, and Sheridan began having their troops apprehend or destroy Confederate civilians' resources to weaken their society's resolve. Armed with an enhanced capacity for destruction, Union soldiers decimated Confederate territories, civilians and all. And they and their Confederate counterparts continued killing each other by the thousands in battle. This totalized style of war also characterized the First World War, the Second World War, and Vietnam.

The previous history points to a third aspect of war: the quantity and quality of war's brutal and dehumanizing effects can vary substantially. The scope of human devastation Sherman witnessed and rightly deplored never appeared in the wars before it. The prior technologies and views of war could not produce the carnage of total war. And in one case, those technologies and views contributed to a yearlong war in which only five people died.

I am assuming, then, that "war" refers to: (1) armed conflict between two or more societies; (2) a practice under human control; (3) a constantly changing mode of human interaction; and (4) a source of varied degrees of brutality and dehumanizing effects.

I am also assuming a certain conception of "government": a government is a person or group of persons with the ultimate civic responsibility and authority to justly rule a society and help maintain the common good— what is genuinely good for every human being, and thus the global human community. On this conception, governments can come in various forms: aristocracies, democracies, monarchies, and the like. Granted, we sometimes use "government" in another sense. We occasionally say that a government is something over and above rulers and the ruled that demands the allegiance of both. In this sense, "government" never refers to any person or group of people; it refers to an abstraction beyond them. But abstractions cannot do anything—including wage war. My conception of government avoids this problem; real people—actual civic officials—can and do wage wars. Let us, then, consider arguments for why, on my conception, governments may *sometimes* wage war.

Two Arguments for Waging War

What does a government's responsibility and authority to justly rule its societies require? For one thing, it requires maintaining a society's peace—its well-being and good order. Maintaining this peace involves protecting a society from internal and external enemies, especially those intending to cause it grave harm. Hence, governments have the responsibility and authority to protect their societies from internal and external enemies.

Sometimes these enemies are societies. And sometimes enemy-societies commit to invading and decimating a perceived adversary. Prior to the First World War (1914–1918), for example, a Serbian nationalist assassinated the heir to the Austro-Hungarian throne and his wife. Multiple Serbian and Austro-Hungarian investigations revealed no link between this nationalist and the Serbian government; he and his accomplices acted on their own. Desperate for vengeance, the Austro-Hungarian government formed an alliance with Germany, Italy, and Bulgaria to crush Serbia. Before attacking, Austria-Hungary gave Serbia an ultimatum of ten demands with forty-eight hours to reply. The Serbian government did so, accepting most of the demands and stating that it would submit to the rest if international arbitration decided it should. Three days later, Austria-Hungary declared war on Serbia and attacked its capital.

In such cases, governments like Serbia have four main options: (1) surrender; (2) allow the enemy to attack, but seek a diplomatic end to the attacks; (3) take up arms to protect their society from the attacks; or (4) take up arms to protect their society from attacks *and* simultaneously seek a diplomatic end to the fighting. Which of these options is consistent with a government's responsibility and authority to protect its society?

Austro-Hungarian-like bloodlust for destruction eliminates (1). Austria-Hungary would have continued devastating Serbia after a surrender—they wanted the Serbians to suffer. Similarly, (2) fails to protect Serbian society from attacks it experiences while its government seeks a diplomatic solution. And although the Serbian government would protect its society against attacks in (3), it would fail to use all available just means to protect it from the brutal, dehumanizing effects of war. Fighting *and* seeking a diplomatic solution could more effectively secure the war's end. Hence (4) is the only genuinely just option in these circumstances.

But (4) has important implications for my argument. By taking up arms against an enemy like Austria-Hungary, governments like Serbia would be waging war—they would establish armed conflict between two or more societies. We have discovered, then, one historic example that, coupled with my conception of government, identifies an instance when a government may wage war. From this instance, it follows that governments may *sometimes* wage war.

For my second argument, recall that I assume governments have the responsibility and authority to help maintain the common good. The widespread practice and praise of government-based humanitarian efforts in other societies reveals that I am not alone, though neither demonstrates that this conception of government is correct. Assume that it is. From this and a few other assumptions, it follows that governments may *sometimes* wage war.

To see how, consider the common good—what is genuinely good for all human beings, and thus the global human community. Note: this is not the same as the greatest good for the greatest number of people; it is the genuine good for all people. Now it is genuinely good for all people to live in peace. Therefore, because governments must help maintain the common good, they must help *all* human beings live in peace. What this help involves varies from government to government, depending on what resources each government's society has, and what these resources enable a government to do.

In some instances, governments have the resources to wage war successfully for another society *and* an obligation to do so to help that society live in peace. Throughout the Bosnian War (1992–1995), for example, Bosnian Serbs committed genocide, killing 100,000 Bosnian Muslim and Croat civilians by the war's end. Despite their pleas, Bosnian Muslims and Croats received relatively little international assistance. American and European governments primarily confined themselves to making sanctions against the Bosnian Serbs, and to urging them to cease hostilities. The minimal peacekeeping forces and airstrikes these governments did provide principally served to aid the transport of humanitarian supplies to devastated towns. All these efforts repeatedly proved impotent: Bosnia's Serbs continued systematically exterminating Muslim and Croat communities. This extermination culminated in two horrific events. On July 11, 1995, Bosnian Serbs captured the city of Srebrenica, and subsequently slaughtered 7,000–8,000 of its Muslim males in mass killing sites. About a month later, Bosnian Serbs indiscriminately shelled the capital to maximize the deaths of Muslims and Croats living there. After this shelling, American and European governments declared and waged war against the Bosnian Serbs. These decisions proved decisive: in three months, a war that had lasted three years—producing 200,000 Bosnian deaths and 2,000,000 Bosnian refugees—was over.

American and European governments had the resources to wage war successfully for Bosnia's Muslim and Croat societies. Military experts agree on this point, and the war's swift end amply confirms it. These governments also had an obligation to do so. Their responsibility and authority to help maintain the common good required that they protect Muslims and Croats from genocide, for genocide is contrary to peace. In this situation, nothing apart from waging war could provide this protection. Sanctions, declarations, peacekeepers, and airstrikes—none of these things could stop the genocide, even after three years. So, American and European governments had an obligation to wage war for Bosnia's Muslims and Croats.

These governments also had an obligation to wage war for the sake of Bosnia's Serbs. Committing genocide is not a genuine human good, but an evil that dramatically dehumanizes victims *and* perpetrators. Indeed, it does not give perpetrators peace, but keeps them from participating in the common good. Attempts to protect the Bosnian Serbs from this evil through sanctions, declarations, peacekeepers, and airstrikes all failed. In this case, then, waging war against this society was the only way to cease its descent into deplorable evil and restore it to peace. Moreover, the American and European governments had the resources to do this. Therefore, these governments had an obligation, and the ability, to wage war for the sake of Bosnia's Serbs. And the combined double, ability and obligation, reveals another instance when governments may *sometimes* wage war.

Just Criteria for Waging War

We have seen two arguments for why governments may *sometimes* wage war. But we have also seen that because war is a practice under human control, societies do not simply wage war; they wage particular kinds of war. The Second Boer War makes this clear. So, what kinds of war may governments wage?

In this section, I propose that governments may only wage wars that meet certain criteria of justice before, during, and after armed combat. I draw these criteria from the Augustinian *just war tradition*. As the name suggests, this tradition begins with Augustine's reflections on justice and war. Though not the first writings on those topics—Aristotle's, Cicero's, and Ambrose's predate them—Augustine's texts have served as a frequent departure point for over 1600 years of reflections on just warfare. Gratian (eleventh to twelfth century), Thomas Aquinas, Francisco de Vitoria (1492–1546), John Calvin, Francisco *Suárez* (1548–1617), and Hugo Grotius (1583-1645)—all these thinkers cite, challenge, and extend Augustine's teachings on just war. They are the primary architects of the tradition. And contemporary thinkers continue to cite, challenge, and extend their teachings. Thus, the Augustinian just war tradition is not simply an historical artifact; it is a living, flexible attempt of previous and present generations to develop an account of just war.

Jus ad Bellum

Like the architects of the Augustinian just war tradition, I hold that five criteria of justice regulate a government's actions before waging war. These *jus ad bellum*—justice to war—*criteria are:* (1) legitimate authority; (2) just cause; (3) right intention; (4) last resort; and (5) reasonable chance of success.

A government's responsibility to maintain peace grounds its *legitimate authority* to wage war. As Augustine writes: "The natural order, adapted to peace for mortal men, demands this—that the authority to wage war and to counsel it lies in the hands of princes."[8] Now this authority has limits. Governments may only wage *just* wars—wars that meet the criteria we are considering. Likewise, governments must seek counsel from wise advisers before exercising their authority to wage war. As Vitoria writes:

> The king is not capable of examining the causes of war on his own, and it is likely that he may make many mistakes, or rather he *will* make mistakes, to the detriment and ruin of many. So war should not be declared on the sole dictates of the prince, nor even on the opinion of the few, but on the opinion of the many, and of the wise and reliable.[9]

Given human fallibility—our liability to err—the prevalence of misinformation and misdirection, and war's brutal, dehumanizing effects, governments must consult wise advisers before commencing war. Thus, the need to consult wise advisers limits a government's authority to wage war. And individuals may also limit this authority: they should refrain from participating in a war that they strongly believe is unjust. Again Vitoria: "If the war seems patently unjust to the subject, he must not fight, even if he is ordered to do so by the prince."[10]

The second prewar criterion is a *just cause*. There are four general just causes for waging war: (a) responding to an imminent and grave threat; (b) repelling an aggressor; (c) recovering something unjustly taken; and (d) restoring the common good. None of these causes is sufficient to make a war just. They simply provide just grounds for commencing war.

Regarding (a), governments may respond to an imminent *and* grave threat to their society by waging war through a preemptive strike. *Imminent* refers to a threat that is almost about to happen—for example, another society's military mobilizing troops along a border in preparation for invasion. *Grave* refers to a threat that, if actualized, would greatly harm its target—the decimation of a border-town, say. Any strike launched against a threat lacking either of these qualities is not preemptive, but preventative. And preventative strikes lack a just cause. As Grotius writes: "I admit, to be sure, that if the assailant seizes weapons in such a way that his intent to kill is manifest [then] the crime can be forestalled. . . . But those who accept fear of any sort as justifying anticipatory slaying are themselves greatly deceived and deceive others."[11]

In the latter case, a government should employ other means to avoid the threat.

Serbia's war with Austria-Hungary is an instance of (b). Serbia's government had a just cause to repel the attacks against its capital, attacks coming after it had expressed a willingness to accept all of Austria-Hungary's prewar demands. The reasoning here is like that supporting just cause (c)—recovering something unjustly taken. During the Bosnian War, the Serbs unjustly captured numerous Muslim or Croat towns. Each time the Serbs did so, they provided Bosnia's Muslim and Croat societies with a just cause to reclaim these lands by expelling those who had wrongly taken them.

Like its historical proponents, I hold that cause (d)—governments may wage war to restore the moral order between or within societies—is a quadruply beneficial punishment. As Grotius argues, waging war to restore the common good (i) corrects the offending society, (ii) aids the unjustly injured society, (iii) reminds the war's witnesses of the moral order uniting them, and (iv) encourages them to uphold it.[12] These benefits obtain in wars rectifying relations between countries (e.g., Serbia and Austria-Hungary) or societies within a country (e.g., the Bosnian War).

The third prewar criterion is *right intention*. Aquinas captures the importance of this criterion: "For it may happen that war is declared by a legitimate authority, and for a just cause, but be rendered unlawful through a wicked intention."[13] With Augustine and his successors, I hold that governments may only wage war from a loving intention for mutual, sustained peace. As Augustine writes: "Peace is not sought in order that war may be practiced—but war is waged so that peace might be acquired. Therefore, in warring be peaceful, so that you bring those whom you outfight and conquer to the advantage of peace."[14] Elsewhere he adds, "As violence is returned to one who rebels and resists, so should mercy be shown to one who has been conquered or captured, especially when there is no fear of disturbance of peace."[15] This intention seeks the peaceful good for all involved in a war— the unjust attackers, the unjustly attacked, and those who come to either society's aid. And like Augustine, I maintain that "the passion for inflicting harm, the cruel thirst for vengeance, an unpacific and relentless spirit, the fever of revolt, the lust of power, and the like" are unjust intentions for war.[16] Hence, Austria-Hungary's war against Serbia was unjust in this respect: Austria-Hungary vengefully wanted to destroy Serbia. This war—which began the First World War—and those started with similar intentions perennially produce mass carnage and inhuman treatment of soldiers and civilians, thus sowing the seeds of future wars. The intention for mutual, sustained peace, however, restricts war's carnage and influence. The Second Boer War makes this clear.

The fourth prewar criterion is *last resort*. Governments may only wage war after all other reasonable means of addressing the just cause for war have been attempted. As Suárez writes, a just war involves an imminent and grave injustice "which cannot be avenged or repaired in any other way."[17] These other means include calling "to the attention of the opposing [society] the existence of a just cause of war and to seek adequate reparation therefore." If the other society offers these reparations, Suárez continues, governments are "bound to accept [them], and to desist from war."[18] Targeted sanctions, multicountry boycotts, adjustment of troop locations—these are some of the other means that may justly help circumvent war.

But any means pursued before waging war must be reasonable, feasible and just. Governments need not try every conceivable way of avoiding war. They need only try the feasible ones. In some cases—for example, repelling an attack—there may not be a feasible alternative to war. In cases where feasible options remain, governments need only try those that are just. For example, general economic sanctions are unjust: they produce widespread suffering among a society's least well-off and rarely affect those producing strife. So, governments should not employ them.

The fifth prewar criterion is a *reasonable chance of success*. Governments may only wage a war that is winnable given the just war criteria. Hence, governments need to consider if a just victory—not merely victory—is likely. For example, if a war is unlikely to secure a mutual, sustained peace, a government should not wage it—even if the government has a just cause for war. As Vitoria writes, "It is clear that one may have a right to reclaim a city or province, and yet find that right nullified by the danger of provoking greater conflict. As I said, wars should be waged for the common good; if the recovery of one city is bound to involve the commonwealth in greater damage . . . [the government should] abstain from war." Likewise, a government should cease waging war and surrender if a just victory becomes highly unlikely. Such surrenders limit a war's destructive scope, and can help establish a mutual, sustained peace.

Jus in Bello

The previous five criteria are just requirements prior to war. If a government does not meet them, it should not start a war. There are also criteria regulating war once it is underway: (1) restricted targeting and (2) proportionality. If governments do not meet these *jus in bello*—justice in war—criteria while engaged in armed conflict, they must alter their conduct—even to the point of withdrawing from war.

According to *restricted targeting*, governments may only wage war against certain people in certain places. Regarding people, Grotius rightly observes that "it does not suffice that we conceive the enemy, by some fiction, as though they were a single body."[19] Instead, governments must distinguish between (a) "combatants" and (b) "noncombatants," protecting (b) and waging war against (a). Both terms are functional: combatants make certain contributions to a war effort that noncombatants do not. These contributions come on a continuum. Whereas soldiers actively executing a war are combatants because they pose an imminent, grave threat, nonactivated reservists or militia-members do not, and so are noncombatants. Similarly, incapacitated soldiers or prisoners are noncombatants since they do not pose an imminent, grave threat. The combatant-noncombatant distinction also applies to civilians. A politician executing a war is a combatant, but a local shopkeeper providing his town with food is a noncombatant. The protection of noncombatants includes ensuring that any injuries or deaths they experience are unlikely, unforeseen, and unintended consequences of attacks on combatant targets.

Protecting certain people requires protecting certain places. Governments may not target locations that sustain the infrastructure supporting noncombatant lives. Farms, grocery stores, hospitals, power plants, and schools—such places are illegitimate targets. So too are roads, bridges, tracks, or airfields, unless the opposing military force is currently using them. But even then, attacks must be directed at the present force without the intention to weaken the society's resolve by making its noncombatants suffer. The lack of this restraint rendered much of the American Civil War's combat unjust.

The second criterion of justice during war is *proportionality*. Governments may only use the minimum force required in combat. As Aquinas writes, it is unjust "to use more violence than is necessary."[20] This principle aims to protect combatants and noncombatants. Nuclear weapons, chemical weapons, and certain forms of ammunition should be prohibited given the unnecessary scale of destruction they release on combatants. And by never using these weapons but employing the minimal force necessary to achieve goals in war, governments and militaries decrease the potential of accidentally killing noncombatants.

Jus Post Bellum

After combat ceases, governments must observe a final criterion of justice: *actualize the right intention*. According to this *jus post bellum*—justice after war—criterion, governments must establish a mutual, sustained peace after war. As Augustine says, they must bring all parties to "the advantage of peace." Any conduct or peace treaty that sows the seeds of a future conflict is unjust. Hence, the Treaty of Versailles, which ultimately ended Austria-Hungary's war with Serbia, was unjust because it mangled Germany and thus paved the way for the Second World War. Even postwar reparation requirements—obligations to remedy the unjustly injured parties of war—must, as Augustine again declares, be formed "in a spirit of love, in the spirit of concern, in the spirit of reform" for all.[21]

Conclusion

Wars—even just wars—are brutal and dehumanizing. As Augustine writes, "If one remembers he is a human being, one will be much readier to deplore the fact that he is under the necessity of waging even just wars. . . . Let everyone, therefore, who reflects with pain upon such great evils, upon such horror and cruelty, acknowledge that [war] is misery."[22] Augustine presses the moral point of this lament upon his readers, adding that one has "lost all human feeling" who can think of war "without anguish of soul."[23]

But a government's responsibility and authority to justly rule a society and help maintain the common good grounds that it may *sometimes* wage war. And when it does wage war, a government must adhere to the criteria regulating justice before, during, and after war, taking up arms to establish a mutual, sustained peace.

Notes

1. As cited in Dave Grossman, *On Killing* (New York: Back Bay Books, 2009), 73 (emphasis added).
2. Thomas Aquinas, *Summa Theologiae* II-II.40.2.co.
3. See *Iliad* Books, 19–23, and Jonathan Shay, *Achilles in Vietnam* (New York: Scribner, 1994).
4. The leniency and mutual enrichment of the treaty ending the Second Boer War (the Treaty of Vereeniging) illustrates this point.
5. See Philippe Contamine, *War in the Middle Ages* (Oxford: Blackwell, 1984), 270–74.
6. Ibid., 256.
7. Quoted in J. Turner Johnson, *Just War Tradition and the Restraint of War* (Princeton: Princeton University Press, 1981), 301.
8. Augustine, *Against Faust the Manichean*, 22.75.
9. Vitoria, *Vitoria: Political Writings*, ed. Anthony Pagden, and Jeremy Lawrance (Cambridge: Cambridge University Press, 1991), 309.
10. Ibid., 235.
11. Grotius, *De Jure Bello ac Pacis Libri Tres*, trans. F. W. Kelsey (Buffalo: Hein, 1995), 2.1.5.
12. Ibid., 2.20.4.
13. Thomas Aquinas, *Summa Theologiae* II-II.40.1.co.
14. Augustine, Letter 189, "To Boniface."
15. Ibid.
16. Augustine, *Against Faust*, 22.75.

17 F. Suárez, *A Work on the Three Theological Virtues*, trans. G.L. Williams, et al. (Oxford: Oxford University Press, n.d.), 4.1.
18 Ibid., 7.3.
19 Grotius, *De Jure*, 3.11.16.
20 Thomas Aquinas, *Summa Theologiae* II-II.64.7.co.
21 Augustine, *City of God*, 19.8.
22 Ibid.,19.7.
23 Ibid., 19.8.

RESPONSES

Response to Alexandra

Nathan L. Cartagena

> **Study Questions**
>
> 1. What commitments do Cartagena and Alexandra share? Wherein lies their disagreement?
> 2. How does Cartagena formulate Alexandra's first argument against a government's waging war? What problem does Cartagena find with the first premise?
> 3. What evidence does Cartagena give for why civil resistance is not always effective?
> 4. How does Cartagena formulate Alexandra's second argument? Why does he think this argument fails?

I have argued that governments may *sometimes* wage war. Andrew Alexandra has argued that they *never* should do so. Given these contrary conclusions, you might conclude that we have little in common. But you would be mistaken. Alexandra and I share several commitments, and I highlight them in the first section of this reply. Nevertheless, we do disagree. And the points on which we disagree lead us to endorse radically different conclusions. But which of these conclusions is correct? Since I have already provided positive arguments for mine, I use this reply's second section to critique the arguments Alexandra gives for his conclusion, thus indirectly reaffirming my own.

Common Ground

Alexandra and I share two fundamental commitments. First, we both hold that governments have the responsibility and authority to protect their societies. As Alexandra writes, "[A]—perhaps *the*—fundamental duty of a government is to ensure the security of both the citizens and the state" (p. 282). Second, we maintain that war is a form of violence that requires justification. There are criteria of justice that regulate when, how, and against whom governments may wage war to protect their societies.

Alexandra and I also share common commitments concerning those criteria of justice. Alexandra explicitly endorses two *jus ad bellum* ("justice to war") criteria—*just cause* and *last resort*—and one *jus in bello* ("justice in war") criterion—*proportionality*—that I champion. Similarly, we both believe that *last resort* entails two requirements. First, governments must "explore feasible, reasonable alternatives to violence, not every possible alternative, no matter how unlikely to succeed or costly they may be" (p. 276). Second, "governments have an obligation to try to find ways to deal with potential threats to their territorial and political integrity without going to war" (p. 279). Given this second requirement, governments considering whether or not to wage war must investigate if "they, or those on whose behalf they are acting, have some responsibility for creating [or allowing]" circumstances that appear to produce a just cause for war (p. 278).

Finally, Alexandra and I also contend that civil resistance can be "effective against violent opposition" (p. 280). Though he never defines "civil resistance," Alexandra does say it includes protests, noncooperation, and interventions. The American Civil Rights Movement (1954–1968) shows that persistent engagement in these practices can produce major civic progress against violent opposition and injustice. Therefore, civil resistance can effectively help governments maintain their societies' political integrity without waging war.

Critiquing Arguments

Given the previous points of agreement, why do Alexandra and I come to different conclusions about war? We disagree on the effectiveness of civil resistance. Considering the arguments Alexandra gives for his position makes this clear.

Alexandra provides two main arguments for why governments should *never* wage war. We can formulate the first as follows:

(1) If civil resistance can effectively protect a state's territorial and political integrity, then governments should adopt civil resistance as the system of national defense, *and* do away with their capacity *and* willingness to wage war.

(2) Civil resistance can effectively protect a state's territorial and political integrity.

(3) Governments should adopt civil resistance as the system of national defense, *and* do away with their capacity *and* willingness to wage war. (From 1 & 2)

(4) Given (3), governments should *never* wage war.

(5) Therefore, governments should *never* wage war. (From 3 & 4)

On this formulation, Alexandra's argument is valid—if premises (1) through (4) are true, then the conclusion, (5), is also true. Alexandra uses the first three sections of his essay to argue that premises (1) through (4) are true. There he contends that, if *last resort* and *necessity* are true, premise (1) is also true.

But this claim has a problem: premise (1) is importantly ambiguous. Does premise (1) merely require that civil resistance can *sometimes* effectively protect a state's territorial and political integrity? If it does, governments lack sufficient reason to adopt it as their system of national defense. They would need to adopt civil resistance and something else (e.g., armed force) to protect their societies when civil resistance proved ineffective. Perhaps, then, the premise requires something stronger: "effectively protect" means that civil resistance can *always* successfully serve as the *sole* method for protecting a state's territorial and political integrity. Given this stronger reading, premise (1) would read: "If civil resistance can *always* successfully serve as the *sole* method for protecting a state's territorial and political integrity, then governments should adopt civil resistance as the system of national defense, *and* do away with their capacity *and* willingness to wage war." Is civil resistance as effective as this stronger version requires?

No. Even the three historic examples of civil resistance Alexandra mentions make this clear. In January 16, 1979, the Iranian shah Mohammad Reza fled Iran due to months of protesting *and* a military mutiny involving an unsuccessful attempt to assassinate him. Having so lost the trust of Iranian citizens *and* military personnel, the shah decided to seek sanctuary in the United States. Similarly, the former Philippine dictator Ferdinand Marcos primarily relinquished power for three reasons: (1) he lost an election; (2) US president Reagan told him to adhere to the election results or face serious consequences; and (3) the New People's Army—a violent communist guerrilla movement—was overtaking large portions of the Philippines. Finally, many East Timor military groups (e.g., Fretilin), waged war against Indonesia's invading and subsequent occupying forces from 1975 to 1999, when those forces finally withdrew because the leader who had deployed them fell from power. During those years, the East Timor government and its international counterparts failed to stop a genocide and unrestricted combat practices that collectively killed 150,000 East Timorese citizens—a fifth of the total population. In these examples, civil resistance was not the lone cause of change. And in each case warfare contributed to that change.

Yet, even if civil resistance alone had worked in these situations, there are still other instances when it cannot do so to protect a society. Even Alexandra admits as much. He states that although civil resistance is superior to armed force, it does not follow "that it will always be effective," adding that "neither is armed force" (p. 283). But, if civil resistance is not always effective, there may be times when governments must wage war to protect their societies. Alexandra admits this, too. He writes: "A government that continues to rely on armed force may find that it has to go to war as the only way to protect the state. . . . It is blameworthy, not for making that choice, but for helping create a situation where it has no other choice" (Ibid.). Alexandra grants that governments relying on armed force may rightly wage war in certain circumstances—they have "no other choice," including resorting to civil resistance—though they will be culpable for partially making these circumstances. Here I add that history contains many cases of genocide and invasion that only war could overcome, including the two world wars, the Bosnian War, and the war against the Islamic state.

History shows (and Alexandra grants) that civil resistance cannot *always* effectively protect a state's territorial and political integrity, and *sometimes* a government may wage war because it has no other way of protecting that integrity. Consequently, this first argument fails, and we need not endorse its conclusion.

Alexandra's second argument for why governments should *never* wage war expands the first, and runs as follows:

(1) If civil resistance is, all things considered, preferable to war, then governments should adopt civil resistance as the system of national defense *and* never wage war.

(2) If civil resistance is at least as effective as war and superior to it, then civil resistance is, all things considered, preferable to armed force.

(3) Civil resistance is at least as effective as war and superior to it.

(4) Civil resistance is, all things considered, preferable to war. (From 2 & 3)

(5) Therefore, governments should adopt civil resistance as the system of national defense *and* never wage war. (From 1 & 4)

This argument, like the first, is valid. But we have seen that premise (3) is false. Civil resistance is not always as effective as war. Sometimes war is the only way to repel invaders or stop genocide. Therefore, civil resistance is not always "at least as effective as war," and premise (3) is false. Thus, this argument also fails, and we need not endorse its conclusion.

Conclusion

Andrew Alexandra provides two arguments for why governments should *never* wage war. Both unfortunately fail. I say "unfortunately," for I sincerely wish that governments could always resort to something other than war to enact justice and establish a mutual, sustained peace. But history shows they cannot. Governments may *sometimes* wage war because they must do so to protect their society. Alexandra surprisingly agrees with me here. Yet I would add that governments also may *sometimes* wage war to protect the common good against evils such as genocide. In either case, governments may only wage just wars—wars abiding by the criteria of justice before, during, and after war.

Response to Cartagena

Andrew Alexandra

Study Questions

1. What ambiguity does Alexandra note in Cartagena's use of the term "war"?
2. What paradox does Alexandra think exists within the institution of war? What does he believe to be the best way to resolve the paradox?
3. Why does Alexandra think that the Serbian resistance to Austria-Hungary in the First World War fails to meet the criteria for a just war?
4. What moral problems does Alexandra have with NATO's intervention in Bosnia?

I agree with much of what Nathan Cartagena says in his chapter, "The Government May Sometimes Wage War." With Cartagena, I think that, if certain conditions hold, a government may be justified in going to war. (Though I am more skeptical than he that these conditions are actually satisfied in modern wars, for reasons I'll sketch below.) And I like his characterization of "government" as "a person or group of persons with the ultimate civic responsibility and authority to justly rule a society and help maintain the common good—what is genuinely good for every human being, and thus the global human community" (p. 287). Finally, as he notes, "*war changes*. 'War' refers to . . . a constantly changing mode of human interaction" (p. 286).

The Paradoxical Institution of War

Despite these agreements, I do have two kinds of problems with Cartagena's chapter. The first arises not from what he says, but from what he does not say—and what I think he should say, given his views about the role of government and the nature of war. Here, it may be useful to note an ambiguity in the way Cartagena uses the term "war." Sometimes, he uses it to refer to particular conflicts: the First World War, or the Second Boer War, say. Let us call this sense of war, *war as event*. But sometimes he uses it to refer to what might be called the *institution of war*. This institution consists of the social, political, and technological arrangements that make particular conflicts possible and determine their nature when they occur, as well as the moral norms and legal rules which constrain their occurrence and course. When Cartagena says that "*war changes*" he is speaking of war in this institutional sense.

There is a paradox at the heart of the modern institution of war. On the one hand, it is making the world more dangerous. As Cartagena notes, technological developments continue to increase the (already enormous) destructive power of modern armies, while the growth of nationalist sentiments and efficient, centralized government allow a state to mobilize all material and human resources of a society to support those armies in times of war. Hence, modern wars, when they do occur, tend to be bloody and costly. And as I noted in my chapter, the "Security Dilemma" whereby the efforts of each state to make itself more secure by increasing its armed capability, are making all less secure. On the other hand, the regulatory framework governing war (international law and the bodies that adjudicate on it) aims to prevent war from occurring, and to limit its harm when it does. The ideal underpinning that framework is a world without war.

Clearly, any government that is concerned with what is "genuinely good for every human being" will want to ensure that that ideal becomes actual. It is doubtful, to say the least, that we can create a world without war while states continue to rely on armed force for their security. If there is, in fact, no way for states to protect themselves without those forces, then we are in a tragic situation, knowing that whatever we do, ultimately we are unsafe. But, as I pointed out in my chapter, we now have evidence that organized nonviolence—civil resistance—is such a method. Cartagena notes that "war is a practice under human control" (p. 287). Like other practices under human control, such as slavery or the subordination of women, which we realized were morally unsupportable, we can and should decide to bring it to an end, and find another way to keep ourselves safe. At the very least we should be having a serious discussion about how to get out of the dilemma we currently face.

Just Wars?

I also find problematic Cartagena's claims regarding particular wars which he sees as just—the Serbian resistance to Austria-Hungary at the start of the First World War, and NATO's attack on Serbia in 1995.

Cartagena thinks that in 1914 the Serbs were justified in refusing the unreasonable demands of the Austro-Hungarians and going to war, while continuing with diplomatic measures to try to resolve their conflict. As he notes, one of the conditions for a just war is that it has a "reasonable chance of success"—thus, the Serbs were justified in going to war only if they had a well-founded belief that they were likely to prevail against the Austro-Hungarians. In fact, they could not have had such a belief. In every respect the Serbs were militarily weaker than the Austro-Hungarians: their army was smaller, less well-equipped, and its capacity had been eroded by a series of recent campaigns; and Serbia, poorer and less industrialized than Austro-Hungary, was less able to support a prolonged conflict. Moreover, Serbia paid a staggering price for its involvement in the conflict, with almost thirty percent of its population, and sixty percent of its military age men, dead by the end of the war. While, of course, no one could have foreseen with any exactness the suffering the war caused, that there would be massive suffering—not just in Serbia, but throughout Europe—was predictable. As was well understood at the time, Austro-Hungary was being pushed by its ally, Germany, to provoke war with Serbia in order to instigate a broader European war at a time that Germany believed would give it a military advantage. Surely no government could justify acting in a way that would cause such suffering to the people on whose behalf it was supposedly acting. This is not to say, of course, that Austro-Hungary was justified in acting as *it* did—both sides acted badly.

NATO's military intervention in Bosnia is Cartagena's second example of a just war. Cartagena presents that intervention as justified, indeed necessary, to halt the genocide of Muslim and Croats by Serbian forces, highlighted by the horrifying massacre of thousands of Muslim men and boys at Srebrenica, and the subsequent shelling of the Bosnian capital. Cartagena's presentation of the facts surrounding these events is, in my view, so incomplete as to be misleading. Obviously, I don't have the space here to provide anything like a satisfactory account of those facts: I encourage the reader to investigate the relevant history, complicated and contested as it is, for themselves. But it is impossible to understand the conflicts that bedeviled (the then) Yugoslavia from the late 1980s on, without a sense of the powerful geo-political forces that came to bear on it in this period. The end of the bipolar world order as a result of the unraveling of the Soviet Union in the late 1980s/early 1990s liberated suppressed nationalistic aspirations in many parts of the old Eastern bloc, including in the republics that constituted the federation of Yugoslavia.

Far from the Western powers, especially the United States, being the benign if largely passive bystanders in the ensuing conflicts, as Cartagena presents them, they fueled and exploited these aspirations for their own expansionist ends, including actively undermining various diplomatic initiatives to broker agreements between the major parties. The massacre at Srebrenica—which the UN had long known was vulnerable—was only one, and not the first, of a series of atrocities that targeted Serbs as well as Muslims. Unlike previous atrocities, however, it became the occasion—in my view, the pretext—for a war that furthered the goals of Western powers. I doubt that the NATO intervention was a just war, because I doubt that it satisfied the criterion of right intention.

The way in which Cartagena attempts to justify NATO's intervention in Bosnia is, I think, symptomatic of a more general problematic phenomenon. The Vietnam War taught that it was impossible for even the most powerful state to win a war if popular support vanished, and that such support depended on the perception that the war was morally justified. Parties to conflicts consequently now engage in strenuous efforts to create and control that perception, making use of the techniques of persuasion developed by advertising and public relations. (All the antagonists in Yugoslavia, for example, hired public relations firms in the United States to try to influence popular opinion.) The presentation of conflicts in which Western states involve themselves tends to conform to a familiar pattern that engages our moral sentiments—on the one side an oppressed population struggling to resist a corrupt, sadistic, and possibly insane tyrant; on the other, targeting of civilians, ethnic cleansing, and massacre. The appropriate response is moral outrage and demand for intervention. The reality is usually far more ambiguous and intervention often does more harm than good.

This is not to claim that no war could be justified—I can't see how such a claim could be established. It is not even to claim that the wars I have discussed weren't justified, though I doubt that they were. It is to point out how difficult it is to be sure that actual wars are justified. And given that difficulty, there is a strong presumption against supporting wars.

Questions for Reflection

1. How realistic or wise do you find Alexandra's claim that civil resistance provides nations with an effective and preferable defense? Why?
2. Do you have any problems or objections to any of the criteria for a just war? Why?
3. What examples of just wars can you think of? Explain why you think they are just.
4. How serious do you think the Security Dilemma is that Alexandra discusses? Does it justify abolishing the military? Why?

Essay Suggestions

A. Suppose that there is a person in your county or city who has refused to pay taxes because he is an anarchist who does not believe that the government has any authority over him. Take the position of either the prosecutor or the defense attorney and write a paper presenting the strongest arguments you can, either for or against this person's view.

B. Supposing that some form of civil government is morally justified, the question remains as to whether the scope of government's authority may extend beyond the minimal state to encompass the nonminimal or expansive state. Write a paper in which you argue that only the minimal state is legitimate or that the nonminimal state is legitimate. Be sure to consider objections from the other side of the debate.

C. Suppose that the area you live in is economically depressed. The local government hopes to improve the economy by granting a permit to a large discount store chain to build a new store in the area. The catch is that the only good location for the store lies on Farmer Johnson's property and he refuses to sell. The government is considering using the principle of "imminent domain" to force Farmer Johnson to "sell" the property and make way for the discount store. Write a paper in which you argue for or against the use of imminent domain in this case. Be sure to discuss what "property rights" you think Farmer Johnson has or doesn't have.

D. Many people today believe that people have a right to healthcare even if they cannot afford to pay for it. Of course, providing people with such healthcare, if they have a right to it, requires that the government redistribute wealth through taxation from taxpayers to the healthcare providers. Do people have a right to healthcare even if they cannot afford to pay for it? Write an essay in which you argue for what you think is the right answer.

E. Consider the US war against Iraq (2003–2011) from the perspective of the just war theory. Write a paper in which you argue that the war met none, some, or all of the criteria for a just war.

F. Can war *ever* be morally justified? The pacifist says "no." Write a paper in which you present what you consider to be the strongest argument in favor of pacifism. Then either defend that argument against potential objections, or present what you think are decisive objections against the argument.

For Further Reading

On Political Philosophy Generally

Cahn, Steven M. *Political Philosophy: The Essential Texts*. 3rd ed. Oxford: Oxford University Press, 2014.
Goodin, Robert E., Philip Pettit, and Thomas Pogge, eds. *A Companion to Contemporary Political Philosophy*. 2nd ed. Malden, MA: Blackwell, 2012.
Nathanson, Stephen. *Should We Consent to Be Governed? A Short Introduction to Political Philosophy*. Belmont, CA: Wadsworth, 2000.
Wolff, Jonathan. *An Introduction to Political Philosophy*. 3rd ed. Oxford: Oxford University Press, 2016.

On Distributive Justice

Allingham, Michael. *Distributive Justice*. New York: Routledge, 2014.
Duncan, Craig, and Tibor R. Machan. *Libertarianism: For and Against*. Lanham, MD: Rowman & Littlefield, 2005.
Pojman, Louis P., ed. *Justice: An Anthology*. New York: Routledge, 2005.

The Ethics of War

Holmes, Robert L. *Pacifism: A Philosophy of Nonviolence*. New York: Bloomsbury, 2016.
Lazar, Seth, and Helen Frowe, eds. *The Oxford Handbook of Ethics of War*. Oxford: Oxford University Press, 2018.
Lee, Steven P. *Ethics and War: An Introduction*. Cambridge: Cambridge University Press, 2012.

Index

abortion   12, 18, 38, 43–4, 48 n.18, 201
Abramovic, Marina   146
actions   40, 50, 60, 61, 62–3, 65, 67–8, 69, 70, 86, 97
   rightness or wrongness of   19, 21–2, 63, 64–5, 77–8, 79, 97, 98–9, 102, 208
   voluntary vs. non-voluntary   252 n.3
Adams, John   39
Adams, Robert   101, 102
aesthetic criteria   143, 148–9
aesthetic experience   130–5, 144, 145, 146, 154
aesthetic judgments   24–5, 130, 142–3, 147, 148, 150 n.7, 151, 152, 153–4
aesthetic moralism   154
aesthetic objectivism   24–5, 139–41, 144–5, 147, 149, 155, 158, 172, 192
aesthetic pleasure   140, 142, 148–9, 154
aesthetic relativism   24, 127, 128, 129, 135, 136, 141, 150 n.7, 151–5, 192
aesthetics   4, 17–18, 24–5, 128, 140, 144, 147–8, 153, 154
aesthetic subjectivism, *see* aesthetic relativism
Allen, Woody   166
American Civil War   284, 287, 294
amoralism   202–3
Amusing Ourselves to Death   134
anarchism, anarchy   199–200, 205–18, 220, 221–2, 223, 226, 227, 228, 230, 231–2, 234, 236, 239
Anarchy, State, and Utopia   213, 242

animals   61, 82 n.2, 91–2, 187–8
Annas, Julia   77
anything goes objection   93, 95, 96, 99, 100, 118
applied ethics   18
Aquinas, Thomas   46–7, 47 n.4, 49 n.22, 52, 54 n.3, 197, 279, 284, 290, 292, 294
arbitrariness objection   95, 96–7, 99, 103, 118
arbitration   212, 213, 225, 234, 279, 288
argument   5, 6–8, 9, 11, 12, 73, 112–13, 148, 258
   deductive   6–8, 11
   inductive   6, 8
Aristotle   31, 41, 42, 45, 61, 77, 89, 91, 157, 161, 197, 225, 290
art   23–5, 27 n.4, 45, 53–4, 127–49, 151, 153–4, 155–8, 168, 177
Art as Experience   131
art objects   24, 128, 131–2
atheism   23, 26, 121, 122–3, 160, 162, 164–9, 170 n.3, 183, 186
atheistic moral realism   171 n.24, *see also* meaning of life—objective optimism
Audi, Robert   173
Augustine   197, 286, 290–1, 292, 294, 295
autonomy thesis   93, 94, 104
axiology   17, 162, 163, 169, 182–3, 184, *see also* value theory

Bastiat, Frederic   253, 256
Beardsley, Monroe   132, 135, 149 n.1
beauty   23–5, 27 n.4, 129, 135, 138–42, 143–9, 151, 153, 154, 155–8, 159, 192
bedrock moral beliefs   22, 71, 73

Bell, Clive 144
Bentham, Jeremy 64, 65, 87, 91, 94
Berkeley, George 94
Bernstein, Leonard 141
Betzler, Monika 78
Bible 95, 164, 192
biology 33, 34, 35–6, 52, 54, 164, 168
Blatchford, Robert 73
Bleak House 35
Booth, John Wilkes 39
Bosnian War 289–90, 292, 300
Boucher, Francois 140
Bourdieu, Pierre 147
Bracho, Varvara 148
Brettschneider, Corey 248
Brink, David 96
Bristow, William 94
The Brothers Karamozov 93, 162
Buddhism 162, 170 n.3
Budziszewski, J. 42
Burgess, Anthony 130
Bush, George W. 5, 42

Calvin, John 197, 290
Camus, Albert 171, 174–5, 178
capitalism 205, 209, 216 n.7, 250
capital punishment 18, 20, 43
Carlson, Allen 156
Carroll, Noel 136
categorical imperative 22, 32, 34, 51
Catholicism 146
character 22, 40, 50, 63, 67–8, 77–9, 100, 122, 130, 227
Cheneoweth, Erica 280
Chesterton, G. K. 73, 82
Chomsky, Noam 140–1
Christianity, Christendom 161, 162, 165, 286
City of God 197
Civil Disobedience 219
civil disobedience, resistance 203, 212, 274, 275, 280–1, 282–3, 297, 298–300, 302, 304
Clark, Kenneth 144
A Clockwork Orange 130
common good 40, 44, 46–7, 163, 199, 284, 287, 289–90, 291–3, 295, 301

composition, fallacy of 212
consent (to government) 199–200, 205, 206, 207–8, 218, 222, 239, 263, 269
consequentialism 5, 21–2, 60–71, 84, 85–6
 core 62–4
Copleston, Fredrick 163
coprophagia 57
core consequentialism, *see* consequentialism
corporate welfare 209–10, 230, 233
courage 38, 39, 40, 41, 42–3, 46
cowardice 38, 39, 40, 41, 42–3
creation 163, 169, 189
creation of value/wealth 209, 255, 256, 259, 267, 269, 270
critic, criticism (of art) 127, 128, 129, 133, 144, 147, 151, 154, 159

Dadaism 147
Daoism 162
Darwall, Stephen 100–1
Darwin, Charles 28, 33–4, 51–2, 56, 168
Darwinian morality 28, 33–6, 50, 51–2
da Vinci, Leonardo 24, 166
Declaration of Independence 164, 199, 208, 222
definitions 8–11, 12, 29, 161
demandingness objection 64–6, 85
democracy 197–8, 238, 250, 282
deontology, deontological 22, 71–83, 90, 183
dependence of morality on God 23, 28, 29, 31, 56, 93–104, 105–6, 107–10, 114–16, 117, 120, 121, 122–5, 126 n.3, 164
Descartes, Rene 139, 141–2
Descent of Man 34, 52, 56
de Vitoria, Francisco 290, 291, 293
Dewey, John 24, 127, 128, 130–5, 151–2, 153–4
Dickens, Charles 35–6
Dickie, George 147, 155, 157–8
dignity, human 22, 26, 52, 69, 72, 79, 80–2, 84, 91, 164

disinterestedness 25, 139, 144, 145–6, 149, 155, 157
divine command theory (DCT) 23, 72, 76–7, 89, 93, 94–9, 100, 103, 117–19, 120, 121, 122, 123, 124, 125, 192
divine right of kings 198–9
divorce 164
do no harm principle 22
Dostoyevsky, Fyodor 22–3, 93
Du Bois, W.E.B. 272
Duchamp, Marcel 147
Dulles, John Foster 35
duties 71, 78, 98, 221, see also moral requirements
  direct 71, 75, 77, 78, 82 n.2, 87
  indirect 71, 75

Ecclesiastes 25
economy, economics 140, 147, 209, 210, 214, 226, 231, 249–50, 253, 280, 305
egalitarianism 90, 201, 240, 241
Emancipation Proclamation 271
environmentalism, *see* ethics, environmental
epistemology 4, 153, 161
equality (of rights) 73, 81, 201, 235–6, 241, 242, 250, 259, 266,
equivocation, fallacy of 97, 121, 123–4
ethical egoism 21, 71, 74–6
ethical theory 18, 21, 22, 62, 63, 71, 72, 73–4, 92, 120, 125
  and iniquitous consequences 71, 74, 75, 76, 86
ethics (morality) 2, 4, 17–18, 19–23, 24, 28, 29–33, 34–36, 37–43, 47, 50–3, 54, 55–8, 59, 61, 62, 63, 65, 70–1, 72, 73, 74, 78, 84, 89, 90, 93–4, 96, 99, 102–4, 105–6, 107, 110–11, 112–14, 115, 117, 120, 130, 146, 165, 167–8, 171, 172, 173, 178, 182, 183, 185, 186, 191, 262, 270, 276–80, 283
  descriptive 107, 110, 114
  environmental 148
  normative 18, 21–2, 29, 50, 51, 72

  objective (*see* moral objectivism)
  religious 100
  secular 93, 99–103, 117, 119–20, 126
  subjective (*see* moral relativism)
  substantive 20, 29–30, 32, 36
ethics of war 198, 202–4, 274–304, 305–6, *see* war, ethics of
eudaimonia 77
eudaimonism 77, 79
euthanasia 43
Euthuphro problem 31, 56, 79
The Euthyphro 31, 76, 79, 95
Evaluating Art 157
evolution, theory of (Darwinism 20, 26, 28, 33–6, 51, 52–3, 59, 106, 110–12, 115, 168, 170 n.18
Existentialism and Human Emotions 166

female genital mutilation 18
Fibonacci series 141, 150 n.6, 155, 156
First World War 203, 285, 287, 288, 292, 301, 302, 303
Flaying of Marsyas 157
Foner, Eric 271
Foot, Philippa 102
Fountain 147
Frankfurt, Harry 178
Frankl, Viktor 168
"A Free Man's Worship" 165
free market competition 200, 209–10, 214, 268

game theory 28, 34, 211
Garner, Richard 101
Gauthier, David 267
Genesis, book of 163, 164
Gert, Bernard 107
Gert, Joshua 107
Giuliani, Rudy 146
globalization 147, 148
God 3, 25, 28, 46, 105, 197, 199, 284
  character, nature 94, 96, 100, 106–7, 122, 162, 170 nn.3, 4
  and ethics 18, 22–3, 29, 31, 51, 54 n.3, 56–7, 76–7, 93–126, 165

INDEX

existence 2, 5, 22–3, 25–6, 29, 45, 93, 102, 109–10, 122, 123, 166, 172, 180, 182, 183–4, 191
  goodness 76, 98, 102, 114–15, 121 n.3, 122, 192
  and the meaning of life (see meaning of life, theistic solution)
  simplicity 115
golden ratio 25, 141
government 2, 81, 197, 200–2, 203, 205–238, 239, 254, 267, 275, 279, 281, 282–3, 284, 285, 287, 288–95, 297–301, 302, 303, 305
  and coercive force, 199, 200, 202, 206–7, 209, 211, 215, 228, 260, 267, 273, 305
  forms of 197–8, 287
  justification of 81, 197, 198–200, 205–38, 239, 305
  monopoly power 200, 206, 212, 213, 219, 225–6, 230–1, 233, 234, 239
greatest happiness principle 65
Greenberg, Clement 153–4
Gyges' ring 75, 83 n.7

Hamlet 25
happiness 17, 21, 26, 60, 61–2, 64, 65, 74, 77, 79, 84, 86, 87–8, 97, 102, 110, 135, 164, 171, 172, 173–4, 175, 178, 180, 184–5, 186–7, 188, 191, 199
Harris, Sam 167–8
Harrison, Gerald 101–2
hate 35, 46–7, 53
Hawking, Stephen 81
hedonism 17, 64
Heraclitus 53
Hilgers, Thomas 145–6
Hinduism 162
Hobbes, Thomas 197, 199, 205, 210–11, 212, 213, 220
Holy Virgin Mary 146
Homer 284
homicide 38, 43, 44, 48 n.18, 209
homosexuality 18
Hume, David 9, 24, 35–6, 89, 127, 128, 129–30, 135, 136, 139, 142, 143, 151, 152, 153–5, 156, 157, 159, 222, 228, 266
Hursthouse, Rosiland 66–8, 77, 78
Hutcheson, Frances 140

ideal advisor theory 119
ideal theory 241, 242, 250–1, 252, *see also* non-ideal theory
identity of properties 118
The Iliad 284
industrial revolution 286
institutional theory of art 139, 147
Islam 161, 162, 300
is-ought problem 160, 167, 168

Jerome, Jerome K. 75
Jesus 164, 170 n.4, 203
Job, book of 31, 56, 161, 255
Johnson, Robert N. 77–9
Joyce, Richard 100, 123
Judaism 162
Judeo-Christian tradition 162, 164
jus ad bellum 204, 284, 290–3, 298
  last resort 280, 283, 291, 292–3, 298, 299
  legitimate authority 291, 292
  just cause 203, 204, 291–2, 293, 298
  reasonable chance of success 291, 293, 303
  right intention 204, 291, 292, 304
jus in bello 204, 284, 293–4, 298
  proportionality 204, 293, 294, 298
  restricted targeting 293–4
jus post bellum 204, 284, 294
justice 73, 80, 81, 86, 88 n.6, 102, 122, 135, 164, 200, 204, 206, 221, 225, 240, 242, 246, 247, 249, 266, 268, 269, 270, 278, 284, 290–1, 293–5, 297–8, 301
  distributive 198, 200–2, 241, 242, 249–51, 265, 271–2, 273
  economic 147, 242, 249–51
  problem of 84, 85–7
  social 81, 147, 249–51
  theory of 242–3
just war theory 203–4, 279, 286, 290–4, 301, 304, 305

INDEX

Kant, Immanuel 22, 28, 31–2, 34, 51, 72, 78, 80, 81–2, 91, 94, 143, 144, 156, 157–8, 161, 225
Kantian, Kantianism 22, 72, 79, 91–2, 183
Kaprow, Allan 147
killing and letting die 60, 69
King, Martin L., Jr. 38, 81
Klimt, Gustav 142, 143
Koran 95, 100
Korsmeyer, Carolyn 130

Lavoie, Don 236–7
law, legal system 38, 39, 41, 43, 44, 46, 80–1, 120, 212, 213, 217 n.16, 220, 223, 227, 234, 302
Leeson, Peter 211
"Letter from a Birmingham Jail" 38, 81
Leviathan 210
Lewis, C. S. 167
libertarianism (political theory) 199, 201, 242, 245, 268
liberty 87, 164, 199, 201, 219, 222, 241, 242, 245–6, 252 nn.3, 9, 262, 263, 265, 266–7, 268
  moralized account of 240, 241, 266
  non-moralized account of 240
Lieber, Francis 287
life 17, 33, 38, 43, 45, 54 n.3, 77, 78, 87, 135, 164, 168, 173, 199, 222, 278, 281
  after death 2, 94, 103, 165
  goodness/value of 17, 43–4, 46, 168, 171 n.24, 186
  meaning of (*see* meaning of life)
  right to 12, 50, 66
life satisfaction view 26, 173–4, 175, 186, 189
Locke, John 94, 197, 199, 200, 205, 212–3, 218, 219, 221–3, 234–5, 268
Lockean proviso 248, 249
logic 6, 13 n.1, 141, 148–9, 158, 161, 172

Machiavelli, Niccolo 197
Mackie, J. L. 23, 94, 99–102, 123, 126 n.3
Maher, Bill 38, 42
Malthus, Thomas Robert 33
Margolis, Joseph 127, 128, 135, 151–3
Marx, Karl 53, 197
materialism 51–2, 53, 59, 167, 168, 183
mathematics 28, 29, 31, 39, 51, 53–2, 56, 139, 141, 148–9, 155, 157–8
Meade, James 250
meaning of life 3, 25–6, 160–90
  objective optimism 26, 178–80
  optimistic naturalism 26, 183–4
  pessimistic naturalism (nihilism) 25–6, 149, 160, 165, 166, 169, 182, 183–4, 189
  subjective optimism 26, 174–8, 186–9
  theistic solution 25, 26, 162–4, 169, 184–5
Mengele, Josef 85, 86, 87, 88 n.3
metaethics 18, 28, 29, 30–3, 51, 102, 103
metaphysics 4
Metz, Thaddeus 173
Midgley, Mary 74
Mill, John Stuart 61, 64–5, 84, 86–7
Mind and Its Depths 133
minimal state 199–200, 219, 221–3, 230, 232, 305
Moby Dick 161
modality 109–10
monopolies 208, 213, 225–6, 228, 230–1, 233, 237, 239
monotheism, *see* theism
moral anti-realism 106, 111, 126
  error theory 111, 122, 123
  expressivism 102, 111
moral disagreements 20
moral epistemology/knowledge 68, 108, 110, 115
moral facts 23, 73, 106, 111, 112, 123–4
moral intuitions 22, 43, 60, 70, 84, 85, 89–90, 92

morality, *see* ethics
The Moral Landscape 167–8
moral law 38, 50, 51–2, 53–4, 55, 82
moral objectivism 18–21, 23, 37–48, 55–7, 58 n.1, 171, 190
moral progress 20
moral realism, *see* moral objectivism
moral relativism 18–21, 23, 28–36, 44, 47, 52, 53–4, 55, 57–8, 167, 183, 191, 203
   conventionalism 19, 20
   implications of 19–20
   subjectivism 19, 20, 59, 183
moral requirements 23, 93, 94–5, 99–102, 122, 124, 126, *see also* duties
moral skepticism 106, 111, 121, 122–3
moral theory, *see* ethical theory
motives 40, 60, 66–8, 69, 71
Murphy, Mark 117–18, 123
myth of Sisyphus 171, 174–8

Nagel, Thomas 85, 165
naïve relativism (in aesthetics) 24, 151
Narveson, Jan 240, 245–6, 252 n.9
naturalism 23, 106, 109–10, 111, 125
natural law, natural law theory 47 n.4, 54, 54 n.3, 56, 57, 81, 107
Nazism 161, 178, 186
necessary conditions 10–11
Nicomachean Ethics 61
Nietzsche, Friedrich 23, 165–6, 169, 183
nihilism, *see* meaning of life—pessimistic naturalism
Nine Muses, or Daughters of the Memory 148
Ninth Symphony 130
noncombatant immunity 204, 293, *see also* jus in bello—restricted targeting
non-ideal theory 220, 226, 241, 251, *see also* ideal theory
nonminimal state 200, 219, 223–6, 230, 233, 305

Nozick, Robert 200, 201–2, 205, 213–14, 219, 222–3, 234–5, 240–1, 242–4, 245, 248–9, 251–2, 252 nn.2, 3, 257, 271, 273

Offili, Chris 146
"Of the Standard of Taste" 128
One Big Idea 53
Origin of Species 33

pacifism 203, 274–83, 298–300, 306
Paine, Thomas 215
pantheism 170 n.3
Paris Can Wait 143–4, 157
Parmenides 53
paternalism 254, 260
Paul (Saint) 35, 36, 58, 163
peace 259, 279, 286, 288, 289–90, 291, 292, 293, 294–5, 301
"peace of God" rule 286
perfectionism 17
personal autonomy 80
philosophical question about morality (PQAM) 71–72, 73–82
philosophy 1–5, 6, 9, 13 n.1, 17, 53–4, 61, 112, 148
Plantinga, Alvin 57, 106, 111–12
Plato 31, 37 n.6, 47 n.2, 76, 95, 141, 144, 146, 149, 150 n.7, 197, 207, 261
Platonism 171 n.24, 262
poiesis 154
political philosophy 4, 17–18, 197–8, 202
Pollack, Jackson 153–4
polytheism 170 n.3
poor, the 200, 202, 205, 210, 214–15, 220, 230, 231–2, 233, 239, 253–4, 257–60, 262, 263–4, 273
Portrait of Adele Bloch-Bauer I 142–3
possible worlds 109–10, 227
Postman, Neil 131, 134
Pratchett, Terry 72
principle of acquaintance 142
principle of benevolence 22
principle of rectification 251, 252 n.2
principle of utility 65, 84, 86
private property, *see* property rights

problem of justice, *see* justice—problem of
problem of moral authority   102–3
problem of moral ontology   99–102
problem of motives, *see* motives
properties   37 n.6, 101, 106, 118, 129, 156, 261
  aesthetic   27 n.4, 128, 129, 146, 148, 153, 154
  moral   23, 54 n.1, 121, 124–5
  natural   23, 101, 109–10, 125
property rights   21, 38, 41, 44, 89, 209, 222, 240, 241, 243, 244, 245–7, 248–9, 250, 251–2, 265, 266, 268, 269, 270–2, 273, 305
  contract model of   269, 271
  libertarian system of   201–2, 240, 244, 245–6
  progressive system of   202, 244, 245–6, 265, 267–8
Protagoras   141
protection agencies   213–4, 222–3, 230–2, 233, 235, 239
public goods   200, 202, 211, 219, 223–4, 228, 234, 235, 254, 260–3

Quin, Philip   117

rape   12, 29–30, 32, 36, 42, 50, 56–8, 72, 73–80, 87, 89–90, 91, 96, 98, 99–100, 125
rationality   88, 91, 183, 262
rational relativism   24, 128, 151, 153, 155, 158, 159
Rawls, John   202, 219, 224–5, 234, 235–6, 247–9, 250–1, 265, 267–9, 273
Ray, Man   147
Reagan, Ronald   219
redistribution of wealth   201–2, 220, 240–73
Republic   146, 197
respect-for-persons principle (RFP)   22, 71, 72, 74, 80–2, 88, 88 n.9, 90–2, 191, 208
Riefenstahl, Leni   157
rights   22, 38, 40, 66, 69, 72, 80–1, 86, 87, 164, 198, 199–200, 205, 220, 221–2, 224, 227, 228, 230, 231–2, 236, 245–6, 247, 250, 266, 273
Rosenberg, Alex   168–9
Rousseau, Jean-Jacques   197, 227
Rummel, R. J.   208–9
Ruse, Michael   52–3
Russell, Bertrand   56, 163, 165–6

Santayana, George   24, 127, 128, 135, 136
Sartre, Jean-Paul   94, 126 n.3, 160, 166–7
Scanlon, T. M.   247
Schopenhauer, Arthur   144
science   53–4, 144–5, 167–8
Scruton, Roger   156
Second Boer War   285–6, 290, 292, 295 n.4, 302
Second Treatise of Government   212
Second World War   30, 43, 279, 285, 287, 294
secular progressivism   53
security agencies, *see* protection agencies
security dilemma   274, 281, 283, 302, 304
The Sense of Beauty   135
sexuality   164
Shafer-Landau, Russ   93, 97–8, 123, 124
Shaffer, Butler   238
Shay, Jonathan   284
Shuzo, Kuki   140
Singer, Marcus   87
Singer, Peter   35
slavery   20, 73, 80, 81, 89, 220, 231, 233
Smith, Adam   234
social Darwinism   168
socialism   201
social justice, *see* justice—social
Socrates   1, 3–4, 25, 95, 150 n.7
Somalia   205, 211
Sophists   141, 150 n.7, 156
soundness   7, 8, 11, 141, 169
Spanish Civil War   212
Starry Night   24
state of nature   200, 221, 222–3, 245–7, 268

Stephan, Maria J. 280
Stirner, Max 186
Stolnitz, Jerome 145, 157
straw man fallacy 182, 183
suffering 61, 62, 64, 65, 67–8, 84, 87, 90, 92, 101, 168, 178, 187, 189, 191, 293, 303
sufficient conditions 9–11
Sullivan, Stephen 97
Swinburne, Richard 118

taxes 199, 200, 206–7, 215, 220, 263, 267, 305
Taylor, Richard 171, 172, 174, 176–8, 179
teleology 162, 163–4, 166, 169, 171 n.24, 182–3, 184
theism 162, 164, 165, 170, 189
Thoreau, Henry David 219
thought experiments 11–12
Titian 157
tolerance 38, 41, 45–7
Tolstoy, Leo 276
total war 286–7
Triumph of the Will 157
Trump, Donald 35
truth 7–8, 11, 32, 41, 44–5, 46, 98, 112, 141, 150 n.7, 165, 175
Two Treatises of Government 221

universalizability 22, 268
US War against Iraq 305
Utilitarianism 61
utilitarianism 21, 61, 74, 84, 87, 90, 183, 191
  maximizing 60, 63, 64–5
  rule 84, 86

vacuity objection 93, 95, 98–9, 118, 121, 122
validity 7, 8, 11, 112
value, values 17, 77, 85, 132, 134, 135, 162, 163, 166, 167, 171, 172, 173–4, 177
  aesthetic 141, 144, 149 n.1, 151, 154, 157, 159, 180
  democratic 282, 283
  economic 202, 244, 253, 256

instrumental 17, 80
intrinsic 17, 26, 183
judgments (*see* aesthetic judgments)
moral 18, 19, 20, 23, 26 n.1, 76, 154, 162
objective 26, 162, 168, 169, 172, 179, 186
value monism 17
value objectivism 17
value pluralism 17
value subjectivism 17
value theory 4, 17, 23, 183, 197
Van Gogh, Vincent 24
Vietnam War 3, 287, 304
violence 203, 213, 221, 223, 233, 266, 268, 274, 275, 276–8, 279, 280, 283, 292, 294, 297
  conditions for 274, 276–8
  presumption against 277–8, 279, 281, 283
virtue, virtues 39, 40, 41, 42, 77–8, 79, 117, 123, 266
virtue ethics 72, 77–9, 89, 110, 183
voting 207, 210

war 38, 43, 45, 259, 276, 278, 285–7, 297, 302, 305–6
  ethics of 198, 202–4, 274–304, 305–6
  as event 302
  institution of 302
War and Peace 179
Ward, Colin 215–16
Washington, George 39
welfare liberalism 199, 201, *see also* egalitarianism
Westminster Catechism 163
What Does It All Mean? 165
Wilson, E. O. 52–3
Wilson, James 80–1
Wilt Chamberlain example 240, 242–4, 248–9, 273
Wittgenstein, Ludwig 29
Wolf, Susan 171, 172–3, 179–80, 185, 188
Wollheim, Richard 127, 128, 131, 133–4, 135, 152